Contents

The South African Game

Sport and Racism

Robert Archer and
Antoine Bouillon

Zed Press, 57 Caledonian Road, London N1 9DN

The South African Game: Sport and Racism was first
published by Zed Press, 57 Caledonian Road, London
N1 9DN in 1982. An earlier version, under the title *Sport
et Apartheid,* was published in French by Albatros in 1981.

Copyedited by Bev Brown
Typeset by Jenny Donald
Proofread by Stephen Gourlay
Cover design by Jacque Solomons
Visuals by Jan Brown
Printed by Redwood Burn Ltd., Trowbridge, Wiltshire

British Library Cataloguing in Publication Data

Archer, Robert
   The South African game, sport and racism in
   South Africa.
   1. Segregation in sport — South Africa
   I. Title   II. Bouillon, Antoine
   305.8'.00968 (expanded)   GV667

   ISBN 0-86232-066-6
   ISBN 0.86232-082-8 Pbk

U.S. Distributor:
Lawrence Hill & Co., 520 Riverside Avenue, Westport,
Conn. 06880, U.S.A.

Chronology of South African Sporting History

Appendices

Bibliography

Index

List of Tables

Terms

The term 'black' refers to all those South Africans classified by the South African government as 'Africans', 'Coloureds' or 'Indians'; the latter terms and the term 'white', are also used because the organisation and practice of sport under apartheid cannot be understood without reference to them.

Preface

The issue of South African sport is raised as often today as it was in 1970 when the Stop The Seventy Tour placed it for the first time on the front pages of the international press. Recent rugby tours to and from South Africa, notably the British Lions' tour in 1980 and the New Zealand crisis in 1981, and the boycott list compiled by the South African Non-Racial Olympic Committee (SANROC) for the United Nations Special Committee Against Apartheid — which nearly capsized the 1981 M.C.C. tour of the West Indies — have ensured that the international campaign to isolate South Africa from world sport remains as lively an issue as ever. Equally, the supporters of South Africa continue to defend their case with the same marvellous illogic they have displayed ever since black South African sportsmen and women began to demand equality of opportunity in sport in the 1950s.

But though we hear how governments and individuals try to promote or stop sporting contacts with white South Africa, we rarely have an opportunity to hear the views of black sportsmen and women within South Africa — those for whom the international campaign is being waged, and who originally called it into being. This book does not claim in any way to be a complete study of sport inside South Africa: the subject has many facets, is saturated in history and is in perpetual movement. But we have tried to present the point of view of the modern non-racial sports movement *within* the country, and to describe the historical and social context within which it came into being — excluded and ignored by white sport, but with a vitality and energy which defy material, social and political deprivation.

We should declare that neither of us have visited South Africa. On-the-spot research would certainly have helped us to grasp the feel of contemporary social relations in sport; we would also like to have been able to spend more time in libraries looking into the history of sport. But would this necessarily have changed our analysis or improved our objectivity? It should not be forgotten that South Africa is a police state, and that those from abroad who try to see 'the other side' do so at some risk to those who help them. Instead, we have interviewed as many South Africans as agreed to meet us, who were able to stimulate and redirect our ideas and give colour and shape to our research. Without their help, we would not have felt able to write the book

i

as we have done. Not all of them can be named. Those who can are: William Beinart, Sadie Berman, Richard Compton, Jasmat Dhiraj, Peter Hain, Baruch Hirson, John Horak, Horst Kleinschmidt, M.N. Pather, Sam Ramsamy, P.B. Singh, Isaiah Stein, Bob Watson. We would like to thank them all for their co-operation and assistance.

Finally, in the hope of avoiding misunderstanding, we would like to state that it has nowhere been our intention to criticize 'sport' as such. We *do* believe, however, unlike many who claim to speak for the sporting world, that sport, as much as other social activities, is subject to contradictions and political tensions. It is part of society, and for this very reason an examination of the evolution and character of South African sport throws light on the character of apartheid and on the contradictory, long and often violent history which gave birth to it.

Robert Archer
Antoine Bouillon
Paris and London
1982

'If You Really Want to Know, Ask the Blacks'

'All I wanted to do was become a sportswoman'

'Sport wasn't very important to me when we first went to school. I don't remember us talking about it. You felt sport was for Whites only, I thought tennis was only for white people until I heard of Arthur Ashe . . . . We played sport because that is all there is to do in the afternoons. We used to go to this very old playground, covered with sand and try to run. We put stones to mark the course. It was all sprints. I didn't know then about long distance.

'At school, there were only two girl runners, one Coloured girl and myself. Perhaps the others weren't good enough and gave up. I don't think in my time Black women were interested in sport at all. Netball was the only thing we were encouraged to play. All girls played netball. We used to play other schools. We were told we ought to have uniforms, and that caused a problem — money. I remember I ran against another school and I had no shoes to wear and I cut my toe on a stone or something: it was the 400 metres and I really hurt myself. That was our experience: first I had no shoes, second there was no proper ground to run on.

'I've never competed with any white people in my life. I used to go and watch them, to hang about the white grounds, because I could go easily on foot from where I lived. Afterwards I would run home and start doing my own thing. I tried tennis because I had seen white children playing. I had friends, older people, who played . . . . They had money of course, because they were working. There was one tennis court in K........ as a whole. It was about then that I started hearing about Arthur Ashe and then about women like Billy Jean King, and we used to see pictures in the paper about how they won. My sister bought me a racket, so I used to hang around there, but I was never a player and they didn't want me. And I was younger than everyone else. Whenever they did try to teach me, they would talk in English, all the terms were in English which I did not understand. I never learnt — and I still feel I could have played well. I wasn't angry about it: I just couldn't understand why I couldn't go any further. I thought I was just not good enough. When I was trying so hard. I was determined to play tennis, to become a champion.

'But I continued to run. That was easy. Sport was important to me. I felt good. When I was encouraged, when I knew I was going to run, I thought I was going to be in the papers, that I would go to the States and become a champion. I used to think like that — all I wanted to do was become a sports-woman.

'But after school I just stopped. It was the end. I went to work. There was nowhere for me to train and I felt discouraged. A friend tried to encourage me, she said we should run home from work without taking the bus — and home was miles and miles from the city. But I felt I was grown up, that I would look silly running through the street, there were not many people doing it and I became aware of myself as a woman, running. What was the purpose of doing such a thing? I *wanted* to run, but the whole thing collapsed. I didn't have the facilities, I didn't have the money to buy what I needed, and even if I found the money, where could I go and train?'

An African woman (25 years old)
Interview, London, February 1980

'One cannot play normal sport in an abnormal society'

'One cannot play normal sport in an abnormal society. . . . For true merit selection everyone has to be given the same opportunities to develop his latent talent. This cannot happen in South African society.

'Consider the extreme example of a boy from Soweto and a boy, say, from Houghton. A migrant worker in Soweto lives in bachelor hostels in the most unnatural conditions. If his wife goes to Soweto she does so illegally and can be arrested. If she obeys the law and doesn't join her husband he inevitably gets involved with women of free virtues, there are hordes of them, and what is worse they are riddled with venereal diseases. Then every two years he goes back to his wife in the homeland. He makes a child. This child is not born normal because he is diseased already. Then the child doesn't get the right food, he doesn't get the right education. If he does, his father has to starve to pay for his fees. He can hardly afford a pair of shoes to go to school, never mind cricket shoes.

'The best time to start teaching a youngster about cricket is at six or seven and at 13 he should have learnt the basics, then you develop what he has. Not so with this chap. He doesn't get any coaching because his teachers know nothing and there are no facilities. As a result his technique is hopeless and he probably does not even know how to grip a bat properly.

'The youngster from Soweto never sees a white person except a Bantu Inspector who comes to arrest his mother and father, a white policeman or someone else in authority who bullies him, or, more correctly, terrorizes him, because to him a man in uniform is an object of terror. All of a sudden he joins a club and his club plays against a white team. He is shoved out of Soweto into the Wanderers. No one in his right mind can expect such a person to give a good account of himself . . . . Say he makes good in spite of all this, because of his innate ball sense, and is selected for his province. He travels by air and stays in an international hotel. After this he must return to life in Soweto . . . . He can't play or live normally under these circumstances. This even applies to my children who live in Cape Town, but never have contact with Whites. There is no relationship except one with authority . . . .

'Only recently did I become aware that to think only about cricket was wrong . . . . I admit now that I should not have fought from a cricket angle. I should have fought from a completely humanitarian angle. I should have carried the fight right down the line.

'People come to me and say what you fought for has arrived, why aren't you satisfied. I can't be satisfied if I was fighting for the wrong thing. My standards were wrong. Probably I've become mature. Probably I've become aware of politics.

'I don't know exactly what caused me to change my views, too many factors are involved, but undoubtedly the riots of last year [in Soweto] were a great influence.

'Nobody in his right sense, even people who are white who saw what was going on, can shrug those events off. Me least of all.

'I saw a nephew who had been shot to death just behind his shop. And I knew in my own mind that this boy was not connected with the riots. He was not made that way. His interests were opening his shop in the morning, running his business and closing up at night. He was shot dead.

'His two brothers were arrested for having petrol bombs in their possession. They were found innocent by the magistrate who said the state witnesses were lying their heads off.

'If the Indemnity Bill had not been passed we would have gone to court on the boy's death. What upset me was that the evidence in court showed that the policeman who shot that boy admitted to killing fifteen other children that same night. Fifteen! One policeman!

'. . . That has had an effect. Not an embittering effect because I very rarely become bitter, but I now have an acute awareness of what the children want. My responsibility is more to them than anything else I think. They want a normal society which is little enough to ask for.'

Hassan Howa 1977
President of the South African Council on Sport (1976-81), President of the S.A. Cricket Board of Control, and of the S.A. Cricket Board
(In A. Odendaal, 1977, pp. 269-70, 276-7)

'When you look at our sport, you see a wall'

'When you look at our sport, you see a wall. You're playing, when you reach that wall you know there's no way out. For instance, you get your Western Province colours — you have to drop down then, because there's nothing else. There's no incentive — like you might represent your country or go to the Olympic Games. Our sportsmen work to a certain point and thereafter they drop dead, hence there's not much enthusiasm for the youngsters or encouragement or some praise: when you're young, you see someone playing, you want to be in competition with them. But they are dying because their heroes don't go up anywhere, they come down.

'And because young people can't play sport, they go for bottles and start drinking — that's what I found when I came home. It was definitely worse. I mean what do you aim for?'

An African (50 years old)
Interview, London, February 1980

'When we talk of non-racial sport, we are also talking of social and economic changes'

'I am extremely bitter. I am not a violent person but I hate every white tennis player or sportsman, however liberal he may be, who participates in any racial sport in South Africa. I blame him for the fact that I am unable to reach my full potential. There are over 6,000 Indians in L..... and they have about six tennis courts to play on. If you go to a white club there will be 15 tennis courts and half a mile further on another 15 tennis courts . . .). There is no way I can be equal to a white man who has more facilities, better housing, better jobs, just because he is white. It is impossible. This is why when we talk of non-racial sport we are also talking of social and economic changes.

'It is very difficult to speak aloud in a country where politics is taboo. When I was a teacher in South Africa I had to teach my pupils about the French Revolution — about Liberty, Fraternity and Equality, the Ancien Regime in France and the class system. This was so clear in our society, where we have first-class and second-class and third-class citizens; it would have been ideal for me to compare France in 1789 with South African society and all my students would have understood at once. But I would have been making them politically aware and I would have been picked up at once. When you talk politics in South Africa you take your life into your hands, no one can be trusted.

'In sport it is different. What is non-racialism? It is equality in sport. I wasn't politically aware when I took up sport but through sport non-racialism becomes alive, you begin to breathe it and eat it, you come into contact with people and, although you are not talking politics but sport, you are all aware that you want equality and once that seeps into your mind you are willing to fight. The pressure is a little less. You're willing to fight for equality in sport and, when you face the sort of problems I had, your political awareness comes automatically, whether you like it or not. When you fight for human rights or human beings, that is politics — and it's a simple notion, you don't have to read books to understand it or experience it and in non-racial sport I think people in South Africa are not only experiencing the word 'equality', they are experiencing what goes with it — sacrifice, pleasure, being deprived of certain things. And at a certain stage the stand you take as a non-racial sportsman inspires your family or your friends, they may take up political struggle. They are bound to do so. Most sportsmen will never take up arms but their fight for equality is always there, in the paper — overseas — and the people can never forget, they are reminded now more than ever that the fight for equality in sport is one with the fight for equality in Soweto, they go hand in hand to a certain extent.

'It is inspiring, too, to know that there are people overseas who are supporting you. It is inspiring when a sportsman overseas says he will not go to South Africa because of its policies, or when white South Africans are thrown out of some international body. We are glad because then they are on equal terms with us, they are as isolated as we are. Why do they make such a big fuss and protest when they are excluded? They expect the Blacks to keep quiet!

'Look, David Samaai was wasted. Herman Abrahams was wasted. I was wasted. And of the 18 to 20 million Blacks in South Africa, thousands are being wasted now. I admire any white sportsman who refuses to participate in a sporting event which is not non-racial. There are a few white sportsmen willing to take a stand and I admire them. But after the game is over they go home to their own townships, they do not live with us, they do not experience the hardships of black sportsmen, they don't know our problems. The white world is a very privileged world and the black world very underprivileged — and unless the white sportsmen will help us to come out of it, are ready to make sacrifices — to sacrifice their sport as we have done, or give up their jobs as we do, or even go to jail as we have to do — I can only feel bitterness. I forgot my Indian tag at a certain stage in my life, I was ready to invite Blacks to my house, to go to their homes. Well, the Whites must also reach that stage, of identifying with the Blacks. Until they do, there is going to be no truly non-racial sport. Personally, I feel bitterness towards every white tennis player who comes overseas, I have no respect for him as a human being — I don't care how liberal they are, their hypocrisy stands out like a bright star in the sky. If they really want to know how the Blacks feel, then ask the Blacks. They have never asked us. When we co-operate they talk well of us, but when we state the truth they reject us — as we were rejected by the International Tennis Federation.

'People ask me sometimes, they say: If you join the white body, you will get coaches and tennis courts and money to go overseas. I am forced to reply to them by saying: Look, we have enough money, we have enough coaches and we can find courts. What we want is competition. We want dignity. We want our rights as South African human beings. And I am positive that if you were to interview one of the white non-racial sportsmen he would feel just as bitter about the injustices practised against black South Africans.

'Yes, we still believe in the principles of non-racialism. We make sacrifices for this principle. I have sacrificed my job and my family has suffered — they still suffer, because the letters I send to them are opened and they are questioned by the police. My friends refuse to write to me because my letters were intercepted and it was dangerous for them. When they come here, they cannot talk to me about what they think because they are afraid. This is the imprisoned society in which we live. We are in a prison in South Africa — and there are so many in my position. So many are suffering, and so many more are going to be destroyed. And the tragedy of it all, and it is a tragedy in the true sense of the word, is that there are not going to be changes until a violent revolution takes place and they overthrow the white government. And you know that thousands of lives are going to be lost.

'So I am very bitter towards white sportsmen — and I have the same feelings towards the French rugby team that is to go out to South Africa, or the British tour. They know why they are going. If they really wanted to know whether to go or not, they should ask the Blacks! The Blacks will tell them fast enough. Go home, we don't want you here, finish. The Whites are not going to oppose them, so ask the Blacks! Those people are lucky that we cannot demonstrate in South Africa. If we could, not a single match would take place. They should be thankful it is a police state!'

Jasmat Dhiraj
South African non-racial tennis champion, in exile.
Interview, London, February 1980

A Sporting Nation?
Introduction

South Africa, sport, apartheid: together these three words compose a political knot which has fascinated the media and tormented the sporting world for over a decade. It has provoked miles of newsprint and hours of discussion. No other sporting issue, perhaps, has generated so much heat and so little light in the last few years, or drawn so many who are not directly involved into the controversy. Why then write more about it?

South Africa, certainly according to white South Africans, is a 'sporting nation'. The quantities of private financial investment, time and energy South Africans devote to sport, its ethos and the public interest it arouses, combine to indicate its social importance. South African sporting facilities are considered to be among the best, if not *the* best, in the world — for white South Africans. Official statistics list 400,000 registered players of major sports[1] and 660,000 players of minor sports (including billiards, fishing, etc.), figures which suggest that about a million white South Africans belong to sports clubs of one kind or another. This means that about one in every four white South Africans — one in every three adults — belongs to a sports club. Excellent public amenities are backed up with a wealth of private sports facilities in clubs, schools and private homes. A swimming bath and tennis court are such normal appurtenances of self-respecting white homes that, according to a director of the Trust Building Society in 1974, 'It is becoming more and more difficult to satisfy the normal demands of our private clients, for private garden, swimming pool, tennis court, two car garage, study, games room, carpet and insistence upon "personalized design", etc.'[2]

White South Africans take full advantage of these opportunities. After school, children are free to spend entire afternoons week-in week-out playing sport, and at the end of the day they are joined by the adult population who profit from the two or three remaining hours of light after work to swim or play tennis. Wednesdays and Saturdays have been devoted to sport and recreation from the earliest days of British colonization. (Nearly 40% of white South Africans claim British descent.) To this luxury of opportunity is added an extraordinary fervour for sporting activity, far more pronounced even than in Britain, whose Victorian ethos effectively brought modern sport into existence. 'Sport is incredibly significant in South Africa, and sports news is *the* news,' according to Bob Watson. 'I well remember an occasion when the local news bulletin was, first, about a couple of leopards that the police had set out after in the mountains to the south of the farms, secondly about the success of the local rugby team the previous Saturday, and thirdly about the devaluation of the currency!'[3] Many authors have claimed that South African sport is almost a 'national religion'. Peter Hain suggests that 'It is almost as if the limits on freedom of thought and expression in South Africa force whites to seek self-fulfilment in sporting achievement, and this, coupled with the general sporting interest found in all ex-British colonies, makes for a formidable sports thirst.'[4] The Afrikaner novelist Andre Brink tells how Mr B.J. Vorster, then Prime Minister, arranged to be interrupted every quarter of an hour during his talks with the American Secretary of State, Henry Kissinger, to be informed of the score of an All-Blacks-Springboks rugby match![5]

The artificial wealth of the white community as a whole[6] and the country's beautiful natural resources and climate both facilitate outdoor activity and together mean that water sports and games like golf are not limited to a restricted and exclusive following as they are in other countries. Another reason for the popularity of sport is the scarcity of alternative cultural activities, which encourages white South Africans to seek relaxation and self-expression in physical activity. In a society which used to offer few opportunities for social contact among families dispersed on farms throughout the countryside, matches and competitions fulfilled from the beginning an extra-sporting function which cannot be underestimated. Even in the towns, white people naturally congregate in their sports and country clubs. In short, for white South Africans, sport probably is and has been *the* characteristic form of social expression.

Its pre-eminent role in white South African social life gives the study of South African sport an interest beyond any intrinsic interest in sport as such. Sport is embedded in South African history and hence in the country's racist traditions and social organization as a whole. Thus it is not merely a question of why sport was in a *position* to become so important, but why in fact it did. And this in turn leads us to examine the history of sport itself.

The first settlers from Holland did not bring sports and sporting habits with them when they settled at the Cape in the 17th Century, for they arrived too early. Modern sport as we know it — with its ethos of effort, of justice and fair play, of peaceable and courteous competition, its appeal to self-discipline and physical performance and to individual will power, and a public ideology that transforms sportsmen and teams into bearers of collective identity, of national and village pride etc. — emerged in Victorian Britain in the second half of the 19th Century.[7] It was brought to South Africa by the British immigrants who annexed and settled the country between 1800 and 1902. Sport and British cultural values, especially those of the public schools, were thereafter inseparably linked. The norm of sport bequeathed to South Africa was attuned to British practice, and black as well as white children remember listening to the B.B.C. sports results as if British sport set the ultimate standards of excellence.[8]

This British model — the model for modern sport — was not of course value-free. Its appearance at the end of the 19th Century coincided with the height of Empire and public school educational ideas. It was a middle-class model derived from traditional and popular sports. One might say that the British ruling class propagated an *aristocratic* ideology of sport to correspond with its aristocratic image of education. The virtues of the sportsman (initiative, energy, bravery, hardiness, collective and individual discipline, loyalty, will power and respect for individual achievement) complemented those of the scholar (literacy, education, obedience, intelligence, adaptability) to produce 'leaders of men'. While sport encouraged virility, academic education — a democratic and democratizing activity — promoted the virtues of obedience and judicious reflection. As P. Bourdieu observes, the British model of sport therefore reinforced a social hierarchy whose structure could not be represented within a hierarchy of pure learning — but which was nevertheless inserted into the heart of the educational structures which were being developed at that time in European societies.[9] This pseudo-aristocratic ideology of sport was in its turn assimilated by the ideology of colonialism.[10] This gave rise to the racist idea that athletes not only represented 'civilization' but were necessarily *white* (and male!).

At the same time, the ideology of sport and Empire naturally influenced the ideas of educated Africans. Sport was part of the curriculum in British mission schools which, from the time of their appearance at the beginning of the 19th Century, had counterposed their assimilationist and elitist conception of education to the segregationist, narrowly religious and slave model of the Boers.[11] When modern sport arrived in South Africa in the last third of the 19th Century, it was also adopted by, and became part of the culture of, the minute assimilated black elite — although not to the same degree as in white schools, where Rhodes' ideal of the rounded man ruled supreme and where facilities were appropriate to the needs of the true *ruling* white elite.

Thus sport was practised by different groups in South Africa's segregated society, where it reinforced and was assimilated into the white ideology of racist supremacy: almost from its beginnings, it both confirmed the racist assumptions of white society and stood for the integrationist principles of the black elite — a contradiction from which South African sport has never been wholly freed, and which is nourished by the peculiarly ambivalent ideology of sport itself.

The initial idealism of Blacks waned as white racism became entrenched, and sport increasingly became one of the points of reference by which Europeans 'proved' their superior 'civilization'. Thus sport came to occupy for white South Africans its present supreme rank among educational and social activities. Emotionally, within South Africa the average white sportsman — and especially the rugby player — has unconsciously elevated sport into a symbol of white virility and superiority.[12] This in turn has ensured that in South Africa, where apartheid gives everything a political dimension, sport has a specific political significance. For Blacks today, a weapon of resistance to apartheid, in the past an expression of colonial values, sport was also politically significant in the growth of South African nationalism among the Boers — the modern Afrikaners. For them sport and patriotism became closely identified.[13] Sporting victories were so many proofs of the truth of their social and political theory of apartheid.[14]

Afrikaners have clothed their sport in the ideology of the State: 'In South Africa,' declares the very Official Year Book for 1977, 'the term "sport" is automatically coupled with competition and rivalry.'[15] This remark would be merely banal, except that in South Africa the sporting ideal of struggle is ascribed not only to individuals but to their racial and national communities. Frequent reference is made in official texts to sport's collective virtues, its promotion of esprit de corps. For example, the role of the Department of Sport and Recreation is defined officially as follows: 'to advise on and encourage activities calculated to develop a strong and healthy nation . . . . Within this broad framework it co-operates with, and assists those sports bodies and recreational associations which seek to build character and encourage discipline as well as physical fitness.'[16]

For white South Africa sport is a collective activity, necessary to the community and instilling values indispensable to its strength and future safety. This attitude is exemplified in the government-sponsored 'National Fitness' campaigns (renamed Trimsa in 1978) encouraging white South Africans to participate in carefully graded mass sporting activities and competitions. Their official purpose is to increase the population's 'determination and perseverance'. It is certainly not by chance that rugby has become South Africa's national sport: a team sport generally assumed to stimulate individual and collective discipline, both South African and foreign observers have been struck by the quasi-mystical identification of the white community with the fortunes of its rugby players.

Thus the official ideology attributes to sport what amounts to a collective morality. Festive and recreational qualities are displaced by an ascetic fervour: the practice of sport becomes an investment of effort, the body — in its social and socialized as well as individual capacities — ascribed a moral purpose. This is what gives sport the exemplary educational virtues emphasized in official circles. Sport reinforces national and international links, improves health and instructs the white nation. It not only implies a *communal* ethic, but a *political* ethic — the affirmation and strengthening of the racial community, a guarantee of its supremacy. 'Defeat in the sports field is treated as a national humiliation for the whites; success confirms their world view of the master race, their heroic image of themselves and justifies to themselves the position of superiority they claim and hold.'[17]

Modern history has, of course, accustomed us to seeing sporting competitions used generally to personify and adjudicate between conflicting socio-economic systems, even though in one way or another, they are in fact the latter's creatures. But South Africa is unique in its systematic use of sports results as disguised votes, sporting relations as overseas publicity and touring teams as ambassadors.

The nationalistic manipulation of sport by the South African ruling class is made more comprehensible by the fact that historically the Afrikaner community consolidated its sense of national identity during the inter-war period when sporting activity was in full expansion, and when Afrikaners were organizing themselves to combat the discrimination they suffered at the hands of the British.[18] To the average Afrikaner, sport was at this time one of the few paths open, outside politics, through which to achieve social distinction.[19]

This nationalist identification was not confined to the Afrikaner community alone. The following experience of Sadie Berman — who held radical and anti-apartheid views — reveals to what extent sport dominated the social and individual values even of those who were critical of Nationalist policy in the 1950s and who had access to a wide cultural tradition.

> Alan was very strong. From the age of four he was swimming like a fish. He was really quite remarkable by any standards and, carried away by the thought of all this glory, we took him to private coaching. So by the time he entered the school in Grade 1 he was already swimming better than the boys in Standard 6. So he was immediately a personality, a hero, he broke all the records, he won all the cups and we — we were thinking people, with cultural interests — even we were so bowled over by all the fuss and acclaim and those endless cups and medals and mentions in newspapers and talk of Olympic Games that we were brainwashed by it. So the emphasis in Alan's very young life was to eat the right food, soya beans, and we had stopwatches and every day we would go to the baths — all the paraphernalia . . . . It really dominated my life, and he was quite keen because of all the glory. Stupidly I was bowled over. It became a very dominant part of our lives, despite the fact that I was very politically conscious. Yet this wasn't to be questioned: this great talent must be developed.
>
> Sure it was a reflection of the social values. Even with ourselves who *abhorred* the social values and the mores of that society. When it came to sport it was nevertheless — I'm ashamed to say it — a very important part of our lives. And everyone who knew us was basking in this reflected glory![20]

Finally, of course, the preponderance of sport in South African society can be seen simply as a form of escape from more disquieting issues. In a society as repressive and contradictory as South Africa, sport's 'neutral' and 'apolitical' image make it a particularly appealing refuge.

> I think sport is a form of escapism in South Africa. Most South Africans aren't political. But more than that. Politics in South Africa is actually a dirty subject — not just as in Europe where people see politicians as cynical: people see politics as a thing which raises too many questions, is a bit nasty, involves apartheid — is just far too complicated and forces them to think about their own situation far more than they want to.

What they want to do is live their lives and have their swimming pools and their second cars and their servants, and sport is a sort of escape route for them culturally. And that is reflected in the absolute obsession with which the sports pages are read in South Africa by the average Whites. The zeal is a hundred times greater — and that of course is one of the reasons why the sports campaigns have had such a phenomenal impact.[21]

Sport Is White

Sport in South Africa has an undeniable moral and political content and its history has influenced its modern social role. What we have said in the preceding pages, however, should alert us to bias: for *whose* sport are we describing when we speak of 'South African sport'? Only white sport? What about black sport? Indeed, should we speak of 'black sport'? What prevents us from speaking quite ordinarily of 'South African sport' as a whole?

The first answer is, of course, that sportsmen and women are identified by the nations they represent, and that in this sense South African sport and South African sportsmen have almost invariably been white. In the eyes of the official, recognized sports associations (all segregated until the 'multi-national' policy was introduced in the 1970s, and even today, all white-controlled) 'national' sport certainly meant 'white' sport. By the same token, it was effectively white South African sport which was expelled from the Olympic Movement for its racism. The existence of apartheid, the policy of so-called separate development for the different racial groups (presented by Whites as so many separate 'nations' with separate futures) *forces* us to consider the divisions and cleavages which have been imposed on South African society and to speak of South African sport not in the singular but in the plural — of several sporting cultures with different histories and characteristics.

If, however, we cannot speak unequivocally of 'South African sport', this should not suggest that the organization of sport in South Africa is not a single inter-related whole which, like other aspects of society, is both unified and decomposed by the laws and ideology of apartheid. The differences and divisons between social classes and communities can only be understood in terms of the historical, social, economic and political entity which we call South Africa — with its contradictions and the characteristic domestic relations of dominance and dependence that assure its fragile equilibrium.

Yet we talk, and always have, of 'South African sport' when what we are referring to is white sport — a not innocent elision of ideas which is committed as systematically inside South Africa as it is abroad. There is of course a degree of truth in the presumption that 'sport' and 'white sport' are one and the same. In comparison with 'non-white' sporting activity (among the African, Coloured and Indian populations), white sport *is* highly developed. It would be astonishing if this were not so: gross exploitation of black labour provides white South Africans with one of the world's highest standards of living and the leisure to enjoy it, while their monopoly of the law and the political process has permitted them to occupy as much space as they desire.[22] White South Africans can devote resources of money, time, energy, space and health to sport which are quite out of proportion to what the pariahs of the system, the Black majority, can afford. Indeed, one could say that in South Africa Blacks work so that Whites can play sport! By the same token, black sport is fostered by white society only as a means of raising productivity, as in the mines: the socio-economic relations which characterize the society are transferred to sport and govern it as they govern other activities. One man's sport is placed at the service of another.

This is a general truth, of course, but it takes a rather special, particularly unambiguous form in South Africa, where the apartheid system *organizes* the domination and exploitation of the black majority for the profit of the white minority, and where, as a result, the *development* of sport among the latter entails the *underdevelopment* of sport among Blacks. Whites have thus been able to appropriate national sport, to such an extent that for nearly a century 'South African sport' has come to be identified with white sport both abroad and by white South Africans themselves. These attitudes help to create the ludicrous, but tragic, situations for which South African sport has become famous:

> Ronnie van der Walt was a moderately successful white boxer until the government decided that he was Coloured. He left South Africa in 1967 to box in England because he could no longer box against those he had been fighting for so many years in South Africa.[23]

> In South Africa it's tough to think of race. The situation there is so hard. Say you just form a club — you don't call it a non-racial club, no, you just let anyone who is interested join. Like we had a boy who thought he was Coloured: then after a while he was classified as white so he had to leave the team! (Laughter) Having swum in polluted water.[24]

> Glen Popham won the gold medal in the South African Games in karate and had been the captain of the Springbok team. While Popham's team-mates were awarded the Springbok colours for winning the silver and bronze medals in that competition, Popham was denied them because it was discovered after the Games that Popham had been classified as 'Coloured'.[25]

Given this context, it is not surprising that no significance was ever attached to the traditional sports of African peoples. Because the institution of modern sport was introduced to South Africa in recent times, and from Europe, traditional skills such as hunting, archery, spear throwing, and numerous forms of wrestling and dance, have never been recognized by Whites as sports except in so far as they conform to European norms. For the same reasons, most commentators and spokesmen for official white sports institutions have held and still assume, quite wrongly, that black South Africans have not adopted and do not enjoy most sports. To hear them one would imagine that no black sportsmen existed before the 1950s, although there is overwhelming evidence that almost as soon as modern sports were introduced into the country, the black population began to play and watch them, as they have continued to do ever since. There is no obvious explanation for the almost complete lack of awareness of this side of South Africa's sporting history, for we have found considerable amounts of accessible information on the subject. In the chapters that follow we present, admittedly cursorily, this other face of South African sport. It represents a picture of the desires and aspirations of black South Africans in the field of sport from the beginning of the century — aspirations systematically refused and even denied existence.

> Of all the curious experiences in observing South African rugby and talking to its leaders and followers, none was more astonishing than that none of them raised the question of African or Coloured players. The matter did not appear to exist in their minds. The African and Coloured Rugby Federations might have been in another physical continent, not merely a separate continent of the spirit. Old Springbok players would talk earnestly, even with passion, about the virtue of rugby in 'uniting the races' . . . but for them the races were Afrikaner and English, the religions Dutch Reformed and Anglican. The blankness with which they responded to the idea that rugby might bring together other races with Whites would be a useful spectacle for those to contemplate who believe that 'tours build bridges'.[26]

The international sports boycott in the 1960s and 1970s undoubtedly forced white South Africans to change this picture. They were obliged to admit that black sport existed and take black aspirations into account. This represented a major concession by the white establishment, and was a considerable achievement; it should not, however, conceal the triviality of the resulting changes, or obscure the degree of control still exercised over black sport. The enforcement of apartheid laws which segregate and reinforce inequality continue, in 1981, to keep sport white. An ambassador, an ex-Springbok captain, Dawie de Villiers,[27] can still declare: 'Don't forget that the Blacks have really known Western sports [only] for the last ten years. They have naturally not yet reached the same standard . . . . Coloured people are taking sport up more and more.'[28] In the same manner, the Department of Sport and Recreation can still issue in 1980-81 what it calls a 'factual statement' to an official commission of inquiry from the British Sports Council, in which it claims that: 'sport in South Africa has evolved methodically in a sustained manner over the past twenty years — when Non-White population groups *also became interested and started to participate* in the wide variety of sports . . . .'[29] The 1977 *Official Year Book* states quite simply:

Blacks, Coloureds, Indians and Whites have always administered and
practised their sports separately at all levels of competition. Moreover,
it is only comparatively recently that the Black peoples have shown a
marked interest in what may be called modern sporting activities. For
centuries they found their recreation in traditional activities, such as
hunting and tribal dances.

It was the White nation, with its European background and tradition,
which participated in the recognized sports.[30]

Implicitly, such spokesmen assimilate the unequal development of sport
among Blacks and Whites, which is a consequence of segregation and of
apartheid policies, to some *natural* difference in the psycho-physiological
character of black people. Not only are the historical facts distorted, for
Blacks began in fact to adopt the major sports at very much the same time
as the white population, but this false history is rationalized by the ethnocentric assumption that sport is at a relatively primitive level among the
'non-white' population because the Blacks *are* relatively primitive. It follows,
of course, that apartheid is in no way responsible for the inequality in social
and economic development which is so marked a feature of South African
society and sport.

In the past, these ethnocentric assumptions, more naively declared, have
led to some quite fantastic conclusions — for example, the assertion by white
members of a surf life-saving team that Coloured swimmers did not like to
get too close to water because surf was a voodoo area; or the celebrated
remark of Mr Braun, a member of South Africa's Olympic Committee, who
explained to a reporter that Africans were generally weak swimmers because
'the water closes their pores so they cannot get rid of carbon dioxide and
they tire quickly'.[31]

These remarks, caricatures though they seem, reveal the underlying significance of the identification of sport with whiteness. Sport represents,
symbolizes for white South Africans, their intrinsic racial superiority. Indeed
the force of this conditioning has been such that, until recently, even black
sportsmen were apparently under its spell.

> Originally black people were withheld from participation in big-time
> sport by a number of factors . . . . As a result the only heroes black
> people knew in the sports they loved best were white people whom
> they saw in white events and in films. With the coming of greater
> organization . . . and the banning of black people from some white
> sports fields, blacks are beginning to develop an allegiance towards
> their own kind and no longer are young blacks very taken up by what
> they read of white sport in newspapers.[32]

White South Africans' ignorance of the existence of black sport in fact
reflects the real position Blacks are permitted to occupy in the society. They
are assumed to be second-class citizens with a derivative culture. White South

Africans therefore take it for granted that it is a privilege for Blacks to watch their games; and since privileges are not rights, when apartheid began to be applied strictly in the 1950s, it followed that Black spectators should be excluded. They were chased from the stands, or permitted to watch only from separate and inferior seating; and in many places, this is still the situation today.

Black servants are scarcely more tolerated than black spectators. A Black on a golf course is almost certain to be a member of the maintenance staff or a caddie, on the race course a stable boy. The huge potential market that black sport represents only seems to have become apparent to white business-men recently, under the pressures of economic constraint. The white press has also lately seized its opportunity and several 'extras' now appear (separate editions of white papers for black audiences). In efforts to reduce its inter-national isolation, even the white sports establishment has recently promoted a few black players to some of its national teams. On the other hand, apart-heid has never forbidden Blacks to spend very large sums of money on horse-racing: this was the reason, no doubt, why the colour bar in South African race-courses was, until the 1950s, less rigid than elsewhere.[33] At all levels, inter-racial contact and participation is vetted according to the social and racial status of individuals and groups, in line with apartheid principles and economic interest.

This is no less true when it comes to actual participation. Players are generally as segregated on the field as they are in the stands; but here again, if we look closely, we see that racial separation is most rigidly enforced in team games and in games which involve bodily contact, like rugby. Individual and non-physical sports, like tennis or golf, are now less subject to an absolute veto on inter-racial competition. The psychological nuances in play show up in the peculiarly rigid enforcement of racial separation in swimming pools, where contact takes place *indirectly* through the medium of water. In fact the playing of sport is shot through with sub-conscious feelings about body contact. Africans are admitted to be adept at certain sports, particularly football, which has been abandoned by the middle classes to the white work-ing class and the Blacks; but it is nevertheless assumed that the African body is exceptionally fitted to perform feats of strength and endurance — and hence for sports like running and boxing, which the mining houses have fostered among their workers. This is a white perception of the black body — powerful, capable of withstanding — if not actually insensitive to — pain, an endurance machine well adapted to the working conditions imposed on and suffered by black manual workers. In 1946, for example, a consultant on black leisure facilities, liberal by belief, concluded from American studies of negro work capacity that:

> In planning a comprehensive physical education scheme for the South
> African Bantu, two physiological facts must be borne in mind: first,
> that the black races of the African continent possess an extraordinarily
> high physical labour capacity, probably higher than that of any other

human race, and that they are singularly well adjusted to the hot and humid climate which characterises large portions of their home continent; secondly, that this high physical labour capacity of the African people is masked by continuous losses of what biologists call 'adaptation energy' caused by a variety of preventable circumstances.

Laboratory and statistical studies in which the performance capacity of Africans has been measured and compared with that of other races bear out the contention that the physical labour capacity of the African is very great.

Professor Dill, of Harvard University in Boston, applied standard physical fitness tests to a number of experimental subjects, among them Negro and white Mississippi sharecroppers. Professor Dill's results clearly point to the conclusion that Negroes are physiologically better fitted than Europeans for strenuous physical work, more particularly in hot environments.[34]

How perfect is natural design! After 1948, indeed, the white authorities systematically encouraged the traditional quasi-sporting activities of African migrant workers (dancing, wrestling and other forms of combat, etc.). In the mines, workers were positively encouraged to keep fit, since this helped to raise productivity below ground. The policies were both produced by and reinforced an image of the black body which closely resembles the white stereotype of black Americans. Virile, brutal, powerful, the image declares the oppressor's fear of the oppressed and faithfully reflects the economic and social relations that bind both parties together.

Socio-economically, the separate and unequal development of black and white sport is closely associated with the system as a whole. There is an intimate relation between sport and apartheid, between sport and discrimination, oppression and racial exploitation in their most political forms. We can clearly see in fact how *white authority has arrogated to itself power over the bodies of its subjects*, by regulations which, in their astonishing extension and grotesque punctiliousness, underline the neurotic preoccupations of the law-makers. The black body is segregated, repelled, isolated from ordinary social intercourse by curfew,[35] confined to the ghetto townships[36] or mining compounds, and kept under perpetual surveillance and administrative control through the pass laws. The system renders black people all but invisible. Their role is to work, to produce, to serve by labouring, whatever their state of deprivation or ill-health and, should they become unproductive, to disappear silently to the Bantustan dumping grounds on the periphery of white South Africa. Even sexual desire is subject to legal limitation: the Mixed Marriages Act reveals hauntingly the degree to which the State has asserted its control over the body.[37]

Song Story

In April 1961, the Minister of the Interior declared that the final criteria of the racial membership of an individual was his or her acceptability to the surrounding community. A man of Chinese origin, David Song, presented a request to become white. His candidacy was supported by 300 local white residents, and he was declared to be white. Several Members of Parliament then asked the Minister whether he was intending to prosecute Mr Song for having married a Chinese woman, in contravention of the Mixed Marriages and Immorality Acts. The Minister replied that the marriage had taken place before the acts became law and was therefore considered to be legal.

The white body too is subject to moral direction, for the image of white sport promulgated by the official establishment also imposes moral obligations and values upon the individual and on white society as a whole — white values which the apartheid system is pledged to maintain against corruption or destruction by the black population or by a 'foreign' ideology (communism).

Under apartheid, which classifies society in physical and racial terms, there is therefore an intimate association between sport (physical exercise) and the body. Although we cannot do more here than gesture towards the psychological mechanisms and implications of this association, it permeates all aspects of the issue and should not be forgotten.

For all these reasons, the appeal of a study of South African sport is not confined merely to those interested in sport, or South Africa. Being the most widespread social activity for all population groups, or at least the three largest (African, White and Coloured), it offers an unusual and revealing point of entry from which to explore the country's hierarchical and segregated social organization and political system. Nor is it of interest solely because we can read the structures of apartheid in its form of organization; for its character and ideology are such that sport reveals almost spontaneously the values which dominate and have dominated social and political organization in South Africa since the country came into being. Its history and organization provide a picture, though partial, of South African society as a whole — in the same way as those we interviewed, in talking of sport, told us about all sorts of other things. It is an activity to which vast resources have been and are devoted — in time, money, space, feeling, words, patterns of behaviour, values; an activity which, as elsewhere, is supposedly apolitical, expressing the simple and purer virtues of the body and physical exercise; it involves the complex psycho-social relations between humans and their bodies, between black and white bodies; it is capable of disclosing the play between individuals and society, and the political forces which in constant friction mould and direct behaviour. In short, we are interested in sport not only because it occupies so prominent a place in society, but also because of its close association with the body, and with physical expression in all its forms — with the body in its social context, as bearer of social and also political values. In this sense, would it not be mistaken to assume that the dramatic experience and history of South Africa's people, which we will discover in the following pages through their sport, is entirely alien to ourselves?

Permits are not needed for road races . . . and cross-countries . . . but if public conveniences are to be used at the start or finish, or if the race ends at a stadium in a 'white' area, then a permit is needed.[38]

In 1962, the S.A. Amateur Athletics Union sent a team selected on merit to compete in a tournament in Mozambique. No black runners had been selected, although two black athletes had run their heats faster than the white competitors who replaced them.

    When Matt Mare, the head of S.A.A.A.U., was asked why Henry Khosi, whose time was 0.1 of a second faster than the white man selected, was not chosen, he replied, '0.1 second does not really count'.[39]

References

1.   Rugby, cricket, football, tennis, hockey, netball, golf, cycling, athletics, boxing, gymnastics, swimming, table tennis, basketball, softball, bowls, motor racing. Of 4,300,000 Whites, some 3,000,000 may be said to be potential sports players, if we exclude children under 9 years old and adults over 60. (The above figures are taken from *South Africa 1977, Official Year Book*.)

2.   In M. Cornevin, 1977, p. 188.

3.   Bob Watson, interview, London, 12 February, 1980.

4.   P. Hain, 1971, p. 43.

5.   Interview, France-Culture (French radio), Parti-Pris, 22 September 1976.

6.   See Chapter 7.

7.   It is not of course true that sport did not exist before, and elsewhere, or that it was exclusively European in origin: nevertheless, the features which characterize sport today do derive from European sport as it was practised in recent times, particularly in Britain at the end of the 19th Century.

8.   S. Ramsamy, interview, Paris, October 1979.

9.   See P. Bourdieu, 1979, pp. 102-3.

10. See E. Weber, *Gymnastique et Sport en France . . .*, in *Aimez-vous les Stades?*, 1980.

11. Descendants of the earliest Dutch settlers who arrived in South Africa at the end of the 17th Century and who are today known as Afrikaners.

12. J. Laurence, 1979, p. 131.

13. Opperman in S.A. Olympic and National Games Association, 1976.

14. See Chapters 2 and 9.
15. *South Africa 1977, Official Year Book*, 1977, p. 808.
16. *South Africa 1977, Official Year Book*, 1977, p. 808.
17. Joan Brickhill, 1976, p. 8.
18. See Chapter 1.
19. Bob Watson, interview, London, 12 February, 1980.
20. Sadie Berman, interview, London, 15 February, 1980.
21. Peter Hain, interview, London, 20 February, 1980.
22. White South Africans, who compose 20% of the population, occupy and own about 87% of the land: Africans, who compose 70% of the population, have the right to live in only 13% of the land area.
23. R. Lapchick, 1975, p. 10.
24. Interview with an African, London, February, 1980.
25. R. Lapchick, 1975, p. 212.
26. John Morgan, *Sunday Times*, 16 November 1969, quoted in P. Hain, 1971, p. 40.
27. Ambassador to Britain 1979-80; Springbok rugby captain 1965-70; Member of South African Parliament 1980-81.
28. *L'Equipe*, 10 March 1980 [Trans. from French].
29. British Sports Council, 1980, p. 8. [Author's italics].
30. *South Africa 1977, Official Year Book*, 1977, p. 807.
31. 'A Flare in the Dark' in *Sports Illustrated*, 3 June 1968, quoted in R. Lapchick, 1975, p. 92.' Mr Braun went on to say that Africans are 'great boxers and cyclers and runners'.
32. *Black Review*, 1972, p. 47.
33. See below pp. 41-2, 46.
34. E. Jokl in E. Hellmann, 1949, p. 449.
35. Africans are forbidden to go out on the streets after 9, 10 or 11 p.m. in 117 South African towns and villages; public thoroughfares are reserved exclusively for use by Whites.
36. Townships are sited at a distance from the cities; all Africans (except a proportion of house servants, watchmen, etc.) are compelled to live in these artificially segregated areas, within commuting distance from their work, but 'safely' distant from the white population.
37. The Immorality Act of 1927 prohibits sexual relations between Whites and Africans, including, of course, within marriage. In 1950, the law was extended to cover sexual relations between Whites and all Blacks, including Indians and Coloureds. Inter-racial marriage was declared illegal in 1949.
38. Brian Scoones, President of the (White) Natal Amateur Athletics Federation, quoted by C.A.R.D.S., 9 October 1976.
39. *Star*, Johannesburg, 30 April 1962, quoted by R. Lapchick, 1975, p. 46.

1. Sport in South African History

My very existence proves the apartheid fallacy. Early Portuguese
adventurers at Goa injected red hair into my Indian ancestry and, on
my mother's side, I can boast a minister of the Dutch Reformed Church
as an ancestor. Chapman of Chapman's Peak married into the family.
Our bond is really very close. How can one be anti-white or fight against
whites under these circumstances, it may be one's uncle you are fighting, your own blood and people. There are people sitting in Parliament
who would blush if they were aware of their ancestry. I am a true South
African. Not a black, white, yellow, pink or green South African.[1]

Hassan Howa

South Africa entered European history on 5 April 1652 when 100 men led
by Jan van Riebeeck landed in Cape Town Bay to establish a port of call for
the Dutch East India Company.[2] Official propaganda and the official histories taught in South African schools declare that the first immigrants, who
went on to colonize the area of what is now Cape Province, found the country without inhabitants, a virgin land:[3] at most, small populations of
'Hottentots' hunted and gathered in the area; the Bantu-speaking peoples
did not descend southwards until later, or until the Europeans moved inland.
It follows, they argue, that Europeans had first rights of possession, as of
April 1652, over the entire territory.

This hypothesis has been widely discredited and no serious independent
historian would defend it today. In fact the Bantu peoples appeared on the
inland plateau (*veld*) and on the coast before the 14th Century. They assimilated the Hottentots who were already there, or drove them, like the Bushmen,
towards more arid areas. Both Hottentots and Bushmen had been living in the
country since at least a thousand years before Christ, and the Bushmen (as
their paintings and other archaeological records prove) for several thousand
years.

When many of the settlers shook off their ties with the Dutch East India
Company and moved inland to herd cattle and sheep, they soon came up
against these 'non-inhabitants'. From 1779 until the end of the 19th Century,
they fought for the land and for supremacy over these peoples and also over
the Xhosa, a Bantu tribe with whom they clashed regularly in the area of the

Fish River after 1702. The settlers called all these African peoples 'Kaffirs' —
and often, like Van Riebeeck, 'stinking black dogs'. The last so-called Kaffir
War took place in 1906.

Early Beginnings

If it is inappropriate to talk of 'sports' in the context of these African societies, their games and physical skills should not be ignored. Drawings of boxers
with gloved hands have been found in a Zimbabwean cave[4] and dancing is a
highly developed art in several South African societies. Unfortunately, we
are unlikely to have good information about these traditional physical attain-
ments until greater freedom of expression in South Africa allows objective
research to be undertaken. All we can do at the moment is signal the presence
of these traditions.

Little is known either about the traditional games and exercises of the first
settlers, who were joined after 1688 by a group of Huguenots fleeing France
after the Edict of Nantes. Folk sports were certainly practised before modern
sport made its appearance in the 19th Century. *Jukskei*, for example, is today
organized by the S.A. Jukskei Board (founded in 1940) which has 20,000
affiliated members and nearly 700 clubs.[5] *Vingertrek*, another traditional
game, now played by children, used to be contested by burly adults at the
religious festival of *nachtmal*.[6] Finally, the horse, which played a crucial part
in Boer social and working life, also featured in many recreational activities.

Of Calvinist faith, and persuaded that they belonged to a superior culture
and race, the settlers fought the Xhosa not only for their lands and cattle but
also to acquire servile labour. The Hottentots who came to work for wages in
the Cape formed the basis of a lower social class to which were added the
slaves imported into Cape Town from India, Java, Madagascar and East
Africa. Mixed with the original settlers, all these groups came to compose
the so-called Cape Coloured population.[7] 75% of the children born during
the first 20 years of the colony's existence had a white father and African
mother,[8] and inter-racial sexual relations apparently continued, because in
1685 a new law forbade Whites to marry their African slaves. At this date,
44 of the 92 Cape Town children under 12 years of age had African mothers.
In 1717, the Dutch East India Company stopped new white immigration,
prohibited inter-racial marriage altogether and encouraged the import of
slaves. This decision was crucial for the future of the Colony, for it identified
skin colour and race with class and status. Henceforth, Whites were to rule
and monopolize economic and political power, while Blacks were to labour,
serve and obey.

> In the long quietude of the eighteenth century the Boer race was
> formed. In the vast, unmysterious, thirsty landscape of the interior
> lay the true centre of South African settlement. When the *trekboers*
> entered it with their flocks and tented wagons, they left the current

of European life and lost the economic habits of the nations from which they had sprung. Though they never became true nomads, the mark of nomadism was upon them, and their dominant traits were those of a restless and narrow existence. They had the nomad's appetite for space and possessed the hardness and courage of men of the saddle who watch their flocks and hunt their meat. Their wealth was in their cattle and in their sons and grandsons, who were born numerously and who thrived amazingly. Their life gave them a tenacity of purpose, a power of silent endurance and the keenest self-respect. But the isolation sank into their character, causing their imagination to lie fallow and their intellects to become inert. Their virtues had their obverse qualities as well. Their tenacity could degenerate into obstinacy, their power of endurance into resistance to innovation, and their self-respect into suspicion of the foreigners and contempt for their inferiors. For want of formal education and sufficient pastors, they read their Bibles intensively, drawing from the Old Testament, which spoke the authentic language of their beliefs and their habits.[9]

In Cape Town, for many years virtually South Africa's only link with the outside world, a narrow urban society emerged; beyond, the small communities of settlers lived in relative isolation, preoccupied by their struggle with nature and with their African competitors. When, in 1794, the Dutch East India Company went bankrupt, and the British occupied the Cape (1795), the Colony was 'economically more undeveloped, politically more inexperienced, and culturally more backward than any of the greater colonies of settlement'.[10] At this date the population numbered 75,000 people, of whom 25,000 were European, 30,000 were slaves and 20,000 free Hottentots. The first British missionaries began to arrive, and as soon as the Cape was definitively annexed, in 1807, attempts were made to stimulate and modernize the economy. Slavery was abolished and in 1834 the colony's 40,000 slaves were freed. Between 1820 and 1860, new English settlers emigrated to the Cape at a rate of more than 1,000 a year. As a result, relations with the Boers deteriorated sharply, for their socio-economic organization, values and way of life were being subverted. In 1834 and, on a larger scale, in 1837, over 120,000 Boers joined the 'Great Trek' inland, at first towards Natal (which the British annexed in 1842) and then into the Transvaal.

From the end of the 18th to the middle of the 19th Centuries, for reasons which have not been fully explained, the African kingdoms in Southern Africa underwent profound transformations. This crisis, called the *Mfecane*, was accompanied by great military and political activity which generated new social and political structures and destroyed others. It so happened that this crisis coincided with the Great Trek, and this largely explains why the Boers encountered so little resistance during their expansion northwards.[11] Only the powerful Zulu state — whose rise lay at the heart of the *Mfecane* — offered serious military resistance.[12]

Nevertheless, the Boers had to fight for the land they took. They were pioneers, too, in having to wrest their living from nature. Hunting, horseman-ship and shooting were therefore of crucial importance to them. Surrounded by wildlife against which they had to defend themselves and upon which they depended for food (elephant, lion, buffalo, springbok and other antelope, leopards and much small game), for the Boers hunting naturally had an altogether different significance from that which the better-born English officers and officials attached to it. The latter found it difficult to understand or tolerate the Boers' 'unsporting' approach. Randolph Churchill wrote in 1891:

> Boer sportsmen never cared to carry home the animals they had slain. Forming themselves into large shooting parties, they shot the beasts down everywhere by scores, by hundreds, and by thousands, leaving the carcasses to be devoured by the vultures, and going a few days afterwards to gather up the skins which the vultures had neglected, and which the sun had dried and tanned.[13]

John Buchan's remarks on the same issue also betray some of the cultural prejudices which have soured Anglo-Afrikaner relations to this day:

> On the lowest interpretation of the word 'sport', the high qualities of courage, honour, and self-control are part of the essential equipment, and the mode in which such qualities appear is a reflex of the idiosyn-crasies of national character. But it is true mainly of the old settled peoples, whose sports have long lost the grim reality in which they started. To a race which wages daily war with savage nature the refine-ments of conduct are unintelligible; sport becomes business; and unless there is a hereditary tradition in the matter, the fine manners of the true hunter's craft are notable by their absence.
> It is worth while considering the Boer in sport, for it is there he is seen at his worst. Without tradition of fair play, soured and harassed by want and disaster, his sport became a matter of commerce, and he held no device unworthy . . . . [The Boers] are not a sporting race — they are not even a race of very skilful hunters.[14]

By contrast, when they took possession of the Cape, the senior British army officers and civilian officials brought with them all the regalia of the hunt, from uniforms to hounds. The Cape and Natal regiments each main-tained a pack, as did Pietermaritzburg in the 1870s. By that time, large game (elephant, lion) had been wiped out in the Karoo (the dry interior of the Cape Province), and the best shooting was to be found in Natal (antelope, eland, kudu and small game). From the end of the 1840s, shooting parties hired large numbers of Africans as beaters. Pheasants were introduced in 1861 and, along with them, closed seasons for the hunting of game birds, hare, etc.

This was not the only form of hunting to take place. Human beings were hunted as well. On the northern borders of the Karoo, Boer *kommandos* murdered Bushmen for sport until at least 1882. The Governor of the Cape ordered a report on this issue in 1862 which revealed that these gratuitous murders probably numbered thousands.[15] It has been estimated that between 1785 and 1795 over 2,500 Bushmen were killed and 700 captured. As many as 10,000 were perhaps exterminated in all, while the survivors were forced to take refuge in the arid, inhospitable mountains and Kalahari Desert.

> The technique is to ride down on your man till you are just outside arrow range, then pull up quickly, sight and fire. If you are lucky he will still be running and it is an easy shot in the back. But they have had experience . . . . What they do is to listen as they run to the sound of your horse's hooves, so that as you pull up you find them suddenly swinging right or left and bearing in on you as fast as they can. You have perhaps thirty yards to get off your shot . . . . My bushman never had a chance to let off an arrow that day: in the end he simply gave up and stood waiting and I killed him with a ball through the head.[16]

This barbaric practice speaks eloquently of the poverty of moral culture among those who preached 'civilization' in the 'dark continent'. The colony for a long time possessed not one library and few books apart from the Bible; there was no theatre; the first newspaper appeared in 1800 (and was censored for the first quarter-century of its existence). Only in Cape Town and one or two other urban centres was there a small leisured class, predominantly English-speaking, whose principal amusements were concerts and card games and dancing:

> Cards, ombre and whist, billiards, draughts, chess and backgammon, were played. The ladies played the spinnet and the harp, and the men the violin, flute, hautbois and other wind instruments. The Cape people had a passion for dancing, and nearly everyone indulged in this form of recreation . . . . Amongst the wealthy . . . the orchestra on such occasions was supplied by the slaves who were excellent musicians . . . . During the meals the slaves, seated on a raised dais at the upper end of the large dining hall, discoursed music.[17]

Besides hunting, two other major sports — cricket and horse-racing — were established once the British occupied the Cape. Needless to say, both are richly evocative of English social life. Horses had been introduced to South Africa for more mundane purposes by Van Riebeeck and his successors; they were imported from Holland's Oriental possessions, and Javanese ponies in particular proved to be well-adapted to the work and hunting needs of Boer life. The Basuto were the only African people to adopt the horse, and bred a pony of their own, named the Basuto pony. They acquired a reputation for horsemanship which they have kept to this day: in 1868, Basuto cavalry repulsed a column of Cape troops sent to subdue them, and they were used regularly by the British to pacify other tribes.

Boer horsemanship was equally famous; but it was the British who turned horse-racing from a form of informal recreation into an organized sport, complete with jockeys, betting and a race-course. The first recorded races, between a group of officers, took place in 1797, at Green Point Common near Cape Town, and races were organized regularly from 1802 when the S.A. Turf Club was created. Shortly before, thoroughbreds had been created by mating British mares with Arab stallions, and Charles Somerset, Governor from 1814 to 1826, imported 34 at his own expense and for his personal use. Further breeding led to the Hantan or Cape pony which later provided the majority of British cavalry mounts in the Crimea and India. Along with making war and horse-racing, polo was also a popular pursuit among officers. Polo was played in East Griqualand, Natal and the Transvaal. From its beginnings in the Cape and Grahamstown, horse-racing spread to Pietermaritzburg and Durban (1852) and then to Kimberley and Johannesburg on the tails of the mining boom. The rules were established in 1859. In 1882, the S.A. Jockey Club was formed, and the first July Handicap, South Africa's premier meet, was held in 1897.

In the early days, at Green Point Common, the competitors apparently rode anonymously under taxing conditions: the course was a field and the riders and their mounts were amicably pursued by the pasturing cows.[18] Hattersley describes a race meeting in Natal, where in the 1840s, 'The race-course was then simply open veld, alongside which would be drawn up the wagons which had brought farmers from all parts of the colony. There were no professional jockeys. The horses were ridden by schoolboys.'[19] The races were nevertheless bitterly contested, and the victors were usually rewarded, not with prize money, but barley or a cow. Boer farmers, excellent riders, took great pride in their mounts. Even though the English officers and gentry imported thoroughbreds, ridden in due course by jockeys, Boer horses could beat the best that the British could put up against them, as a letter in 1862 from Lady Duff Gordon amusingly describes:

> Mr Jamison drove me to the Capetown Races, at Green Point, on Friday. As races, they were *nichts*, but a queer little Cape farmer's horse, ridden by a Hottentot, beat the English crack racer, ridden by a first-rate English jockey, in an unaccountable way, twice over. The Malays are passionately fond of horse-racing, and the crowd was fully half Malay: there were dozens of carts with the bright-eyed women, in petticoats of every most brilliant colour, white muslin jackets and gold daggers in their great coils of shining black hair . . . . Their pleasure is driving about *en famille*; the men have no separate amusements.[20]

In short, the sport was popular throughout society. The Cape Malays and Coloureds specialized in horse-training and provided the majority of stable boys and jockeys and a proportion of owners. Some of the richest Hottentot families possessed up to 20 horses at the beginning of this century.[21] Africans also ran races in the main urban centres, at Kimberley and on the Rand, some of which were as 'bent' as racing elsewhere if the evidence from Matatiela District is representative — here, the entrepreneur who organized them was a celebrated horse thief.[22]

The Cape pony was decimated during the Boer War (1899-1902) when, faced by the Boers' superior horsemanship, the British massacred them in large numbers. They were further reduced by epidemics, until in 1908 scientific breeding methods began to raise the standards of stock, which have continued to improve since then.[23]

Cricket was the other organized sport to establish itself early on. The game was already popular in Britain when it was introduced into South Africa at the turn of the 18th Century. The first known match also took place on Green Point Common, on 5 January 1808; the first club was formed in 1843. The sport was to have an important socializing and ideological influence upon the emergent African and Coloured elite who aspired to its 'gentlemanly' values at the end of the century.[24]

There is some evidence that some other sporting activity took place at the time, of variable quality and uncertain significance — like the exhibition of running described by A.F. Hattersley in Natal in 1852, when 'Albion's Little Wonder' challenged all-comers to a 50-mile race, giving them a one-mile start, and threatening to 'repeat his herculean feat of walking 72 miles a day for 16 successive days on the sands of Africa'. Most people appear to have enjoyed less flamboyant forms of physical recreation, however, such as shooting and walking.[25]

Overall, until rugby/football arrived in the early 1860s, hunting, horse-racing and cricket remained the three principal sports, played essentially by the British immigrants and the military. Located in the Cape and to a lesser extent in Natal, they were already beginning to be adopted by the Boer and Coloured populations, and to some extent by Africans. After rugby/football, all the other major sports followed rapidly, their arrival coinciding with the discovery of diamonds at Kimberley (1867) and of gold on the Rand (1886). Rapidly disseminated through the sprawling new mining towns which sprang up as South Africa industrialized, closely associated with urban culture, sport was part and parcel of the tumultuous social change that swept the country during the Imperial era.

The Imperial Age

In 1867, the country could be divided politically into three zones — the Cape and Natal, under British authority; the Boer Free States of the Orange Free State and Transvaal; and those areas over which the Zulus and other African tribal states still retained partial sovereignty.

The supply of labour in the European areas was already preoccupying the authorities, for Africans remained unwilling to sell their labour at the low wages offered. The British therefore introduced laws against 'vagrancy' which forced all Hottentots to acquire a registered address and place of work, and pass laws which required Africans to remain within defined geographical areas unless they were specifically authorized to travel by the Administration. The boundaries of eight such areas were drawn in 1854 and they have served as a model for the Nationalist regime's present-day 'Homelands' or Bantustan policy. Economic production within these areas being insufficient to supply the needs of the African population settled in them, many Africans were forced to migrate in search of work to the so-called European areas, where they henceforth had no legal rights of residence. The logic of this system has remained unchanged to this day, and the policies of subsequent regimes, including the policy of apartheid, are merely refinements of the system of forced African migrant labour which generates the wealth of the South African economy.

The establishment of sugar plantations in Natal exacerbated the need for labour. With the agreement of the British Administration in India, indentured labour was therefore imported into the Colony, and between 1880 and 1886, 30,000 Indians were shipped in. By 1905, the number of Indians had risen to 122,000.[26] At the end of their first contract, the terms of the agreement allowed them either to return to India, or to renew their contracts, or stay on in South Africa as colonial subjects. In fact it was nearly a century before the status of those Indians who opted for the latter course was officially recognized by the Administration.

The status of Africans varied from province to province. In the Cape they had in theory had the same rights as Europeans, but access to the province was increasingly subject to control. In Natal, quota controls had been more severe from the beginning. Nonetheless, no formal colour bar existed within these two provinces, in contrast to the situation in the two Boer republics, which were organized on semi-feudal economic lines.

Table 1
Creation of the First Sports Clubs and National Federations

First Sports Clubs	Date	First National Federations
Horse Racing	1802	
Cricket (Port Elizabeth)	1843	
Rugby (Cape)	1876	
Football (Pietermaritzburg)	1879	
Athletics (Port Elizabeth)	1880	
Cycling (Port Elizabeth)	1881	
Tennis (Natal)		
Bowls (Port Elizabeth)	1882	Horse Racing
Professional Boxing		
Croquet		
		Rugby
Gymnastics (Johannesburg)	1889	
	1890	Mountaineering

Table 1 (Continued)

First Sports Clubs	Date	First National Federations
	1892	Football
		Cycling
	1894	Athletics
	1903	Tennis
	1904	Bowls
	1909	Golf
	1923	Hockey
	1928	Rifle Shooting
	1931	Motor Racing
	1937	Roller Skating
	1939	Badminton
	1940	Jukskei
	1947	Squash
	1948	Smallbore Rifle Shooting
	1949	Archery
		Fencing
		Softball
	1951	Gymkhana
	1953	Clay Pigeon Shooting
	1954	Equestrianism
	1962	Judo
		Trampoline
	1964	Body Building
	1965	Surfing
	1968	Karate

These differences in status naturally affected the adoption and practice of sport by black people in the different provinces. In the Cape and to a lesser extent in Natal, they were not excluded from the towns or from access to education as they were in the Transvaal and Orange Free State, and here the nascent elite took up sport from an early date. Cricket is particularly associated with their attempts before the First World War to assimilate and adopt white culture.

With the exception of cricket and horse-racing, all the major sports made their appearance between 1860 and 1900, therefore coinciding with the most active period of imperial expansion. Table 1 gives the evolution of sporting activity. It shows that:
1)   All the major sports apart from rugby/football (1862) — athletics, cycling, golf, boxing, tennis — appeared between 1880 and the end of the century;
2)   Sport became a social institution between 1875 and 1885. During this decade the first clubs were formed in rugby, football (now a separate sport),

23

athletics, cycling, horse-racing (jockey club), golf and tennis;

3)   Sports were subsequently taken up so fast that the first national federations appeared only ten years afterwards and were established in all the major sports before the 1920s;[27]

4) The development and institutionalization of sporting activity continued, with two particularly active periods, during the inter-war years, and again in the 1950s (see Chapter 4).

What influence did these economic and social developments have upon the adoption and transmission of sports, in different sections of the population? To answer these questions we need to look a little closer at political developments in the colony. The discovery of diamonds in Kimberley triggered a process of social and economic change which dramatically restructured South African society and reinforced the traditional segregation and racial exploitation. These became essential institutional features of the economy and the State.

On the discovery of diamonds, Kimberley was claimed by the Orange Free State. It was nevertheless rapidly taken over by the Cape Government[28] and in 1877 British troops occupied the Transvaal. Zulu power was finally destroyed in 1879. The Transvaal was gradually encircled. After taking possession of Basutoland (Lesotho) in 1868, Britain occupied Bechuanaland (Botswana) and Swaziland in 1884, while Rhodes christened Rhodesia after himself (1895). Occupation of the Boer republics provoked strong anti-British feeling and brought to life the incipient nationalism of the Boer communities. United by their common cultural and linguistic identity, Boer nationalism in all the provinces expressed itself in the semi-mystical Calvinistic terms which have informed Afrikaner nationalism ever since.[29] Boer resentment was further inflamed by the influx of foreigners (*uitlanders*), who poured into the Transvaal to make their fortunes in mining. During the last quarter of the century the white population doubled, and the Boers were themselves outnumbered by other whites. At the same time, the mining industry destroyed traditional individualized master-servant relations and replaced them with the *collective* subjugation of the black 'races' to the white.

Two models of government and two kinds of society were effectively in competition for mastery: one British, industrial and capitalist, based upon profit and intent on unifying South Africa under its control; the other Boer, patriarchal and agrarian, more segregationist and determined to resist imperial pretensions and preserve its independence and traditional prerogatives. War finally broke out between them in 1899, and after a prolonged struggle the Boers surrendered (1902), irrevocably embittered. The Boer War has been described as one of the first modern wars: the Boers used guerrilla tactics and to subdue them the British created concentration camps, introduced the machine gun and resorted to widespread material destruction.[30] They also made the first military use of the bicycle, when 161 men (later 361) were incorporated into the 26th Middlesex Cyclist Volunteer Rifle Corps.[31] Elsewhere, vestiges of chivalry surfaced in unlikely circumstances, as on the occasion when, from Concordia on 28 April 1902, one S.G. Maritz addressed a letter to 'The Hon. Major Edwards' suggesting a rugby match. 'I, from my side,' he wrote, 'will agree to a ceasefire tomorrow afternoon from 12 o'clock until sunset, the time and the venue of the match to be arranged by you in consultation with Messrs. Roberts and Van Rooyen who I am sending to you.'[32]

Surrender marked the end of the Boers' dream of political independence. Their struggle was henceforth to be conducted from within the Union of South Africa (1910), and their racial system of political and economic organization was not to be fully realized until the Nationalist Party took power in 1948 and enforced the philosophy of apartheid. It should not, however, be assumed that British victory secured justice or equality for the black populations or that the Constitution of the Union took African interests into account. Rhodes spoke for the white population as a whole when he declared to the Cape Parliament that for so long as the natives were uncivilized, they should be treated as subjects and that the key to the South African question was the supremacy of the white race, not because of its colour but by virtue of its civilization. The Constitution of the Union of South Africa institutionalized this racial supremacy and the privileges of the white population and marked the official birth of 'white' South Africa. Boers and English representatives took four months to negotiate the Union agreement but devoted just two days to discussion of African interests. 'There is no need,' remarks Rene Lefort, 'to negotiate what has already been agreed.'[33]

The preceding period had seen tremendous social change and population movement. In 1891, the Cape Province was still the most populous, ahead of the Transvaal, the Orange Free State and Natal. Its white population had risen from 180,000 in 1865 to 237,000 in 1875 and 377,000 in 1891. Ten thousand black workers were flooding into the Kimberley mines every year. The growth of Johannesburg and the Witwatersrand was even more phenomenal. By 1900 only 15 years after the discovery of the Reef, over 100,000 black migrant workers were employed on mines in the area. Ten years after its creation in 1896, Johannesburg itself had mushroomed into a city of 100,000 people.

To discipline this mass of labour, to prevent desertion and theft, the mine owners organized the compound system, a series of huge enclosed camps within which the black miners, recruited from all over South Africa and from neighbouring states, were virtually imprisoned for the duration of their contract. It was in these camps, as we shall see, that some of the most determined efforts to introduce organized sport were to be made. The mine owners encouraged physical recreation and traditional dancing – if only to vent the miners' frustration at being cooped up – though in general, in the early period, facilities and living conditions were so primitive that few cultural and recreational activities were likely to prosper. Perhaps significantly, boxing was one of the first sports adopted by the miners: it came to South Africa via Basutoland in the person of a policeman named R.J. Couper who in 1889, in the 27th round of a famous professional contest, defeated W. Bendorf for the magnificent prize of £4,500. Until that year, public prize fighting was illegal, although the professional boxing federation had been founded in 1882, and the sport had already spread from Kimberley to Johannesburg.

On its side, the white working class was composed of poor Afrikaners ruined by the Boer War, and poor immigrants from Europe. In the 1890s they united to defend their privileges against encroachment by black workers. They prevented the employers from hiring or training skilled black workers at lower wages, and the first steps were taken after 1896 to institutionalize the colour bar which has guaranteed to Whites a monopoly of skilled work ever since.

Urbanization and schools were the two most powerful forces for the propagation of sport. Before the British arrived, the Boers had created virtually no schools for their own children, let alone for their African workers. In the rare institutions which existed, black pupils were segregated by order of the Dutch Reformed Church,[34] and the Boers were unhappy about the founding of Genadendal College in 1797, where Moravian missionaries hoped to provide Xhosa children with manual and agricultural training.

The London Missionary Society opened a number of schools soon after its arrival in 1803, on an explicitly integrationist policy. Mission schools were free and open to all races, they provided the only educational facilities for Africans until the inter-war period, and were instrumental in the training of a skilled and semi-skilled African workforce, adapted to the needs of a market economy, and the creation of a small assimilated black elite which could lead and communicate African opinion. Towards the middle of the 19th Century, the missionaries began to train African clergymen and teachers: Lovedale, then Healdtown and St Matthews colleges were built, providing an exceptionally good education and deeply influencing the ideas of the nascent African elite. At about the same time, the State also began to encourage and support black education. In 1865 2,827 African pupils were enrolled in mission schools in the Cape, receiving elementary education in reading, writing and arithmetic, with an emphasis on manual training. By 1885 this number had risen to 15,568 pupils in about 700 schools.[35]

At the end of the century, as industrialization progressed, the white population demanded the provision of separate and superior education, appropriate to its higher status. Officially schools had fostered (at least in the Cape) an assimilationist ideal; henceforth they were to reinforce the supremacy of the white settler population. With the creation in 1905 of state schools for white children, segregation was imposed in the Cape Province, bringing it into line with the rest of the country. In Natal, a circular of 1856 laid down a school curriculum for Africans composed of religious instruction, rudimentary English and manual training, financed by local authorities. 232 African schools trained 18,000 pupils in 1912, and the province also ran five industrial centres and three training colleges for African teachers. The Indian population received little education[36] but between 1885 and 1905 Indian children were permitted to attend white schools; in the Transvaal, their education was undertaken by the missions.

In the Transvaal and the Orange Free State, where the Boers attached little importance to the formal education of their own children, there was generally no education for those they had dispossessed and used as servile labour on their farms. The first missionary schools were not founded until 1842. In 1901, 201 schools provided the rudiments of reading and writing. In 1904 a separate curriculum was imposed on African children, followed in 1907 by the opening of the first state school for Africans.

In 1900, therefore, the African elite was tiny, and concentrated almost exclusively in the Cape. In 1884, the first black paper *Imvo Zabantsundu* (Native Opinion) was edited by John Tengo Jabavu. It represented the opinions of the African petty bourgeoisie which appeared at Kimberley at the same period, composed of postal workers, clergymen, teachers, translators, officials etc., who enthusiastically took up sport and other cultural activities in the towns where they settled or the mission schools in which they taught. From the Cape and Durban, their ebullient progress can be traced through the mission schools, to Kimberley, then at the end of the century to Johannesburg and the gold mines of the Witwatersrand. Though their rights were gradually to be whittled away, the African petty bourgeoisie preserved its faith in British rule and the promise of equality before the law for all subjects of the Crown.

> There existed the strong belief that the survival of the non-racial Cape franchise — which provided both the hope and means for their incorporation into Cape colonial society by institutionalizing 'civilization' rather than race or colour as the crucial set of criteria for this — depended upon the maintenance of direct imperial control. Accordingly, expressions of loyalty and attachment to the 'imperial factor' were frequently on their lips, particularly at times when local colonial interests were pressing for more repressive 'native policies'. 'Direct Imperial control', as *Imvo* put it in 1897, 'is the talisman engraved on the heart of every Native in the land.'[37]

These values and ideals — regarding 'civilization', 'progress', the Empire, Christianity, etc. — were propagated and expressed in a wide range of clubs and associations, many of which were sporting. Membership and rank within these societies was an obvious sign of social success, which explains to a large extent their vivid and tumultuous activity.

Social classes were formed in urban black society according to a complex mixture of factors including type of employment, place of origin, level of education and wealth. The evolution of sport, both in terms of its organization and its values, is intimately linked with this process. Some sports, as we have seen, were associated with compound life, others were learned in the mission colleges and schools; their performance required different levels of economic investment or apprenticeship, and incorporated different social values. One only has to think of cricket, which was played almost exclusively by the black elite, and football, which was adopted by all classes and spread even beyond the towns to certain rural areas, to understand this.

But the playing of all sports offered to team members, and even more to their managers, an opportunity to declare publicly their allegiance to colonial society and to the values of 'civilized life'. Nor was the relation between sport, education and urbanization confined to the African or black populations: it existed in all parts of the country and was true of all races, which explains why it was the towns like Cape Town and Port Elizabeth, in particular, which were sporting pioneers in the early period and why, after gold was discovered, sport spread rapidly to the Transvaal and Orange Free State.

Perhaps surprisingly, for some time sport was not placed officially on the curricula of white schools.[38] The Afrikaans and English-speaking students of the South African College (Cape Province) had been accustomed for 20 years to playing rugby and cricket on a corner of meadowland before, in the mid-1890s, their sporting activities were given official encouragement and financed by a levy on the students. In Natal, under the influence of teachers freshly arrived from England, sport had been introduced rather earlier into the secondary schools. Rugby, cricket and athletics were the main sports.[39] Girls were confined to more decorous activities. 'Violent exercise was not thought becoming for girls in the sixties and seventies. Girls' costume admitted of little freedom of movement. Croquet, introduced in the sixties, was not played at school. In private gardens it gave girls the sensation of playing a game on Sunday. Riding was the principal outdoor recreation for colonial girls and boys alike.'[40]

The British officers who introduced most of these sports were usually themselves the products of British public schools, and merely took their sports with them on active service, in Natal, in the Transvaal, to the Zulu wars, often passing them on to the surrounding populations. The first identifiable athletics competition matched a team of British soldiers against local runners at the Natal Wasps Football Club in 1870, and similar examples can be found in other sports.[41]

The role of English-speaking immigrants in carrying sport into South Africa was almost as important as that of the military. For obvious reasons, their influence was particularly great in the mining and industrial towns of the Transvaal, but it can be detected much earlier in Natal and Cape Town. With the exception of rugby, however, which Afrikaners made their own, most sports were as English in their following as in their origin, for the resentment against Britain which was then spreading among the Boer population, as Afrikaner nationalism crystallized, combined with class differences to inhibit their adoption. Sport was associated in this sense with a way of life and with values to which the Afrikaner population was opposed.

As a general rule, and for obvious reasons, sport did not generally cross the colour line either, until the 1920s. There were nevertheless exceptions. We have seen that the nascent black elite played cricket and football and that boxing and dancing were encouraged in some of the mining compounds; the American Board Missions also encouraged games among the black population of Natal and successfully fostered football. Finally, the Coloured population — and particularly the Cape Coloureds — enthusiastically supported and played rugby and cricket from an early date, and by 1900 some were already of national standard. Their pre-eminence is not surprising, for their lifestyle, culture and values more nearly resembled that of Whites than did any other black groups: they dominated black sport as they did the small black petty bourgeoisie which was then making its appearance. For most, however, sports were essentially spectacles organized and performed by Whites – although for a growing minority, active sport meant football.

As for the Indian population, concentrated in Natal except for a small number in the Transvaal, their only contacts were really with the Coloureds, in sport as in other social activities. Their principal game was football, but as the Indian petty bourgeoisie and trading middle class grew, some began to play higher-status, more expensive sports, like cricket and tennis.

The relative slowness of Blacks to adopt modern sports should therefore be interpreted in context, in relation to the dependent, subordinate status of the black population, cast in the role of unskilled labour in the mines and in agriculture. Between 1856 and 1904 a number of Acts – the Masters and Servants Acts – were passed, further defining their position. It became a *criminal* offence for unskilled workers to break their contracts.[42] Sport, one of the most typical expressions of leisure and rank in white imperial society naturally became one of the dividing lines between the races, one of the symbols of white status. Not by chance were the first clubs and federations from the beginning *exclusively white*. Reflecting this, the black clubs which were spawned in their wake catered, with rare exceptions, for an exclusively Coloured, Indian or African membership.[43]

The Consolidation of Apartheid and the Development of Sport

In 1910, when the Act of Union was passed, there were just 100,000 Coloured voters in the Cape (4.7% of the electorate) and 9,000 in Natal. The new constitution left this situation intact; nevertheless, in spite of the representations of black leaders, it was accepted by the British Parliament.

A number of discriminatory laws were subsequently enacted which extended and strengthened the forced labour system. In 1911, the Mines and Works Act definitively legalized the colour bar in the Transvaal and Orange Free State. In 1913, the Native Land Act forbade Africans to rent or buy land outside the reserves – which then covered 7.3% of the total land area (an amount later increased, following the Native Trust and Land Act of 1936, to 13%). In 1923, the Native Urban Areas Act decreed that urban areas lay in European zones and that black city dwellers were to reside in 'locations' (later renamed 'townships'). In 1927, the Native Administration Act gave to the Administration and the forces of order further powers over the African population, and invested more authority in the hands of tribal chiefs.[44] Other laws were passed in the 1930s, further reducing the number and influence of the small number of black voters in the Cape; in 1936, they were removed from the white electoral roll and henceforth voted separately to elect three white M.P.s who represented their interests. The establishment during this period of the Native Representative Council (which was never recognized by the black population), furthered the process by which the white minority gradually stripped the black majority of all their political rights.

Opposition to this battery of legislation was organized from an early date. A crucial influence at the turn of the century was Mahatma Gandhi, who formed the Natal Indian Congress and from 1883 to 1913 put into practice his theories of peaceful disobedience and passive resistance. When the African National Congress (today the most important of the South African liberation movements) was founded in 1912 by elements of the African elite, it adopted the same tactics that had been used so successfully by the Indians to protest against racial discrimination. The first African passive resistance campaigns against the pass laws date from 1913.

The First World War and the subsequent Great Depression accelerated the movement of Africans and Boers into the towns, increasing competition between them and hardening white racial sentiments. The rallying cry of white miners during the great strike of 1922 on the Rand — which the Government finally quelled with troops and air-strikes — is justly famous, for it reveals poignantly the violent confusion of loyalties within the white working class: 'Workers of the World, Fight and Unite for a White South Africa!' From 1904 to 1936, as the white urban population doubled, the black tripled — doubling its size relative to the African population in the country as a whole.[45]

The Growth of Afrikaner Nationalism

General Hertzog founded the Afrikaner National Party in 1914, when he broke with Generals Botha and Smuts who had agreed to co-operate with the British in the context of the Union. It was the first of a series of major splits between Afrikaner politicians, which until 1948 always operated to the advantage of the more extreme nationalists. From the beginning, Hertzog's line presaged the future development of apartheid: the Party's 'native' policy prescribed 'the dominance of the European population in a spirit of Christian trusteeship, with the strictest avoidance of any attempt at race mixture'.[46] In the 1930s, political and electoral vicissitudes led Hertzog to join his party with Smuts' South Africa Party, to form the United Party. It was then Malan's turn to refuse to follow him. A 'Purified' Nationalist Party was formed in opposition, while several semi-clandestine organizations were created, around which Afrikaner political nationalism cohered. The best known among them is the *Broederbond* (the Brotherhood), an organization created to champion Afrikaner interests, to which a majority of the Afrikaner elite rapidly affiliated. Their aim was to win Afrikaner supremacy, and thereby guarantee the perpetuation of white 'civilization'.[47]

Afrikaner nationalism accelerated during the 1930s, influenced by European fascism, inspired by Afrikaner history and haunted by the spectre of black competition. In secret debate, nationalist para-political organizations evolved the ideology of apartheid — separation of the races. In public, the Nationalists organized popular demonstrations of Afrikaner solidarity, the most dramatic of which was the 1936 re-enactment of the Great Trek, when thousands of Afrikaners made the pilgrimage along the route followed by the Boer trekkers, spreading nationalist sentiments and proclaiming their independence from anglophone Whites and the black population alike.

The ideological ferment of the 1930s was mirrored in sport, which leapt in popularity during the decade. The role rugby was to play in cementing Afrikaner perceptions was already clear, while immense numbers of working-class Africans took up football. Liberal opinion was experimentally promoting sport in the hope that it would divert and diffuse the mounting alienation of black leaders and urban workers (see Chapter 5) while some prophesied that sport would bridge the gap between the two white communities. This lyrical quotation from a British colonel, P.A. Silburn, writing in 1927, captures the style:

> The Boer and the Briton . . . follow the same sports with equal fervour and skill, they belong to the same clubs and play in the same teams . . . . This love of the same sport is gradually eradicating racial antagonism, and it will be upon the sports field that it will eventually expire and be decently buried. The postponement of that day is mainly due to the non-sporting, self-seeking politicians of both races, gentlemen whose stock-in-trade is racialism.[48]

It is interesting to find that such texts have the same strategic blindness to black sport and black interests as modern exponents of 'sport not politics' bridge-building, and resound with the same pleasant illusions. Needless to say, the combination of apolitical good cheer and racial amnesia made no more headway in the 1930s than it does today. For the most part, sport remained segregated, not only between the races, but between the white communities — as the efforts of a Hofmeyr to take cricket to the Afrikaners demonstrates.[49]

Afrikaner nationalism was naturally antagonistic to all such aspirations. At the end of the 1930s and during the 1940s, the nationalists were forming their exclusive Afrikaans-speaking cultural organizations all over the country (among the railway and post office workers, in the police, nursery school-teachers etc.), and their student movement was also particularly active. In 1933, Afrikaner students had left the National Union of South African Students to form the *Afrikaanse Nasionale Studentebond*, which, influenced by Nazism, was disbanded at the end of the War, to be replaced in 1948 by the *Afrikaanse Studentebond*. Dr Diederichs, first President of the A.N.S. and later a prominent Minister, studied Nazi theory in Germany; and many other nationalist intellectuals not only sympathized with Nazism but gave support to anti-Jewish campaigns. In 1936, for example, the Nationalist Party officially backed a greyshirt (fascist) demonstration against the arrival in South Africa of Jewish refugees fleeing Germany[50] and during the War the Nationalist newspaper *Die Transvaler*, edited by Dr Verwoerd, the future Prime Minister (who had also studied in Germany), campaigned against the Smuts Government's support for the Allied cause. A minority of nationalists went even further and formed an organization of armed subversion, the *Ossewa Brandwag*, to support the Nazi war effort and take power in South Africa by violent means. The president of the *Ossewa Brandwag* at one time was B.J. Vorster, another future Prime Minister (1966-78). Between 1942 and 1944, Vorster was interned for organizing sabotage against the Government, along with his future Chief of Security and head of BOSS, H. van den Bergh. In 1942 Vorster declared: 'We stand for Christian Nationalism which is an ally of National Socialism. You can call this anti-democratic principle dictatorship if you wish. In Italy it is called fascism, in Germany German National Socialism and in South Africa Christian Nationalism.'[51]

Anti-semitism is still detectable today in South African sport and the society in general,[52] although the number and influence of Jews in public life and the economy has helped to inhibit its open expression. In the 1930s Jews were among those who hoped that sport would reconcile them with the white community, and from the beginning they were among South Africa's prominent sportsmen.

> By 1908 there were four Jews on the Olympic Committee. There were Jews on the Johannesburg Amateur Gymnastics Association. Jews played chess and a Jew was described as 'the best pigeon shot in South Africa'. When Israel Hayman first began to play for Wanderers in 1902, he was the only Jew interested in cricket. In 1907 there were three in the team and many more were playing the game.[53]

In 1939, Joseph Brauer published a short and enthusiastic essay about South Africa's Jewish sportsmen; his conclusion, written in the shadow of Nazism, and without mentioning black sportsmen, is a tragi-comical illustration of the state of mind sporting ideals can create in a repressed, racist society like South Africa:

> The sports field of South Africa knows neither politics nor racialism; and there is no ghetto, nor will there ever be as long as sanity reigns. When politics clash with sport, the high ideals of sportsmanship are lost. And as long as there will be no segregation in South African sport, there will be understanding. The Jewish sportsman will go out and mix with his fellow human beings and between them and him the bonds of fellowship will be woven . . . .
> The Jewish contribution to South African sport, as will be seen, is no mean one. The Jew in this country is part of the country. He has worn the football jerseys, he has played on the cricket pitches, he has represented South Africa. He has rubbed shoulders with the sturdy Afrikaner and the sun-burnt Briton. He has done his share in the administration of the various branches of sport. There is no need for me to enumerate the list of cups, trophies and shields he has presented, and the donations of Jewry to South African sport are well known. The future of the Jewish sportsman in South Africa is bright. It will always

be bright as long as the true South African spirit of sport exists. The true spirit of sportsmanship and the high ideals of Olympia thrive in this great sports-loving country. And long may it thrive. South Africans are known for their sportsmanship the world over, and the song of our sportsmen — Jew and non-Jew — is an echo of the Olympian Games on the banks of the Alpheus held some twenty-five centuries ago.[54]

Organized within the *Federasie van Afrikaanse Kultuurvereenigings* (FAK), the Afrikaner cultural organizations continued their campaign in defence of the Afrikaans language by demanding — as the *Broederbond* had always demanded — separate education for English-speakers and recognition of Afrikaans as one of the two official languages of the country. In 1938 it was the FAK which organized the Oxwagon trek mentioned above; in 1939 a major conference on Christian National Education was convened to set out an official Nationalist policy on education. On all these questions, the Dutch Reformed Church gave to the Nationalists its full and weighty support. 'It is the firm policy of our Church, reiterated with emphasis at our last synod,' declared one of its spokesmen, Mr Nicol, on 5 March 1941, 'that our children must be educated in separate schools with Afrikaans as the medium . . . . Not only the salvation of our *volk*, but the preservation of our Church, depends in large measure on separate schools.'[55]

Sport and Youth
Great significance was attached by the Nationalists to the recruitment and organization of young people to their cause and ideals.

The Afrikaner teachers will then demonstrate to Afrikanerdom what a power they possess in their teachers' organizations for building up the youth for the future republic. I know of no more powerful instrument. They handle the children for five or more hours daily, for five days each week, while at hostels and boarding schools the contact is continuous for longer periods. A nation is made through its young being taught and influenced at school in the tradition, customs, habits and ultimate destination of its *volk*.[56]

The inter-war period saw, of course, a general movement in European countries in favour of the organization of young people, through educational, religious and secular institutions whose activities and ideals tended to reinforce moral values and stimulate patriotism. And, as elsewhere, sport was heavily involved in this moral education. Victor Stiebel's wry recollections of his schooldays paint a picture no less telling for its humour:

[My] inability to learn spread like a disease into my attitude to school sports. In South Africa this was an even more serious defect than being a numbskull at work. South Africa was, and I believe still is today, fanatical in its enthusiasm for sport — particularly rugby and cricket —

and this enthusiasm was shared by every man, woman and child — white, beige or black — dog, cat, bird, lion, zebra, antelope, giraffe, impala buck, cheetah, wart-hog, wildebeeste, crocodile, elephant, hippo and rhinoceros. At the Prep, where games were not compulsory, my disinterest passed unnoticed, but at later schools it was to prove a dangerous handicap . . . . School life was pigeonholed to a degree that was suffocating. In an unchanging pattern week followed dreary week and, except for the holidays, there was seldom anything to look forward to. A week-day consisted of classes, compulsory games — only rugby and cricket were played — prep and meals, with a dose of chapel at each end. Free time was restricted to the morning half-hour break, a short period for lunch, and the few hours after games and before supper; but there was no place in which one could enjoy it in privacy; only the classrooms or the playing fields were available. On Saturday afternoons, unless one of the chosen few, one watched matches instead of playing in them. Watching, like playing, was compulsory and a merit of the rugger season was that a match was soon over, and one had therefore a little more leisure afterwards. But watching rugger matches had its hazards. It was the duty of every non-player to demonstrate loyalty to his school by bellowing from the bottom of his lungs. If a covey of prefects considered that our applause was unsatisfactory, after the visiting team had bathed and changed, been given tea and departed, we would be ordered to parade once more on the rugger field where, toeing the touch line of the empty pitch, we would scream and yell until our superiors were satisfied.[57]

Clubs and camps for white boys were first organized around 1910, in the Cape by Oswin Bull who had previously set up student camps. Roundabout 1925, several other young men — among them Alan Paton — brought them to Natal. Rather later, camps were set up for Coloured boys. Bob Watson of the Cape remembers:

The churches ran the clubs I took part in. At school we were encouraged to take part in outside activities, one of which was the local boys' club, which was really sponsored by the school. They played boxing, gym, table-tennis; they were mixed, but mainly for boys, and, understandably in the Cape, Coloured boys . . . . Sport was not particularly stressed in the clubs. It was a night out — something to be enjoyed.[58]

The State first involved itself in sports education in 1938 when the Government launched a National Plan for physical education, in line with other European countries. Over a period of six years, £95,000 was granted to develop physical education; it was shared by the armed forces, the railways and harbours, the five education departments, local authorities and various welfare institutions. The initial aim was to make sport and physical exercise more accessible to the public. 'At present, physical education, sport and recreation,' declared the author of a report on this subject, written in 1946 and published in 1949 'are available in a satisfactory manner only to a small fraction of South Africa's population. It is significant that it is this small fraction which is distinguished from the rest of the people by a superior standard of material welfare, and, generally speaking, also of social conduct.'[59] Social and economic performance was to be enhanced, and unemployed, unskilled youth trained for the modern world by means of physical exercise — like the young soldiers whose physical training the report also describes:

> Experiences collected in different parts of the world and in this country, particularly by the Special Service Battalion, the Youth Training Brigade, the Physical Training Brigade, and the Non-European Army Corps, leave no doubt that physical education — this term being understood in its broadest sense — is an essential formative educational technique to assist in the transformation of raw, inexperienced, clumsy, undisciplined and purposeless youths into useful members of a modern integrated society who can make a valuable contribution to the economic life of the nation.[60]

In 1939, physical education was made compulsory in Government schools, and appropriate basic equipment provided. The black population, however, was scarcely affected by these provisions — not least because at this period only one-quarter of the black children of school age were enrolled.

The Social Role of Sport
The introduction of physical recreation into school programmes, military training and youth activities was only one aspect of sport's development during the inter-war period. Expansion was rapid throughout the society, particularly in the 1930s and 1940s, when the South African economy began to take off after the serious crises of the 1920s: living standards rose and the Afrikaner poor whites benefited particularly. New federations were founded in hockey, shooting, motor racing, basketball, roller skating, badminton, jukskei, professional boxing[61] (see Table 1); and sport generally, evidence of growth and prosperity, was increasingly patronised by Government. Afrikaners began to play sport in large numbers, and international sporting ties were extended to other countries apart from Britain. (The South African Olympic and Empire Games Association[62] had been founded in 1908, and South Africa participated for the first time that year in the Olympic Games: she was to take part regularly until 1960 — on all occasions fielding an all-white team — and win a total of 17 gold medals in athletics, tennis, cycling, boxing and swimming, 28 silver and 27 bronze.)

In short, it is to this period that we can date both South Africa's appearance in international sport and the development of popular, mass sport within the country.

Predictably, sport boomed most in the industrial growth areas — above all on the Rand, which until the First World War had been relatively backward in comparison with the Cape or Natal. The phenomenal industrial growth of the area, which today accounts for 40% of South Africa's industrial production[63] financed the installation of fine leisure and sporting facilities for the white workforce.

Bob Watson describes the role sport played in white social life at the end of the Second World War and during the early 1950s, when the major sports most people indulged in were swimming and tennis, followed by rugby and cricket.

There would be a barbecue. The whole thing actually had a ritual to it . . . . Some of the neighbours would be over the day before to help the farmer's wife to prepare, getting meat cut up, bake, and do a lot of traditional dishes. People did not normally see a lot of each other but they would know each other very well. At weekends, you would go to somebody else's farm and swim in the dam, or you might go to the tennis club where you would see virtually everyone, from a larger area.

Most tennis clubs predated World War II. I went to three or four in the late '40s. Mature trees were planted round the courts and provided a very nice setting. There was the social side to tennis, but tennis was also competitive: you would have a tennis ladder in which most of the younger men would take part. But I wouldn't say that it dominated the club: people played because they enjoyed it. The attitude towards rugby was not dramatically different. I played rugby in a number of different areas, in the Western and the Central Cape and in the Transvaal. It was always very relaxed. You went intending to win, or petrified that you would be annihilated — you would have a few bruises, but there wasn't the same violence then. During ten years of playing rugby I was never injured.

If we played at Beaufort West, for instance, the families would all be there, plus the local supporters. Afterwards you would go to the clubhouse or local hall and eat. Beaufort West was probably large enough for the catering to be done professionally, but if you took a smaller village like Nelspoort, it would be just the families. The match was an occasion. You would meet old friends. Older people who served together in the First World War or against the British would get together. A number of sports teams were in fact made up of Old Comrades — *Moths* (Memorable Order of Tin Hats) — associations. This was particularly true of white working class areas of Johannesburg (where) the Old Commie Association would be the social centre.

Marriages started from these social meetings and sports matches, because the youngsters could meet people outside their immediate neighbourhood at these occasions — and you would meet your parents-in-law perhaps for the only time during the year. Tennis matches would sometimes take place on the Saturday before *nachtmal*, and you would stay over with the family and all go to *nachtmal*. In Johannesburg and in the Cape coaches were coming in, but in the rural areas everyone had to come in from their farm, with their family, and came by car.

People worked very long hours and so although there were social visits they were nothing like as frequent as in a commuter area where you were seeing a lot of other people every day socially. In the country you would probably meet once or twice a week. The teams would train Wednesday afternoon, or on a Saturday. But not that much. I don't remember training. If you had played together for ten years you knew each other well, and the young lads had seen the team playing as children and when they eventually came to play themselves, it was really a matter of growing up.

The drinking was nothing like as significant as it is here in England. In cricket there may have been a lot more drinking, but in athletics which was my main sport there was virtually none at all — perhaps cool drinks or a beer. Cross-countries were another social occasion where whole families sat down together. Athletics was a far less popular sport — and tended to be a town sport. Once on the Rand, you had hundreds of athletics clubs. Otherwise, the meet would be in the local town, where there would be a sports field. Local clubs would train and have their own games, but in a place like Beaufort West, farmers who took part would train on their own, around the lucerne fields or along the tank of the dam.

In my area, the mile and marathon were the most important distances. Sprints were not the emotional event. If you won the mile, you were definitely the local hero for the day, whereas if you won the 100 yards, unless you won in a provincial record time, your name would just be in the results. My personal feeling is that this was because you liked to see two people straining against each other and in a sprint you do not see this.

In field events standards were low. It was all track, with long jump and occasionally the javelin or hurdles. From about 1948-49 there was I think a Danish pole-vaulter who emigrated, and a gymnast — both had won medals at the 1948 Olympics, so people became interested in these events for a time. But it didn't last.

In the same way, when South Africa was very successful at world tennis in the beginning of the 1950s, there was a tremendous resurgence of interest in playing tennis. Lots of little clubs were started up by professionals. Women played tennis particularly — and also netball, bowls, hockey, a little athletics. There was women's cricket in the cities, but it was not very developed. Women swam a lot too. You have really got to translate yourself into the California situation where *everybody* swims Saturday and Sunday and lunchtime if they're near enough. Because it's a pleasure and you are out in the sun and the sea is there, and the pools are fresh. Swimming is almost second nature. Everyone in the rural areas had a dam. Most farms had two or three. In the cities the well-to-do had swimming pools. There were also a large number of municipal swimming pools, which were very well kept. In all the mining villages along the Rand every mine would have its own pool — as well as its own squash courts, its own cricket team, football and rugby team. I don't think any of the pools I saw were as bad as any I have been to in England.

So on Saturday afternoon you'd swim or play tennis with your friends and in the evening you would have a barbecue. That was a city activity — it would be completely mixed, mixed dances were very popular in the Free State and the Karoo. You might sleep over and the next day all go off somewhere together — if you were near, you would go to the coast, swim in the sea, have a barbecue and then go your separate ways. In the Karoo, Free State and Transvaal, you would go to Sunday morning church; in the English-speaking areas, if you went, you would go on Sunday evening. But it was not that hard and fast. In the cities you might play on Sunday — but for fun, no competitive sport. Golf, and horse racing were popular.[64]

Visitors like Wright Noel (in 1929) or A.W. Wells (1939) are largely in agreement as to the order of popularity of different sports at this time.[65] Both would agree with Bob Watson that tennis was the principal social game. Noel calls it the 'national sport', because it was played everywhere, in town and village, by all ages throughout the year. Then followed rugby, clearly on the rise, and cricket, which preserved its traditional high status. Bowls was an extremely popular game as well: clubs and greens existed in all towns of any size and competitions were frequent. These were followed by golf, surfing (very popular on the Durban coast, at Plettenberg Bay, at Port Elizabeth and the Cape), motor racing (which began at East London in the 1930s), yachting, hunting, fishing (fresh and seawater), climbing etc. The range of sports played was wide, reflecting the very different economic and natural climates in which white South Africans lived. If urban games like squash, ice hockey and water polo acquired large audiences in the burgeoning cities on the Rand, in the wide spaces of the farms shooting remained a major recreation: 'In the Karoo, the Free State, the Transvaal, everyone had their rifle range, and rifle teams would compete locally and nationally if they were good enough. Very competitive. People would go out to the range on Saturday afternoon, or you would have your own target practice on the farm.'[66]

As for competitive games and spectacle sports, rugby, cricket and tennis, followed by athletics, were the most important. Rugby's strength lay then in the Cape, where up to 5,000 or 8,000 spectators would attend a big match, against 1,000 for football; but elsewhere, even before the advent of professional soccer in 1959, football was the most popular game for the white working class and for the African and Indian populations. Horse racing — perhaps indeed, 'bent as a dog's back leg'[67] — also had a long tradition in South Africa and a large following among all social groups.

The July Handicap is the biggest horse race in South Africa, and people all over the sub-continent are interested in it . . . . The 'July' really

means more — much more — to South Africans than the Derby means
to England. It is a very convenient excuse for scores of thousands of
people in Johannesburg and the interior of South Africa, where ice and
frost lie thick on the ground, and waterpipes may be bursting, morning
and evening, in the rarefied winter air at five thousand feet, to say, and
feel in their bones, that nature never meant any self-respecting South
African to keep too many weeks out of a bathing costume; to sigh and
long for the sun, and the sea, and the sands, and they go — to see the
'July'.[68]

Inequality and Segregation in Sport in 1948

While white sport began during this period of rapid expansion to acquire its
modern form and characteristics, and to make its name abroad, black sport
also began to evolve as it spread through the townships. At all levels, however,
segregation was almost always the rule, which is one reason why white people
remained so entirely unaware of the range and quality of black sport.

> The only Blacks who would be around the tennis courts and clubs [in
> the late 1940s] would be serving drinks. They would work during the
> week bringing the court up to standard, but they were not even really
> present . . . . If I was waiting for my partner to arrive and there was a
> black man sweeping, I could say, 'Do you feel like knocking the ball
> around until they arrive?' and he could do so as long as he got off the
> court as soon as anyone else turned up and without them saying
> anything.
>   A good black or Coloured player was invariably confined to his own
> league and to breakout was almost impossible. Where a good black
> sportsman did take part in inter-racial activities, and there were some
> at that time, he would eat separately — which was more pathological
> than not taking part.[69]

As we have seen, sport had been assimilated by non-Whites in schools and
then in the urban centres, particularly on the mines and among the urban
elite. It should be remembered, however, that social conditions were far from
ideal for cultural life of any kind. Bob Watson recalls the state of one of the
older mines on which he worked:

> Facilities for Whites were good. For Blacks they were non-existent. If
> you had put chickens in the mine I was on in this country now, you
> would have had the inspector in from the RSPCA . . . . There was a
> beer hall and an open area which was called the dance floor where there
> would be traditional dancing — for their own, not public entertainment.
> They would drink beer, come out on Saturday which was a short shift
> and drink beer and get drunk until they fought, then collapse into their
> concrete coffins and the next day they would drink beer again and
> dance and fight. It sounds an exaggeration but there was never a

Saturday or Sunday when there was not a reasonable sized fight, including at least five people out of 2,000. And you can see why. I never saw any sporting facilities for Blacks.

Mind you, I was on an old mine. But the same would be true of all the old mines which dated from 1900-10. On the newer mines everything was better, for Whites as well, and dramatically better for Blacks. In 1963, on our mine, there were no mattresses for the men to sleep on, just coir mats. [The mine closed in 1963.] [70]

The situation in black schools was no better. The proportion of children attending classes rose from 18.1% of children of school age in 1936 to 27.1% ten years later, to reach 30% in 1951 — but the vast majority of these pupils had no more than four years of primary education at the end of which most were not literate. [71] In 1946, only 173 of the 4,587 African schools taught at secondary level: there was just one college of further education, Fort Hare, opened in 1916, which also took Coloured, Indian and some white students as well. In 1939, 90 degrees were awarded — a measure of the minute size of the black elite, almost all of whom studied at Fort Hare or at the mission colleges of Lovedale, St Matthew's or Healdtown. It is therefore startling to discover that, in spite of poor nourishment, the virtual absence of education, the lack of recreational and sporting facilities and poverty, the standard of black athletic achievement could be very high.

Outside school, Blacks had virtually no opportunity to play sport. The very gifted could try their luck and skills abroad, and among those who succeeded, more than a few made successful careers for themselves. Among these, a handful — of whom the best known are Jake Ntuli (Olympic and Empire Boxing champion), Precious McKenzie (Olympic and British Empire Weight-lifting champion) and Basil d'Oliveira (English test cricketer) — achieved national honours. But this was possible for only a short period, from the beginning of the 1950s until South Africa left the British Commonwealth in 1961; and very few black players had the opportunity or resources to travel abroad. (Many white South African sportsmen, particularly footballers, also left South Africa during this period to seek better prospects abroad.)

The rare sporting facilities which did exist in the townships were generally financed by the sale of beer and spirits. Indeed the huge profits from the sale of alcohol were almost the only funds which the municipalities running the townships made available for social and housing development. 'The more an African community drinks, the more profits there will be available to spend on housing, rent subsidization, and recreational and social amenities. This amounts to a penalty being placed on a low-drinking community as well as an over-reliance on the profits of drink.' [72] This conclusion, reached by a modern student of the beerhall issue, was put more energetically in 1941 by three African residents of Grahamstown who protested that it was morally and socially unacceptable to finance their tennis courts with profits derived from the alcoholism of the mass of African workers. 'Are we expected to enjoy any game or entertainment knowing full well that we owe [them] directly to the financial and moral degradation of some unfortunate fellow African? . . . . We say without hesitation — the price is too high. We would far rather be without sport and entertainment, which we do love dearly, than that we pay this price.'[73] Their objections have not been heeded to this day; the situation has in fact worsened since the Government removed all restrictions on the sale of alcoholic drink to Blacks in 1961 and 1962. A high proportion of the budget devoted to education, health care, housing and sport in the townships continues to depend on the alcoholic intake of township residents.

No *formal* law was directed specifically towards preventing black and white sportsmen at this time or later from playing sport against each other — and Coloured and white teams did occasionally organize informal matches — but in general organized sport was subject to the same racial segregation as other social activities and most clubs had racially exclusive membership rules. Where Blacks were permitted to watch alongside white spectators, as in football and horse racing (until the 1950s), they usually more than paid their way for their enjoyment.

> Theatres and cinemas usually do not admit non-Europeans . . . . For the most part, natives are debarred from seeing or listening to European artists who visit the Union . . . . When the circus comes to town . . . white and black are separated into roped-off enclosures, and the Natives pay their money at a separate entrance; but the point is that they are admitted to the same show as the Europeans . . . . Racing provides another example where the social colour bar is partly broken down. Even in those provinces where colour feeling is strongest, non-Europeans are admitted to race-courses as backers, as owners, and as jockeys, and only slight distinctions are made. The annual report of the Turf Club in 1939 referred to the fact that about one-third of cash receipts for the year was obtained from Natives, and the report stressed the fact that Natives were playing an increasing part in the local racing and that Native owners would have to be given more privileges in the future.[74]

In 1936 the Rev. Ray Phillips, an American Board Missionary who was extremely active in promoting black and inter-racial sport in the 1920s and 1930s, even made an informal survey of African betting on the Reef.

> There is a total of ninety racing days on the Witwatersrand during the year.
> A normal Saturday race meeting at Turffontein attracts from two to four hundred Native men; two or three-score women; several score Indians and Eur-Africans. A stand is reserved for non-Europeans, but there is no barrier preventing them from visiting the large European stands if they wish. 'What we like about this,' Africans told the writer, 'is that there is no bar based on colour.' No liquor is served, but non-

Europeans have a tea room where tea and minerals are obtainable . . . .

At the writer's request the officials of the Johannesburg Turf Club kindly placed an official at the totalisator to record the total amount of Native bets at a normal race meeting. The Club Secretary reported the results as follows: 'The meeting on Saturday last (9 March 1935) was a normal one and there were about 250 boys present, and on the seven races they put some six hundred pounds through the totalisator. That probably works out at about £50 a race allowing for deductions' [Letter to the writer from Major J.J. Henley, 11 March 1935].

Inquiry into the extent of participation in the Dublin Sweep indicated that probably fifty per cent or more of the educated Native men on the Witwatersrand buy tickets on these lotteries.[75]

Financial interest, therefore, helped to temper racial segregation on the race courses and the football stands until the 1950s. Conditions of club membership, on the other hand, were an altogether different matter. Here segregation was very strictly applied – for many years the Wanderers Club in Johannesburg was even closed to Afrikaners[76] – and the Indian Weightlifting Federation which permitted members of all races, including Whites, to practise their sport together was probably a unique exception to the rule.

Black sports federations had nevertheless made some progress in this regard before 1948, for in several major sports (notably in football and cricket) they had formed Inter-Race Boards which regularly organized interracial contests between Indian, African and Coloured teams belonging to the different federations. These Boards foreshadowed the creation a decade later of the first unified non-racial sports federations which replaced the racially constituted black federations when apartheid legislation was applied to sport after 1956 (see Chapter 8).

Apartheid

When the Nationalist Party took power in 1948, it therefore had little need to impose apartheid on the playing of sport because it was already segregated. Nevertheless, a certain number of general and specific laws were passed which, without imposing an explicit ban, effectively rendered the playing of multiracial sport, as it would normally be understood, illegal. The rights and opportunities of black people were reduced in all domains, and therefore in sport as well.

To understand the future evolution of the sports issue and black demands, in fact, it is essential to remember that from the beginning apartheid laid hands not just upon the playing of matches, but on the *social and economic environment which conditions and makes the playing of sport possible and enjoyable.* By savagely curtailing black access to education, urban residence, employment, wealth, and the freedom to associate, to travel and to free expression, the Nationalist Government necessarily stunted the natural development of sport and dealt a crippling blow to the attempts of black players to improve their standards of play and organization.

At the beginning, some disciples of Nationalist dogma, particularly in the Cape, appear to have applied themselves with idealism to the 'separate development' of the subject peoples. For example, I.D. du Plessis, the Afrikaner poet, was appointed to the Cape Department of Coloured Affairs and organized, with other liberal Nationalists, several sports and boys clubs for the Coloured population. Bob Watson, who was present at some of these, recalls that:

> They saw the role of the Coloured Affairs Department as building up the organization, the administration of a semi-independent federated Coloured State. Their boys camps were very successful. They took old army and navy camps and got international sportsmen to come up for two weeks in the summer and sometimes for a week-end. They would have anything from 200 to 500 kids — Cape Coloured — who were coached in their particular sport, athletics, rugby, football . . . .
>
> I remember that Danie Craven was invited to coach rugby on one of them . . . and he was billeted in the same room as me by coincidence. When he got there, he unpacked his bags and took this revolver out of his briefcase and stuck it underneath his pillow and said, 'You can't trust these people you know, you don't know what's going to happen at night.' It was quite incredible, completely laughable, but he believed it and believed it each time he came back . . ., to about three camps. When I was in University, I was an Afrikaner Nationalist myself, a member of the Nationalist Youth Party.
>
> It took about five years for the bureaucrats to decide that liberalism was not what was intended, and they put in some Pretoria government officials.[77]

Any illusions which the Coloured community may have had as to the real intentions behind apartheid were thus rapidly dispelled. For the other two black communities, there had never been any question of temporizing, for the purposes of the new policy were starkly visible: immediately after 1948, the Indians were categorized as foreigners and plans were put forward for encouraging their return to a country which their forebears had left several generations earlier. There was even less ambiguity about the consequences of apartheid for the African population: it would shear away whatever derisory rights remained to them and subject them definitively to the servile status of labour power for the Whites.

In contrast, the Nationalist Party's victory led to substantial improvements in the lifestyle and living standards of Afrikaners. Having won political power, Afrikaners sought and gradually obtained a major share of the economy. They did so in the first instance by extending state ownership[78] and encouraging the formation of Afrikaner capital and Afrikaner enterprise. The growth of an Afrikaner bourgeoisie had been inhibited by the sovereignty of English-speakers in industry, commerce and finance, but after 1948 the combination of state patronage and an education policy designed to promote Afrikaner interests transformed the social structure of the Afrikaner community. By the 1960s over 70% of Afrikaners lived in towns, and bankers, businessmen, financiers and senior civil servants had joined the older elite of intellectuals and soldiers.[79] Their rise in wealth and status during an economic boom of record levels — a Japanese-style growth-rate of around 7% a year between 1960 and 1970 — also encouraged the further adoption of sport, which boomed in South Africa after 1955. Afrikaners not only adopted sport en masse but took to games which had previously been monopolized by the English, like cricket. The English-speakers themselves, of course, benefited from the same prosperity and devoted themselves more than ever to sport too. Numerous new sports federations representing modern and minority sports joined the Sports Federation which, created in 1951, saw its membership rise from 14 to 90 affiliates (1977) in the space of 25 years.

Overall, one can say that *the initial principal effect of apartheid was to widen the gap which already existed between the white and black communities — and between the social classes within each community.* A black elite on a significant scale did not surface to enjoy the fruits of South Africa's wealth until the 1970s; even then, the presence of a handful of black petty plutocrats in Dube (Soweto) and elsewhere has only served to underscore the terrible impoverishment of most of their countrymen.

In essence, the elections of 1948 turned around the place Blacks and particularly Africans were to occupy in the society. It went without saying that the all-white electorate would vote to keep South Africa white: but there was dispute over how the shortage of skilled and semi-skilled labour was to be resolved.[80] This problem had been created by the colour bar which prevented black labour from acquiring qualifications. Whereas the United Party and liberal opinion was in favour of recognizing the urban status of those black workers necessary to the efficient functioning of the national economy, the Nationalist Party claimed that the migrant labour system should be reinforced, the subject status of the reserves and the African population confirmed, and repressive political and economic legislation forced through Parliament to guarantee the preservation of white supremacy.

With a mandate in favour of apartheid, the Nationalist Government pushed through a barrage of segregationist laws in its first years of office, which reinforced white privilege, extended Government authority and reduced the rights of Blacks and opposition groups of all kinds. The legislation governing migrant and temporary labour was strengthened and extended; the pass laws were reinforced; racial zoning of residential areas (so-called 'group areas') was accelerated and the inhabitants of 'black spots' (Blacks living on white farms) removed; the black population was further concentrated in urban slums and townships while massive numbers of urban Africans were deported to the reserves; the political and civil rights of Blacks were further eroded or removed — and even the rights of Whites to protest were subjected to legal repression. In 1949 mixed marriages were prohibited; in

1950, racial classification of all members of the population was made statutory (the Population Registration Act); in the same year the terms of the Suppression of Communism Act made illegal not only the South African Communist Party but any organization which, in the view of the authorities, had a propensity to subvert the State;[81] in 1953, secondary and primary schools were racially segregated by law (higher education institutions were segregated in 1959); the Group Areas Act (1950) which established the conditions according to which different racial groups were assigned to separate dwelling zones, finally expunged once and for all the rights of Africans to own property in urban areas, and accorded wide powers of expulsion and resettlement to the authorities.

All these 'fundamental' laws indirectly affected the playing and organization of sport. Other laws which had an even more direct impact included the Urban Areas Act (1923, 1930, consolidated 1945, and subsequently amended) which reserved sporting (and other social facilities) for exclusive use by one racial group; the Reservation of Separate Amenities Act (1953) which imposed racial segregation in stadiums and public places; the Native Laws Amendment Act (1957) which regulated segregation within various organizations (sports federations, clubs, schools, churches etc); and the ubiquitous pass laws (redefined in 1952, 1956, 1957, 1959, 1963, 1964, 1966, 1967, 1968, 1969, 1970 . . .) which oblige every African over 16 years of age to carry on his or her person at all times a pass book which can be demanded at any moment and which indicates whether or not he or she is entitled to be present in a white zone (no African may leave the white area or Homeland to which he or she is attributed for more than 72 hours without having previously acquired a formal authorization from the authorities to do so).

The Group Areas Act was extended in 1965 (Proclamation R.26 amended by Proclamation R.228 of 1973) so as to exclude black spectators from sports matches and other public entertainment. Blacks had been banned intermittently from stadiums, and strictly segregated within them, from the middle 1950s. The first reported case occurred in 1955 when Bloemfontein municipality and rugby club decided to exclude black spectators from their new stadium; their initiative was widely followed during the next few years. Peter Hain recalls the introduction of Proclamation R.26 at his local club, Arcadia United, in Pretoria, when non-white spectators, already partitioned off, were finally expelled from the ground altogether: 'The carnival atmosphere engendered by their enthusiastic support disappeared. But crowds of Africans still gathered outside the ground, listening to the match. Others tried to watch from trees adjoining the ground: this so angered local white residents that in September 1966 police dogs were used to drive them from their vantage points.'[82]

The proclamation of 1965 banned black spectators from social or sporting events at which other racial groups were present, unless a permit allowing racial mixing had been granted. The same proclamation gave the Administration powers to ban the playing of multi-racial matches on private land in the presence of spectators.[83] White stadiums which wished to accommodate black spectators were obliged to construct separate entry gates and toilet facilities for them and build partitions to keep fans of different races apart. It was decided, for example, that the barrier at Newlands should be at least two metres in height.

During the same period, the barrier of apartheid descended on the race-courses. In 1950 separate enclosures and entry gates were introduced in Durban. Natal also became the first province to ban inter-racial athletics contests between schools — several years before the Government introduced legislation to this effect in 1966.

The Liquor Amendment Act (1963, after the Act of 1923) should also be mentioned. It forbade Whites, Indians and Coloureds to consume alcoholic drink with Africans except on premises they owned, and effectively prevented people — and sportsmen — of different races from drinking and mixing together socially, for example after matches.

These laws and regulations comprehensively control the social environment in which sport is played although they do not address themselves directly to sportsmen or sporting organizations. As a result, their application is uncertain and in general has had to be tested before the courts. Whenever the applicability of apartheid legislation to inter-racial sport has been questioned by the courts or by sporting practice, however, the Government has generally intervened to define official policy.

The first such statement was made in 1956 by Dr Donges, then Minister of the Interior, at a time when several black federations (football, table tennis, cricket, weight-lifting) were pressing for international recognition, within or outside the official (all-white) South African Associations. The principles he advanced informed official policy until 1971 (indeed they are still applicable to many aspects of the official 'multi-national' policy today):[84]
1) Whites and non-whites must organize their sport separately;
2) No mixed sport would be allowed within the borders of South Africa;
3) No mixed teams would compete abroad;
4) International teams competing in South Africa against white South African teams must be all-white, according to South African custom;
5) Non-white sportsmen from overseas could compete against non-white South Africans in South Africa;
6) Non-white organizations seeking international recognition must do so through the already recognized white organizations in their code of sport;
7) The Government would refuse travel visas to 'subversive' non-white sportsmen who sought to discredit South Africa's image abroad or contest the Government's racial policies.

In 1966, the Government created a Department of Sport and Recreation, to organize and stimulate white sport; black sport remained the responsibility of the appropriate black department (Indian, Coloured or Bantu Affairs) until 1978.

Apartheid measures were particularly damaging in the field of education which, as we have seen, was one of the nurseries of black sport. This is not surprising for the Nationalists attached particular importance to education, which was to assure the survival of Afrikaans and of Afrikaner culture, and thereby of white 'civilization' and power. The *Broederbond* had created a committee to deal specifically with this issue and the theory of Christian National Education preoccupied the Nationalists throughout the 1930s and 1940s.

Early statements of principle were so fundamentalist, however, that even ardent Nationalists had to discard them.[85] Nevertheless, formulated more subtly, the same ideas subsequently informed official education policies and were translated into law during the 1950s. In all cases, the role allotted to the black population was unambiguous. In June 1954 Dr Verwoerd, then Minister of Native Affairs, declared to the Senate:

> There is no place [for the Bantu] in the European community above the level of certain forms of labour . . . . For that reason it is of no avail to him to receive a training which has as its main aim absorption in the European community . . . .
> Education must train and teach people in accordance with their opportunities in life . . . . It is therefore necessary that native education be controlled in such a way that it should be in accordance with the policy of the State.[86]

In obedience to this view, the Government set about destroying the influence of the mission schools which still taught a minority of African and other black children to a high standard and were continuing to create a small intellectual elite. In 1953, African education was placed under the responsibility of the Department of Native Affairs,[87] and schools which had not been officially approved were forbidden to open; the following year, grants to private schools were cut back and soon afterwards withdrawn altogether. As a result, the number of mission schools fell from 5,000 in 1953 to 438 in 1971 and 132 in 1977 — a decline of 97.3%. These last remaining schools are obliged to teach the official curriculum.

The effect on physical education and the spread of sport was dramatic, for it was at school that African children first played sport — and school frequently provided their only opportunity of doing so. Official Government schools paid less attention than the mission schools to physical education (see Chapters 5 and 6) and the farm schools, introduced by the Nationalist Government to replace the mission schools in rural areas, were subject to the whim of the white farmers responsible for them and, apart from offering little or no sport, generally provided the lowest possible quality of primary education. Indeed no better was intended, the purpose of such schools being 'to fit [the child] for farm work'.[88]

At the other end of the system, the Nationalist Government closed the English-speaking universities to African students[89] and created in their stead three 'tribal' universities (Fort Hare for Xhosa, Ngoye for Zulu and Swazi, Turfloop for Sotho and all other African language speakers). Westville University College (Durban) was reserved for Indians and the University of the

Western Cape for Coloured students.

A new era was reached when Verwoerd became Prime Minister in 1958. As the European imperial powers began the process of decolonization in Africa, the South African Government decided to confer 'self-government' on the 'Homelands'. The Government was then able to pursue its neo-tribal and forced labour policies while claiming at the same time to 'free' black South Africans from white rule. Apartheid became 'Separate Development' and by the terms of South African law all Africans became, actually or potentially, foreigners in their own country — migrant workers without the rights or title of citizenship except in the 'tribal Homeland' to which they had been assigned by the Administration. In 1970 Prime Minister Vorster stated that the bantustans could be accorded 'independence', and that the South African citizenship of *all* Africans (including those who had never lived in or been born in one of the 'Homelands') would be withdrawn and replaced by passports from the bantustan of which they were the registered dependents.

By a parallel process, the Indian and Coloured minorities also became second-class citizens. In 1956, the South African Parliament had removed Coloured voters from the electoral rolls altogether and recreated the old Coloured Advisory Council which offered no more than indirect representation. South African nationality was finally accorded to the Indian population, but without political rights; the Indians were also to be represented by an Advisory Council. The latter not only had no power but until 1977 was nominated, not elected.

Within a decade, all black people in South Africa had lost whatever political rights they had possessed. The entire black population (80% of South Africans) had been disenfranchised. In the face of this threat, black political leaders succeeded for the first time in uniting their forces and organizing concerted resistance. Pushed by its youth wing, the African National Congress (A.N.C.) had adopted a much firmer line from 1945 — demanding universal suffrage, abolition of all laws restricting the free movement of Africans, and restitution of the rights of ownership and residence. In 1946 the party organized a major strike, and in 1948 a series of national protests and civil disobedience campaigns against the Nationalist Government. In 1954 the A.N.C. also organized a boycott of official schools and created a series of education centres under the guise of social clubs.

In the Cape[90] after 1943 the young Coloured petty bourgeoisie organized a heated campaign against the Advisory Council within the Anti-CAC committee or Anti-CAD or within the Unity Movement (under Trotskyist influence). Without co-ordinating their protest with the mass campaigns then being organized by the A.N.C., these organizations called upon the Coloured community to boycott all institutions which recognized official authority.[91]

In 1954, finally, the executives of the A.N.C., the South African Indian Congress, the South African Coloured People's Organization and the South African Congress of Democrats,[92] convened a Congress of the People under the chairmanship of the A.N.C. which took place in June 1955. Three thousand delegates from all over the country adopted the Freedom Charter which established the aim of creating a non-racial South Africa. The Charter, which states *inter alia* that South Africa belongs to all who live in it and that all are equal before the law and that all have equal political and social rights, remains the fundamental statement of principle of South Africa's major liberation movement.

'The main demands,' wrote Basil Bunting in 1964, 'would have been unnecessary in any civilized democratic state . . . .'[93] Nevertheless, a series of new laws were added to those already passed to counter the spreading influence of the A.N.C. and other opponents of apartheid. Political demonstrations were banned; the Government gave itself power to rule by decree if it declared a State of Emergency, which could be prolonged indefinitely (Public Safety Act, 1953); banning orders made it possible, upon issue of an administrative instruction, to confine an individual to his house and force him or her to suspend all public activity. Hundreds of people were arrested and tried in the period after 1955 under these and other punitive laws, but without halting the movement of protest.

Finally, on 21 March 1960, 69 people were shot dead and hundreds wounded when police opened fire upon peaceful demonstrators at Sharpeville and in Langa. The massacre provoked huge protests within and outside the country. The A.N.C. and P.A.C.[94] were banned. Both organizations went underground, established military commands and began to organize armed sabotage. New laws reinforced official powers of repression: it became legal to detain suspects for up to 90 days without trial or judicial control, subsequently extended to 180 days (in 1965), then one year, then one year indefinitely renewable . . . .

In 1963, the principal political and military leaders of the A.N.C. were arrested at Rivonia. Nelson Mandela, Walter Sisulu and six others were tried and condemned to life imprisonment. While they served their sentence on Robben Island opposite Cape Town, during the 1960s the white electorate moved steadily towards the Nationalist Party, their racial anxiety fuelled by its racialist programme and propaganda. Not until the end of the 1960s did a new black generation emerge to lead resistance to apartheid. The Black Consciousness Movement confronted the white regime's policy of cultural dislocation and physical separation by unifying all Blacks – Indians, Coloureds and Africans – on the basis of a common awareness of their dignity and cultural equality. The Movement's principal leader, Steve Biko, who was first president of the South African Students Organization, was murdered in detention in September 1977, a year after the riots in Soweto: shortly afterwards the Black Consciousness organizations were proscribed and their leaders banned or arrested. The series of strikes and school boycotts in 1979-80, and the recent acts of sabotage against SASOL and other official and military installations are the latest expressions of political resistance to a regime which has not ceased, since it took power in 1948, to reinforce itself against threats of any kind, and to force upon the South African people, by

all means to hand, a philosophy and economic system which is racist, undemo-
cratic and unjust.

Black sportsmen and women also organized during the same period. We
have seen that Inter-Race Boards had been created by African, Indian and
Coloured sportsmen during the 1940s. In the 1950s, a number of black sports
organizations coalesced, to create national federations in football, cricket,
weight-lifting, athletics, table tennis etc.; and black sportsmen formed their
first national organization – the South African Sports Association (1959).

The creation of SASA paved the way for the establishment of the *non-
racial principle*, upon which, after 1959, the unified black sports institutions
increasingly based their constitutions. As a result, their representatives and
their teams were banned from leaving the country and harassed in systematic
fashion by the white sports establishment.

The creation in 1963 of the South African Non-Racial Olympic Committee (SANROC), whose purpose was to seek recognition for black sportsmen
and women and to defend non-racial principles abroad, constituted the third
major development for black sports during this period. First within South
Africa and then, from exile, in London, an enormously successful campaign
was launched to isolate South African racial sport, which began with South
Africa's exclusion from the Olympic Games in 1964 and culminated in 1970
with her exclusion from the Olympic Movement. A formidable amount of
international support for non-racial sports organizations operating inside the
country was mobilized and henceforth black sportsmen and women rarely
suffered the same degree of repression that they had to endure between 1960
and 1965.

The 1970 crisis forced white South Africa to adapt its sports policy and in
1971 the Government revealed what has become known as the 'multi-national'
policy. This policy, refurbished and ameliorated, was formally adopted by the
Sports Minister Dr Piet Koornhof and by the Government in September 1976
(see Appendix 1).

Long before this, however, the superficial nature of the changes involved
had been denounced by a powerful new sports organization within South
Africa, the South African Council on Sport (SACOS), created in 1973 and
representing all the non-racial sports federations. SACOS called for a complete moratorium on all tours to and from South Africa and the boycott of
all official institutions for so long as apartheid laws remain on the statute
book. The story of the struggle between 'multi-nationalism' and 'non-
racialism' is the subject of the latter part of this book; first let us look in
greater detail at the history and character of black and white sport up to
the 1950s.

References

1. Hassan Howa, President of the S.A. Council on Sport in A. Odendaal, 1977, p. 275.
2. This is a book devoted to sport not a general study of South African history. For those who wish to read more widely, we refer the reader to the general bibliography at the end of the book. This chapter is intended to situate the development of sport in relation to the principal events and developments in the country's history. We emphasize the history of black sport, because it has been largely ignored: Chapters 5, 6 and 8 are devoted to it, and parts of Chapters 2, 3 and 4. Many books have dealt with white sport: the reader will find a certain amount of information in Chapters 2-5. For easy reference the reader is invited to refer to the Chronology in the Appendix.
3. This myth has been widely disseminated and has given rise to some bizarre conclusions. 'South Africa is evolving,' declared M. Jean de Beaumont, ex-President and member of the French Olympic Committee, in 1979. 'She must be allowed to broaden a constitution which was made at a time when there wasn't a single black man in South Africa, only Whites.' *(L'Equipe*, 6 November 1979).
4. *Encyclopaedie moderne du sport*, No. 1, January 1980.
5. *South Africa 1977, Official Year Book*, 1977, p. 828.
6. The game was played by two adversaries who crooked their little fingers together and tried to pull each other off balance.
7. The Coloured population rose from 445,000 in 1905 to 2,368,000 in 1975. This group also includes the Cape Malays, imported from Java and Bali between 1667 and 1749, who have retained their cultural identity.
8. Goguel and Buis, 1978, p. 9.
9. de Kiewiet, 1941, p. 17.
10. Ibid., p. 30.
11. Official South African histories also gloss over this important crisis in African society and claim that the territories occupied by the Boer trekkers were virtually uninhabited. The argument serves to justify the subsequent seizure of African lands and the restricted size of the African reserves which are alleged to represent the areas occupied by Africans when the settlers arrived.
12. The Boer victory at Blood River on December 16 is today a 'national' holiday for South Africans. The Zulus continued to resist European encroachment until the beginning of the 20th Century.
13. R.S. Churchill, 1892, p. 75. Other observers, however, detected real love for wild game among the Boers, some of whom fenced in areas for springbok and blesbok within which it was forbidden to hunt.
14. J. Buchan, 1903, pp. 49-50.
15. S. Thion, 1969, p. 35.
16. From *Dusklands* by J.M. Coetzee (1974, p. 14), an imaginative reconstruction of a Bushman hunt, based on archival research.
17. C. Graham Botha, 1970, pp. 51-52.
18. D. Child, 1967, p. 33.
19. A.F. Hattersley, 1940, pp. 99-100.

20. Lady Duff Gordon, 3 May 1862, 1927.
21. D. Child, 1967, p. 33.
22. W. Beinart, interview, Oxford, 11 February 1980.
23. F. Alderson, 1974, pp. 138-9.
24. The history of cricket is described more fully in Chapter 3.
25. A.F. Hattersley, 1950, p. 333.
26. The Indian population in 1975 numbered 727,000.
27. Compare the assimilation of these sports to the situation in France, where the first 'English' clubs were founded in 1882 and 1883. They merged and subsequently gave birth to the *Union des Societes Francaises de Sports Athletiques* (U.S.F.S.A.), which represented all the players of rugby, tennis, cycling, football, rowing, etc. However, sport was almost exclusively the preserve of students and the upper classes until the First World War, and individual national associations were not set up until the 1920s.
28. From 1872 the Cape was self-governing under a Prime Minister who replaced the British Governor. Natal became self-governing in 1893.
29. See Chapter 2. According to Thion, the emergence of the concept of *Afrikaner* can be traced to this period (1967, p. 65).
30. It has been estimated that some 26,000 Boers died in British concentration camps during the war — about 10% of the entire population.
31. J. Edmunds, 1975, pp. 303-7.
32. Caffrey, 1973, p. 89.
33. R. Lefort, 1977, pp. 30-31.
34. In 1678. The first European school for the children of slaves had opened in 1658.
35. These and subsequent figures are taken from B. Hirson, 1979, p. 15.
36. The Indian Commission Report of 1872 found that, of 930 children of school age, only 88 were enrolled (9.4%) (R.S. Naidoo, 'The Indian Community and Education', in *Race Relations News*, November 1976.)
37. B. Willan, *An African in Kimberley*, (the reference is to *Imvo*, 13 May 1897, Natives of the Jubilee).
38. Physical education was an obligatory item on the state school curricula after 1938; African schools even today have little organized sport, although sport was played in the mission schools and reached a high standard in the large mission colleges and Fort Hare. See Chapters 5 and 6.
39. The rules of rugby were still evolving at this time: in the 1870s 14 played on each side — 2 backs, 2 three-quarters, 2 halves and 8 forwards; players of association football were still to be seen with the ball in their hands.
40. J.F. Hattersley, 1940, p. 202.
41. For examples in cricket and rugby, see Chapters 2 and 3.
42. This principle was incorporated into the 1911 Native Labour Regulation Act. It was of course illegal for black workers to strike.
43. See Chapters 5 and 6.
44. The system of reserves (or bantustans) and the role of the tribal chiefs are central to understanding the South African Government's neo-tribal policies and modern apartheid. By artificially stimulating tribal and racial structures and incorporating them into its own organization,

the Administration is able to divide the black, and within it subdivide the African population, into tribal groups living in separate areas which are, in effect, so many pools of migrant labour. At the same time, the population in the reserves reproduces itself (though to a steadily decreasing extent), thereby freeing the Administration from the many social costs of maintaining its work force – education, health care, pensions, sickness and accident benefits etc. This neo-tribal policy allows the white authorities to exploit the black labour force at the lowest possible cost while claiming to recognize and respect the cultural specificity of different peoples. Separate development serves merely to conceal the fact that white development is systematically at the expense of black underdevelopment.

45. 1904 – 10.4%; 1936 – 19.0%; 1946 – 24.6%.
46. Bunting, 1964, p. 24. See also pp. 25-6.
47. We will later have occasion to examine the important role played by the *Broederbond* in the elaboration of South Africa's official 'multi-national' sports policy in the 1970s (see Chapter 9). The importance of this secret organization should not be underestimated, despite its cloak-and-dagger reputation. Since 1948 every one of South Africa's Prime Ministers has been a member. Membership has risen from 37 in 1920 to 1,980 (1940), 3,362 (1950), 5,670 (1960) and 12,000 (1977) – a progression which measures to some degree the growth of the Afrikaner elite itself. In 1968 20.36% of *Broeders* were teachers, 7.12% in the Church and 4.35% senior officials in the Administration. In 1977, in addition to 24 university and college chancellors and principals, 171 professors, 176 lecturers, 468 headmasters, 121 school inspectors and 647 teachers, there were 22 publishers, 26 judges, 13 barristers, 156 solicitors, 67 magistrates, 154 managing directors etc. Women are not admitted; nor are non-Afrikaans speakers. See Wilkins and Strydom, 1980.
48. P.A. Silburn, 1927, p. 75.
49. See pp. 86-7.
50. A. Kum'a N'dumbe III, 1980, p. 287.
51. B. Bunting, 1964, p. 88. For the background to Afrikaner anti-semitism and sedition during the War, see B. Bunting, 1964, pp. 54-93, and Wilkins and Strydom, 1980, passim.
52. 'It is well known that certain social and sporting clubs do not admit Jews to their membership.' H. Lever, 1968, p. 85. See also p. 103 below
53. Saron and Hotz, pp. 225 and 396.
54. Joshua Brauer, August 1939, pp. 44-5.
55. Nicol, *Kerkbode*, 5 March 1941, in Wilkins and Strydom, 1980, p. 258.
56. Statement of a schools inspector to the Congress on the National Language, held in December 1943, in Wilkins and Strydom, 1980, p. 258.
57. V. Stiebel, 1968, p. 60, pp. 144-5.
58. B. Watson, interview, London, 12 February 1980.
59. E. Jokl in Hellmann, 1949, pp. 442-3.
60. Ibid., p. 449.
61. Professional boxing had been banned again until 1923.
62. S.O.E.G.A.: this organization later took the title of the S.A. Olympic

Games Association (S.A.O.G.A.), in 1961, when South Africa left the Commonwealth, and is now known as the S.A. Olympic and National Games Association (S.A.O.N.G.A.).

63. In 1938, gold mining accounted for 87% of the value of all mining production in South Africa, trailed by coal (4.7%), diamonds (3.7%), copper (0.6%). In the same year, 386,607 of the 474,588 workers in the mines were gold miners.
64. B. Watson, interview, 12 February 1980.
65. Wright Noel, 1929, pp. 206-15; A.W. Wells, 1939, passim.
66. B. Watson, interview, 12 February 1980.
67. Ibid.
68. A.W. Wells, 1939, p. 258.
69. Interview, (Bob Watson), London, 12 February 1980.
70. Ibid.
71. See Chapter 7.
72. Savage, September 1976. During the Soweto riots in 1976, large numbers of beerhalls were burned down in protest.
73. Bokwe, Foley, Th. Nkosinkulu, in *South African Outlook*, September 1976.
74. J. Burger, 1943, p. 190. The author adds: 'On the other hand, it is highly improbable that anyone would promote a boxing match or a wrestling match in which a non-European was billed to perform against a European, though there is no law against this, and though such a match would prove highly profitable for the promoter.'
75. R. Phillips, 1936, pp. 220-3.
76. R. Compton, interview, 18 October 1979.
77. Bob Watson, interview, London, 12 February 1980. Danie Craven is President of the South African Rugby Board.
78. The South African state sector is today the largest in the country, both in capital investments and turnover.
79. About 60% of the white population are Afrikaners: according to Mitchell, cited by H. Lever, 1978, p. 18. Afrikaners nevertheless now hold 90% of jobs in the public sector.
80. This problem preoccupies employers and the Government to this day and remains a fundamental contradiction of apartheid. South Africa cannot industrialize effectively without raising the productivity and skills of its labour force — which entails training black labour. Nor can the domestic market be extended to increase demand for South Africa's products without paying (black) labour better wages, which implies higher productivity, and again, a more skilled African labour force.
81. Clause (b) of the Act, for example, states that an organization may be banned 'which aims at bringing about any political, industrial, social or economic change within the Union by the promotion of disturbance or disorder, by unlawful acts or omissions or by the threat of such acts or omissions . . . . ' See B. Bunting, 1964, pp. 164-7.
82. P. Hain, 1971, p. 40. The introduction of Proclamation R.26 was linked to the white sports establishment's campaign to destroy the growing influence of the non-racial sports movement. See Chapter 8.
83. Previously such matches had not been subject to control, which permitted a certain amount of multi-racial sport to be organized. This law

effectively prevented non-racial sportsmen from playing before the
public and thereby seriously undermined their finances, since no
tickets could be sold. The complexity of this and other acts is such
that detailed explanations have to be furnished by official spokesmen.
In this case, the sports unions were informed that, according to the
Proclamation, white facilities could only be used by white people; but
that if separate gates, lavatories and services had been installed, Africans
might be invited to watch international and interprovincial games, and
Indian and Coloured spectators matches below this level – provided
white spectators did not object!

84. See Chapter 9 and Appendix 2.
85. Wilkins and Strydom, 1980, p. 261.
86. Verwoerd, quoted in B. Bunting, 1964, p. 206.
87. The Department of Bantu Education was created in 1959.
88. The Minister of Bantu Education, 1959, in D. Herbstein, 1978, p. 92.
89. Until then, they had accepted a small minority of black students. They
    scarcely had an 'open' policy, however, for segregationist principles
    were rigidly applied by students and staff in most college activities,
    including sport. (See below p. 132) and UNESCO, 1972, p. 101; also
    Apartheid-Non! Du cote noir du tableau, 1980.
90. Where in 1951 the number of Coloured people overtook for the first
    time the number of white, reaching 46.35% of the total population.
    (S. Patterson, 1953, p. 15).
91. Sports associations were also involved. When the C.A.C. was created in
    April 1943, 'The fight was on. It was a bitter fight with no quarter
    given. It was carried into all spheres of communal life – football clubs,
    cricket clubs, tennis clubs, cultural clubs, societies, churches, and even
    into domestic life . . . . Never before had the Coloured community
    experienced the like.' A.C. Scholtz, *Cape Times*, 8 July 1949 (in
    S. Patterson, 1953, p. 312, note 90).
92. A small white party, communist in sympathy; the S.A. Communist
    Party had been banned under the terms of the Suppression of Commu-
    nism Act (1950).
93. B. Bunting, 1964, p. 172.
94. P.A.C.: Pan African Congress – a rival nationalist liberation movement
    born of a split within the A.N.C.

2. Rugby: The Chosen Sport of a Chosen People

> Rugby is one of the three cultural activities of the white
> population, the other two being lying in the sun and eating.[1]

'A South African thinks: Tell me how you play rugby and I'll tell you what
you're like — if you play good rugby, you are a great people.' With those
words the French coach Serge Saulnier addressed the French team before it
left to play its first official South African tour in 1958. 'You have the opportunity to prove that France is still a major power. I am not exaggerating,
believe me, you're going to find out what rugby is like over there — it's a
religion with temples, high priests and the faithful .... Every moment will
be a battle which, for yourselves, for our rugby, for our country, it is your
duty to win.'[2]

Here is our first image of South African rugby — a game of semi-mystical
status. Indeed this image permeates our general idea of the country as a
whole. Rugby is the national sport, South Africans are devoted to it and
their play has the grandiose qualities of myth.

Yet football (or soccer) is undoubtedly the number one sport in terms of
players among the country's four population groups as a whole. Well over
half a million adults play it, compared with the 215,000 senior and school
rugby players. Moreover, although rugby is the second most popular game
for the Whites and Coloured minorities, it is played by few Africans and
scarcely any Indians. Why then do we, and South Africans, attach such
importance to it? The answers to this question tell us a good deal — and
about more than just rugby.

Rugby-football developed over the same period of time in South Africa
and Great Britain. Tradition dates the birth of the game to 1823, when
William Webb Ellis took it into his head to pick up the ball and run with it
during a game he was playing at Rugby School in Warwickshire. The sport
was baptized in 1841-42 and the rules first written down in 1846. By the
1860s, it was being played in the majority of English and Scottish public
schools where it had already earned its reputation as a game to harden
gentlemen.

The sport was introduced to South Africa in 1862, by Canon George
Ogilvie who had played it at Winchester before he emigrated to South Africa

in 1861 to take up the post of Director of the Diocesan School. His version of rugby-football[3] was nicknamed the Winchester Game or 'Gog's Game' after its founder, and it seems reasonable to assume that the same rules were played when a team of British soldiers met a team of civilians on Green Point Common (Cape Town) on 23 August 1862. It was certainly this version that was played by the pupils of the South African College on a corner of paddock and in the unenclosed municipal squares of Cape Town. Two pairs of oaks served as goals and the rules of the game were described as follows by an old boy, Sir Henry Juta, in 1909:

> Whether it is the Worcester or Winchester game I know not, but the principle was that a player was not allowed to touch the ball with his hands unless he caught it after it had touched one of his opponents and before it reached the ground. If so caught, there was a choice either of taking a free kick or of running with the ball. The latter was round as in soccer. The goal-posts were placed as in the Rugby Union game, but there was no cross-bar and a goal was scored whenever the ball passed between the posts and over a line drawn between them. The game began with a scrum, but, when the ball found touch, the two sides, saving a few, formed two single-man lines, shoulder to shoulder, and it was push when the ball was thrown in. Shouldering was a great feature, but the finesse of the game lay in dribbling. In spite of the apparent simplicity of the game as compared with Rugby Union, my experience was that it was quite as dangerous.[4]

In 1879 the Winchester Old Boys helped to form the first two rugby clubs, Hamiltons and Villagers R.F.C.,[5] which recently celebrated their 200th match against each other. They appear to have adopted modern rules in 1879. British regiments also played against one another during the Zulu and 'Kaffir' wars of 1877-79 when Britain invaded the Transvaal and occupied the rest of present-day Natal.

To these years can be dated the game's adoption by the two high schools of Natal and Hilton College. The first recorded match in Natal had taken place on 26 September 1866 in Pietermaritzburg market place, when a garrison side took on a town team led by a Balliol man,[6] and by the 1870s the schools were beginning to play seriously — as we can judge from this lively description of one early encounter quoted by A.F. Hattersley:

> Rugby-football was the winter game . . . from the earliest days, played under rules and conditions which differed considerably from those at English schools. Teams sometimes numbered fourteen, with two backs, two three-quarter backs, two half-backs and eight forwards. There were usually two referees. Knee breeches or shorts extending below the knee were worn by the players. The first Hilton versus Bishop's match to be fully reported in the press was played at Hilton on 21 June 1879. 'The Red Maltese crosses of the Bishop's College and the black fleur-de-lys

of the Hiltonarians showed up well against their jerseys as the ball was kicked off,' wrote the reporter, 'though, before the match was over, many of them bore witness to the heat of the contest. During the first "half-time", the Hilton XV managed to score two goals (a drop by Wirsing and a place kick by the same player, from a touch down by Middlebrook). After the change, the Bishop's College team tried hard to prevent a defeat; but they were outweighted, their opponents scoring another three goals (two place kicks by Wirsing from a maul in goal, and a run in by himself), and a touch-down by Giles, the try from which was not successful. There was some good play on both sides; but though the Red Crosses played up very pluckily, they were unable to make up the lost ground. At one o'clock no side was called, the match resulting in a victory for the fleur-de-lys by five goals and one try, besides touch-downs.[7]

The arrival in the 1880s of the English international W.H. Milton (later Sir William Milton) further stimulated the game, and it spread rapidly throughout the country. The first provincial rugby unions appeared in 1883, when first the Western Province Union and then, a few months later, the Eastern Province Union were created; Natal soon followed (though soccer was to remain more popular) and Griqualand (Griqualand West Union, 1886) and the Transvaal (1889) in their turn. The South African Rugby Board was formed to administer the sport nationally in 1889, one year before the creation of the International Rugby Football Board in November 1890, of which South Africa was a founder member. By the end of the century, rugby seems already to have acquired much of its modern ethos for the white population. It was already seen to be above politics and to express symbolically the superiority of one people over another — as the match organized in 1902 between teams from the British and Boer armies at the bitter end of the war perhaps shows.[8]

The Development of Black Rugby

As the game spread, it was adopted by new strata of the population in new areas. The Coloured population of the Cape had taken to the sport almost at once and were enthusiastic spectators when Newlands was opened in May 1890. In comparison, the Africans working in Cape Town had little social contact with Whites and few of them adopted the game. However, at Kimberley rugby and cricket were both played by the African petty bourgeoisie: during the 1890s the Native Rovers Rugby Football Club competed with the half dozen black clubs (most of them Coloured) grouped in the Griqualand West Colonial Rugby Football Union (1894) and the Union's flamboyant President, Isaiah Bud Mbelle, persuaded Cecil Rhodes to donate a cup to African and Coloured rugby, which was then awarded every year to the best team in the colony. Bud Mbelle was also instrumental in the creation in 1896 of the South African Colonial Rugby Football Board, which was also dominated by Coloured teams.[9]

At the beginning of the new century, the S.A.C.R.F.B. became the South African Coloured Rugby Football Board, which ran all Coloured rugby until the 1950s (when a minor secession occurred), and administered African rugby until the 1930s. The Coloured Rugby Board's policy was throughout this period open with respect to race, and in areas where no African club existed, African players continued to play within its teams. Bud Mbelle himself was the Board's first Vice-President.

No doubt under similar pressures to those which fragmented cricket along racial lines at the same period (see Chapter 3), after 1929 a group of African players formed a separate association, called the South African African Rugby Board (1935), which ran a biannual national inter-provincial tournament for African teams in Kimberley. The Board was not apparently known for its probity.[10] African rugby nevertheless continued to grow, particularly in the Eastern Cape (where the first club had been formed in Port Elizabeth in 1887, and an Eastern Province Native Rugby Board formed in 1905). According to a survey in 1946,[11] the S.A. Bantu Rugby Union (no doubt the S.A. African Rugby Board) had affiliates in Eastern Province, Western Province, Border, Griqualand West, the Midlands and the Transvaal, while the S.A. Rugby Sports Board of Control (no doubt the S.A.C.R.B.) covered the same areas, excluding the Midlands, but distinguishing Northern Transvaal from Transvaal and Cape City from Cape Suburban, and claiming affiliates in Boland and South West Districts. No affiliates of either were recorded in Natal or the Orange Free State.

Indian rugby remained virtually non-existent, although the talented Baboollal Maharaj from Transvaal appears to have played in friendly matches for white teams during the 1920s.[12]

In Transvaal, for which we have statistics for the 1940s, the Transvaal Coloured Rugby Union claimed 500 players and ran 9 teams; it was affiliated to the Johannesburg Sports Board of Control, which co-ordinated all Coloured sport in the area. The African union, the Transvaal Native Rugby Football Union, claimed for its part to have 32 affiliated clubs, including 16 school teams, and its activities extended across Springs, Randfontein and Pretoria; it had access to 20 pitches. The schools belonging to the Johannesburg Bantu Inter-Schools League also had a rugby section, with four teams (1946) which played occasional matches against senior sides.[13]

These figures confirm that rugby was played essentially by the Coloured population in the Western Cape and by Africans and Coloureds in the Eastern Cape and Transvaal. Virtually no rugby was played by Blacks in Natal or in the Orange Free State. In spite of the lack of facilities — further reduced by the Nationalist Government after 1948 — African schools also played rugby.

Until the end of the 1950s the white S.A. Rugby Board accorded little attention to black rugby, which organizationally evolved rather more slowly than some other major sports. It was not until the middle 1960s that a clearly identifiable non-racial organization emerged — the South African Rugby Union — and not until the 1970s that it began to take its present important place as one of the most powerful and multi-racial sports federations in the

South African Council on Sport. At the end of the 1950s, the Coloured rugby players were grouped in two organizations, the S.A. Coloured Rugby Board (which later became the S.A. Rugby Union) and the S.A. Rugby Federation which represented a group of teams from the rural areas of the Western Cape. The African players were organized within the S.A. African Rugby Board, whose strength lay in the Eastern Cape, in the mining compounds of the Transvaal and in the police force. At the beginning of the 1970s significant numbers of African teams in the Eastern Cape and Natal disaffiliated from this racial organization to join the S.A. Rugby Union; there they were joined by teams from the S.A. Rugby Federation and by some white players.[14] The S.A. Rugby Union is today South Africa's second largest rugby federation, regrouping around 20 provincial unions, representing about 230 senior clubs and a similar number of school and student players.

The Transvaal and Western Cape are, for both Black and White, the heartlands of South African rugby. In 1976, the white S.A. Rugby Board claimed 9,840[15] and 3,630 members in each respectively. Over 5% of the entire white population belongs to rugby clubs (37,000 adults and 180,000 school players), a statistic which confirms the comparative importance of the game to the different racial groups, since — as we have seen — virtually no Indians play the game and few Africans (less than 0.1%) while the number of Coloured players is high enough (at least 2.4%) to justify comparison with the Whites. This fact helps to explain why the white community has adopted the game so completely: many white South Africans find it difficult to believe that Africans have any knowledge of, or interest in, the sport, as an incident concerning Steve Biko illustrates:

> His interrogators had been astonished by his interest in what they regarded as exclusively 'white' matters. For example, a rugby tour by the New Zealanders was in progress at the time, and the Security Police asked if he was following the tour. He told them he was.
> What did he think of the Springbok team?
> Steve replied: 'I wouldn't have Bosch at fly-half, I'd pick Gavin Cowley.' This, he said, appeared to flabbergast them. Such black knowledge of white sport . . . .[16]

The Rise and Fall of White Rugby

Until very recently, no Coloured or African players or teams were permitted to compete in either of South Africa's 'national' championships — the Currie and Pienaar Cups — or to represent the country at international level. General ignorance of the existence of black rugby both inside and outside the country has been reinforced by the policies of the S.A. Rugby Board and the International Rugby Board (I.R.B.) which both refused to recognize the claims of black players. South Africa's international rugby record is therefore all-white; and, until the boycott put an end to tours the Springboks competed almost exclusively with the 'white' British ex-colonies, the four home counties and France.

Rugby began to take root in Australia and New Zealand soon after it did in South Africa. The first British tour went to New Zealand in 1888 and was shortly followed by a Maori tour to Great Britain, which prompted the British Rugby Union to lay down two rules of touring which were to have a major influence on the future of the game. It was decided that no player or official should earn money from a tour and that no unofficial tours to or from the colonies would be recognized.

Immediately afterwards, an English team was invited to South Africa, at the expense of Cecil Rhodes, then Prime Minister of the Cape. South Africa therefore hosted the first official international tour of the Rugby Union, in 1891, when the British won all 20 of their matches — including three tests — and totted up the astonishing score of 226 points for 1 point scored against them. Their captain, W.E. MacLagen, who had been asked by Sir Donald Currie to award a cup to the best team they had played, selected Griqualand West who immediately entrusted the Currie Cup to the S.A. Rugby Board. Ever since, it has been South Africa's premier tournament.

South Africa's closest international ties for many years were with Britain and between 1891 and 1980 18 tours took place between the two countries. Bilateral contacts with other members of the I.R.B. did not occur before the inter-war period. New Zealand's first major tour took place in 1919. Australia opened relations from 1933, though the Springboks combined their Australian visits with tours to New Zealand until 1971. Finally, although France had unofficial and club contacts from 1906 onwards, the French Rugby Federation did not send a representative side to South Africa until 1952 and organized its first major tour, as we have seen, in 1958. After that contact was close. Since 1958, France has organized more tours to and from South Africa than any other member of the I.R.B. except Britain (see Table 2).

This is not without political significance, for the S.A. Rugby Board's close co-operation with the French Rugby Federation began at the same time as international resistance to South Africa's racial policies in sport. The first demonstrations occurred in 1960 during a New Zealand tour; South Africa's next tour with the All-Blacks, planned for 1967 was cancelled; huge demonstrations ruined the Springboks' tour to Britain in 1969-70, and to Australia in 1971. Twice during this period, the French team stood in at the last minute, for the All-Blacks in 1967 and again in 1975, in both cases saving the S.A. Rugby Board from embarrassment and insulating white opinion from international disapproval.

During the 1970s, South Africa's isolation was such that the Springboks were rarely able to tour abroad. The S.A. Rugby Board therefore opened relations with Latin American and North American sides, with whom several short tours were organized in both directions even though their standard of play was inferior.

The South African Springboks — who first adopted their colours for the tour to Britain in 1906 — dominated the small world of international rugby

Table 2
Chronology of Tours to and from South Africa by Member Countries of the
International Rugby Board

Date	Great Britain	Australia	New Zealand	France
1891	x			
1896	x			
1903	x			
1906-07	+			+ *
1910	x			
1912-13	+			+ *
1919			x	
1921		+ *	+	
1924	x			
1928			x	
1931-32	+			
1933		x		
1937		+	+	
1949			x	
1951-52	+			+ *
1953		x		
1955	x			
1956		+	+	
1958				x
1960-61	+	x	x ●	+ *
1962	x	x		
1964				x
1965		+	+	
1967			cancelled	x
1968	x			+ (*)
1969-70	+ ●	x	x	
1971		+ ●		
1972	x			
1974	x			+ ●
1975			cancelled	x
1976			x	
1979	+* (Barbarians)			cancelled x
1980	x			
1981	x (Ireland)		+ ●	

(x) Tours played in South Africa
(+) Tours played abroad by South Africa
(*) Non-official tours
(●) Tours during which demonstrations occurred

for half a century. From 1903, when they won their first victory over the British, until 1956, when they were humbled by New Zealand, they did not lose a test series, and it is this magnificent record which has given them their extraordinary reputation.

For a decade after their defeat in 1956, the Springboks went into relative decline; and because of the international boycott it has since been difficult to judge whether a revival has taken place. In 1980-81, the results of three highly controversial tours — with New Zealand, the British Lions and the French — indicated that the Springboks remain internationally competitive — and that South African rugby remains racist. In purely rugby terms, however, the recent quality of their play has still to be tested.

As early as 1913, observers were impressed by the size, strength and discipline of the Springbok pack. 'The successful part of their history,' writes Maurice Golesworthy, 'has been founded mainly on the tradition of great, heavy, albeit highly skilful forwards apotheosized by such as A.S. Knight, M.M. ('Boy') Louw, M.J. Mostert, P.J. Nel, Chris Koch and Hennie Muller, who have rucked and scrummaged their opponents almost literally into the ground, before bringing their own backs into the game as an attacking force.'[17]

From 1931, under Bennie Osler, but essentially after the Second World War under Danie Craven, South African rugby players adopted a new style of play that minimized the number of possible mistakes giving advantage to opponents. Their technique 'had its basis in a powerful pack of forwards as the main striking force, with the backs as "support troops" kicking accurately to touch until they had gained enough ground to handle with comparative impunity.'[18] Henri Garcia argues that Craven's methods opened 'a new era in rugby, of continuous play. The traditional movement from forwards-to-backs was carried on by the forwards who, brought back into play by the backs, became crucial attackers. Athletic . . . excellent ball players, the South African forwards were the prototypes of modern forwards.'[19]

Commentators have often tried to link the pre-eminence of South African forward play with the fact that they are mostly Afrikaners, whereas most of the backs have been English-speakers. The Irish international Andrew Mulligan, for example, argued that Afrikaners have such a talent for the game because of their farming tradition, which makes them reject city ways in favour of the satisfactions of an open air life which in its turn has given them a certain physique and mental outlook. Such an ethnically centred argument[20] is appropriately located in a chapter entitled 'Of Rugby and Anthropology':

> Demographically they are of Dutch origin or descended from emigrant French Huguenots. Towns have never attracted them: they make up the rural population of the South African Union. They are athletes with long bones and big thighs; almost invariably they form the core of the South African pack; Piet du Toit, Avril Malan and Johann Claasen represent the tradition of huge Springbok forwards.
> It is relatively rare to discover English players in the South African

scrum — except perhaps in the back row, where players like Stephan Frey, Basil Kenyon and Doug Hopwood can be found.

In the back line, the roles are reversed and names with a British ring to them are more frequent: Danie Craven, Geoff Harris, Paul Johnson, Keith Oxlee and John Gainsford . . . . French influences are also to be found, as the names of Francois Rouch and Michel Antelme go to prove. The name of a player like Van Vollenhoven is rather the exception proving the rule.

It is enough to read the composition of a Springbok fifteen to realize the truth of these remarks. In the Union of South Africa, most English-speaking citizens work in the towns and particularly in the tertiary sector.

In contrast, the Afrikander has a strong predilection for the open air life and the profession of farmer which, in addition to any genetic inheritance, has given him his height and strength. The difference is clearly visible at matches between the provinces. The teams from Natal and the Western Province play a far more lively form of rugby than those from the Eastern Transvaal or the Orange Free State.[21]

Given his approach, it is not surprising to find the author describing the huge Johann Claasen as a living symbol of the 'perfect Afrikander'.[22]

Rugby and Afrikaner Nationalism

So rugby *is* the national game in South Africa — if 'nation' is taken to mean the Afrikaner and more generally the white minority. The main features of Afrikaner society have been defined by a sociologist as

characterized by heightened in-group solidarity combined with an unfavourable attitude towards certain out-groups, especially the non-Whites. The Afrikaans-speaking White is apt to be more ethnocentric than his English-speaking counterpart. There is considerable homogeneity in the Afrikaner community and the gap between the least tolerant or ethnocentric members and its most tolerant or polycentric members is far less than in the English-speaking community. There are striking pressures to group conformity and those who deviate from the norms are likely to be treated very severely . . . . The strong sense of Afrikaner nationalism . . . is perhaps the most salient characteristic of this group. Religion appears to play a far greater role in the life of the Afrikaner than in the lives of the English . . . . It is not surprising, therefore, to find Afrikaner nationalism imbued with religious overtones.[23]

Why then did the Afrikaners, who until recently played very few of the sports introduced by the British to South Africa, adopt rugby so early and so enthusiastically that today they dominate the game? Several factors seem to have played a part.

We have already seen that until 1948 the Afrikaner population was, and felt itself to be, subjugated by the British; and that the British occupation of the Transvaal (1880) and the Anglo-Boer War which followed (1899-1902) gave birth to a political and cultural nationalism among Afrikaans-speakers which was profoundly anti-imperialist (in relation to the British) and 'anti-capitalist'. What it expressed was the antagonism between a rural society of farmers, suddenly deprived of power, a society whose wealth was derived from cattle and land ranged against an industrializing urban economy, capitalist in structure, which had been introduced and was dominated by the British.

The period during which Boer nationalism took shape corresponds almost exactly with the period during which rugby appeared and spread across the country.

Defeated and impoverished, after the Boer War (and again after the Great War) many Boers began moving to the towns where they joined the growing white working class. Here they fought to maintain their privileges against the English employers on the one hand and against the competition of black workers coming into the mining and industrial areas on the other. The standard of living of Afrikaners at this time was certainly very much higher than that of black employees; but Afrikaners were poorer than the majority of English-speakers, whose living standards were protected by the political and economic supremacy of British capital.[24]

Economic factors therefore also contributed, alongside nationalism, to inhibit Afrikaners from adopting an 'English' way of life, and those sports which were one of its ingredients. If many Afrikaners were able on their own farms to swim and shoot and perhaps to train for the annual athletics competition, only two major team sports were probably accessible to them: football and rugby. And of the two, rugby had the advantage that it can be played more easily on rough, unlevelled rural terrain.

But, beyond practicality or technique, or economic considerations, rugby also had a *symbolic* significance which predisposed Afrikaners not merely to play it but to *identify* with the game, in such measure that to some extent they have transformed it in their own image. To avoid misunderstanding, this remark should be explained a little more fully. All sorts of reasons may induce social groups or individuals to adopt one sporting activity rather than another. Some of these influences are symbolic in character. The choice of one sport rather than another implies certain social choices, for different sports have had different social attributes attached to them: they are not played the same way by the same people, they do not involve the same economic costs or the same length of apprenticeship, they do not take place in identical climatic or technical conditions, etc. If we think of polo on the one hand and soccer on the other, the existence of such social differences is immediately apparent.

For both individuals and social groups, sport is therefore a complex social phenomenon, and at a given time in any society we can try to describe the structure of sporting practice and the different values attached to various sports. Such a description is not simple; several layers of values have to be distinguished. An 'old' sport, for example, has a history, a tradition, a given code of practice which interacts with contemporary social mores and with technical factors (ease of access, cost, status, difficulty, etc.). We can also chart the sociological distribution of a sport, which will not be played with the same enthusiasm, or as generally, or in the same way, by different social classes and groups. An understanding of social distribution in turn widens our understanding of a sport's significance or status.

Thus, the tradition of rugby-playing among Afrikaners certainly helps to explain its very wide distribution (throughout schools, in both town and rural areas) as well as the importance Afrikaners attach to it. Rugby has a unique historical dimension for Afrikaners, for other sports are associated with other groups — football with the Africans, cricket with the English, etc. — while Afrikaners have excelled at rugby from its earliest appearance in the country.[25]

If we now go back to the late 19th Century, the symbolic significance of rugby's adoption by the Afrikaner community becomes clearer. The form of game introduced by the British had been derived from a ball game played originally in the Middle Ages ('soule') and banned from the 14th Century onwards both by Church and State in France and Britain. In the 18th Century a 'wild' form of the game survived in Picardy, Normandy and Brittany and flourished in England and Scotland, where vain attempts were made by governments to suppress it. In the 19th Century it was transformed from an essentially popular game to a sport for aristocrats — a morally improving form of exercise for gentleman pupils in the public schools. Thomas Arnold, headmaster of Rugby School from 1828 and one of the principal advocates of this conversion, encouraged rugby to improve his pupils' moral conduct. Victorian England became the nursery of modern sport.

Stamped as it was by the mark of a foreign and conquering elite, why then did rugby appeal to an Afrikaner community which had very little in common with the ideology of English gentlemen? The reason surely lies in the game's character, in the essential *ambivalence* it had acquired during its long history of social transformation. Rugby is a collective sport of combat, which values physical endurance, strength and rapidity, the warrior virtues of struggle and virility, fellowship and shared effort. All these belong to its popular origins. At the same time these qualities lent themselves peculiarly well to appropriation by a social elite with aristocratic ideals, who were able, in the 19th Century, to transform rugby (like boxing) into a school of moral discipline for future leaders.

This ambivalence explains why rugby lent itself so perfectly to the physical, emotional and ideological needs of the Afrikaner people. It is a sport ideally suited to 'ideological investment' and the Afrikaners, who considered themselves to be a civilizing elite, a pioneer people conquering barbarism, recognized an image of their own ideology in its symbols.

By this we certainly do *not* mean that rugby as such is to be identified with a certain ideology, for this would be absurd, but that certain of its historical and technical characteristics are susceptible to interpretation by people who, like the Afrikaners, have a specific vision of the world. Rugby cannot be called an ideology — it does not carry a political message — but it can be likened to a language which lends itself better than many other sports to certain kinds of ideological interpretation. The heady and far from value-free discourse which surrounds rugby is the best evidence of this. In the absence of more scientific material, we shall use it to illustrate the often disquieting correspondence between the values this discourse promotes and the characteristics of Afrikaner nationalism.

Afrikaner nationalism was born of a conviction that Afrikaner culture and language were threatened, from without by British imperialism and from within by African barbarism. It is rooted in the assumption that Afrikaners were elected by God to defend civilization in Africa.[26] Serge Thion describes this vision. 'In their own minds,' he says, 'Afrikaners are good, united, industrious, faithful to God and to their word, simple and warm-hearted; they dispose of a quite unique tool — *die Taal*, the language, Afrikaans . . . . All the virtues of the people are present in its language, which perfectly embodies both its limitations and its character.'[27]

The concept of 'Afrikanerdom' encapsulates these values: it denotes 'the body of people who are conscious of being Afrikaners, the traditional values contained in the Afrikaans language and society, and the political and historical movement which aims to recover independence and sovereignty'.[28] Pioneers, an 'indigenous advance guard of Christian civilization on the Black Continent,'[29] conscious of their divine mission, Afrikaners perceived the world in the strict Calvinist terms of their Church, with its dogma of predestination. The 'master people' (*herrenvolk*), created by God, are naturally separate from the subject peoples, which include all the black races. At no time were 'black pagans and white christians to be treated on terms of equality'.[30] White and Black were to remain in their allotted states of master and servant.

A few historical examples will help to show how far the process was taken. When members of the *Broederbond* (see Chapter 1) first put forward the theory of apartheid, they claimed to find philosophical justification in the Bible:

> Rejecting liberal individualism, these theoreticians considered the nation a divine creation with a 'vocation' of its own, as the supreme form of the human community, and declared themselves in favour of a type of State which was corporative and authoritarian . . . . It did not seem to them that they were committing an injustice in relation to the Africans by forcing the latter to develop within their tribal society, under their 'responsible guardianship'.[31]

The essentials of the Nationalist programme were already to be found in the *Broederbond's* seven-point ideal, as I.M. Lombard expressed it in a series of articles he wrote for the *Transvaler* in 1944-45:

1) The removal of everything in conflict with South Africa's full international independence;

2) Ending the inferiority of the Afrikaans-speaking and of their language in the organization of the State;
3) Separation of all non-White races in South Africa, leaving them free to independent development under the guardianship of the State; . . .
5) The rehabilitation of the farming community; . . .
6) The Afrikanerization of public life and education in a Christian National spirit.[32]

The concept of 'Christian Nationalism' had already been defined in a Draft Constitution drawn up in 1941 by members of the *Broederbond*, the *Ossewa Brandwag* and other nationalist groups on the fringes of the Nationalist Party:

> The Republic is grounded on a Christian National foundation and therefore acknowledges, as the standard of the government of the State, in the first place the principles of justice of the Holy Scriptures; secondly, the clearest direction of the development of the national history; and thirdly, the necessary reformation of the modern government of states . . . .
>
> Every coloured group of races, Coloured, natives, Asiatics, Indians etc. will be segregated, not only as regards the place of dwelling or the neighbourhoods dwelt in by them, but also with regard to the spheres of work. The members of such groups can, however, be allowed to enter White territories under proper lawful control for the increase of working power and also for the necessary increase of their own incomes.
>
> To each of these segregated race groups of coloured subjects of the Republic, self-government will be granted within their own territory under the central management of the general government of the country, in accordance with the fitness of the group for the carrying out of such self-government for which they will have to be systematically trained.[33]

Apartheid is not the ad hoc extension of an armchair philosophy: it expresses a precise vision of the world and is a detailed project of social engineering. Paternalistic but strict control was to be exercised over the 'Kaffirs' and 'Bantu' as defined by *baasskap*, and over the *'uitlanders'*, within a *republic of freemen* whose decisions would be sovereign, and whose security would be guaranteed through a system of militia (*kommandos*). Social relations would be governed by the principles of the Bible. 'The idea of the Republic', writes Serge Thion, 'takes its ideal from the most elementary, simplest Helvetic forms of democracy. Her history contributed to making this the "natural" political structure adopted by the *volk*. Crushed by the English, it symbolized revenge over the English and over Imperialism (or the idea of Imperialism entertained by the Boers' descendents).'[34] In short, the Afrikaner ideal was a form of republican democracy in which the elite, the chosen people alone, would be competent to exercise political rights.

We seem very far away from rugby: yet perhaps not, for the ideology of the Afrikaner people, which traverses the events and themes of their history and informs their social and moral universe, is echoed in the discourse which surrounds the game. Rugby, say the experts, is a sport for pioneers, played, as Lucien Mias puts it, by young males in a state of 'hormonal pugnacity'.[35] Unlike football — 'a simple quasi-geometrical game [which] requires the strict application of an unchanging code' — rugby is 'subject to interpretative rules'.[36] It is 'an intelligent game' (Francoise Sagan), 'in essence a university sport',[37] wherein 'intention counts for as much as action'.[38] Rugby claims to be a more varied, fertile sport than football, a sport whose performance involves interpretative traditions that are both 'technical and gestural . . . historical and oral'.[39] Rugby tolerates, indeed encourages, creative players whose innovations rejuvenate the game and prolong the revolutionary gesture of W.W. Ellis when he seized the ball with his hands: 'Rugby has evolved by a process of leaps and bounds at the instigation of "discoverers" who . . . have opened new approaches. In contrast to other sports with fixed rules, this is one of rugby's attractions.'[40]

For Anglo-Saxons in search of a game to reanimate 'the heroic colonial adventure',[41] rugby was obviously a suitable candidate: it was also eminently qualified to attract the valiant Boer farmers of the Great Trek.

> As in other new countries [rugby met] an exceptionally favourable reception among the rough pioneers in Southern Africa, as much among the Boers on the highlands of the Transvaal and Orange Free State as among the new British colonies on the coast, in the Cape, at Port Elizabeth, or Durban. Having rapidly become the 'sport elect', rugby was just about the only thing capable of uniting the two white communities . . . . Men of character, courageous (white!) men, South Africans were all conquered on the spot by a sport of bravery and character. Even today, in spite of the vicissitudes it experiences internationally, rugby remains the 'sport elect', the sport which every young [white!] South African must play to become an accomplished adult.[42]

So in the eyes of the experts, rugby is for pioneers, for the elite; unlike football, which is a 'universal sport', it is 'the game of a social group, the expression of a certain form of civilization', able to 'raise itself to the height of becoming the shared language of an elite'.[43] Moreover, the British had voluntarily restricted its extension, with a mind to creating a 'club reserved for a few chosen members'.[44] Is it surprising that in South Africa rugby has developed into a sport which is intrinsically 'white', reserved for the white minority and the 'civilization' to which it lays exclusive claim?

> No-one should regret the fact that the pleasures of rugby are reserved for an elite. Oh yes! An elite, don't think I am afraid to say it! No

amount of beautiful and sly speeches addressed in our direction about the universality of football will subtract an iota from rugby's royal crown. If rugby is not a universal game then, by Heaven, it is because rugby players did not choose to make it so! Gentlemen only. Rugby, a sport for ruffians, would be a dangerous game if ruffians were allowed to play it. In the hands of mad Latin Americans or the greedy sportsmen of Democratic Republics it would become unplayable.[45]

Why? Because rugby, being a combat sport, involving physical contact, requires self-control if it is not to collapse into brutality.[46] In its requirement that players stay this side of violence and exercise a fine restraint over their aggression, rugby stands on the border-line between barbarism and civilization. The ethic is almost chivalric. 'One does not play rugby, one *is* rugby, absolutely.'[47] It is a game which remains itself only by virtue of its moral rigour. The hardness, toughness, virility, which make it a sport for men who are not afraid to fight, and licenses bruising physical contact, 'requires something impalpable to sublimate and transform pain into a feat of arms'.[48]

The game's warlike aspects do not cease there, for rugby also resembles a struggle for conquest. Garcia calls it 'the only team sport in which physical possession of the ball remains essential. And before anything else, as in ancient games, the ball has to be conquered . . . all its structures turn upon possession.'[49]

Before the ball can go forward, the team must mass its strength behind it. It is therefore entirely logical that the key man, the torch-bearer, should be the one in possession of the ball, and that a pass can only be made to someone placed behind him. For the same reason, after a kick ahead, only those who are behind the kicker can immediately follow up and participate in play, the others must wait until they have been overtaken . . . .

Rugby, a combat sport, has conserved from its old customs the right to seize an adversary and throw him down. Indeed, this act is essential and gives to the game its rigour, its difficulty, its character and virtues. Here again the laws of rugby become clear and logical as soon as one realizes that for all his adversaries it is the man carrying the ball — conscious and alert to the responsibilities he bears — who must be brought down, but that anyone who is not carrying the ball is taboo.

[As a result, the frontier] between virility and brutality is often reduced to intention. This is why rugby is a difficult game for it requires respect for the opponent and a sense of humour. These qualities are sufficiently rare to make those who control the destiny of rugby hesitate before universalising it.[50]

It was not therefore arbitrarily decreed that rugby should be confined to the elite: the decision was assumed by the young nobility of the British establishment who in accordance with their definition of proper behaviour and manners, made rugby a means by which a young man could prove his title to the aristocracy of gentlemen.

'Its roughness automatically engenders moral rigour,' writes Henri Garcia again, 'in that, according to the time-honoured phrase — and unlike football, "a sport of gentlemen played by ruffians" — it seeks to be "a sport for ruffians played by gentlemen". Rugby has elected to conserve the difficulties of a team combat sport in order to remain more than simple physical exercise, in order to remain truly a school in which the good man may seek to prove his character and discover the meaning of communal life.'[51]

South African rugby has emphasized the combative aspects of the game to the point of caricature and their teams have frequently been accused of brutality by foreign opponents; but if they have seemed to deprive the game completely of humour and turned touring into a form of national campaigning, they have also elevated it by their invariable moral and collective discipline. 'Their approach was entirely realist: a series of passes down the three-quarter line which goes backwards is not an attack, a prop who drives forward one metre is an attacker, a tackle made on the other side of the advantage line constitutes an offensive. These new ideas were to deeply influence modern rugby.'[52] It is now possible to place this distinctive style within the historical context of the development of the game in South Africa.

Its chivalric virtues are honesty, humour, fair play and pursuit of excellence: for its admirers, rugby contains 'all the joy of a game wherein the unfinished individual completes himself through others':[53]

> No other discipline requires its followers at one and the same time to be athletes, because it is an athletic skill, to have character and courage, because it is a rough struggle, to have the generosity needed for participation in a collective activity and finally to remain serene during what remains a game. This is obviously a lot to ask of a single individual. This is no doubt why, throughout the world, schools and universities have been its natural breeding grounds and why wherever it has gone graduates have been its first disciples.[54]

It is essentially a team game, a group sport. Whereas football encourages individualism and showmanship, rugby insists on 'altruism and modesty':

> Everything contributes to making play as communal as possible. The pass backwards, for example, makes teamwork essential to all advance, to the precious conquest of ground. None of which would exist if the ball could be passed forward. The ball is oval to make holding and passing it more difficult. Individual exploits are rare and unprofitable because progress is difficult. As a result collective play is encouraged. At kick-offs and drop-outs, the ball is not handed to either side. The kicker must kick the ball to the opposite team and send it at least 10 yards. Thus the ball is put in competition and won by the best team. It is for the same reason that when the ball goes off or is stopped by a

71

technical fault which does not contravene the spirit of fair play, it is replaced in play by a line-out or a scrum which are both group confrontations to win the ball.[55]

A. Blondin aptly describes this team sport as a 'democracy peopled by nobles'.[56] Created after the elitist ideals of the British establishment, it corresponded perfectly to the ideals of the republic of free men dear to Afrikaner nationalists. *Personal self-denial* in the service of the group, *collective discipline* in the prosecution of a general cause, all explicit components of Afrikanerdom, were among the implicit virtues of rugby — a game which the Springboks have conquered above all by their ferocious collective discipline. The international rugby code even forbids all practice of the game for money or profit, a principle which finds echo in the traditional disdain and fear felt by Boer culture for all that was capitalist. It is surely no coincidence that in South Africa (unlike Australia) Rugby League has never taken hold.[57]

It is the same moral virtues which make rugby an eminently educational sport — according to that famous tradition stretching unbroken from the 19th Century British public schools to the modern Afrikaner education system which attaches at least as much importance to rugby instruction as Thomas Arnold. Once again, it is prized as a team sport which cultivates the manly virtues of discipline in collective action, of disinterested devotion to the interests of the group, of pluck and daring and self-control.

In my high school in Johannesburg where I studied in the 1960s football wasn't permitted as one of the official sporting activities, although the best local football team had its pitch there. We had to play a minimum of two hours of rugby or hockey twice a week in winter, and of cricket or tennis in summer, and in addition, twice a week, we had classes of gym or swimming. Football wasn't allowed because the school authorities wanted to keep up the school's sports reputation, as the best rugby school.

There were very many competitions in Afrikaans schools, particularly in cross-country and rugby. They were very well organized too, and the pupils took part in them regularly. It was these Afrikaans leagues rather than the English teams which were chosen to play in the Craven League, after provincial play-offs between the high schools. I remember that when I was chosen to play for the first team, the attitude of some of my teachers changed — that of my maths master for example. They became much more interested in my progress.

In Afrikaans schools sport, like everything else, was used to inculcate a spirit of discipline and authoritarianism that you didn't find to the same extent in English schools.[58]

A sport for frontiersmen, a combat and conquest sport, a sport reserved for the physical and intellectual elite, above all a *moral* sport; the king of sports 'because nowhere else is to be found such fertile ground for the fine human qualities which make Man reveal himself',[59] the embodiment of civilization and all that is noble, encouraging the elite to cultivate devotion to the group but refining at the same time its sense of special status; democratic but not common, an egalitarian community for aristocrats .... What sport could represent more perfectly to white South Africans, and above all to Afrikaners, their proper image of themselves? In symbolic terms, rugby bears the print of Afrikaner culture — its convictions, aspirations and dreams: attached to their Voortrekker past, proud of their civilizing mission in a savage land, perceiving themselves as elected and created by God to reign on earth, conscious of their vocation as warriors — not soldiers but freemen under arms — inspired by faith and an uncompromising moral ethic to defend the cause of their people and their God, the Afrikaner people did more than adopt rugby. They conquered the game.

According to Denis Lalanne, 'English-speaking people reproach the Nationalists for having changed many things in their lives and above all their dear old rugby. The British love rugby. For the Nationalists it is a wild passion.'[60] His remarks are reflected in the following remarks of John Horak (1960s) and Sadie Berman (1930s):

> Rugby is the Afrikaners' game: they got their kick nationally, as a people, out of playing it. And they were hard, they pushed it: when you were playing an Afrikaans school, those guys played in a kind of way we English schools didn't. They used to play it hard and they used to play to win, they were dour about it and they were always rough. We never used to play to kill, just to win ....
>
> The big match of the year was always Wits versus the Tucs — Tucs being the Afrikaans university at Pretoria. They always used to beat us. You used to have this hysteria build up. We used to meet at the Amphitheatre and have sing-songs, the cheerleaders used to go on about the 'Hairy Backs', that is the Afrikaners — they had hair in their teeth, growing out of their ears, disgusting animal type of people. We used to be the *Rooineks*, red necks — we were white-skinned and they were dark and swarthy. The night before you'd get pissed and go about looking for some Hairy backs to beat up; and you'd get beaten up after the game, they'd find you in their cars. And this happened every year.[61]
>
> When Witwatersrand played Pretoria, it wasn't just rugby they were playing, there was an enmity and a bitterness and a hatred of each other. The overtones were quite clear. The major goal was to beat the other university *not* only in the game. I think the competition between two such universities was naturally bitter ... because it was the child of the hatred of the Afrikaans for the English-speaking. It certainly didn't dissipate the tension.[62]

The Nationalists have not diluted the qualities of rugby as a result of their wholesale conversion to the game: on the contrary, they have concentrated and reinterpreted the game, transformed it into an image of the South African soul — as John Morgan's description of Northern Transvaal's defeat by the British Lions in 1969 tellingly reveals:

> I had travelled to the match with a crowd of farmers from a small town called Brits, few of them able to speak English, all convinced they were kind to their workers . . . all believing their workers loved them . . . . And until ten minutes from the end of the match this astonishingly kindly false view of themselves endured. At which point the British team took the lead.
>
> In thirty years of watching rugby I have never known any experience comparable to the chilling transformation of spirit among that multitude. The silence was that of a people witnessing a tragedy rather than the normal disappointment of a home crowd.
>
> When the game was lost and over, the crowd did not cheer or groan. Without a word or a sound of any kind, they shuffled out into the dusk and away back to the farm lands and their enchanted dreams and unspoken fears.[63]

Many indices signal the Nationalists' extraordinary identification with rugby, but it is worth noting the particular correspondence between the evolution of South Africa's international relations in rugby and official sports policy. It is not for nothing that supporters and opponents of the boycott of South African sport have always paid particular attention to rugby tours, for 'rugby crises' have probably influenced South Africans and South African policy even more than exclusion from the Olympics. In 1965 Verwoerd's 'No' to an All-Black team including Maoris marked the high tide of pure sports apartheid. In 1967, Nationalist circles divided over the same issue and three years later rugby was directly implicated in the formation of Hertzog's 'Herstigte' National Party. The dramatic tour of Britain in 1969-70, which coincided with this crisis, led Vorster in 1971 to permit the Maoris to enter South Africa along with black French winger Bougarel. In 1975, the first 'multi-racial' rugby match with a foreign side was considered a test for the Government's 'multi-national' policy. In 1980, the entry of a Coloured team to the Craven Schools Rugby Championship caused another crisis in the Nationalist establishment.

Nationalist political investment in rugby is also clearly visible in the number of famous *Broeders* who adorn its history — Avril Malan, Johann Claassen, Dawie de Villiers, Hannes Marais (all Springbok captains), Dutch Lower, Piet du Toit, Mannetjies Roux, Wilhelm Delport (Springboks), Fritz C. Eloff (President of the Northern Transvaal Rugby Union), Jannie le Roux (President, Transvaal Rugby Union), Sid F. Kingsley (ex-President Northern Transvaal Rugby Union), Kobus Louw etc. And also in attempts by the *Broederbond* and by Afrikaners to wrest control of the game from more liberal non-*Broeders* like Morne du Plessis or Danie Craven, who have had to defend their positions from such attack, for example in 1975.[64] The same preoccupation also finds expression in Parliament, where M.P.s declared their concern in 1979 because young people were deserting rugby for television and other sports, as if rugby was a test of the nation's moral condition.[65] Perhaps Serge Saulnier was not merely indulging in rugby hyperbole when he lectured the French team before the first test in 1958 and told them that rugby in South Africa was 'an affair of state'.[66]

Rugby League

Virtually no rugby league is played in South Africa. In the past it seems only rarely to have been played in the Cape and confined to the Transvaal. Attempts were made in the early 1950s to promote professional rugby. A Mr Ludwig Japhet met the Secretary of the British Rugby League, Mr Fallowfield, and it was agreed that the French and British teams in the 1957 World Championships should play three matches in South Africa on their way back. The games were played at Benoni, Durban and East London and the British won all three by such wide margins that, as Gaulton records, 'the South Africans, who like a serious and hard-fought game, were not interested'.[67]

Another attempt was made in 1961 with the creation of two separate and rival organizations, the Rugby League of South Africa and the National Rugby League. A British team (which included several 'guest' South Africans) toured the country in 1962, winning all six of its matches. It was followed in 1963 by a mixed New Zealand/Australian team led by ex-international Dawie Ackermann, which was equally victorious. Since then, the game has not prospered.

A number of very good South African players have nonetheless signed for rugby league teams abroad. Among them, the most famous are Van Vollenhoven (St. Helens, 1957), Fred Griffiths (Australia, 1963) and Trevor Lake (Australia); others include Anthony Shene, Jan Prinsloo, Charlie Nimb, Oupa Coetzer, Colin Greenwood, Wilf Rosenberg etc.

References

1. Richard Dowden, *Irish Times*, 21 February 1980, Many of the references in this chapter are to French sources, as this book was originally written in French: the English-speaking reader may judge from his own experience whether Gallic and Anglo-Saxon visions of the game correspond.
2. In H. Garcia, 1973, p. 395.
3. It must be remembered that the rules of rugby and association football were not formally distinguished before about 1863, and differences of opinion lasted until 1871 when the English Rugby Union was founded.
4. In Ritchie, 1918, p. 692. The South African College soon began to organize matches against the Bishop's College (Cape Town) and

Victoria College, Stellenbosch, which was to become the Mecca of
South African rugby.

5. R.K. Stent in Rosenthal, 1973, p. 489, mentions that another club,
    Swellendam (South Western Cape), claims to be the oldest, dating back
    to 1865; since fire has destroyed the club's archives, however, the proofs
    supporting this claim no longer exist.

6. A.F. Hattersley, 1938, pp. 95-96. For a description of the game, see
    pp. 98-9 of the present volume.

7. *The Natal Witness*, 28 June 1879, in A.F. Hattersley, 1940, pp. 200-1.
    From this description it appears that at this time only the conversion
    counted for points, a touch-down serving merely to give a player the
    opportunity to 'try' to convert.

8. See above pp. 24-5.

9. B. Willan, *An African in Kimberley*.

10. *Work in Progress*, April 1981, p. 2.

11. E. Jokl in Hellmann, 1949.

12. Mr P.B. Singh, interview, London, 22 April 1980.

13. See Chapters 5 and 7 below. Bloemfontein at the same time had neither
    a rugby club nor a rugby pitch for Blacks; Pretoria had one pitch for
    Coloureds (population 4,500) and one for Africans (population
    100,000).

14. A full description of the development of non-racial rugby is given in
    Chapter 11.

15. Transvaal — 2,715; Northern Transvaal — 3,270: South Eastern Trans-
    vaal — 1,665; Western Transvaal — 1,335; Eastern Transvaal — 885.

16. In D. Woods, 1977, p. 130.

17. M. Golesworthy, 1976, p. 125.

18. M. Golesworthy, 1976, p. 126.

19. H. Garcia, 1976, p. 52.

20. A. Mulligan, 1965, p. 33. 'One can clearly discern,' Mulligan writes
    (p. 28), 'the individual characteristics of different races on the rugby field
    .... The French are generally caucasoid, but most of their players
    come from the Midi, and are mainly of Alpine or Mediterranean descent.
    They are big men . . . .' [Trans. from French].

21. A. Mulligan, 1965, pp. 33-4 [translated from the French]. Similar
    remarks may be found in S.G. Millin, 1936, pp. 165-6, or in R.F. Avery
    and T.J. Haarhoff, 1930, p. 28.

22. A. Mulligan, 1965, p. 167.

23. H. Lever, 1978, pp. 18-9.

24. Even today, Afrikaners outnumber English-speakers in labour-intensive
    sectors of the economy (agriculture, mining, transport, etc.), and domi-
    nate the police and army. On the whole, their standard of living remains
    lower than that of the English-speaking white population.

25. The recent tendency of Afrikaners to widen their sporting interests
    may be interpreted as evidence that the elite, whose standard of living
    has risen to match that of the English-speaking elite, now considers
    itself fully competitive with them, fully part of the South African
    ruling class.

26. 'In obedience to God Almighty and His Holy Word, the Afrikaans
    people acknowledge their national destiny, as embodied in their

Voortrekker past, for the Christian development of South Africa . . . .'
Article 1 of the Draft Constitution prepared by Nationalists from
various organizations.

27. S. Thion, 1969, p. 172.
28. S. Thion, 1969, p. 154.
29. R. Lefort, 1977.
30. R. Lefort, 1977, p. 19.
31. A. Goguel and P. Buis, 1978, p. 27.
32. In B. Bunting, 1965, pp. 49-50.
33. The quotation is from the Draft Constitution, cited in B. Bunting, 1965, p. 96. Though subsequently disowned officially by the Nationalist Party, there is no doubt that the principles announced in this document expressed the sentiments of a large section of the Nationalist leadership.
34. S. Thion, 1969, p. 182.
35. L. Mias, Preface to H. Garcia, 1978, p. 3.
36. G. Meyer, *L'Equipe*, 26 March 1979.
37. H. Garcia, 1976, p. 32.
38. G. Meyer, *L'Equipe*, 26 March 1979.
39. L. Mias, Preface to H. Garcia, 1978, p. 3.
40. Ibid.
41. H. Garcia, 1976, p. 31.
42. H. Garcia, 1976, p. 50. Our approach and H. Garcia's should be distinguished. The above description takes beliefs at their face value (i.e. assumes that the settlers really were courageous pioneers, etc.) whereas we have tried to analyse an ideology. The distinction is important because rugby commentators still play with the idea of 'national character', with the racist penumbra such an approach involves, whereas our intention is to describe the links and parallels between the ideology of rugby discourse (including the idea of 'national character') and Afrikaner ideology.
43. A. Blondin, Preface to H. Garcia, 1973, p. 7.
44. H. Garcia, 1976, p. 31. The 'club' is of course the International Rugby Football Board, now the International Rugby Board, founded in 1890. Membership is confined to the four Home Countries, England, Wales, Scotland, Ireland; to three ex-colonies, South Africa, New Zealand and Australia; and France.
45. It is rare to find opposing views, but see Mulligan, 1965, p. 65. Elitism has marked rugby from the beginning. More than any other sport it is associated with the ideals of the gentleman amateur, E. Weber (in *Aimez-Vous les Stades?*, 1980) shows how the *Union des Sociétés des Françaises de Sports Athletiques* took over this idea and excluded 'mechanics, workers and craftsmen, teachers and monitors of physical education from their number, and refused for some time to countenance the discipline of football, because of its lower-class standing.' According to Harri Roberts (*Le Monde de Dimanche*, 28 December 1980), Wales is the rare exception to social segregation, for 'coal miners are used to playing alongside barristers, and steelworkers with university lecturers', though the officials, he observes, are as conservative as those to be found elsewhere, not least in South Africa.
46. Football in contrast creates formal geometrical patterns but allows

freer reign to the emotions. G. Meyer cites the theory of G. Hanot (who
created the European Champions Cup) who compares scoring a goal to
coitus, to rape, thereby explaining the embracing which generally
follows and which rugby players avoid, because rugby is by nature far
more direct, requiring the rationalization of performance.

47. H. Garcia, 1973, p. 13.
48. L. Mias, Preface to H. Garcia, 1978, p. 5.
49. H. Garcia, 1973, p. 15.
50. H. Garcia, ibid., p. 13.
51. H. Garcia, ibid., p. 14.
52. H. Garcia, ibid., p. 341
53. H. Garcia, in the introduction to his book *Le Grand Combat du XV de France* (1962).
54. A. Blondin, Preface to H. Garcia, 1973, p. 90.
55. H. Garcia, 1973, pp. 16-17.
56. A. Blondin, in Preface to Garcia, 1973, p. 10.
57. See the end of this chapter.
58. Interview with a South African, London, October, 1979.
59. H. Garcia, 1973, p. 14.
60. D. Lalanne.
61. John Horak, interview, London, 9 February 1980.
62. Mrs Sadie Berman, interview, London, 15 February 1980.
63. John Morgan, *Sunday Times*, 16 November 1969, in P. Hain, 1971, p. 44.
64. See Wilkins and Strydom, 1979, p. 245.
65. See the speech of Mr Cuyler to Parliament in the South African *Hansard*, 21 May 1979, columns 6974-5.
66. H. Garcia, 1973, p. 439.
67. Gaulton, 1968, p. 115.

3. Cricket: Gentle Game for Gentlemen Only

Every good cricketer should have one golden rule: keep your promise, keep your tongue and keep your wicket up.[1]

Until the 1950s both Afrikaners and the English themselves considered cricket an English game, and many still do. The fact that black cricket is heavily concentrated in areas of strong British influence — the Cape, Eastern Cape and Natal — seems to confirm this view. Nevertheless, the history of the game within South Africa during the 19th Century shows that during the second half of the century, Boers and Blacks also played cricket and the social values attached to the game were far from monopolized by the English.

As early as 1854, for example, ten years after the first clubs were formed, a match took place in the Cape between 'the Hottentots and the Boers Afrikanders (sic)' — which the 'Hottentots' apparently won.[2] John Sheddon Dobie, a Scot who emigrated to Natal in 1862, recorded camping near to a farm on the edge of a small town during a journey he made to Queenstown to buy sheep. 'After dinner,' he noted in his journal, 'the farmer paid us a visit, a good-looking fellow but decidedly, like all I have seen, having a deuced seedy appearance, boots all worn out on the sole! Had been amusing himself by playing cricket with Kaffirs.'[3] Afrikaners went on playing the game until the Boer War at the turn of the century and black cricket has steadily expanded since the 1880s.

How true, then, is the truism of the 'Englishness' of cricket? Before we look at the game's social values and at what cricket may symbolize for South Africans, let us begin by mapping out its history, the historical tradition of which cricketers are so conscious and proud.

History of the Game

The first certain reference to cricket dates from 1478, in Northeast France, near St. Omer in Flanders, then ruled by the House of Burgundy. Usually derived from the Anglo-Saxon 'cricce' (a curved stick), 'cricket' may also be French, from 'criquet' which denotes the wicket rather than the bat.[4] At all events, the game is ancient, and was played from an early date throughout

Britain and Europe. The first descriptions of play date from the beginning of the 17th Century. At this time it was already on the decline; in France, for example, it was confined to rural areas, since the nobility, assembled at court, played only the royal game of tennis and disdained all popular pastimes.[5] In Britain, by contrast, cricket had penetrated throughout society, including urban life.

In the 18th Century the game can be traced from Flanders to North America. It was played in Aleppo (Syria) in 1676, had reached the American colonies before 1709, India by 1721, Canada by 1785, to reach South Africa following the British occupation in 1795. In 1766 it was played in Austria and Holland, in 1792 in Italy and in 1796 in Germany. In 1811 Murat, King of Naples, created a cricket club with his French and Neopolitan officers, and an ancient version of the game was apparently introduced to St. Lucia in the West Indies while the island was still under French control. The game played in Europe at this period was indigenous and there is no reason to believe that it derived from the British game or was imported from the United Kingdom.[6]

In Britain itself, cricket had become a major sport. Some of the most important clubs date from the 1760s, including the famous Marylebone Cricket Club (M.C.C.) — whose Lords ground is so aptly named. Slowly, over a long period (for the rules of the game were not really established until the end of the 19th Century), the M.C.C. arrogated to itself legislative authority and responsibility for the organization and administration of the game. At the same time, it sought to raise the game's social standing by confining M.C.C. membership to the nobility and gentlemen.

Nevertheless, of the three great sports of the period — cricket, horse-racing and boxing — cricket, the only team game, was also the only one to have attracted a truly popular following. The popularity of the game was unrivalled until the appearance of football at the end of the 19th Century.

By then, the revolution in the English education system had transformed cricket from a popular field game to one which was also urban, upper class and modern. It was this newly regulated game which was played throughout Britain and by all classes. This explains why British colonial immigrants introduced it so readily into the colonies with their other social habits and why it took such deep roots everywhere from the West Indies to Australia. It was played virtually wherever there was a British presence. The creation of the English Cricket Board of Control, the first South African tour to Britain, the spread of cricket to the West Indies, cricket's heyday in Philadelphia, the origin of the first great competitions and the founding of national federations in India, Australia, New Zealand and South Africa all date from one short dazzling period — 1890-1914. The Age of Empire is also the golden age of cricket.

Cricket in South Africa

Cricket was brought to South Africa by British troops, between 1795 and

1802, when Britain occupied the Cape. The earliest known match took place in 1808 on Green Point Common, between the officers of the Artillery Mess and the Colony — for a prize of 1,000 dollars. A second match was held in 1810; then no more is heard of the game for 30 years, until the 1840s and 1850s by which time quite a number of British settlers had arrived. Their interest in the game was part of an attempt to re-create the English society they had left. Unhindered by competition, cricket followed the spread of colonial occupation across the Cape and inland.

The game appeared in Maritzburg in 1843, the year after Natal had been annexed by Britain,[7] and during the next 30 years it was widely and enthusiastically adopted across the whole country. The first club was formed in Port Elizabeth in 1843, the second in Wynberg (Cape) in 1844, the third at Maritzburg in 1851; Bloemfontein (O.F.S.) followed in 1855, the first Transvaal club opened in 1863, the Western Province Cricket Club in 1864, Queenstown club in 1865, and so on. Johannesburg Cricket Club was founded in 1887, one year after gold had been discovered.[8]

The first regular competition was set up in the Cape in 1862 when a team from the 'Mother Country' took on a team of 'Colonial Born' in an annual contest which attests to cricket's socializing and integrative vocation in these early years. By 1875 there were so many teams that the town of Port Elizabeth presented a trophy — the Championship Bat — for a competition held at the Cape of Good Hope. Precursor of the Currie Cup, this competition further focused public interest on the game and it was around this time that the first cricket annuals appeared.[9] By the end of the 1880s, school cricket was also organized, the Coloured population was becoming actively involved in the game, the first international links abroad had been formed, and white and Coloured national cricket federations had been established.

In 1888 the first British tour of South Africa took place. The English team played and won two tests against a representative South African side at the Wanderers Club in Johannesburg. The Currie Cup was born as a result. The following year the all-white South African Cricket Association (SACA) was formed, shortly before the Coloured cricketers, who were already organizing their own competitions, formed a federation of their own.

The British returned in 1891-92, 1895-96, 1898-99 and 1905-06 (first M.C.C. tour), while South Africa toured England in 1894, 1901, 1904 and 1907. Australia toured South Africa for the first time in 1902-03, and hosted South Africa in 1910-11. In 1909 South Africa became a founder member of the Imperial Cricket Council, alongside Australia and the M.C.C.[10]

School cricket — essential to the standard of adult play — developed during the same period. Its quality may be divined from these recollections of Henry Juta, old boy of the South African College (Cape), writing in 1909:

> Football and cricket were played in the Municipal paddock, and our principal, if not only, opponents were the boys of the Diocesan College. Season after season we were beaten, and no wonder. There was no ground to practise on, and no one connected with the College staff

took any interest in our sports. Still we pegged on, taking licking after licking, until we succeeded in getting the right to play in what is now known as the Rosmead paddock.

For years [the paddock] had been kept sacred for the grazing of His Excellency the Governor's cows . . . . It was in fear and trembling — for Sir Henry [Barkly] had not exactly a sympathetic manner towards boys — that we ventured to urge, with much circumlocution, no doubt, that the physical development of the S.A.C. boys was of somewhat greater importance than the small saving in the grazing of His Excellency's cows . . . . The Governor, it is true, would not give up his grazing rights, but . . . he was pleased to allow us to share the paddock . . . . And so for years the boys and the cows ran together, until Sir Hercules Robinson became Governor. He willingly gave up all his rights, and the paddock was given up to the College.

Old Boys will remember how cricket scores were kept. A score book or a loose leaf was handed to some unfortunate follower. After a great deal of persuasion he was induced to score, then a pencil was commandeered and for a few minutes the unfortunate scorer kept his promise. Thereafter he would induce someone else to take it on, and so it went on the whole day . . . . Matches started at ten in the morning and continued until each side had completed two innings each . . . . [They] were played on grass, veld, or any fairly level spot that could be found on the Green Point Common, Bishop's Camp Ground, Sea Point etc. Matting was out of the question in those days.

Before a match it was quite the thing for the Captain of the side to ask each member of the eleven for a shilling to buy the ball, which had to serve the team to dismiss twenty men. There were usually two bats belonging to the College, which were used by most of the team.[11]

The first grass pitch was laid in 1926 but matting wickets predominated until after the Second World War, although by the inter-war period almost every small town and mine had its football and cricket club, playing in leagues and competitions. When it was decided to compulsorily purchase the Johannesburg Wanderers Club for South African Railways in 1948,[12] this was met by an outcry from the white population. Until the club was rebuilt, tests had to be played in that sanctuary of Transvaal rugby, Ellis Park.

Until the 1950s, cricket was not widely played by Afrikaners whose nationalist revival made them unreceptive to a game with such imperial overtones. As in other sports, attempts to use cricket to reconcile the white communities were rare and generally unsuccessful. However, during the 1960s, a number of factors — South Africa's international cricketing successes, higher living standards and the new dominance of Afrikanerdom — combined to create a cricketing boom in which Afrikaners joined. It touched black cricket as well. This period saw a general movement among black cricketers in favour of unification and non-racialism, and the emergence of several outstanding individual talents, of whom the best known is Basil d'Oliveira, the Coloured player whose selection to play for England against South Africa in the 1960s sparked a Government crisis and eventually led to South Africa's exclusion from the international cricket circuit after 1970.

Character of the Game

Cricket has a unique historical dimension which sets it apart from the other major team sports like rugby and football. More perhaps than any other single factor, it has helped to create the 'universe' of cricket, its special world, to which all cricketers belong and by virtue of which cricket has acquired its capacity to assimilate across social class and, to a degree, across race.

Cricket is an acquired skill and an acquired taste. Indeed, it is one of the basic premises of the game that it takes a long time to learn and this accounts for some of the social attitudes attached to it. The length of apprenticeship reinforces the sense of tradition and historical continuity, and the very rules themselves take outsiders an unconscionable time to understand. In this way social class gets a purchase, for a sport which requires the investment of so much free time and skill — as well as material cost — inevitably privileges the rich and leisured. Thus cricket has always held up a mirror to society and this is revealed in the division between amateurs and professionals. Even though they played side by side in the same teams, their status was different, and this is in turn crystallized in the terms by which individual performances and styles of play are judged. Batsmen are 'noble' or 'workmanlike', 'strokers of the ball' or 'run getters' — while in England it was possible until recently to find clubs with separate changing rooms for 'gentlemen' and 'players'.

From at least the 18th Century, cricket has been at one and the same time a popular and a select sport, and both these faces are to be found in its traditions and practice. We associate the game both with elegant gentlemen and public schools — with leisure and privilege — and with hard-nosed professionals, whose contribution to the sport has undoubtedly been as great and as ancient. Having a grasp of cricket therefore involves coming to terms with its history. Cricket is at one and the same time an integrative force — welcoming all those who can learn its code — and exclusive: all may enter — but all must prove they are worthy. And in South Africa as elsewhere, this ambivalence has encouraged two tendencies which co-exist side by side: one has been exclusive, tending to reserve the game to a pre-defined elite; the other, meritocratic, has assumed that an elite defines itself and has been relatively tolerant towards black cricketers. Played throughout the Empire, cricket was virtually unique during the colonial period in that the subject peoples not only adopted it but came to play the game at least as well as the British or their settler masters. Its moral and assimilationist qualities, which soon inspired a series of famous English aphorisms, were transmitted across the world; but, at the same time, it is a game which has a long tradition of segregation and has always been played in a most paternalist and racist manner.

The 'fascinating and complicated' arithmetic of cricket[13] reinforces this historical and exclusive tradition. Experts amass endless statistics about cricketing performances and scores dating back to the earliest years and covering all aspects of play from left-handed batting and under-arm bowling to the performances of substitute wicket-keepers, in which even the quality of the light, the weather, or the umpires, may be recorded. Yet if performances are obsessively quantified, equal attention is paid to the *quality* of play — quality which is traditionally translated into excellent prose. A team sport requiring a high degree of organized co-operation, cricket is also uniquely *individualist*, for it revolves around a struggle for supremacy between a single batsman and a bowler supported by his team. As a result, achievement may be computed in both individual and collective terms. Although conditions of play and technical standards have changed radically since cricket began, every score may finally be judged in absolute terms — in relation to a batsman's career best, or the fastest century of the season, the highest score in history, or the achievement of W.G. Grace. It is not unusual to read that in '1882-83 Winburg made 505 for 5 wickets versus Brandfort in the Orange Free State, the first known score of over 500 in South Africa.' Or that 'in 1902-03 Kotze for Transvaal v Griqualand West at Port Elizabeth became the first South African cricketer to do the hat-trick in first-class cricket.' Or that when South Africa made 692 runs versus Cambridge University at Fenners in 1901, this was 'the highest score to this day by a South African team overseas and the highest in first-class cricket'.[14]

The open-ended character of a game which can last from one to five days also privileges the leisured and select as does the cost of equipment. In comparison with rugby or football, cricket tends naturally to be seen as a 'game for gentlemen played by gentlemen' or, as Thornton expresses it 'a game that only gentlemen could play' and 'only great gentlemen could play really well: one of the few things, indeed, that a gentleman was permitted to do really well.'[15]

A game which forbids physical contact between players, in which the pleasure of spectators comes as much from intellectual appreciation of the play as team loyalty, cricket requires from those who play it a combination of courage, authority, speed, aggression, tactical skill and finesse. Unlike rugby, cricket highlights individual dignity by requiring the batsman, alone and surrounded by hostile fielders, to master and dominate a ball delivered towards him at speeds of up to 100 miles an hour. Mastery of personal fear, indeed mastery of the self, combine with skill and concentration to create in players of the highest class a unique appearance of grace and serenity. The image of the bowler, while less striking, also displays a wide range of qualities — courage, aggression, guile, stamina, persistence, invention — ranging from the disciplined physical violence of the pace bowler to the wiles of spin.

> For Hofmeyr it was the purest and completest of joys . . . . Cricket satisfied utterly his moral sense, for here was a human activity, governed by the rule of law, competitive in nature, yet devoid of rapacity or fear or cruelty, and pleasurable to enjoy.[16]

One of the greatest forms of social contact between the white men in Basutoland is the playing of cricket. Before the war (and no doubt the practice will be resumed) men rode for long distances and over difficult country to take part in the games that were held on Sundays for the reason that it took many of the players the greater part of a day to get there, and the best part of another to get back. . . . But at the morning tea interval a religious service is sometimes held — and has been known to be conducted by the Anglican bishop. The 22 players, spectators, and those providing tea, gather in the shade of a tree, have prayer, a short address, sing a hymn, and then the game goes on again.[17]

In the last 20 years, South African cricket has been widely commercialized, like other sports,[18] but until then, more perhaps than anywhere else, it was played according to the highest amateur tradition. 'It is an ideal kind of pre-1914 amateur cricket that is to be found in "white" South Africa,' writes Bowen, 'and it produces a remarkable number of fine cricketers, few of whom however play in the top class for more than a few years. They know they have to earn a living and in this respect they do not resemble the pre-1914 amateur English players, so many of whom did not need to earn a serious penny all their lives.'[19]

We can see in the following incident the anxiety of South Africans to be part of the white international cricket world. It occurred during a tour led by Hofmeyr in 1929, at a dinner given to his team by the British Empire League:

Eric Louw paid tribute to the role played by sport in bringing the two white races together. Mr Taberer recalled, amid much laughter, that after taking part in a freshman's cricket match at Oxford in 1889, the *Sportsman* described him as 'a coloured gentleman from South Africa', while the *Field*, with less reserve, called him a coloured cousin from across the waters. 'My Lords and Gentlemen: that will indicate to you how we have progressed, for those incidents will reveal to you how we in South Africa were at that earlier time regarded by the people of England. If a person had been born in South Africa, it was confidently assumed that he had coloured blood in his veins. If you examine the finger-nails of the boys representing the South African cricket team, you will not find any indication of coloured blood.'[20]

It is this combination of elitism and racism in South African cricket which helps to explain why the English-speaking minority who dominate the game, as its 'natural guardians', neither disseminated it among the Afrikaner and black communities nor recognized it where it did exist.

In the early years there was natural segregation in South African cricket, the same as elsewhere in British Colonial Africa. In Kenya, Nigeria, Ghana and other countries separate bodies also existed for white and black cricketers. Sometimes, on select Sundays and festival occasions, the paternalistic white hand would open the door of a club — for instance Green Point and Claremont in the Cape — for the back-yard cricketers and their enthusiastic entourages. Then, for a day, there would be play, and at stumps the doors closed again until some hazy date in the future. Sometimes whites ventured into the dustbowl territory of the other side for a match.[21]

Afrikaners and Cricket

In the early years there was a definite Afrikaner presence among South Africa's cricketers. Wells speaks of Johannesburg's 'first cricket team, formed in the year gold was found [1886], captained by O.J.J. van Wyk, and containing as many Dutch-speaking men as English',[22] while Bowen records that a team of Boer prisoners of war, exiled to Colombo (Sri Lanka), played cricket against a multi-racial local Colts XI in 1901.

The decisive event occurred when, on the initiative of the South Africans themselves, the Imperial Cricket Conference was formed in London in 1901. Membership of this body, cricket's regulating institution, was henceforth confined to imperial subjects. This had a general effect of stifling the spread of cricket in places like Holland and the Nordic countries and in Philadelphia where the game, played under slightly different rules, was at the time more popular than in South Africa itself. But it was particularly offensive to the Afrikaners, who were scarcely likely, at the very moment of their recent and bitter defeat, to take up a game that had voluntarily and explicitly chosen to identify itself with British imperialism.

J.H. Hofmeyr's efforts in the 1930s to bridge this chasm were rare exceptions confirming the rule. Famous son of a famous cricketing family,[23]

Hofmeyr organized an Administrator's Eleven [which] used to play Saturday afternoon matches against the high schools of Pretoria and Johannesburg . . . . Hofmeyr's team also visited the Volks High School in Heidelberg, and other Afrikaans-medium schools. The cricket teams representing South Africa have always been overwhelmingly composed of English-speaking players, and the rugby teams very largely of Afrikaans-speaking players. Hofmeyr used his team for the express purpose of seeking out Afrikaans-medium schools who were anxious to encourage the game. In the last year of his administration he was approached by a number of the masters in these schools . . . to see whether the Administrator's Eleven might not go further afield. Hofmeyr needed no persuasion; he promised a team of first-league standard, and both the Eastern Province and the Border Cricket Unions jumped at the idea. Hofmeyr organized the entire venture . . . . The team played nine matches in nineteen days, winning seven and drawing two. At each place there was a lunch, and sometimes a dinner too. No one except Hofmeyr was acceptable as a speaker . . . . The tour produced another joke for him . . . that on this tour he had compiled what he believed to be a world record, namely of making more speeches than runs . . . . After Hofmeyr had told a joke or two, he would grow serious and pay tribute to the game itself, especially its power to draw English and Afrikaans-speaking men together.[24]

Nevertheless, until the early 1960s, few Afrikaner schools played cricket or encouraged the game and most senior cricket was organized around Old Boys Clubs which naturally recruited among the English-speaking community. Some clubs, like the Johannesburg Wanderers, for many years actually excluded Afrikaners from membership.

I played for Old Parktonians which was Parktown School's Old Boy Club. They had grounds and a club house and played cricket, hockey, tennis and bowls. They never played rugby or soccer . . . because rugby was not organized on an Old Boy network . . . rugby and football were on a club basis . . . . Cricket was more or less an exclusively English game . . . . Cricket is a game that takes a long time to learn, it's not like rugby or soccer which you can learn quite quickly . . . . You have to start playing very young. Afrikaner schools did not promote it in junior school level and it needs to be promoted right through. I started learning when I was five or six and Afrikaners never learnt it till they were 13 or 14 which is why they were never very good. For example, the University had a rugby team and there you would get a certain amount of mixing of language, but not in cricket, because not a lot of Afrikaners played. Most of the Old Boys' Clubs were from English schools. I suppose it had to do with the English education system, based on public schools, where Old Boys' Clubs are important.[25]

The first book in Afrikaans on cricket — *Amper Krieket Kampioene* (Almost Champion Cricketers) by Werner Barnard — was not published until 1955 and Afrikaners only started playing the game in any numbers after 1960, when South Africa's departure from the Commonwealth had freed the game from its imperial connotations, and when the Springbok team was for a decade — until the boycott put an end to foreign tours — perhaps the best in the world. 'The game is no longer an English and therefore an alien institution,' wrote Bowen in 1970, 'it is a South African game, and now that the political connection with England has been severed, the Afrikaner can play cricket with a quiet conscience. He can do more: he can read about it, to the tune of several pages in each issue of his daily paper, when a Test match is on, a coverage equalled perhaps nowhere in the world today.'[26] Between 1955 and 1970 the number of white cricketers more than doubled[27] and, stimulated by the successes of the national side, Afrikaner schools and the Nationalist authorities both encouraged the game:

Until from about 1960 until the boycotts took hold, South Africans were very good in cricket internationally. You had the Pollocks, the Barry Richards and Proctors of this world . . . . They got a lot of kudos for South Africa. They used to beat England and Australia and so on. I think that Afrikaners for that reason got interested, they realized cricket could be a national game, it could be nationally important and so it began to be promoted. Administering cricket actually became an important thing, and cricket was promoted in Afrikaner schools.[28]

South African cricket was marketed abroad and became a political asset like white rugby. 'Many South Africans,' wrote Bowen again, 'disturbed at the prospects of political isolation, are using every endeavour to keep the country's name prominently before the eyes of those abroad who, they think, will support their cause. The result has been a flood, compared with what happens in respect of every other country, of club teams and schoolboy teams visiting England, and in turn being invited to visit South Africa.'[29]

The boycott which froze South Africa's international cricket from 1970 had a number of effects. Cricket has been inhibited by the boycott more than other sports. At the same time, the game has become more acceptable and popular among all sections of the white community than at any time in the past. Both effects were to influence the evolution of black cricket.

Black Cricket

If one of cricket's characteristics is its ambivalence — its double tradition, both popular and aristocratic, both professional (competitive) and amateur (social), both integrative and exclusive — this ambivalence finds political expression in the equivocal posture of the white liberal and cricketing establishments towards black cricket.

Until the end of the 19th Century, cricket had been a social game played popularly by all groups, including Africans and Coloureds. Its transformation into an 'imperial' sport for an elite, conscious of its 'civilizing', integrating mission in the world and in Africa, sharply reduced the game's audience among Blacks, the majority of whom were excluded from playing by material costs and their lack of education, and attracted away by football, which was on the way to becoming a mass sport among Africans and Indians by the beginning of the new century. By the time Mweli Skota came to compile his *African Yearly Register* (1932), cricket was already a game which among Blacks was played, if not followed, almost exclusively by the African, and black, elite.

This elite crystallized in the last decades of the 19th Century, in the mission colleges and the burgeoning new mining towns like Kimberley. 'The birth of African cricket proper,' writes Andre Odendaal, 'found its cradle in educational institutions such as Lovedale, Zonnebloem and Healdtown. From there the game was spread by the students to their respective centres. Children in primary schools were introduced to cricket and as the organization of white cricket became greater, so the European influence on African cricket increased.'[30] Brian Willan fleshes out this description with his account of the African petty bourgeoisie at Kimberley:

> Cricket was the game that Kimberley's African petty bourgeoisie really made its own. That this should have been the case is perhaps not at all surprising. Cricket, after all, was not just a game. Rather it was a uniquely British institution that embodied so many of the values and ideals which, individually and collectively, they aspired to. Cricket provided for them an opportunity to inculcate these values and ideals, and to demonstrate that they were capable and worthy of doing so. Cricket was a social training ground: the analogy between cricket and life generally was widely accepted, its value in character development unquestioned. 'Caution, care, patience and decision,' so one writer in the *Diamond Fields Advertiser* claimed in 1893, 'are inculcated by cricket's manly toil.'
>
> The game was widely played by educated Africans throughout the Cape Colony. During the cricket season, every issue of *Imvo* contained columns of cricket results, reports, batting and bowling averages. In Kimberley, the two African clubs (they ran several teams each) were the Duke of Wellington Cricket Club (usually referred to simply as 'Duke'), and Eccentrics Cricket Club: even their names are suggestive. both symbolizing qualities upon which the British Empire was built. During the 1890s these two clubs competed with eight other (Indian, 'Malay' and Coloured) teams, firstly in the Griqualand West Coloured Cricketers Union (from 1892-95), and thereafter in the Griqualand West Colonial Union. Fixtures between 'Duke' and Eccentrics came high up on the social calendar of Kimberley's African petty bourgeosie. It was the major entertainment, for example, of Christmas Day, 1895.[31]

During this period, the same missionary paternalism that led certain Whites to play cricket occasionally with Blacks and expressed itself in the donation of the Barnato Cup, offered to black cricket in 1897 by Sir David Harris (President of De Beers Consolidated Mines) in the hope that it would foster and improve cricket standards among all sections of the black community,[32] co-existed with the most rigid segregation and a conscious refusal by white cricketers to recognize black cricket within or outside the country. South Africa played 172 tests between 1888 and 1970: not once did the Springboks play the West Indies, India or Pakistan, and a player of the calibre of d'Oliveira had to exile himself to Britain before he could achieve international honours.

It should be said that racism has by no means been confined to South Africans. The record of visiting English cricketers is not exactly exemplary. On the single occasion on which an English touring side have ever agreed to play a black side in South Africa — in 1891-92, against a Malay XVIII — the English amateur players refused to take part. And no black cricketers were

allowed to play against a first-class visiting side before 1973, when Derrick
Robins financed a tour of the country by an international team, most of
whom were white . . . in order to break the boycott.

There are numerous stories of white racism in South African cricket. In
1894, the Coloured cricketer, T. Hendricks, one of South Africa's best players
at the time, was not included in the party which toured Britain. The reason
was certainly not form but race, for he was not included either in the 'Colonial Born' side against the 'Mother Country' XI for 1894-95. At that time the
question of his selection was raised officially for discussion, but 'at the meeting it was moved and carried that that item on the agenda be ignored and the
next business taken'.[33] Similarly, an uninformed British army captain selected
his servant to play in an army match, only to be told that his action conflicted
with custom, while C.B. Llewellyn, the only Coloured cricketer known to
have played for South Africa, was ostracized and bullied by his team mates
when he toured Australia in 1910-11.[34] During their 1929 tour of Britain,
the Springboks even succeeded in imposing their racism on others: they
objected to playing against the Sussex captain, K.S. Duleepsinghji, an Indian
educated in Britain, and he played in the first test match but was subsequently left out of the English side.[35] When finally the 'd'Oliveira affair' broke in
England in 1968, and the South African cricket and political establishment
vetoed his presence in the English side to tour South Africa, British public
opinion was no longer so tolerant; more important still, the West Indies, India
and Pakistan had votes on the I.C.C. South Africa was banned indefinitely
from international competition.

The history of black cricket shows evidence of the same ambivalence
characteristic of white cricket. Although black cricketers began in unity,
helped by their common membership of the elite, for much of the 20th
Century they played separately in racial leagues. After repeated attempts
at inter-racial co-operation, they finally reunited in the 1950s within the
South African Cricket Board of Control (SACBOC), which dominated black
cricket until SACBOC's dissolution and the reorganization of cricket structures in 1976, under the impact of 'multi-nationalism'.[36]

Coloured Cricket

From the beginning Coloured cricketers have been prominent in black cricket.
In the Cape, their clubs were recognized as better organized and more experienced than their African counterparts,[37] and their enthusiastic interest in the
game was renowned in the 1930s.

> Not only is a special stand erected for them [the Malays] at the famous
> rugby ground at Newlands, where they will go into ecstasies over the
> sudden breaks and drop-kickings of their favourite Springboks, but for
> long hours hundreds of them will stand in St. George's Street, which is
> the Fleet Street of Cape Town, waiting anxiously for the fall of every
> wicket to be posted outside the newspaper offices of some test match
> in which South Africa is engaged six thousand miles away.[38]

Records of organized black cricket go back to 1876, at which time
Coloured cricketers already predominated. In that year the South End
Cricket Club of Port Elizabeth was created out of two pre-existing clubs,
and cricket was started in Kimberley, which was to remain the undisputed
capital of the game for black cricketers until the 1940s.

In 1889-90, while white cricketers were setting up a national organization,
the first major Coloured tournament took place, at Newlands, between Malay
teams from Cape Town, Port Elizabeth, Johannesburg and Claremont. The
following year Kimberley hosted the event, in which three teams took part.
Then in 1890-91, a Malay team played and lost the only — and therefore
historic — match ever played by a black cricket team against a first-class
national touring side. On this occasion the black pace bowler, 'Krom' Hendricks, distinguished himself.[39]

In the 1890s, the Griqualand West Colonial Cricket Board organized an
inter-provincial competition and from 1897 (with a break during the Boer
War) awarded the Barnato Trophy to the winning Coloured (or African)
side. Soon after the War, in 1902, the first national Coloured cricket association was formed, the South African Coloured Cricket Board (S.A.C.C.B.),
which soon afterwards inaugurated the first formally constituted competition
between representative provincial sides.[40] In 1926 a rival organization split
off, the South African Independent Coloured Cricket Board, to which Sir
David Harris also gave a cup. (The Independent Coloured Cricket Board was
renamed the Coloured Cricket Association in 1948.)

African Cricket
As we have seen, Africans had played cricket from early days, although never
to the same extent as the Coloured community. The Boers had played a
'Hottentot' team in the 1850s, and African sides took part in the 'native'
tournament held at Port Elizabeth in 1890-91 between four teams from the
Cape Colony. A match at Kroonstad had pitted an African club team against
a Potchefstroom side. African teams were also members of the Griqualand
West Colonial Union and, until 1932, of the S.A. Coloured Cricket Board.
For the first 30 years of the century, in fact, black teams played together
within a single inter-racial organization.

Relations were certainly not always easy, however, and the extension of
segregation and racial legislation certainly exacerbated already existing
strains. Brian Willan notes that as early as the 1890s 'the participation of the
two African clubs in the Union was on occasion a source of tension: when
Mr J.S. Moss was elected to the position of Vice-President of the Union in
November 1895, three of the Coloured clubs temporarily pulled out, although
Moss was, as Isaiah Bud Mbelle pointed out in a letter to the local paper, 'a
cultured and respectable native gentleman of whom any sensible community
can be proud.' The ideology of segregation and the ever encroaching destruction of African status, in particular, caused the standard of African cricket to
decline steadily — it remains the game's poor relation — and eventually forced
the black cricket organizations apart. At the beginning of the century, it was

91

played almost exclusively by the African elite. Subsequent extension of the game was virtually confined to the mines, where segregation was particularly severe — but which could provide facilities:

> The mining houses were greatly responsible for getting African cricket on its feet in the Transvaal. Facilities which the Africans themselves would not have been able to afford were made available by the mines. Roro, Nteshekisa, Gwele, Mlonzi, to mention only a few names which will endure in African cricket history, learnt to play and administer the game as a result of their opportunities.[41]

There is no doubt that the increase in social and physical segregation contributed to the succession of splits which between 1926 and 1932 took African cricketers out of the Coloured Union. In 1926 five clubs, dissatisfied with their treatment inside the South African Metropolitan (Coloured) Union, formed the Western Province Bantu Cricket Union,[42] and in 1932 all the African clubs which had been affiliated to the South African Coloured Cricket Board resigned to form the South African Bantu Cricket Board. Six areas were involved — Western Province, Border, Eastern Province, Transvaal, Griqualand West, and Natal — and they played for a cup offered by the Chamber of Mines, the Native Recruiting Corporation trophy, which remained the highest national trophy for Africans until 1976. The Transvaal dominated the championship, winning six of the ten tournaments held between 1932 and 1952 (against two victories by Western Cape and two by Border).

There is certainly a link between the reorganization of black cricket along racial lines and its development on the Rand, and in particular its sponsorship by the Native Recruiting Corporation and the mining companies, and by the Joint Councils Movement which attempted between 1920 and 1948 to influence social and cultural activity among the black, and especially African, communities.[43] Several key figures behind the formation of the Bantu Cricket Board were in the Joint Councils or closely involved with the mines. One of the principal organizers of the 1932 split, Mr H. Masiza,[44] for example, was General Secretary of the S.A. Coloured Cricket Board at the time and also a member of Kimberley Joint Council, while Mr Piliso, president of the new Association, was a headman at Modder B Compound and President of the Native Recruiting Corporation Cricket Union[45] — whose patron was Mr H.M. Taberer, himself a prominent member of the Johannesburg Joint Council.[46]

Between the wars African cricket produced at least one great player — Frank Roro, 'probably the finest African cricketer of all time' according to Odendaal.[47] After travelling from his birthplace in Kimberley to take employment on the Rand mines, like so many other Africans of his generation, he scored over 20 centuries during a long career whose tail stretched into the 1950s and he became President of the Bantu Cricket Board.

Indian Cricket

The earliest mention of Indian cricketers occurs in 1896 when the indentured labourers brought to South Africa from India created their own union. They had begun to form football and then cricket teams from about 1890. Cricket, however, a game even more expensive than tennis, was played almost exclusively by the educated elite, traders and members of the professions. Membership of some clubs was also confined to particular religious groups. In 1922, during a football tour of India, an Indian team played a cricket match at Calcutta.[48] In 1940, the Indian Cricket Union was created, with unions in the Transvaal, Eastern province and Natal: affiliates played for the Christopher's Trophy.

Between the wars, according to Bowen, 'non-white cricket started to flourish on a scale comparable with Indian cricket in India.'[49] Confined, because of its cost and ideology, to the black petty bourgeoisie, it constituted an important common reference for this group. As a result, it was no doubt easier for black cricketers — who after all had played together until 1932 — to reunite their forces at the beginning of the 1950s.

Persistent attempts to do so had been made between 1936 and 1952. 'Inter-race boards' in the Transvaal, Eastern Province and the Northern Cape had organized competitions between teams from the different racial unions — including apparently some white sides,[50] and from its creation the Indian Union had campaigned for a single national cricket body, an aim which was finally achieved in 1952, when the South African Cricket Board of Control was born. The leaders of this new organization, one of the first unified inter-racial bodies, had to overcome resistance within their communities and of course from the white sports establishment and the Government. By the end of the 1950s, SACBOC had been drawn into the campaign to boycott all cricket tours, and persuaded to cancel a tour it had arranged with a West Indian side led by Worrell (which would have played all-black sides). Nearly ten years later, from these small beginnings, the cricket campaign erupted into the 'd'Oliveira Affair', with its spectacular results.

D'Oliveira's talent had been recognized in the 1950s and in 1957-58 he was named captain of the first representative black South African cricket team to tour abroad (to Rhodesia and East Africa). In 1960, however, with no possibility of playing first-class cricket in South Africa[51] and frustrated by the non-racial movement's campaigns in favour of a moratorium on all tours, d'Oliveira left for Britain.[52] In due course he became eligible for the England side and successfully toured the West Indies. When it seemed he would be chosen for the English team which was to tour South Africa in 1968-69, the South African Government intervened to state that his presence in the visiting side would be unacceptable. However, for the first time in its history, the M.C.C. refused to step down: d'Oliveira *was* selected (after initial confusion), the Nationalist Government protested,[53] the tour was cancelled. In 1970 the I.C.C. imposed a moratorium on all tours with South Africa so long as cricket there continued to be organized on racial lines.[54]

Almost despite himself — for he has never publicly identified with the non-racial movement — d'Oliveira had finally discredited white cricketers' claims that no black players were good enough to play for South Africa. The d'Oliveira Affair became a symbol of white South Africa's racist sport. No official tours have taken place since the Australians visited South Africa in 1971, although in 1973, 1975 and 1976, Derrick Robins brought an international scratch side to South Africa to break the boycott and Wilf Isaacs has also organized several private tours abroad.[55]

Since 1970 important changes have overtaken South African cricket, which has accepted large-scale commercial sponsorship and the introduction of one-day cricket, financed by the Gillette Company and then by Datsun. The Currie Cup has also been sponsored to the tune of 150,000 Rand over five years, by South African Breweries, the country's major sports sponsor. South Africa's highest cricket trophy now goes under the overloaded title of the South African Breweries Currie Cup Competition. Commercial interests have promoted theatrical cricket played by the 'stars' of the game, professional players whose charisma guarantees the crowds. Racially mixed cricket has been introduced at top level — athough only a handful of black cricketers are involved — and the S.A. Cricket Union (SACU) is the most racially mixed of the official 'multi-national' sports bodies. Of more significance, because it implies a much greater commitment to non-racialism, about 10% of the non-racial S.A. Cricket Board's members are reported to be white.[56]

This should not disguise the fact, however, that it is white cricketers and the white cricket establishment who are overwhelmingly responsible for the racism and racist practices which characterize the game. When the Nationalists took power in 1948, cricket was already segregated, and organized on apartheid lines. To understand what the Government means when it attempts to defend the racialism of its sports policy by reference to the 'customs and traditions' of the country, one need look no further than the history of cricket. And this is particularly significant for a game that is played and run by English-speaking South Africans with their reputation for being more 'liberal' and 'enlightened' than Afrikaners.

References

1. *Diamond Fields Advertiser*, 8 November 1893 in B. Willan, *An African in Kimberley*, p. 15.
2. R. Bowen, 1970, p. 277.
3. A. Odendaal, 1977, pp. 305-6.
4. See R. Bowen, 1970, p. 32.
5. Tennis derives from the 'jeu de paume' (hand game) which reached its apogee in Britain and France during the 16th Century, after Louis X had made it a royal sport in the 13th Century. The name 'real tennis' is thus a distortion of 'royal tennis' and the word 'tennis' itself a distortion of the French word 'tenez' called by the server before opening play. Like other sports, tennis reappeared in Victorian Britain after a

period of obscurity. The Revolution and Napoleonic era had virtually ended the playing of tennis in France and it was reimported at the end of the 19th Century from England.

6. See R. Bowen, 1970, pp. 71-3.
7. A.F. Hattersley, 1950, p. 333, refers to a famous match between the 'West End' and 'East End' of Pietermaritzburg on New Year's Day, 1852, and describes the first cricket match to be played in Alexandra Park, in 1863 'between teams representing Richmond and Pietermaritzburg. Richmond batted first and compiled 60. "The town boys then took the willow, Messrs. H. Shepstone and Pearse leading off. These two made very good average scores (7 and 11), but several of their successors could not obtain anything beyond duck's eggs, Ling doing great execution with his underhand bowling." On the two innings, Richmond emerged victors by 40 runs.' A.F. Hattersley, 1938, p. 95.
8. Matches were played earlier of course: tradition dates the inaugural games as follows — Bloemfontein (1850), Potchefstroom, then capital of the Transvaal (1867), Queenstown (1862), Pretoria (1870), Kimberley (1871) Botswana (1879), Lesotho (1881), Johannesburg (1886-87).
9. *The South African Cricket Guide*, 1871-72 (Cape); *Natal Cricket Annual* (1885) became after 1888-89 the *South African Cricket Annual* which appeared until 1892 and then recommenced from 1905-06.
10. Between 1886 and 1976 South Africa played 328 times against England, Australia and New Zealand. South Africa's Springboks (all-white, see pp. 89-90 below) have never played India, Pakistan or the West Indies, or any other of the black cricketing nations. During the same period 839 matches were played in the Currie Cup.
11. W. Ritchie, 1918, pp. 682-3 and p. 684.
12. Bowen, 1970, p. 214, goes so far as to suggest that 'there are plausible grounds for believing that the arrogant manner in which the Smuts Government displaced the Wanderers Club from their long-established ground — from that concession granted by President Kruger — in what had become the centre of Johannesburg, lost that government a good many votes . . . . If so, it is interesting that one of the world's political tragedies should have developed as it did because of the inept way in which a cricket ground was appropriated.'
13. R. Bowen, 1970, p. 68.
14. R. Bowen, 1970, pp. 291, 313, 311 respectively.
15. This has not prevented cricket crowds from rioting in the past: see R. Bowen, 1970, p. 71.
16. A. Paton, 1964, p. 140.
17. A.W. Wells, 1949, p. 232.
18. R. Bowen, 1970, p. 215.
19. Ibid.
20. A. Paton, 1964, p. 159.
21. A. Odendaal, 1977, p. 23.
22. A.W. Wells, 1949, p. 131.
23. His father, Jan Henrick Hofmeyr (1845-1909), leader of the liberal wing of Smuts' United Party, had captained a cricket team in Stellenbosch in 1895-96, composed entirely of members of his own family.

24. A. Paton, 1964, pp. 140-1.
25. John Horak, interview, London, 9 February 1980.
26. R. Bowen, 1970, p. 216.
27. R. Bowen, 1970, pp. 215-6.
28. John Horak, interview, London, 9 February 1980.
29. R. Bowen, 1970, p. 216. The number of national tours was also remarkable. In 1963-64, the fourth S.A. tour to Australia and New Zealand took place; in 1964-65, the tenth M.C.C. tour to S.A.; in 1965, the thirteenth S.A. tour of England; in 1965-66, the first M.C.C schools team toured S.A.; in 1966-67, the seventh Australian tour of S.A. took place; in 1967 a S.A. universities team toured Britain; in 1967-68, an Australian schools team toured S.A. . . . etc.
30. A. Odendaal, 1977, p. 307.
31. B. Willan, *An African in Kimberley*, p. 15. For the important social position occupied by cricket among the African elite, see pp. 115-6 below.
32. Odendaal, 1977, p. 307.
33. P. Hain, 1971, p. 74.
34. Llewellyn's family contest to this day that he was Coloured; certainly he did not play with black cricketers. The dispute itself is symptomatic of the problem. Odendaal, 1977, pp. 325-6.
35. P. Hain, 1971, pp. 74-5.
36. This later period is examined in Chapter 11.
37. M. Wilson and A. Mafeje, 1963, pp.114-5.
38. A.W. Wells, 1939 (1949), p. 44.
39. According to Odendaal, 1977, p. 325, 'the fastest bowler in the country at that time,' and according to 'English test players George Rowe and Bonnor Middleton . . . one of the fastest in the world'. Indeed, it would be a mistake to underestimate the individual skills of some of the black cricketers of the period, although it was probably true that they could not compete in depth with white representative teams. Nicholls, another Coloured cricketer, was 'the fittest and most feared left-arm pace bowler in the Cape' (Odendaal, 1977, p. 326). 'Plum' Warner, captain of the first M.C.C. tour in 1905-06, wrote of his performance when he was hired to give the tourists net practice (10 gold sovereigns for three afternoons): 'One young Malay with a fast left-hand action hit my middle stump nearly every other ball and Denton began his South African career by being caught and bowled by the first three balls and clean bowled by the next' (P. Warner, 1906, p. 2).
40. The Eastern and Western Provinces and Griqualand West were joined by the Transvaal after 1904. The competition was suspended during the First World War.
41. A. Odendaal, 1977, p. 307.
42. Home Bachelors, Oriental, Far East, Wanderers and Great Powers.
43. See Chapter 6.
44. Odendaal, 1977, p. 308. Mr Masiza was an old boy of Healdtown College, Lovedale and Fort Hare, and headmaster of the United Mission School in Kimberley.
45. Odendaal, 1977, p. 308; Mweli Skota, 1932, p. 447.
46. See Chapter 5. Mr H.M. Taberer was Labour Adviser, Chamber of Mines. The N.R.C. Cricket Union Board was: President Mr B. Piliso, headman

of Modder B Compound (and one of those responsible for the 1932 split); Vice-President, Mr Ntontelo, clerk Block B Compound Langlaagte; Secretary, Mr P.S. Kekane, clerk, Robinson Deep Compound; Assistant Secretary, Mr P. Gwele, Durban Deep Compound, Roodepoort; Treasurer, Mr S.C. Mbatsha, Central News Agency (Mwele Skota, 1932, p. 447).

47. A. Odendaal, 1977, p. 309.
48. Mr P.B. Singh, interview, London, 22 April 1980. Mr Singh played in this match and subsequently umpired the 1926 M.C.C. tour of India.
49. R. Bowen, 1970, p. 134.
50. A. Odendaal, 1977, p. 309.
51. His exclusion from the Springbok team which toured England in 1960 excited some protest: see Lapchick, 1975, pp. 33-4.
52. Like a number of other good black cricketers in the 1960s, including the Abrahams' brothers, John Neethling, Tiffie Barnes, Omar, Abed, etc. d'Oliveira's ticket was financed by a benefit match staged between a white and black team in defiance of apartheid and Government policy.
53. On hearing of the selection, Prime Minister Vorster made the astonishing statement, on 17 September 1968, that 'the team as constituted now is not the team of the M.C.C. but the team of the anti-apartheid movement, the team of SANROC and the team of Bishop Reeves.'
54. For further details, see P. Hain, 1971, pp. 75-83; R. Lapchick, 1975; and A. Odendaal, 1977.
55. In February, an unofficial tour by a party of English cricketers, including a number of Test players, and complete with 'tests' was heavily promoted, and subsidized by the white cricket establishment.
56. For an analysis of the current situation in cricket, see Chapter 11.

4. Social Sports

Football

It may seem surprising to find football in a chapter devoted to social sports, when it is the most widely played game in South Africa – with up to half a million adherents – and represents a powerful professional sector attracting several tens of thousands of spectators every week. However, for white South Africans football has never had the prestige of rugby or indeed cricket; nor has it been monopolized in the past by any single community – although today the game is undoubtedly dominated by Africans, who of course form the great majority of the population and play soccer in large numbers all the year round, particularly in the Transvaal.

Thus football is included in this chapter precisely because it is the *most* social game in South Africa, played by the greatest number of people over the country and at all levels, for exercise and pleasure. It is also the most popular game, played from its first appearance by the working class, both white and black.

The rules of rugby and football were not formally distinguished until the 1860s in Britain, and the 1870s in South Africa. Before the first football club, Pietermaritzburg County, was founded in 1879, it is therefore difficult to trace precisely the history of the game.

The first recorded football match was played on the market square between the City [of Pietermaritzburg] and the Garrison on the 26th September 1866. It had been agreed that the game should last one and a half hours and be played between sides numbering fourteen. According to a spectator 'the rules were systematically disregarded by both sides through the whole game', but it should be remembered that the laws of Association Football were only formulated in England in the year 1863. The Town side captained by J.D. Burnett 'looked like a lot of little boys' in comparison with the strapping figures of the military. Nevertheless, they nearly won. We are told that 'a well-contested and plucky game ensued, and lasted for about half an hour, when all at once the game came to an end, and shouts were heard in the distance but no one knew why. In a word, the garrison had nearly kicked a goal, missing by about six feet, and their umpire, Sergeant Clark, cried 'game', although his own men admitted that it was no goal. However, after an interval, the game was eventually restarted. R. Erskine kicked a goal for the Town, and a draw was the result. 'We can hardly call it football,' wrote a correspondent, 'as almost every player used every part of his body more than his feet.'[1]

The first real attempt to establish football was made in 1881, in Port Elizabeth, by a Scots player from Queen's Park. But he died,[2] and it was in Natal — where the game had already been played for some time — that the first official football association was created, in 1882. To its first four affiliates — Pietermaritzburg County, Natal Wasps, Durban Alpha and Umgeni Stars — the association added six more the following year, and the game spread rapidly to other towns. The Football Association of South Africa (FASA) was founded in 1892, the year which also saw the first Currie Cup played off between only two teams, Western Province and Griqualand West. The Western Province Association was founded in 1896 and Transvaal Football Association three years later.

The first foreign tour was made in 1897 by an English side, the Corinthians. A South African team was then invited to Argentina in 1906, and toured several Latin American countries, winning 11 of its 12 matches. It was not until 1924 that a second South African tour abroad took place, this time to Britain. The first professional tour by a British team had occurred in 1910.

From the beginning, football was the most popular sport among the white community as a whole, played particularly by the working and lower middle classes on the Witwatersrand. Many of the most gifted players made football their career; but to do so they had to travel abroad, generally to England or Scotland. 'Boksburg, a place of less than twenty thousand white inhabitants,' records Wells in 1939, 'has contributed no less than nine players to first-class English and Scottish soccer in the last eighteen years.'[3] The tradition continued — and continues today, for although a professional sector has existed since 1959, opportunities and rewards remain relatively limited compared with those to be had abroad.[4]

The popular character of white football distinguishes it from all the other major sports, which until the 1950s were controlled and socially marked by the more prosperous and privileged sections of white society. From its beginning, in South Africa as in many other countries, soccer was seen to be an essentially working-class game. It was therefore virtually ignored by 'good' white society: Sadie Berman does not remember having seen a football match before coming to England and John Horak recalls how rarely football was covered by the press until the early 1960s when the professional game got into its stride.[5] It was a game for the poor, white as well as black — one of the few remaining contacts between the two communities after the Second World War.

Football was also played by the black population from an early date. Indians and Africans were playing it in Natal before the turn of the century, and the game boomed during the inter-war years, particularly on the Rand. In the 1920s, the best teams were Indian: a representative side successfully toured India in 1921 (before the sub-continent had formed a national association), stimulating the game there and defeating a number of the best Indian clubs, including Mohan Bhagan, in front of 100,000 spectators. In 1933, the Indian footballers sponsored a return tour sent out by the All-India Football Association.[6]

Huge numbers of Africans began playing football in the 1930s, particularly on the Witwatersrand, where club membership shot up dramatically.[7] Football (with rugby in the Cape, and boxing and horse-racing) became a truly mass sport in all communities — though significantly, as we have seen, less so among the Coloured and white populations than among the Indians and Africans. For the African working class, it would not be exaggerated to say that football *was* sport: no other game showed soccer's remarkable ability to penetrate among the poorest, most exploited group in the society.

It is surprising therefore that the first professional soccer league was not formed until as late as 1959, on the initiative of the S.A. Soccer Federation, which in 1952 had regrouped all of the black racial federations into a single union (and was to become fully non-racial in 1962-63). The official white federation retaliated immediately by creating the (all-white) National Football League in the same year. Almost at once, in 1961, the Football Association of South Africa became independent of the British Football League when South Africa left the Commonwealth. Because of its racial policies, the white association was then suspended by FIFA.

Isolated internationally and threatened from within by the S.A. Soccer Federation, the Football Association of South Africa, supported by the Government, embarked on a campaign of intimidation: racial Indian, Coloured and African federations were artificially created or resurrected, non-racial teams were excluded from municipal pitches, and a third professional league was created, for Africans — the S.A. National Professional Soccer League. The white association also created and controlled a football council composed of all the racial federations, (thereby prefiguring the 'multi-national' confederations established in the 1970s). Having bought time for itself, white football remained solvent and in command until the middle 1960s.[8]

The introduction of 'multi-nationalism' after 1971 upset this artificial equilibrium. Commercial sponsorship and the numerical predominance of African players and spectators caused a major crisis after South Africa's formal expulsion from FIFA in 1976. After prolonged disruption, the Nationalist Party and the African Football Association emerged victorious.

The importance of football can be summarized as follows: (1) It is easy to play and inexpensive, and as a result spread rapidly and was adopted by all sections of society, in rural as well as urban areas, in the mines of the Transvaal and Orange Free State as well as in the Cape and Natal, and by adults as well as children (both in and out of school). (2) Being cheap and a team game, it was the most accessible sport for the poor and underprivileged;

but it also encouraged individual talent, which, when the game was profession-alized, made it a sport of hope for those without a future, as well as relatively 'integrated' at the highest professional (but *not* amateur) level. (3) The very great popularity of football has increased the effects of isolation; but its association with the working class has also tended to reduce the political impact of football compared with more prestigious sports (notably rugby and cricket). After table tennis, football was the first South African sport to be isolated and South African teams have not taken part in serious official international football since the early 1960s.

Tennis

This ancient game reached South Africa soon after its revival in Britain during the 1870s. It was played by L. Neville in Natal and was already being widely adopted when the first Wimbledon championships were played in 1877.[9] The first known South African tournament took place in 1881. In 1884 the South African E.L. Williams reached the final of the Wimbledon Men's Doubles, partnering an Englishman against the Renshaw brothers.

The first clubs were founded in 1882 in Durban and Port Elizabeth. A match between Grahamstown and Port Elizabeth is recorded in 1884, and four years later tennis club associations had been formed in Natal and the Cape, while the Wanderers Club in Johannesburg inaugurated its tennis section the same year.

In 1891, the Port Elizabeth Club, assuming the role of national association, organized the first national South African tennis championships. The South African Lawn Tennis Union was created in 1903. The first British tour took place in 1908, and South Africa took part in all the Olympics (in 1908, 1912,[10] 1920) until tennis was dropped as an Olympic sport. In 1913 the S.A. Union was one of the twelve national associations which founded the International Tennis Federation (I.T.F.). In the same year, South Africa entered and won the Davis Cup (played off between eight nations) but, apparently for financial reasons, participation was irregular until 1929, after which she participated biennially until 1959, and then annually until her suspension in 1972.

Until 1928, the Union's international contacts were restricted to tours with Britain. In that year, a tour was arranged with an Australian women's team, and from then onwards foreign visits frequently took place. The South African women's team took part in the Federation Cup from its inception in 1963; they won it in 1972, in Johannesburg, between two international bannings.

The two most important domestic competitions are the South African Championship and the Sugar Circuit. The former has been 'open' since 1969 and is played in Ellis Park, Johannesburg. It is one of the five international championships recognized by the International Tennis Federation's constitution. The Sugar Circuit, a five-round contest, also attracts a number of international players.

Competitive tennis was largely dominated by English-speakers. Play, particularly in doubles, has been generally of a high standard, and the international success of South African players like Drysdale, Hewitt and MacMillan helped to stimulate a boom in white tennis during the 1960s.[11]

Because of its racial policies, South Africa was suspended from the Davis Cup from 1971-72 (and from the Federation Cup after 1972). It was then permitted to play in 1972, 1973 and 1974, when the South African team won by default because India refused to contest the final. In order to facilitate South Africa's participation and avoid such disputes, the I.T.F. had elected to transfer South Africa to the Latin America division! In 1980 South Africa's suspension from the Davis Cup was confirmed by the I.T.F. but the white Union still remains a full member of the international body and its members are free to play in any tournament abroad; I.T.F. members are also free to play in South Africa.

Individualist, with a long aristocratic tradition, involving no physical contact, tennis is not a mass sport. Compared with Europe, however, tennis in South Africa is, alongside swimming, the white minority's principal social recreation. It was played by both men and women and socially (though not competitively) by Afrikaners as well as English-speakers.

Nonetheless tennis remains an expensive sport, requiring well-laid and well-maintained courts, costly equipment (rackets, balls, net) and considerable practice before it can be played enjoyably. It is also one of the sports marked by the social values of the elite which originally propagated it, and club players are expected to wear white and conform to certain standards of etiquette. For all these reasons, tennis has remained somewhat exclusive and certainly 'white'.

This does not mean that tennis has not been widely played by Blacks. Although its distribution and popularity have been severely inhibited by material cost, lack of courts and the racially exclusive practices of white clubs, tennis is played by more black people than cricket, golf or swimming — although it trails behind the mass sports like football and rugby.

No doubt for technical and financial reasons black tennis associations appeared relatively late. However, their evolution paralleled their equivalents in other sports. The first tennis association was Indian, created in the 1920s, and the game spread from there to the other communities. The different racial federations (African, Coloured and Indian) were organized on separate lines, but championships were increasingly open and they came together in the late 1950s to negotiate unification. In 1962-63, they finally amalgamated when the non-racial Southern Africa Law Tennis Association (SALTU) was founded.[12] In the 1970s, professional tennis changed the face of the game, which became highly commercialized and 'star' oriented. As in cricket and football this permitted a limited amount of mixed competition at the highest levels of competitive tennis. After prolonged dispute, Arthur Ashe, the black American champion, was permitted to play in South Africa in 1973, for example, and a black tennis player, Peter Lamb, was selected for junior Wimbledon in 1972. But professionalism brought no advantage to black tennis players as a whole and probably handicapped them financially. In 1978, following the African tennis union's decision to repudiate its association with the white union, a new non-racial federation was created, the Tennis Association of South Africa (TASA), which today brings together all but a handful of South Africa's black tennis players.[13]

Golf

Golf is a sport which mirrors even more faithfully the hierarchy of social class. Another expensive game which takes time to learn, it also possesses a powerful professional sector and is heavily sponsored. Like tennis it is an international and individualist sport, which reinforces its commercialism and liberates its 'stars' from many of the organizational and official restraints inhibiting the independence of players of team sports. For all these reasons golf, like tennis, is one of the sports which it has been difficult to isolate internationally.

> Golf was a very serious matter to people. Their handicap was a serious matter, and the club to which they belonged because there are clubs which are more prestigious because they have better facilities and more beautiful surroundings and they are a bit more difficult to get into because the committee is selective.
> The most prestigious golf club in Johannesburg was I think the Royal. I mean they simply did not have any Jewish membership.
> This was not very widespread. The Royal was blatantly so. The most snobbish, the most elitist club was then the Country Club. It wasn't so blatantly anti-Jews as the Royal Johannesburg because they did have Jewish millionaires . . . . You couldn't show this, but it was almost impossible for any other Jewish person to get in.
> Of course we're not talking about Blacks!
> Money was the criterion. Money *is* class in South Africa. We didn't have any class other than a money class. There was no aristocracy.[14]

Golf is also the only sport directly associated with *service*, where caddies perform the role of servants hired to carry the clubs and equipment of players.[15] This already peculiar social relationship, combined with the classy image of golf, is inevitably exaggerated in South Africa, where caddies are almost all black and usually adolescent while the players are predominantly white and as often as not middle aged or elderly. Players may not appreciate the symbolism of this relationship; the caddies surely do.

The game was officially introduced in 1882, when the first club was sponsored in the Cape by a number of prominent figures and directed by the Garrison Commander. By 1886, it had appeared in Natal (the Pietermaritzburg Club), by 1890 on the Rand, and soon it was played throughout the country, by women as well as men. The first national championships date back to 1899, though they were not made official until the end of the Boer War (1902). The first women's competition — the Ladies' Championship — was played in 1909, the year in which the S.A. Golf Union was founded. The game spread rapidly because the climate is ideal. There are now over 300 courses: if you are white, South Africa is a golfing paradise.

Both caddies and professionals appeared at an early date in South Africa. The first professionals' championship was held in 1923 and Bobby Locke, one of the greatest golfers of all time, was a professional in the 1930s. As for caddies, in 1938 a study of the Johannesburg area showed that 14 of the major clubs employed 646 full-time caddies and numerous part-time caddies at the weekends. Most of the full-time caddies were recruited in the rural areas (in eight of the clubs studied) and lodged in compounds comparable to those built for adult migrant workers. They received a low wage (compared with other black adolescents) but substantial tips, which doubled their income and raised their wages to the highest levels for boys of their age — less than boy waiters in hotels and cafes, but more than houseboys, and more than all kinds of productive manual workers.[16] Apparently, service in South Africa is of more value than productive work.

The 1960s boom and the arrival of mass sport, among Blacks as well as Whites, and among Afrikaners as well as English-speakers, transformed golf by 'democratizing' it in the white community. As in Britain, its elite ethos has been somewhat effaced by its new image as an ideal Sunday sport, particularly for those elderly sportsmen no longer able to withstand the buffets and rigours of rugby. As golfers, they have less need of reflexes and breath and can score over younger men by their guile and experience.[17]

From the beginning it was extremely difficult if not impossible for Blacks to play golf — let alone play it well. The statistics explain why. The first 18-hole course for Africans was opened in 1968, and in 1977 there was just one course for every 484,025 Africans in the population and every 608,000 Coloureds![18] Yet astonishingly, black golfers have not only been organized for a considerable period but have achieved remarkably high standards. In the 1930s they were already organizing competitions, although they had to borrow a white course to do so,[19] and, in the teeth of logic, by the early 1960s black golf had produced a national champion.

Papwa Sewgolum's achievement was indeed remarkable. A poor and uneducated caddy, his gifts were so outstanding that his employers sent him abroad to polish the golfing skills he had acquired without training or facilities. In 1959 and again in 1960 he won the Dutch Open and was finally allowed, against strong opposition, to play in the otherwise all-white Natal Open in 1963.[20] South African Radio was so shocked by the decision that broadcasts of the event were cancelled. Sewgolum won, defeating 103 white contestants, but was unable to receive his trophy in the Royal Golf Club in Durban because the laws of apartheid made it illegal for an Indian to enter the building (except as a servant). Plans had been made to hold the ceremony out of doors, but since it was raining, the white officials and players trooped inside for shelter and the cup was handed out to the champion through a window! Papwa Sewgolum won the Durban Open the following year as well — and was then refused the right to take part in competitions involving white golfers. He returned to the impoverished life of a black golf coach.[21]

Since 1971, like other major sports, golf has adapted to international and commercial pressures. In 1979 the organizers had to raise a million rand to maintain the status of the South African Open and pay the winners the 100,000 rand in prize money they expected. Golf receives a great deal of commercial sponsorship, and its 'stars' travel the world as tirelessly as tennis players, their fame and fortune illuminating South Africa's name abroad. Millionaire Gary Player did not hesitate to hire a helicopter in order to make the start of the South African Open in 1979.[22]

A handful of black professionals ply their trade in this plutocratic rat-race: four or five participate regularly in international tournaments, and Vincent Tshabalala won the French Open in 1976. But the vast majority of would-be golfers have no opportunity and no place to play, and their only hope at the moment lies in the first national non-racial golf organization, SANRAGA, created in 1979 and now representing the majority of black amateur golfers.[23]

Swimming

If one sport represents for white South Africans the quintessence of leisure, it is clearly swimming. In the sea, in farm dams, in numerous private and public pools, wherever there is water, South Africans swim — at all times of day, but not in any company! We have seen how Bob Watson compared South Africa to California, and spoke of swimming as second nature. More than tennis for the young or golf for the ageing, swimming is omnipresent, cheap, adapted to the climate, a physical pleasure, non-technical. It permeates this culture surfeited with leisure, and one might have expected it to be as accessible to Blacks as Whites.

Yet, at the heart of white social life swimming is subject more than any other leisure activity to a pitiless, indeed pathological segregation. For unlike tennis or golf, swimmers are in indirect physical contact with each other, through the medium of water; far from separating swimmers of different races (or sex) water dissolves the physical barriers between them. Innumerable stories describe the 'pollution' which white South Africans fear will result from mixed bathing, and the outrage they feel when it occurs. Bob Watson recalls being thrown out of an acquaintance's house when he bathed in the sea with an African friend. 'Many people,' Sadie Berman remarks, 'wouldn't have minded if the children were playing cricket on the lawn and the black servant batted — but those same people would find it totally offensive to have allowed that same Black to have used their swimming pool. It's got something to do with the water and that somehow they're not clean — I am sure it's not even a conscious thing — but it would have been totally unacceptable to normally kindly people who were not politically conscious and who accepted the order as natural.'[24]

The 'Japanese Affair' offers as grotesque an illustration of the complexities of South African double-think as one is likely to find. In 1961, a Japanese trade delegation visited South Africa to negotiate several important contracts and for this purpose they were declared by the Nationalist Government to have honorary 'white status'. However, a Japanese swimming team followed in the delegation's wake. These swimmers were denied access to Pretoria's Olympic pool by the City Council which refused to extend white rights to 'white' Japanese swimmers. A quite serious political incident blew up, and Prime Minister Verwoerd was obliged to express his disapproval of the Council's decision before the visitors could take to the water again.[25]

Very little progress has occurred since then in a sport which remains as amateur as rugby, and relatively uncommercialized. In 1979, for example, the management of Balkumar Singh Baths in Asherville (Durban) — a pool reserved for Indians — barred the wife of an Indian swimmer on the grounds that she was 'Coloured', though her children 'looked' Indian. The Indian Advisory Council (an official body without power) contested this decision and called vainly upon Durban City Council to open the pool to all who wanted to swim there, as the local population desired.

In the same year, Johannesburg City Council refused to open a new sports complex to swimmers of all races, as a black swimming association, supported by the Progressive Federal Party (P.F.P.) had demanded. Embarrassed by adverse publicity, the Government intervened to persuade the Council to change its mind, and another pool, at Ellis Park, was subsequently opened . . . on four days a week, for two hours a day, between 7p.m. and 9p.m. to *'proven'* swimmers! Opposition parties — the P.F.P. and the N.R.P. — had a majority on the Johannesburg Council.

This unbending segregation underlines the flagrant disparities between the facilities available to white and black swimmers. While the white population has access to very large numbers of public as well as private pools, and the advantages of a solid organizational structure which promotes adult and school swimming,[26] black swimmers have virtually no opportunity to swim for pleasure, let alone reach competitive standards in a sport which requires specialized and above all consistent training. The officially recognized racial associations claim only 1,500 African swimmers (in 14 clubs, with access to 28 pools) and 2,000 Coloured swimmers (in 26 clubs, with access to 24 pools) and no official statistics are even available of the number of officially recognized Indian swimmers.[27]

The non-racial swimming body, the S.A. Amateur Swimming Federation (SAASwiF), is one of the most energetic and expansive organizations in the non-racial movement, however, and claims a membership of 7,000, of which the vast majority are black, even though their members are barred from most official public pools. If the spread of non-racial swimming has undoubtedly been hampered by this discrimination, the wit and invention of the swimmers themselves have not:

What sort of facilities did we have when we started the club? There was a pool — a bat-shaped pool, specially built with a large area of shallow water and a very small deep area. That pool was built in 1962. Then in 1963 they built the pool in Guguletu. Now there is one pool in Langa and there are two in Guguletu.

We had difficulties because it was a Council pool and, when it leaked out that we were swimming with Coloureds, they clamped down on some of our privileges. The Council had allowed us to use their van to go to matches for example, well, they stopped that.

Most of the early members were children. Many Africans simply don't know swimming as a sport as such. I had to go to the parents and say to them that their son was a good swimmer — but the children liked it from the beginning.

Some funny things happened. Once, when we went to Durban . . . they held a reception for us at the Admiral Hotel. The mayor was there to meet us and we were introduced to him and then he says: 'But these look like Blacks [i.e. Africans] !' And we said, 'No, no, they're not Blacks but Cape Coloured!' (laughter) You see it was illegal and thought to be immoral to allow Africans into hotels, so we used to change our names and give ourselves Indian names, for example.[28]

The situation on the beaches is no better. Racial zoning of the coastline and segregation of beaches was imposed from 1966. It goes without saying that the best and most beautiful stretches have been reserved for white use, whilst those furthest away, least attractive and, above all, most dangerous have been set aside for the black majority. A weekend expedition to the beach for a black family in Cape Town is no mean affair:

The bus that takes you to Nandi beach, well, it's a 40 minute ride before you get there, it goes from stop to stop and never gathers speed, and goes from the townships starting at Langa and going through Guguletu and then on to Nyanga and then . . . . Well you can imagine, you're packed solid like sardines. There's one bus an hour.

On big holidays most people don't go because it gets too congested and you only get friction there — you can hardly swim, you can hardly stand!

Nandi beach is also very dangerous. There are surf lifesavers on all the white beaches but where the Blacks swim — which is in much more dangerous places — there's nothing. A lot of people are drowned.

When I was at home in 1978, people were being allowed to go to those white beaches again.[29] On Boxing Day, people went with their picnic baskets because everyone in Cape Town and South Africa on Boxing Day packs all the food left over from Christmas into a hamper and goes down to the beach. Well, I saw them all chased away by the police. The police are always there, everywhere.[30]

The President of the European Athletics Federation, Arthur Gold, who was a member of the British Sports Council's fact-finding delegation to South Africa in February 1980, came across similar attitudes. Walking on the beach with a school friend now teaching at Cape Town University, he stopped to watch some black women dancing.

> It was a quiet civilized little party, disturbing nobody, when suddenly this aggressive young security guard arrived, snatched a bottle away from one of the women and threw it on some rocks where it smashed. As he chased the women away, I clearly saw him punch one of them in the face. Quite involuntarily I said loud enough for him to hear, 'now, that was unnecessary.' He came up to me and shouted angrily, 'I will lock you up too; you British don't even know how to deal with your strikers.'[31]

The gap between Black and White in competitive swimming yawns ever wider. When South Africa was excluded from international competition and from the Olympic Games in the 1960s, her swimmers — Karen Muir, A. Fairlie, L. McGregor — were among the best in the world. But whereas in weight-lifting, boxing, tennis, cricket, golf, athletics, football and other sports, outstanding black athletes have been able to fight successfully for recognition, no black swimmer from South Africa has ever excelled at national or international level. This is a measure of the degree of deprivation they suffer.

On the other hand, according to the white swimming union, international isolation is seriously damaging the quality of white competitive swimming, which is an amateur and far less commercial sport than most of the other major games. In 1979 the white association was in such a state that the South African Government was persuaded to fund a campaign to raise enthusiasm for competitive swimming throughout the country.[32]

Social Sports and 'Multi-Nationalism'

After a boom period in the 1960s when sport became widely popular and subsequently acquired an even bigger mass following in the 1970s, white sports associations passed through a period of self-doubt and financial crisis, under the impact of the international boycott. One partially successful strategy has been to stimulate professional and spectator sports and exploit commercial sponsorship on a large scale. It is at this level that a certain amount of racial mixing has been allowed to occur between 1971 and 1976, under the approving eye of the Government which introduced after 1971 a new 'multi-national' sports policy designed to make South African sport acceptable to world opinion without becoming truly non-racial.

Below the level of professional and top-class competitive sport, little change has taken place. Wherever sport is played socially and for recreation, and particularly in schools and sports clubs, segregation is still generally and legally enforced: none of the major laws governing racial mixing which affect sport have been repealed. Tennis, golf, cricket and rugby clubs remain pivots of social life for white South Africans, the places where they meet and relax, and where their racial and cultural values are articulated and confirmed. And this is precisely why the introduction of truly non-racial sport is so problematic, for it would carry non-racial relationships into the family and into the core of white South Africans' human contacts.

Commercialization of sport is beginning to change the place sport occupies in society in certain crucial ways, however, although the process is very recent and the transformations it is bringing about are still barely discernable. Until as late as the 1950s South Africa was a country in which, for both urban and country people, sport was the major form of recreation. The advent of television (1975), commercial sponsorship and the 'professional star' have turned increasing numbers of South Africans into spectators — as preoccupied as ever by their games, perhaps, but essentially passive observers of high quality performances achieved by exceptional athletes. This process has already been registered as alarming in political circles, conscious not only of being guardians of the nation's health and of its 'pioneer' trekker tradition but also responsible for the military defence of a society whose principal enemy is bound finally to be its own, black, population. White South Africa requires a fit white male population.

To reverse the trend and stimulate popular, non-competitive sport and physical health programmes, the Government has promoted 'Run for Your Life', 'Swim for Your Life', 'Walk for Your Life' campaigns, and Trim Parks, etc., with some success for a cross-section of the urban population. They have not, however, removed the essential contradiction of official policy, as practised by the Government and the white sports establishment. Trapped by a sports issue which is of marginal political significance but which has refused to go away, these bodies continue to support policies whose effects ultimately give further ammunition to domestic and international protest. They encourage highly commercial, professional sport, which is financially profitable and resistant to international isolation, and technical, minority sports which virtually no black South Africans can afford to play. But these policies can only further erode the white amateur sporting tradition while widening the gap between white and black sportsmen. It is too early to judge how far the process will be taken, or what its effects will be, but they will certainly be felt within South Africa, by sportsmen and women of all races, and by those outside who are campaigning for or against the international boycott.

References

1. A.F. Hattersley, 1938, pp. 95-6.
2. E. Rosenthal, 1973, p. 529.
3. A.W. Wells, 1939 (1949), p. 373.

4. In recent years, about 15 players have travelled abroad every year to play professionally.
5. 'Until I came to England I had never seen a football match. There was no television and the grounds were much smaller — in no way could you have 20,000 spectators, let alone 70,000. In the newsreels there were a lot of shots of the rugby matches . . . and horse-racing and motor-bike racing, but I can't remember football. Of course I am talking about the economic group in which I lived and the area in which I lived.' Sadie Berman, interview, London, 15 February 1980.
6. P.B. Singh, interview, London, 22 April 1980. Mr Singh played in and helped lead both tours. He was instrumental in organizing the All India Football Association and for many years remained a football and tennis official in South Africa.
7. See Chapter 5.
8. For the repression of the non-racial footballers, see Chapter 8. From 1960 to 1975 the FASA's N.F.L. controlled the best and largest grounds and therefore kept the best gates: spectator turnover rose from 500,000 in 1960 (the first year) to a peak of 1,500,000 in 1976, before being bankrupted. This crisis (1976-79) is described in Chapter 11.
9. M. Robertson, 1974, p. 318.
10. C.L. Winslow won the Olympic Men's Singles in that year and, with H.A. Kitson, the Men's Doubles, at Stockholm.
11. M. Robertson, 1974, p. 319.
12. See Chapter 8.
13. See Chapter 11.
14. Sadie Berman, interview, London, 15 February 1980. She adds: 'There was aristocracy among Afrikaners, by the way. It was not a blood aristocracy so much as an aristocracy that started because you were an early governor of the Cape or because your great great grandfather was a leader of one of the Boer treks . . . or first President of the Orange Free State.'
15. Professionals also played the flattering role of hired technical advisers.
16. E. Hellmann, 1940, pp. 11, 115-6, 117.
17. At 44, Gary Player, champion of golf and the South African way of life, is a keen disciple of this approach. 'The young man has energy and strength,' he wrote in the *Sunday Times* of 13 January 1980, 'but envies the experience of the man of 50; while the man of 50 envies the young man his energy and strength. But the older man has a much better chance of holding on to his strength than the younger man has of acquiring self-discipline, maturity and experience. It is if you like *easier* for the older man — if he can view the matter in this positive way. Really golf is only reflecting life itself.'
18. See Chapter 7.
19. 'Golf clubs have been formed by Native caddies and ex-caddies living on several locations [around Johannesburg] . . . . Tracts of land have been roughly prepared as golf courses. Remarkable records are made on these bumpy grounds . . . . Annual championships are held, that in 1937 being held over the Stirtonville course at Boksburg. There were 32 entries.' Phillips, 1937, p. 309.

20. He had been prevented from playing in 1961 and 1962.
21. In January 1966, when Papwa Sewgolum played Gary Player in the Professional Players Golf Championship, 'Government officials took a personal hand in trying to segregate crowds who watched Papwa and Gary Player . . . . Following Papwa and Player were two inspectors of the Department of Community Development – sent to make sure that Indian and Coloured spectators remained separate from whites.' (*Rand Daily Mail*, 7 January 1966.) Even when the ban was relaxed, segregation was not.
22. *Star*, 26 May 1979.
23. South African Non-Racial Golf Association. See below Chapter 11.
24. Sadie Berman, interview, London, 15 February 1980.
25. Peter Hain, 1971, p. 41; R. Lapchick, 1975, pp. 41-2.
26. The S.A. Amateur Swimming Union (white) claims 14,000 adult and some 20,000 school swimmers, organized in twelve regional unions, each of which organizes its own galas and annual competition. The SAASU is only concerned with competitive swimming; the number of social swimmers is far greater.
27. The most that can be concluded from the *1977 Year Book* is that Indian swimmers have access to 6 pools. There is reason to believe that these figures, and those for the other racial federations, should be treated with some caution.
28. Interview, London, 12 February 1980 with an African from Cape Town.
29. The reference is to beaches like parts of Muizenberg which used to be reserved for Africans or Coloureds but which were occupied by Whites because they presented several advantages.
30. Interview with an African woman, London, 12 February 1980.
31. *The Times*, 18 February 1980.
32. See Chapter 11.

5. Charity and Neglect: Black Sport, 1900-50

We saw in the first chapter that, apart from hunting, horse-racing and cricket, modern sports arrived and spread in South Africa during three major periods: in the last two decades of the 19th Century (which saw the introduction of most of the major sports); between the wars, and particularly during the 1930s; and then in the 1960s, which saw a consumer boom and the spread of a number of highly technical and minority sports.

As one might expect, black sport evolved in much the same way but with a slight time lag, and with the exception of those minor or technical sports which require resources black people do not have — such as yachting, motor racing, power-boat racing, skiing and all the aerial sports. Certain sports, notably shooting, were also forbidden to the vast majority of black people.

Coloured sportsmen were pre-eminent from the 1880s until the 1940s. Feeling closest to the Whites in lifestyle and values, they soon provided themselves with sporting competitions and organizations, so that among black sporting associations during the first decades of the 20th Century theirs were superior in range and quality in all sports except football. Football had already become a mass sport among the Indians and Africans, whereas it was relatively neglected by the Coloured population in favour of rugby.

As for the earlier period, the available sources are unfortunately too rare and too vague to give an accurate picture of physical recreation before colonization or before the advent of organized popular sport in the 1860s. All we can say with certainty is that horse-racing was popular among the Coloured community, and that cricket was the major popular sport until it was overtaken by rugby and by football.

By the 1930s, most of the major sports — football, rugby, cricket, tennis, athletics, golf, boxing, weight-lifting, cycling, gymnastics — had taken root in one or more of the black communities and sport in general had filtered down from the elite into the townships where in Kimberley, Port Elizabeth, Cape Town, Johannesburg, Durban and East London, it was becoming an activity central to social life.

Black sport took a further leap forward during the 1950s and 1960s, when black sports associations decided to unify and seek recognition nationally and internationally on the basis of their non-racial principles. This process occurred at the same time as Afrikaners, profiting from their new power and confidence, began adopting sports previously played by the English, while white sport itself became more commercialized and professional. In establishing the non-racial movement, black sportsmen were effectively responding to specific sporting pressures and injustices and to the imposition of apartheid.

In this and the following chapter we shall outline the principal influences on black sport during the inter-war years and try to portray the sharp flavour of social life during this period of intense activity and experiment marked by the Afrikaner revival and the Nationalist victory of 1948. A word should first be said, however, about the traditional African sports or games which existed in pre-colonial times and which have come down to us in distorted or folklore form. The rich tradition of tribal dancing, practised extensively on the mining compounds from the end of the 19th Century, provides the best known example; or *amalaita*, a form of stick fighting promoted in Johannesburg and elsewhere (see below pp. 125-6). Unfortunately, it is difficult to know in detail the original 'sports' from which these forms are descended, or define their role and place within the social systems which created them. They have either been deformed for social or political reasons, or their original meaning has been transformed by the ethos of modern sport.

That sport-like activities existed in pre-colonial South Africa, however, there can be no doubt. A wrestling tradition is found all over Southern Africa and competitions still take place between the champions of different villages, who wrestle to throw one another to the ground according to certain rules of combat. The winner declares the subsequent feast open, and the losers provide the food![1] To prove and harden their young men, the Zulus apparently organized races rather similar to modern orienteering, in which competitors had to cover the distance between two points as best they could in the fastest possible time.[2] Other sport-like activities were also practised by the Zulu people as part of military training: javelin throwing, *amalaita*, dance, etc. The Basuto riding skills should also be mentioned.

Children's games are relevant, too, if sport is defined as a peaceful physical activity practised according to certain rules and in a spirit of competition. One African woman[3] described how they had been played by her mother and probably by generations of children before her. In addition to knuckle-bones (*madlopa*), forms of hopscotch and other universal games, the children played a sort of wide-game, between teams of boys and girls who had to defend their territory and capture flowers and other property from the other side without being caught. Another game required competitors to jump as far as they could from a fixed point on the branch of a tree, while a third, played on riverbanks, was even more adventurous, for the child held onto a supple tree which his or her friends bent to the ground and released, flinging the child far out into the water! In a letter written from Genadendaal mission school in January 1862, Lady Duff Gordon describes the skills shown by African boys in a traditional stone game:

> On Monday I saw all the schools, and then looked at the great strong Caffre lads playing in the square. One of them stood to be pelted by

five or six others, and as the stones came he twisted and turned and jumped, and was hardly ever hit, and when he was he didn't care, though the others hurled like catapults. It was the most wonderful display of activity and grace, and quite incredible that such a huge fellow should be so quick and light . . .[4]

A tradition of physical skill and agility was undoubtedly in existence when the British started playing games in South Africa. No doubt it contributed to the rapidity with which the black populations assimilated and adopted European sports.

Sport and the Elite

The earliest identifiable African communities to adopt sport and other European cultural activities were almost certainly the *Mfengu* — a name given to the first groups of Africans converted to Christianity, who became literate and settled around the mission centres, usually as traders. In the second half of the 19th Century they spread throughout South Africa and for a time monopolized the clerical and subordinate jobs which became available as Britain extended its colonial control.[5] It is therefore in the British administrative and commercial towns that we find the first references to black sport — naturally enough, for it was the British soldiers, settlers and officials living in these towns and educating their children in them, who introduced sport into the country. By the late 1880s, sport was no longer an occasional activity, but was in the process of becoming organized and in certain places had already become institutionalized, both among the African petty bourgeoisie and the Coloured community. Brian Willan describes the role sport played in Kimberley:

The values and ideas which they [the African elite] held in common — whether these were notions of loyalty to the British Empire, or the desirability of 'progress', 'education', or regular church attendance — were shaped, sustained, and disseminated, not in a fitful, haphazard manner, but through a network of regular activities and involvement in churches, clubs and societies. It was the existence and functioning of these that created a sense of class and community out of the cosmopolitan group of education Africans who lived on the diamond fields. And it constituted, too, the most important mechanism for the socialization and incorporation of new members . . . .

Sport, too was important in the life of Kimberley's African petty bourgeoisie, providing — in addition to exercise and enjoyment — a further bond of association and the means of disseminating the hegemonic values of the society in which they lived.[6]

The vigour of Kimberley social and cultural life was remarkable; it is also noteworthy that at this early period, when segregation had not yet acquired the force of law, the Coloured and African elites organized themselves on multi-racial (if not non-racial) lines. African clubs played with Coloured clubs and affiliated to the national organizations for rugby (1896) and cricket (1902), which Coloured sportsmen had created. In contrast, although regional football associations were solidly implanted by the First World War, notably in Natal, no national association was created before the 1920s and the first national African body did not appear until the early 1930s, when nationalism and segregation were leading to the formation of separate African associations for rugby (1928) and cricket (1932).

In 1915, when Fort Hare was founded to provide further education for the most gifted graduates from the mission colleges, one of the first acts of the new students (according to the college's official historian) was, without prompting from the staff, to lay out football and cricket pitches under the direction of one of their number, Hamilton M.J. Masiza.[7] Proof indeed of the extraordinary influence exercised by the public school ethos, which produced 'gentlemen' on an almost industrial scale throughout the British Empire. The physics master responsible for sport between 1935 and 1950, Mr Davidson, considered that the annual inter-college athletics competition 'for years produced the best athletics performances among Africans in the country' and that in football 'play was of a high standard . . . in the June-July holiday, touring football teams have held their own with the best teams on the Rand'.[8] Conscious that they were training the elite of a people reduced to the status of servants, the college staff attached far more importance to academic standards than to sport: 'Sport has never been overdone,' wrote the official biographer again. 'Studies took first place and no one came to college just for sport.'[9] Nevertheless, the Fort Hare graduates were trained to be leaders, a Christian and intellectual elite for whom accomplishment in sport was a component of Western civilization.

It was this elite that was to mediate between the Europeans and the mass of Africans between the wars, and as a result it is not surprising to find that a large number of the African personalities included in Mweli Skota's *African Yearly Register* (1932) mention sport among their principal leisure activities. In doing so, they also give us an idea of the status of different sports at this date.

The presence of cricket and tennis at the top of the list in Table 3, both sports which are more costly to play and take longer to learn than either rugby or football, supports the view that the elite already followed white settler society in ascribing class attributes to sporting activity. The surprisingly marked preference for cricket is a clear sign of this, for as we have seen, cricket was explicitly a 'gentleman's game', with gentlemanly values. In addition, several sports traditionally associated with the European aristocracy (riding, shooting, horse-racing and motoring) were apparently practised exclusively by a small minority of 'tribal chiefs'.

Interestingly, however, the association of sport with social accomplishment or status was apparently also reversible, for a handful of Mweli Skota's

Table 3
African Personalities and Their Sporting Interests (1932)

Sport	Number of times mentioned	Proportion of all people who play sport	Women
'Sportsmen' (no details)	10		2
Cricketers	22	44.5%	
Tennis players	15	30.0%	
Footballers (rugby & soccer)	11	22.4%	
Athletics	1		
Riding	3*		
Shooting	1*		
Horse-racing	1*		
Motoring	1*		
Total number of entries mentioning sport as a leisure interest	49	100.0%	2
Total number of sports mentioned	65		

* Sports played exclusively by royal families or the families of tribal chiefs.

Source: Mweli Skota, 1932.

celebrities appear to have been selected *because* of their sporting accomplishments. M.Z. Jumani, for instance, was a baker: born in 1884, he is described as 'one of the best batsmen of the Eccentric Cricket Club and captain of the same club on several occasions. Is now playing for the Duke of Wellington Club.' Mr F. Ntshoko, a shoemaker from Kimberley who became a Crown Mine clerk, is likewise described as 'one of the best batsmen of the Africans in the Union of South Africa. He played with much success in many tournaments.'[10]

By the First World War, however, football, which had been relatively ignored by the elite, was becoming a mass game. Indian indentured labourers seem to have been the first to have played it in any organized way, in the 1890s, even before they set up associations for cycling, boxing, cricket, tennis, table tennis, swimming and athletics in the early part of the new century.[11] As we saw earlier, an Indian football team toured India in 1921 and hosted an Indian tour of South Africa in 1933.[12] Africans in Natal had also begun playing football before 1900, encouraged by the American Board missionaries. In 1916, the Durban and District Native Football Association[13] was founded, and during the 1920s it campaigned for a national football body and promoted the development in Natal of tennis, cricket and boxing.[14] It

116

continued to grow until, at its peak in 1959, the Durban and District African
F.A. administered 5,000 players in 256 clubs.

Although football came later to the Witwatersrand, it is in the Transvaal
and Johannesburg in the 1930s that we can see how soccer invaded the
African working class. In 1932, the Johannesburg Bantu Football Association,
with 33 clubs, was already the largest organizing body.[15] It administered as
many clubs as the Transvaal Rugby Football Association (seven clubs), the
Native Recruiting Corporation Cricket Union (13 clubs) and the African
Tennis Association (13 clubs) combined. Only five years later, in 1937, the
same body was apparently administering no less than 153 adult teams plus
282 junior teams; and a rival association, the Johannesburg African Football
Association, an additional 86 clubs.[16]

As for Whites, soccer was a working-class game. Non-technical, relatively
cheap to play, a team sport without any of the exclusive elitist associations
of rugby, it was the natural choice for the mass of African workers who
flooded into the Rand between the end of the 19th Century and the 1920s.
Observed by missionaries, social workers and mine officials whose job it was
to interest themselves in African social life, black football burgeoned in the
ghettoes. It was largely ignored by white society (and by much of the black
elite) until it emerged at the beginning of the 1950s as one of the most
organized and ambitious, and certainly the largest, black sports associations.

In the Cape, which had a different and more ancient sporting tradition,
rugby fulfilled a comparable role for both the Coloured population and the
Africans of the Eastern Province and Border. Rugby, too, was a relatively
cheap, non-technical team sport, accessible to the majority of the population:
the extraordinarily high membership attributed by researchers to rugby clubs
in the Cape and in East London in the 1950s (and today) suggests that Blacks
took it up every bit as enthusiastically as football in other parts of the
country.[17]

Other sports, which were technical, or more expensive, which took longer
to learn or had exclusive class associations, developed unevenly and far more
slowly between 1920 and the 1940s. After the War, as the application of
apartheid reduced the living standards of black sportsmen and women and
their access to leisure time and facilities, new and technical sports (hang-
gliding, water-skiing, etc.) became virtually inaccessible.

The appearance and evolution of modern sport is intimately associated
with urbanization, literacy and the emergence of an industrial culture, and
both black and white sport in South Africa conforms to this rule. With the
major exception of football, sports were first assimilated by a relatively
prosperous minority of urban dwellers, educated and comparatively leisured,
open to Western culture and in contact with colonial society. For this minority, the elitist cultural values attached by Europeans to sport were not found
offensive; on the contrary, sport expressed the values of a novel and attractive
way of life, which (until the 1940s) held out hopes of assimilation and progress. Though it bore an ethic, sport could still claim to be a 'politically
neutral' institution: during the inter-war period it was used to *divert* political

tension, before black sportsmen and women began in the 1950s to use it as a weapon in their struggle for recognition and justice.

Sport under Liberal Influence

Black sport and social life in the townships was neglected by the white community until its power to influence black attitudes was recognized at the end of the First World War, with the first signs of urban unrest. The spread of vast mining camps and compounds, and the mushrooming slums in the townships of the Rand caused the authorities serious disquiet, turning to actual alarm during the recession of 1918-22, when not only the black but the white working class threatened government authority. Leisure activities of all kinds seemed to offer an admirable way of defusing and channelling the political pressure which was beginning to make itself felt.[18]

The conditions of life in the mine compounds and slums were also unacceptable to a current of liberal white opinion. Up to 2,000 miners were crowded into each compound[19] while the slums seethed with an unemployed, uneducated and rightless sub-proletariat. The meteoric rise of the radical Industrial and Commercial Workers Union (I.C.U.) in the 1920s[20] seemed to provide the clearest warning that political aspirations and poverty were combining to create an explosive situation.

Liberals, therefore, put their minds to creating channels of communication between the black elite and white opinion, to improving racial understanding and making the lives of the mass of Africans more tolerable. Departments of Bantu Studies and Social Anthropology were opened in the major universities. In 1920 the Chamber of Mines launched a new black newspaper *Umteleli Wa Bantu* to counteract the political success of the A.N.C. Inter-racial discussion groups (Gamma-Sigma clubs) were organized by American Board missionaries from 1918 to bring literate Blacks into civilized contact with white ideas.

In particular, in the early 1920s, a number of influential liberal personalities in Johannesburg, led by Professor Rheinallt-Jones, set up the Joint Councils Movement, an association which attached great importance to the advancement of cultural and leisure activities among Blacks and which was to influence the character of black sport among the elite during the inter-war years.

The Johannesburg Joint Council was the first to be created, in 1921, and it remained by far the most important. Ten years later there were 26 and by 1935 40 councils were distributed throughout the country. Each was composed of an equal number of Africans, or Coloureds, or Indians, on the one hand, and of Europeans on the other, and their aims were 'to promote co-operation between Europeans and Natives in South Africa', 'to investigate and report on matters relating to the welfare of the Native peoples', 'to make representation on behalf of Natives and to the relevant public bodies, to publish such investigations as thought desirable and to enlighten the[white] public on native questions.'[21]

Some idea of the Movement's political complexion and backing may be gauged from the list of the 18 European members who founded the Johannesburg Joint Council: they included 'academics, lawyers, priests and missionaries ... directors of a mining company and of an insurance company, the former chairman of the Stock Exchange, chairman of the Chamber of Commerce, the manager of the Native Recruiting Corporation and the President of the Typographical Union'.[22] It was planned to invite, to represent African opinion, five members of the Transvaal Native Congress, three representatives of the Mine Clerks Association, two members of the Native Teachers Association, three from the Native Ministers Association and five others; it is suggestive of the hesitancy of the black response to the initiative that the Transvaal Native Congress finally declined to take part.[23]

The principal aim of the Movement's European leaders was to raise the level of African cultural life and thereby attach the mass of African workers, via the elite, to the values of European civilization. Improvement was perceived in essentially *moral* rather than political or economic terms: the aim according to Rheinallt-Jones was 'the cleansing of the moral and public opinion',[24] while the missionary Ray Phillips sought, in his own words, 'to devise a social gospel' which would resolve 'the whole great problem of moralizing the leisure time of Natives in city and country alike.'[25] Their gospel was therefore non-political; but their readiness to intervene in social affairs and recruit among the African elite necessarily had political effects. Critics argue that the Joint Councils tended to fudge whatever consensus existed in African political circles on combined opposition to white racial policies, at a time when many of the basic rights of the black population were being removed by legislation.

The Joint Councils gave birth, in Johannesburg, to a series of organizations, among which the most important were the South African Institute of Race Relations — the research and publications wing of the organization — and two institutions which are of particular interest to us: the Bantu Men's Social Centre, built in Eloff Street in the heart of Johannesburg (1924) became the headquarters of the Movement and housed the J.H. Hofmeyr School of Social Work; and the Bantu Sports Club, built on a dozen acres of wasteland donated by a mining company in 1925, which opened in 1932. We shall see below that the Joint Councils, through Professor Rheinallt-Jones and his wife, also promoted youth activities and an African Scouts and Guides movement.

Responsibility for the promotion of sport was largely confined to the American Board missionaries, who believed that physical exercise had a particularly salutary moral effect, as can be seen in the Reverend Dexter Taylor's speech to the National European-Bantu Conference (Joint Councils) in 1929:

> As a missionary, perhaps one may be permitted in this company to indulge in a little sense of gratification that it was the missionary who first recognized the necessity for recreational activities for Natives as

119

part of a thorough redemptive programme . . . from the point of view
of what was good for the Natives and not what was good for the Church
. . . . The Church and community ought to interest itself in the play life
of the Native, not in order to induce him to be willing to be saved but
as an agency itself in large measure a saving force . . . .

Proper and adequate provision for Native recreation would mean
better workers, keener mentally and physically, better citizens less
likely to be criminals, better neighbours, less likely to be anti-white,
more likely to possess a true sense of community values . . . .

There are obvious dangers in the over-emphasis on sport by Native
youths and obvious advantages in maintaining the closest relationship
between the play life of the Native and the religious, educational and
community efforts for his betterment . . . .

The most important element in the extension of the saving influence
of recreation is the provision of the necessary *leadership*. A trained,
enthusiastic and wise director of social activities is worth more than
any provision of plant or equipment.[26]

Emphasis was given to forming leaders rather than providing material equipment or facilities — although it remains difficult to see how African workers,
however well led, could play sport without either balls or pitches. Ray
Phillips' experiments in the early 1920s perhaps supply part of the answer.
In the face of initial official resistance, he had pioneered the introduction of
pastimes into the mining compounds, and, in a lyrical passage in one of his
books, he describes how his approaches were received by the workers. Initially
he had planned to set up volleyball, football and athletics matches but he
found that, having finished their shift and eaten a heavy meal, the men were
too lethargic. Attempts to introduce tiddly winks and board games met with
an equally lukewarm response. But when he took in a film show, he received
a rapturous welcome — from both miners and mine owners,[27] and 'bioscopes'
rapidly became an institution and occasionally (according to Phillips himself)
a political sedative.[28]

The Bantu Men's Social Centre created a forum where members of the
racial elites were able to meet informally. The same emphasis was placed
upon forming and influencing leaders, who would be able to mediate between
European opinion and the mass of African workers. The Centre had an African
director, a library, a conference room capable of seating 1,000 people, 'advanced night school classes, a study club, a literary society, tennis and football
tournaments, concerts, lectures'.[29] Members were nominated (there were 584
in 1936) and as a result were 'mainly of the educated type of native'.[30] The
Centre's club-like exclusiveness naturally influenced its public image, and
Phillips himself ingenuously admits that the Centre was 'looked on by the
masses as a "high hat" club of the White Man's "Good Boys".'[31] As so often,
the popular comment was acidly exact, and a necessary supplement to other,
sympathetic, descriptions: 'There is in Johannesburg,' Hellmann wrote on the
eve of the Nationalists' electoral victory, 'a Bantu Men's Social Centre where

any mention of tribal loyalties is deprecated and where English as a language medium is assiduously fostered in the belief that a common language will help to merge natives of different tribes, each with its different language, into a Bantu Nation.'[32] The Centre certainly was a welcome refuge for men who, it must be remembered, were subjected every day of their lives to petty and grave racial humiliation. Peter Abrahams' description of his first visit to the Centre breathes a sense of human relief and speaks volumes for the absence of cultural amenities elsewhere: 'It was a long room, spacious, and with big windows that let in light. At one end was a billiard table. Two men, in short sleeves, played. At the other end were shelves filled with books. Comfortable settees were ranged about the room. Men sat reading or talking. Others watched the game. They all spoke English here.'[33]

The Centre's formal sporting activities were limited by space, but 'its tennis section . . . counts well over a hundred members' and 'there is a modern gymnasium [where] a variety of indoor games are played, such as badminton, basketball, volleyball, skittles and box-hockey. Table tennis and billiards are also popular. Classes in boxing and physical training are held every evening.'[34]

The major team sports were played from 1932 at the Bantu Sports Club, which was equipped with two football pitches, several tennis courts and a stand which held 2,000 people (and served for meetings as well as matches). With the aim of furthering social relations, occasional contests were organized between African and European sportsmen. Mixed tennis matches were played at the opening of the Bantu Sports Club, and 15,000 spectators watched a cricket match between a European and an African side on the same occasion. Europeans were also invited to the Bantu Men's Social Centre or Bantu Sports Club to coach: the white referees' association agreed to train some African football referees, for example, and, in agreement with the Bantu Sports Club, the Transvaal Boxing Association staged a number of competitions for black boxers.[35]

There is no doubt, however, that inter-racial contacts were essentially informal and irregular, and always inspired, as far as Europeans were concerned, by a moralizing paternalism. 'With a little encouragement,' wrote Phillips in 1936, 'the cordial relationships which have developed in the field of sport will, undoubtedly, continue, and will act as a positive factor in shaping the attitude of the hundreds of Africans who are finding an outlet for their energies on the Witwatersrand playing fields.'[36]

The ambivalence of European attitudes is revealed clearly by an incident which occurred in 1926, when G.H. Dodd, who had been South African tennis champion in 1912, played several matches at the Bantu Men's Social Centre against African tennis players, including the Centre's director, M.R. Senaone.[37] As in a similar incident involving a rugby match between African and European delegates at a Christian students' conference several years later,[38] the event excited adverse criticism in the press. Significantly, the (white) S.A. Tennis Association at once 'placed the responsibility entirely on Mr Dodd's shoulders' while Dodd himself effectively disowned his own behaviour by arguing that he regarded 'his actions as an exhibition, merely, and as having no inter-racial significance whatever'.[39]

Contacts were therefore one-way, and there was never any question (for the Europeans at least) of establishing relations of equality. Indeed there were occasions on which the liberal attitude was almost a parody of itself. With his customary lack of guile, Phillips describes a workers' outing arranged by the *Star* newspaper for its employees and their families (290 people in all). 'Refreshments were provided on arrival,' he writes. 'Then a programme of athletic sports for all, after which lunch is served by a caterer. An orchestra plays during the afternoon while couples dance on a tarpaulin . . . or there is swimming in the dam. A trophy is presented to the winning tug-of-war team . . . . A dozen European ladies and gentlemen were hosts and hostesses.'[40] The whole scene, with its reversal of roles as European masters serve their servants and employees, captures marvellously the spirit of condescension marking European relations with their African 'partners' within the Joint Councils. And it must be remembered that this is an attitude not towards the mass of uneducated and impoverished African workers but towards the educated African elite.

Nevertheless, the Joint Councils and liberal circles did succeed in raising the issue of black sport and recreation and the Government was asked to formulate policies for the development of sport and the provision of adequate sporting and recreational facilities for the black population. The 1929 European-Bantu Conference convened by the Joint Councils resolved, for example:

> **Recreational Activities:**
> (1) This Conference urges upon municipal authorities, large employers of Native labour, Missionary Societies and Native Welfare Associations, the provision of recreational facilities for Natives in the following ways:
> (a) Athletic fields and Children's playgrounds, equipped and directed;
> (b) Paid directors of Recreational facilities;
> (c) Social centres and Community Halls for indoor sports, concerts and other entertainments;
> (d) The training of Native Recreational Directors and the giving of special courses for training in Social Service to all Native Students in Training Colleges;
> (e) The liberal financial support of all properly organized and similarly directed recreational efforts as one of the most effective contributions to community welfare.
> (2) Pathfinder and Wayfarer Movements:
> The Conference gives hearty endorsement to the Pathfinder and Wayfarer movements as very effective means of character development, of health propaganda and of adaptation to the new environment of Native youth in both rural and urban areas.[41]

The attention given to youth needs and to the Pathfinder and Wayfarer movements (African Scouts and Guides) was by no means merely pious, for the

Joint Councils attached particular importance to their youth programme, which deserves to be examined separately.

Influencing Black Youth

The African Scout movement was launched in 1918 and led by the principal animator of the Joint Councils, Professor Rheinallt-Jones, Chief Pathfinder, and his wife, Chief Wayfarer.[42] Scouting, like sport, was intended to 'moralize' the cultural environment of Indian, African and Coloured adolescents and children. Most Scouts and Guides were urban schoolchildren and therefore literate and relatively well off. The influence of this initiative was therefore limited in much the same ways as the Joint Councils Movement itself. Scouting is interesting for our purposes, however, because it provides, as early as the 1930s, an example of the way in which white associations systematically blocked the demands made by black organizations for recognition or greater independence — thus prefiguring by two decades the conflict between sports organizations.

Like the Olympic Charter, the world Scout movement's constitution is unequivocally non-racial.[43] Nevertheless, the white Scout movement, which was the recognized affiliate of the international body, refused to integrate with the Pathfinders and Wayfarers or permit them to seek independent international recognition. Just like the white sports associations in the 1950s, the white scouting body ordered the African body to set up an organization which was separate from all the other racial Scout groups (white, Indian and Coloured) but to channel all its international correspondence through the white organization.

The reactions of Pathfinder and Wayfarer officials to this ultimatum varied according to their class and background. White officials generally accepted it, but a large number of black Scout leaders, many of whom were teachers, appear to have resigned from the movement rather than recognize white hegemony. A sizeable block of black Wayfarer leaders seceded over the same issue in the 1930s, when European leaders (mainly in the Churches) accepted the terms of the white Guide movement's 'offer of affiliation to the Wayfarers as a branch of the S.A. Girl Guide Association'.[44] The Wayfarers demanded international recognition no less than four times before 1936 — providing another parallel with the persistent efforts of sports organizations in the 1950s. They were finally rewarded in 1945 when the world body recognized that the Wayfarers were a legitimate representative of the South African Guide movement.[45] Unfortunately, the Nationalists came to power very soon afterwards and no further progress was made. This is no doubt the reason for the sharp fall in Guide and Scout membership recorded between 1948 and 1950 in the African and Indian branches of the movement.[46]

Scouting reinforced among schoolchildren a body of values — ideals of justice, equality and fair play — that the white Scout movement signally failed to observe. Like sport a generation later, the *moral* ethos of Scouting seemed to offer the black elite a relatively favourable opportunity to claim its rights. Nevertheless, at a time when many of the previous opportunities for inter-racial contact and organization no longer existed, scouting did at least provide inter-racial contact at the camps and jamborees to which adolescents and children came from all the black associations across the country.[47] Here again, there is a parallel with sport. In addition, scouting made a limited contribution to the development of sport among children, promoting the physical and moral qualities of courage and self-help so beloved by Baden-Powell, and celebrating 'healthy deeds of daring — even in make-believe — and . . . acts that go to form manly character.'[48]

For the young black unemployed and children out of school, on the other hand, there was no opportunity to learn or to play sport. The brief history of the Wednesday Football team in Johannesburg illustrates the problem. It was created specifically for unemployed adolescents, but so great was the demand for sport that it was almost immediately submerged by adult players.[49] For the swelling band of deprived children, recreation consisted of street games (stone throwing, marbles), betting, smoking *dagga* and various gang activities, and work was confined to petty theft, or one-off jobs running errands, selling newspapers, or, for a minority, caddying.[50]

To provide for this neglected and vulnerable group, a number of Boys Clubs were organized during the 1930s, principally in Johannesburg and elsewhere on the Rand and in Cape Town. Once or twice a week, boys had the chance to try their hand at boxing, weight-lifting, table tennis and gymnastics, and girls, in their own clubs, at needlework, drama and gymnastics. At the end of the War, the 32 boys clubs and 22 girls clubs on the Rand, catering for 2,892 members,[51] were led by 76 voluntary leaders who had received training at the Wemmer Barracks, at the Bantu Men's Social Centre or at the J.H. Hofmeyr School of Social Work.[52] In the beginning these clubs were financed by grants from the Department of Social Welfare, the National Advisory Council for Physical Education, the mining companies, the Bantu Welfare Trust and municipal councils; but after 1946 a proportion of costs was recovered from the members, who had to pay an individual contribution before they could attend.

A number of holiday camps for black children and adolescents were also organized, on the same lines as white camps which had been started in 1910 in the Cape and 1925 in Natal. For a short time after 1948, liberal Nationalists carried on this tradition, as we have seen.[53]

White Nationalism and Neo-tribal Sport

These youth projects show clearly that the liberals who initiated and ran them sought to make bearable the appalling social problems faced by black children and adolescents in the cities. They had no intention of combating racial segregation and prejudice but wished to make its effects more palatable for a small minority of those who suffered from them. The weaknesses of this policy were cruelly revealed by the Nationalists who at once overturned liberal social reforms and suppressed the civil and political rights of the black population altogether. During a period of intense political activity between 1948 and 1953, important sections of black opinion finally rejected the paternalism of the liberal movement, and the movement itself broke up into several conflicting tendencies. One, represented by the South African Communist Party, which was banned in 1950 but whose former members remained politically active in various other organizations for some time afterwards, called for outright opposition to apartheid, while two others formed the cores of the Liberal Party (created in 1953) and the United Party, a centralist grouping whose electorate and leadership soon accommodated themselves to Nationalist policies.[54] The liberal movement could only make headway and remain politically useful when the aims of government were themselves reformist: it is dubious whether this was so before 1948, and it was certainly not so afterwards.

The black organizations which had given support to the liberal movement also divided, over the question of whether or not they should collaborate with, or boycott, the new regime and white rule in general. Organizations split at every level, with profound effects. African political opinion divided between sympathizers of the A.N.C. Youth Wing, which had begun to radicalize its parent body, and followers of the All Africa Convention. A similar division split the Coloured community between the pro-CAD and anti-CAD (Unity Movement) factions. Cultural, religious and professional organizations were also drawn in: as we have seen, an organization as far down the political spectrum as the Scout movement was affected, and in due course the same political split within the sports associations was to stimulate the creation of the non-racial sports movement.

After 1948, at least for the black population, almost all activity became explicitly political, including sport — a fact that was recognized by all political parties. Sport became politicized as the whole society became politicized: under apartheid, a racially mixed game of tennis is seen by all to be a political act, and can no longer, as the liberals had envisaged, *replace* political action.

Once in power, the Nationalists imposed their own idea of social order. Far from trying to improve the lives of urban Blacks, they introduced apartheid legislation and reinforced the system of migrant labour. Their programme and dogma required the *retribalization* of African society, including African social and cultural life and sport. From 1948, therefore, games and sporting activities with a 'traditional' or 'tribal' content were officially encouraged and financed by the Government. The 1950s witnessed the promotion of organized tribal dancing, which had thrived in the mine compounds from the early years of the century but which had been declining in favour of modern sports like football. Several dance troupes were sent abroad to represent 'African culture' and provide reassuring publicity for the regime, and inside the country tribal dancing was generally commercialized as a tourist attraction.[55] The official encouragement of a degenerate popular form of *amalaita* was even more suspect. Originally a kind of formal stick fighting practised in certain African societies at initiation ceremonies, by the 1950s *amalaita* contests had become 'semi-gladiatorial mass fights between gangs of young male Africans, held under armed police supervision and attended by Europeans of both sexes'. As the author of this description pointed out, 'the primitive savagery of these fights is of course not disturbing to European stereotypes concerning the inferior and barbarous African.'[56] Tolerated by the Administration, who claimed that such fights (like the regular brawls in the mining compounds) were an integral part of 'African culture', these brutal spectacles regularly attracted crowds of up to 2,000 people in Johannesburg. They took place in Cape Town as well, where apparently up to three-quarters of the spectators were European.[57]

'Coon Troops' provide another example of the way in which the white Administration promoted popular traditions in order to reinforce racial stereotypes. The Coloured community in the Cape has celebrated this ancient New Year festival since the 18th Century: every year, teams of Coloured participants prepare floats and dress up as Negroes ('Coons').[58] Great publicity was given to the festival which was recognized to be an occasion on which Coloured people let off steam.[59] In the 1950s, Coon Troop tours around the country were financed and organized by the Government. At the same time, the evident ambiguity of an occasion which required real Blacks to dress up as caricatures of Blacks — and black slaves at that — was increasingly denounced by Coloured political organizations.[60]

Sport and Social Life, 1945-55

It should already be clear that all the organized sporting activities described above — in the Scouts, the boys clubs and youth clubs, the Bantu Sports Club and adult sports associations — affected only a tiny proportion of the black population, generally confined to the educated urban elite. There was an acute lack of material facilities and adequate organization for black sportsmen and women, which meant that most could not even *begin* to play sport. This must be borne in mind while reading the information we have compiled below about black sports facilities and associations on the eve of the 1948 elections. The need was overwhelming, commented upon by all contemporary observers.

> The existing clubs [in the Rand in 1940] are only reaching a handful of the boys who so greatly need them. There are playing fields in all the locations, but for the boy who has left school or has no or only part-time employment — there is no equipment, such as footballs, available.[61]

> When the cry of *amalaitus* was raised in Johannesburg [the Bapedi football club] was changed to a social club. We had to do something to keep people out of the streets on Sundays, and keep them away from drink.[62]

Sport for Africans in the Cape has been very seriously hampered by lack of playing fields. According to Father Botto, 'only a fraction of the demand for sports facilities is being met'. During the years 1954 to 1959, matches were played on the few available fields from 1 p.m. on Saturdays until the light failed [i.e. on Sundays].[63]

When speaking of black sport, therefore, it must be remembered that we are speaking of a minority. The vast majority of black people simply had no facilities or training opportunities available to them. This is the backcloth to all discussion of the issue — today as much as it was in the past[64] — and means that judgements upon black performances and black sports participation cannot be made without reference to the lack of facilities, officials, money, health services, good diet etc. from which they suffer.

Dr Jokl, an adviser to the Industrial Development Corporation of South Africa, who became something of an expert on the sports issue in Johannesburg during the 1940s, calculated that according to the criteria employed by the I.O.C. and the sports authorities in the United States, Europe and the U.S.S.R.:

Johannesburg with its 300,000 non-Europeans would need about 600 acres of ground for organizing play activities and recreational pastimes for this section of the population alone. Actually, there are not more than perhaps 20 acres available.

The pressure on the few available sports fields is such that matches begin as a rule at 8.15 a.m. every Sunday and continue throughout the day. In the later months of the season play often begins as early as 7 a.m. It is obvious that only a fraction of the demand for sports facilities is at present being met . . . . The population of municipal hostels and compounds alone numbers approximately 200,000, most of whom have today no facilities for recreation at all in the respective districts.

The situation is quite similar in respect of the Coloured, Indian and the small Chinese communities in Johannesburg.[65]

Father Botto's conclusions, several years later, regarding needs in the Cape, were similar. He wrote that 'not more than 30 acres were available for fields in 1954 for 44,300 Africans, whereas by the standards of the United States and Germany 220 acres would be required.'[66]

Because they were so rare, pitches and other facilities were automatically over-exploited and at the same time — with the introduction of legislation depriving Africans of the right to own property in white areas[67] — under-maintained:

Some matches were played outside the town. There were no changing rooms, you came with your attire or changed behind a bush. Many people came to watch. The balls were provided by the clubs: sometimes they changed the balls at half-time . . . . The so-called stadium at

> Guguletu . . . was an oval ground surrounded by planks. Langa had a
> better stadium, but it was small, there was only one rugby field and
> one soccer field; if we played cricket, we made up pitches on these
> fields.[68]

Many black sports associations cleared grounds for themselves, at their
own expense, taking over waste or marginal land over which they had no
right of tenure.

> Golf clubs have been formed by Native caddies and ex-caddies living on
> several locations. With the more or less active support of location super-
> intendents, tracts of land have been roughly prepared as golf courses
> . . . . The Bobby Jones Golf Club of the Western Native Township[69]
> was the premier African club on the Reef in 1937. Annual golf cham-
> pionships are held, that in 1937 being played over the Stirtonville
> course at Boksburg. There were 32 entries.[70]

Ray Phillips suggests here that the authorities were relatively tolerant towards
this form of appropriation, but this would not be a fair impression. The black
sportsmen who laid and maintained their pitches in this way, at great cost
and effort to themselves, could be expelled at any time, without compensation – and were indeed expelled, in Johannesburg and elsewhere. It is
scarcely surprising that relations between the sports associations and municipal and city councils (which were, of course, all-white) were characterized
by extreme mistrust. The Durban and District African Football Association,
for example,

> is extremely sensitive to any suggestion of white patronage. And it is
> vigilant in maintaining and asserting its independence, and highly
> suspicious of the Durban Corporation, which has the means to inter-
> fere with the autonomy of the Association through its control of
> playing fields. Relations have been guarded since the earliest days. The
> Association would clear land and prepare grounds, only to be moved
> out again into the bush. A white official of the Native Recruiting Cor-
> poration, donating a trophy to the Association, commented that the
> Native footballers had been booted out by the Durban Corporation
> from one football ground to another, from Western Vlei to Lords
> Ground and from there to the Eastern Vlei, and that each time this
> happened, Europeans or Indians followed to occupy the ground.[71]

The extraordinary density of sporting activity on these over-used, self-help
pitches is the clearest evidence, if proof were needed, of the vitality of black
sport, which in spite of all handicaps, bubbles out at all levels of black society.

> I used to watch the games at Riverlea, which is a Coloured location
> near Johannesburg. This was around 1960. They had five football

fields, four sand and one grass pitch, all of which had been cleared by the community. The matches began at 7 a.m., with the Under-7's. An older child would referee and then he would play in his own team later on in the morning — and so it went on until ten at night, when the top teams would have quite a large crowd supporting them. By that time the matches were floodlit. It was much the same in Soweto. The teams were organized by the children themselves who would ask an older man to train them — they organized themselves into leagues all the way up.[72]

In Johannesburg, the 127 school football teams shared their eight pitches with 145 adult sides. In 1947, for a total of 380,000 Africans living in Johannesburg, there were just 30 football pitches, five rugby pitches and 26 tennis courts (three football pitches, four tennis courts and one athletics track were under construction).[73] The facilities available in 1944 to the 112,000 Africans living within the city itself covered the needs of just 7,000 people (6.25%).[74] The state of these facilities can easily be imagined.

Youth Sport
These statistics and the problems they reflect relate to the urban areas in general. In the heart of the slums and in the wastes of the rural areas, however, the problems are even more acute: the need is not for sports facilities or training, but for basic health and physical education. Provision of these services depended in the first instance on schools. How did apartheid affect the school system, and what sort of physical education programme was envisaged for black children by the Nationalist Government?

We have already seen that it was in schools that most black sportsmen and women first learnt to enjoy playing games. This was even more true of the rural areas than of the towns, where as least a certain number of independent and adult sports associations existed. Until 1939, physical education was not a statutory component of school curricula; sport was not even obligatory in white state schools until 1938. The first courses for black physical education teachers were established in 1941 at Healdtown College; the J.H. Hofmeyr School of Social Work followed suit soon afterwards, and in 1942 the Johannesburg City Council authorized courses for black youth leaders working in the boys clubs.

Sporting activity before the War was left to the initiative of teachers and the pupils themselves. This naturally tended to advantage the children sent to better schools which sought to model themselves on public schools and therefore took pride in athletic achievement. As a result, it was virtually only in the English-speaking mission schools that pupils could expect to be taught sports and to play them regularly. This is one reason why so many South African black sportsmen preferred to use English as their means of expression, since sports associations tended to coalesce around relatively educated and relatively prosperous black sportsmen and officials, who had usually been educated in English-medium schools. (Some degree of political resistance to Afrikaans should also be taken into account.) A number of sports associations even went so far as to oblige their members to speak English.

As we have seen, the education changes introduced by the Nationalists in 1955 destroyed the independent and mission schools network and severely damaged the standard of African education in general, including physical education.[75] Thereafter, the majority of African (and Coloured) children learnt all their sport in state schools, and only a very small proportion continued their studies to secondary level.

The official timetable in primary schools at the beginning of the 1960s divided the pupils' time as follows:

> Roughly 25% of the time is spent on religious instruction and health parades in the lower primary courses . . . . Children in Standards I and II [the 3rd and 4th year] follow a curriculum spread over 1,650 minutes, double the time allocated to the lower standards. The school day lasts 5½ hours. Religious instruction and health parades take up 300 minutes (18%), English, Afrikaans and the vernacular 600 minutes (36%), arithmetic 200 minutes (15%), environmental studies 120 minutes (8%), gardening, handicraft, needlework, singing and writing 420 minutes (25%).[76]

Even if we have only a rather vague idea of what 'health parades' involved, it is unlikely that they took the form of organized sport. In fact, given the almost complete lack of equipment in most black schools, almost all sporting activity would have been confined to foot-races. In any case, after 1948 many of the best black teaching staff were hounded out of their jobs, forced to resign or systematically passed over for promotion for their educational beliefs.

Amid such disheartening neglect, the enthusiasm shown for sport is all the more moving. For many young South Africans, growing up in a society obsessed with sport yet frustrated by their inferior conditions of life, sporting achievement was a dream, a fantasy of escape from a society which imprisoned them and ignored their existence. The feelings of the young African woman quoted at the very beginning of this book capture some of their incomprehension and confused ambition, the dreams of children unable to square their conventional ambitions with the personal injustice of their oppression.[77] If Magnane is right in believing that the modern athlete is at heart inspired by a desire to conform,[78] the refusal of white society to allow black children even this right must further reinforce their sense of alienation, the 'self-negation' of which Steve Biko spoke or the violent frustration expressed by Jasmat Dhiraj in the Introduction.[79]

> Your school is not the same as the white school. The white kids always have uniforms. You find, for instance, even the organization of sport (those are things you notice as a kid) at white schools is absolutely so thorough and indicative of good training, good upbringing. You could get in school 15 rugby teams. You could get from our school three

rugby teams. Each of the white teams has got uniforms for each particular kid who plays. We have got to share the uniforms among our three teams. Now this is part of the roots of self-negation which our kids get even as they grow up.[80]

It would probably be wrong to suppose that anxiety is confined to the oppressed, on the other hand. Many young white children must have had to come to terms (and forget) the nagging guilt Dan Jakobsen describes, when he first recognized his place in the racial hierarchy:

> The Afrikaner children went to Afrikaans schools; the English-speaking to English-medium schools; the Cape Coloured went to Coloured schools; the African children . . . well, most of them at that time did not go to school at all but wandered around the streets in ragged bands . . . . They stood in little groups and watched us in our 'English' school-caps and blazers as we cycled or walked home from school; beyond the fences around our school grounds they were the spectators of our games of cricket and rugby. One was always aware of being under the scrutiny of these excluded groups that one could never finally exclude from one's own consciousness.[81]

The games of still younger children were not so frustrated by poverty, as Ellen Hellmann pointed out in 1940:

> Stone games, *madlopa*, in which one pebble has to be thrown up and caught while other pebbles have to be scooped from a hole in the ground, are popular girls' games. The boys continue to play at flicking one stone at another. The player continues flicking until he misses his aim when the next player has his turn. Skipping is a favourite pastime of both girls and boys. Hardly any toys of European manufacture are to be seen in Rooiyard. The poverty of the children prevents them from indulging their tastes in this respect.[82]

Original use is made of what lies to hand to create relatively sophisticated team games which can be played without equipment on slum street corners. Joyce Sikakane describes one[83] called the pyramid game, which 20 children can play with a single ball. One player throws down a pile of empty tins and his team have to build it up again before the ball can be fielded and thrown by the opposing side to hit one of them. From the organization of such games to the management of seven-year-old football sides is not a great step!

The research carried out by Jokl into black sport in 1947 revealed clearly how actively black schoolchildren could be involved in sport. In Bloemfontein, for example, the judicial capital of the country, notorious for its ferocious application of sport apartheid, more than 1,500 of the 5,000 schoolchildren belonged to the African schools' athletics association. In Johannesburg, the inter-schools league ran 127 football and 144 basketball teams.[84]

If we can safely say that school and children's sport flourished wherever it was encouraged, it is much harder to estimate the standard of performance. Pupils of different races scarcely ever competed against one another, times and scores were rarely recorded and black pupils received almost no formal training. It is not even possible to compare the performances of black and white students at English-speaking universities, for black students were usually refused permission to use sporting facilities and were certainly never proposed for selection for a college team.[85] The small minority of black students who were able to play sport in moderately good conditions, at the four major mission colleges, seem to have achieved surprisingly good individual performances, however. The Fort Hare football teams played some of the best teams on the Rand, and the times recorded by black students at the annual athletics match between Fort Hare, Healdtown, St. Matthews and Lovedale compare favourably with national records, when the small pool of athletes and their numerous handicaps are taken into account.

Table 4
African College Athletic Records Compared With National Records (to 1949)

Event	Best Performance by African Student			Best National Performance		
100 yards	Manana (St Matt)	9.9 secs	1946	Joubert	9.4 secs	1938
220	Manana (St Matt)	21.7 secs	1946	Theunissen	21.1 secs	1935
440	Tiso (Ft. Hare)	51.0 secs	1946	Shore	47.0 secs	1938
880	Lule (Ft. Hare)	1min54.3 secs	1939	de V. Heyns	1min53.6 secs	1946
Mile	Manpunye (Lovedale)	4min34.0 secs	1946	Wessels	4min16.0 secs	1937
2 miles	Zondan (Lovedale)	9min49.9 secs	1946	Green	9min44.6 secs	1939
120 yards (hurdles)	Nyati (Ft. Hare)	15.7 secs	1946	Lavery	14.3 secs	1937
High Jump	Njoroge (Ft. Hare)	5ft 11 ins	1942	Arnes	6ft 7½ ins	1943
Long Jump	Lango (Ft. Hare)	21ft 8½ ins	1941	Viljoen	24ft 2½ ins	1939
Javelin	Jack (Lovedale)	160ft 2½ ins	1940	de Bruyn	215ft 2½ ins	1939
Shot	Cetu (St Matt)	37ft 0½ ins	1938	Hart	51ft 7½ ins	1931
Discus	Bosnell (Lovedale)	108ft 6 ins	1945	Hart	147ft 6 ins	1931

Source: Jokl, in E. Hellmann, 1949, p. 450.

White South African sports officials who complain today that standards are falling in South Africa because of their exclusion from international competition will of course understand that the above performances by Black athletes were certainly not a true reflection of their potential, for at no time were they allowed to train or run against the best white or foreign athletes of their generation. It is not surprising either that track standards were higher than those achieved in field events which require more technical facilities and sophisticated training.

Adult Sport

Three types of organization offered sporting facilities to Blacks: the mines and parastatal companies; the armed forces and police; and private clubs and associations. After the Second World War the first two groups each received from the Government a grant of £5,000 towards a physical education programme, and were often supported as well by the municipal or city authorities which provided many private clubs with pitches and equipment. The powers of municipal and city councils were further augmented by the decision taken in 1940 to nationalize the distribution and sale of alcohol in the townships and to spend the disproportionate profits realized from alcohol sales on social and community programmes and in particular on leisure and housing facilities. The policy was naturally much criticized on moral grounds,[86] for in essence it consisted of encouraging alcoholism among one section of the population in order to improve the living standards of another. At all events, it further increased the dependence of African sportsmen and women and black sports associations in general on the local authorities who controlled most of the sports facilities.

As large employers of generally unskilled labour, the mines and parastatal organizations like the Railways and Harbour Administration, the armed forces and the police force, all had an interest in promoting sport. This was particularly true of the mines which required the vast numbers of uneducated men they employed to be at the peak of physical fitness. Their sports programmes have consequently expanded since the beginning of the century, when the first generation of miners, locked in their compounds, had little to do except dance and drink. Nowadays, athletics facilities at mines like Welkom are the equal of any in Europe[87] and the best black and white athletes are permitted to train together. Even in 1955 'a young African employed by the mines at Welkom beat the South African running record for the three miles by 21.1 seconds at the Bantu athletics meeting held during May'.[88] On the other hand, the standard of facilities was uneven and the social policies at many older mines were far from enlightened.[89]

The paternalism shown by some major employers to the black workforce was positively lavished on their white employees, who frequently had access to quite superb sporting and social facilities. The South African Railways and Harbour Administration, for example, which in 1948 was South Africa's largest single employer, ran 47 social and sports clubs, with 20,000 members.[90] Railway teams competed in the rugby and football leagues in the Cape and elsewhere, and most of the mines and major commercial companies ran company leagues in football, athletics, cycling and other sports. The police and armed forces did likewise. Some competitions were on a large scale: the police organized a provincial athletics meet every year, and in 1955 500 African athletes employed by South African Railways met at Durban to compete in a multi-sport tournament including athletics, football, weightlifting, boxing and traditional dancing.[91]

The major companies also promoted some of the minority sports, like tennis. On the Witwatersrand in 1947, the mine companies provided free tennis balls to African players using company courts, thereby stimulating the spread of a game which was expensive and arduous to learn.

Such patronage by Government and company was double-edged, of course: the employers and municipalities who built and maintained sports facilities acquired the right to determine who could use them, and as a result it became increasingly difficult for black sportsmen and women to question the discriminatory and unequal conditions under which they were asked to play. Boycotts were even more difficult, for alternative facilities were simply not available. In 1947, for example, 12 of the 14 tennis courts set aside for use by African players on the Witwatersrand (with 12 clubs, 25 teams in all) were the property of the mine companies.[92]

In the armed forces and the police, physical education was also an important feature of training programmes. Most units had service teams, both white and black[93] and particularly after the recession of the 1920s and 1930s, army policy reflected the view that 'physical education — this being considered in its broadest sense — is an essential formative and educative technique' to civilize black youths and make them economically productive.[94]

The Nationalist Government put an end to most black participation in the armed forces, but shifted greater responsibility on to the police, which was expected to use African constables to keep order in the African areas (and Coloured police to control the Coloured population, etc.). The police therefore continued to organize sporting competitions and to participate in the black football and rugby leagues.

Relations between the police and the population were to change profoundly, however. Up to the middle 1950s, the policeman was a figure of authority, whose role was obviously delicate but who was personally tolerated and even respected. The image of Can Themba's Ten-to-Ten comes to mind — a giant with powers of life or death over the inhabitants living on his beat, a dangerous mediator between white injustice and the anarchy of the slums, but a man who could at the same time be a pillar of the local football team, pleasing the crowd with his witty play.[95] No such tolerance appears to have survived the first decade of apartheid:

> The country clubs all wish to beat the townsmen of the Langa Blues, but town and country alike are united in their determination to beat the police team. Most members of the Langa police force are town residents, and therefore the townsmen are their home boys, but the migrants can abuse the police as much as they like and the townsmen will not come to the aid of the police but join the attackers. When the police team plays, the onlookers all support their opponents and jeer at the police; indeed a game against the police team commonly develops into a fight, and the spectators make no objection to deliberate assaults on police players, whereas in any other match they would protest at such foul play . . . . The tension has increased very considerably during the last five years, for in 1955 a fieldworker was told that 'there is no stigma on the police team, owing to the fact that the feeling between

police and Africans is much better at the Cape than in other South African towns'. The attitude towards the police team now is comparable to that of non-whites towards the Springboks when they play a visiting team from overseas; nowadays the non-whites always support the visitors, whoever they may be.[96]

References

1. Interview with an African woman, London, February 1980.
2. Sam Ramsamy, interview, Paris, 20 January 1980.
3. Interview with an African woman, London, February 1980.
4. Lady Duff Gordon, 28 January 1862, in Duff Gordon, 1927, p. 110.
5. William Beinart, interview, Oxford, 16 February 1980.
6. B. Willan, *An African in Kimberley*, pp. 8 and 14. To give a better idea of the wealth of associational life and its social significance, Mr H.C. Msikinga was President of the Come Again Tennis Club, Secretary of the Eccentrics Cricket Club, member of the Rovers Rugby Football Club, member of the South African Improvement Society. A still more notable example was Mr Isaiah Bud Mbelle, a *Mfengu*, teacher, the first African to pass the exam into the civil service, an interpreter, who was director of the Philharmonic Society, Captain of the Rovers Rugby Football Club, Secretary of the S.A. Colonial Rugby Football Board, Secretary of the Griqualand West Colonial Rugby Football Club, committee member of the Eccentrics Cricket Club, and journalist, with many articles on the community life of Kimberley to his name.
7. A. Kerr, 1968, pp. 247-8.
8. A. Kerr, 1968, pp. 249-50.
9. A. Kerr, 1968, p. 250.
10. Mweli Skota, 1932. Allowance should be made for the fact that the author was frequently describing his friends; nevertheless, the partiality of his selection is itself significant, and indicates the status of sport.
11. H. Kuper, 1960, p. 74.
12. P.B. Singh, interview, 22 April 1980.
13. Renamed in 1932 the Durban and District African Football Association.
14. L. Kuper, 1965, p. 452.
15. Formed at the end of the 1920s, with the backing of the Bantu Men's Social Centre, the Chamber of Mines and the Municipality.
16. Mweli Skota, 1932, p. 445; Ray Phillips (an American Board Missionary and Secretary of the J.B.F.A.), 1936, p. 308. Jokl in Hellmann, 1949, p. 457, claims that in 1946 the Johannesburg African F.A. was running 113 teams, the Alexandra African F.A. 16, the Johannesburg Bantu F.A. 145 — a total of 274 teams.
17. See below pp. 141-2.
18. 'In Johannesburg there had been the strike of men who removed night soil in 1918, and the A.N.C. had initiated a passive resistance campaign against the passes . . . . In 1920 there were strikes at the Cape Town

Docks, riots and considerable damage at Kilnerton Training College and Lovedale School; a strike on the gold mines involving 40,000 to 70,000 African workers; shootings in Port Elizabeth which left 21 dead and many more injured after the detention of the I.C.U. leader, S.M. Masabalala; and then, in May 1921, the crowning tragedy when police killed 120 Israelites at Bulhoek, near Queenstown.' B. Hirson, 1978, p. 4. The great white mining strike, of course, took place in 1922.

19.   See pp. 39-40 above.

20.   In 1927 the I.C.U. claimed a paid-up membership of between 50,000 and 80,000, composed of 'the ill-defined groups of dissidents characteristic of early industrialization. Landless peasants, rural squatters, domestic servants, unemployed migrants and other *lumpens*, even aspirant rural and urban entrepreneurs, were its bases, as well as workers *per se*.' Legassick in Callinicos & Rogers, 1977, p. 43; P. Walshe, 1970, pp. 93-4.

21.   B. Hirson, 1978, p. 4; Phillips, 1936, p. 347.

22.   B. Hirson, 1978, p. 6.

23.   B. Hirson, 1978, p. 6. The I.C.U. was even more critical.

24.   Rheinallt-Jones, Second Annual Report of the S.A.I.R.R., 1931, Appendix A, in Hirson, 1978, p. 9.

25.   R. Phillips, 1930, p. 58, cited in Couzens, 1979, p. 32.

26.   Report of the National European-Bantu Conference, 1929, pp. 195-6 and 200.

27.   The Chamber of Mines offered the American missionaries £1,500 worth of bioscope equipment and £5,000 a year for administrative costs and overheads.

28.   In 1922, when the black mine-workers refused to join the strike of the white miners, a group of white miners threatened to attack a compound in New Primrose. Ray Phillips sped to the mine with a film by Charlie Chaplin and as a result the black miners remained tranquil while order was restored. As Phillips puts it, 'there was no murder that night at the New Primrose', Phillips, 1930, p. 150 in Couzens, 1980, p. 11.

29.   Report of the National European-Bantu Conference, 1929, p. 199.

30.   Dexter in Report of the National European-Bantu Conference, 1929, p. 199.

31.   R. Phillips, 1930, p. 303.

32.   E. Hellmann, 1948, p. 114.

33.   Peter Abrahams, 1954, p. 192.

34.   Jokl in E. Hellmann, 1949, p. 457.

35.   R. Phillips, 1936, p. 353.

36.   Phillips, ibid., p. 304.

37.   Mr Senaone was later to become director of sports for the Johannesburg Municipal Council and a member of the executive of the Johannesburg Football Association, based at the Bantu Sports Club.

38.   Described in A. Paton, 1964, p. 173.

39.   R. Phillips, 1936, p. 353.

40.   Ibid., p. 305.

41.   Report of the National European-Bantu Conference, 1929.

42.   It was thought inappropriate to give African Scouts the same title as European Scouts. They were therefore called Pathfinders and Wayfarers.

Indian and Coloured Scouts and Guides retained their right to the European names. Sheila Patterson observed wryly that: 'In the case of Brownies, the name was changed to Sunbeams for non-European children. "It might have been thought offensive," said a European guider.' S. Patterson, 1953, p. 156, note 9.

43. This fact obliged the white South African Scout movement to rewrite its constitution in the following terms: 'Here then is the true conception of the inter-relation of colour. Complete uniformity in ideals, absolute equality in the paths of knowledge and culture, equal opportunities for those who strive, equal admiration for those who achieve; in matters social and racial a separate path, each pursuing his own race purity and race pride, equality in things spiritual, agreed divergence in the physical and material. And whereas it is recognized that it is not possible in South Africa to form one association embodying the principle of the International Scout Movement, which provides that there shall be no distinction of race, each of the sections of the Movement within the Union will be self-contained, self-governing and entirely separate from the other, save as hereinafter set forth . . .' Patterson, 1953, note 87, p. 136.

44. R. Phillips, 1936, p. 301.
45. S. Patterson, 1953, p. 138.
46. Membership of the Scout and Pathfinder Movements, 1948-50

Date	Europeans	%	Coloured	%	Indians	%	African Pathfinders	%	Total
1948	14,830	41.0	2,067	5.7	1,562	4.3	17,531	48.7	*35,990*
1950	15,496	48.1	2,288	7.1	1,062	3.3	13,376	41.5	*32,222*
Difference	+666		+221		-500		-4,155		*- 3,768*
% Difference	+4.5%		+10.7%		-32%			-23.7%	*-10.5%*

Source: S. Patterson, 1953, p. 136, note 88.

47. 'Indians (in Pretoria) had no scouting group so we, as Indians, all joined the Coloured group. And they suddenly realized that we were just like them, especially when we went to camps together. Scouting teaches you about fraternity and brotherhood and I think the contact we had then broke many barriers. Later on, it was the people we had contact with that we accepted in our [sports] teams. My parents also let us join the scouts, and before I was fourteen I went out on a camping trip that was hundreds of miles away.' Jasmat Dhiraj, interview, London, 1980.
48. Report of the Native Economic Commission, paragraph 781, sd, in R. Phillips, 1936, p. 245.
49. E. Hellmann, 1940, pp. 44-5.
50. E. Hellmann, 1940, pp. 44-5.
51. Report of the South African Conference on the Post-War Planning of Social Work, 1944, p. 227.
52. Jokl, in E. Hellmann, 1949, pp. 457-9.
53. See above p. 43.
54. The South African Institute of Race Relations survived to provide an

invaluable chronology of developments during the period in its research documents and annual surveys.

55. These remarks are not intended to disparage the quality of the dancing, which is well-known, but to underscore the political (and commercial) purposes to which the dancers — and their contemporary equivalents, such as Ipi Tombi — have been put.

56. S. Patterson, 1953, p. 130, note 33. *Amalaita*, as described above, is still practised today.

57. S. Patterson, 1953, p. 130, note 33.

58. This is apparently another example of the influence of the United States upon black values and culture in South Africa, which may be found in the vigorous jazz tradition, in black South African writing in the 1930s, or in the influence of Dubois, Marcus Garvey and Booker T. Washington in the 1920s. Also in sport, where it is noticeable in the names chosen by black clubs. See T. Couzens, 1980, passim.

59. 'The police do give us a lot of privileges at New Year. It is the only sport we can indulge in to our hearts' delight and we look forward to it', Leader of the Spes Bona coons, *Cape Times Magazine*, 20 January 1951, in S. Patterson, 1953, p. 156, note 56.

60. S. Patterson, 1953, p. 156.

61. E. Hellmann, 1940, pp. 40-6.

62. J. Maketa Thema in Phillips, 1936.

63. Wilson and Mafeje, 1963, p. 125: the report by Father Botto dates from 1954.

64. See Chapter 7 below.

65. Jokl, in Report of the South African National Conference on the Post-War Planning of Social Work, 1944, pp. 236-7. In a later article in Hellmann, 1949, p. 457, he provides different figures, no doubt referring to a larger area. 'The non-European population requires about 850 acres for recreational purposes whereas less than 75 acres are now at their disposal.' His figures are based on I.O.C. standards (1938), which set the needs for recreational space at 2.5 hectares (6 acres) per 1,000 people, and on the work of Dr Diem who considered that individuals require between 3 and 5 square metres of recreational space.

66. Botto, in Wilson and Mafeje, 1963, p. 125.

67. This statement requires qualification: after 1937 it was illegal to establish churches, schools or recreational centres, which were destined for African use, outside the townships or locations. Africans were also forbidden to buy land in urban areas. In 1946, legislation was passed severely restricting the right of Indians to acquire property in Natal or the Transvaal.

68. Interview with an African, London, 12 February 1980.

69. The Western Native Township comprised part of the inner-city area of Johannesburg, from which Africans were expelled in 1967. The area became a Coloured zone. The Group Areas Act and Nationalist policy have caused huge forced movements of population, particularly from the inner-city areas. As a result, it is impossible to make realistic comparisons of facilities over time. Generally, figures of facilities should be lowered except where new facilities have been provided for the displaced African population.

70. R. Phillips, 1936, p. 309.
71. L. Kuper, 1965, p. 458.
72. Interview with a white South African, London, October-November 1979.
73. E. Jokl in E. Hellmann, 1949, p. 456.
74. Jokl, in Report of the South African National Conference on the Post-War Planning of Social Work, 1944, p. 229. In 1945, municipal facilities for the 500,000 Africans in Johannesburg included 33 football pitches, 4 rugby pitches, 24 tennis courts, 8 club houses, 3 athletic tracks, 6 playgrounds, 2 swimming pools (one privately financed) and a number of basketball courts, cricket pitches and boxing rings. In Durban (200,000 Africans), there were 5 recreation halls, 15 football pitches, 2 cricket pitches, a dozen tennis courts, 2 banked cycle tracks, 2 Ngoma dancing areas, 7 children's playgrounds and several boxing rings. Bowling greens were under construction. *SAIRR Survey 1944-1955.*
75. See above pp. 46-8.
76. Unesco, 1972, pp. 63-4. This regime was slightly modified after 1968: a science course replaced environmental studies.
77. See pp. iii-iv.
78. Magnane, 1964, pp. 43-4: 'Sport is the principal pole of attraction towards acceptable activities, which are approved, consciously social and in widest sense of the word, docile . . . . Well-controlled freedom is what sporting discipline offers them . . . . The athlete in training is a well-behaved young man, with a quiet conscience . . . . Consciously or not, he behaves like a son ought to behave.'
79. See pp. vii-viii.
80. S. Biko, testimony at the SASO-BPC trial in May 1976, in Biko, 1978, pp. 100-1.
81. D. Jakobsen in P. Wastberg, 1967, p. 89.
82. E. Hellmann, 1948, pp. 66-7.
83. J. Sikanane, 1977.
84. Only 8 schools played rugby at this date; 38 took part in the annual athletics tournament. Jokl, in E. Hellmann, 1949, pp. 453 and 458.
85. Sadie Berman, interview, 15 February 1980.
86. See the protest of Messrs Bokwe, Foley and Nkosinkulu in 1941, p. 40-1.
87. Report of the British Sports Council, 1980, p. 80.
88. S.A.I.R.R., 1955-56, p. 226. As if to disarm a certain scepticism among his readers, the author hastened to add that 'He ran this distance in 13 minutes 54.7 seconds on a properly surveyed track with three official European time-keepers in charge.'
89. See above, pp. 46-8.
90. G. Norton, 1948, p. 129. The South African Railways employed 142,000 people of whom 60,000 were black. A high proportion were from the poor white working class, for whom a substantial number of jobs were reserved.
91. S.A.I.R.R. 1944-55, p. 226.
92. E. Jokl in Hellmann, 1949, p. 460.
93. The relevant units were the Special Service Battalion, the Youth Training Brigade, the Physical Training Brigade and the Non-European Army Corps.

94.   E. Jokl in E. Hellmann 1949, p. 449; for the complete quote see p. 35 above.
95.   Can Themba, 1972, pp. 46-57.
96.   Wilson and Mafeje, 1963, p. 123.

6. Sport and Social Life in the Townships

Sport in the Townships

In the 1950s, sport already occupied a central place in African urban life and that of Blacks generally. At this time, a number of important studies in urban anthropology were written, which devoted particular attention to associative activities and to the role associations, including sports clubs, played in the social movement of migrants from rural to urban life. These studies permit us to sketch in some detail the role sport played in the townships at this time.

After the churches, sports clubs involved more people than any other form of association. Their membership was in fact astonishingly high. According to Father Botto, who conducted a survey in 1954, one-quarter of the 11,300 Africans in Cape Town belonged to a club or association, and at least 2,095 people belonged to the 22 rugby clubs, 13 football clubs and 9 cricket clubs in the Cape. This suggests that, when the 394 registered members of other sports clubs (tennis, golf, weight-lifting, boxing and netball) are included, about 2,500 Africans played sport — 5.6% of the African population of the Cape (44,300). This figure does not include the most ephemeral or marginal associations, nor spectators who, according to Wilson and Mafeje, numbered about 10,000 a year, or 700 for an important match.[1]

Even when allowance is made for the fact that many players belonged to two or more clubs, the figures are high. Neither children under 10, nor the aged, nor women (as a group[2]) played organized sport, and the African population of Cape Town had a high proportion of migrants, who were generally less likely than settled urban dwellers to join clubs or play sport regularly. In all, probably 15% or more of the adult African population likely to play sport appears to have been actually involved in some sort of sporting activity, and this proportion was no doubt much higher in townships like Langa, where the African community was settled and relatively prosperous.

A survey of East London in 1955 gives support to Botto's figures.[3] Nearly half the African men aged between 15 and 30 and born in an urban area, claimed to belong to the Gompo Rugby Football Union which brought together the district's 11 rugby clubs. Of migrant workers, more than 25% of the men aged between 15 and 25 and about 15% of those aged between 25 and 39 (including a majority of the educated men) also belonged.

It would certainly be foolhardy to suppose that such figures were necessarily representative of the proportion of Africans involved in sport during this period. For one thing, the Cape has a large Coloured population; for another, the figures concern rugby, whereas most Africans played football. Nevertheless, supported as they are by eye-witness accounts, these figures do suggest that in the townships and wherever the urban population was settled and stable, sport was followed and played by very large numbers of people.

A number of other factors which support this view need to be given some explanation. Towns in South Africa had been traditionally segregated into racially separate zones, for Whites, Africans, Coloureds etc. Apartheid formalized and reinforced this process and in the 1950s the Nationalist Government attempted, particularly in the towns, to establish definitive, racially exclusive zones. The rights to urban residence of three of the four major racial groups (White, Coloured, Indian) were then recognized, but under the Group Areas Act each was regrouped into areas which were exclusively reserved for one of them. Africans, on the other hand, were refused this general right to urban residence and subjected to a different regime.

The urban African population, both before and after 1948, could be divided into two categories. Migrant workers, the majority, had work contracts but no residence rights; they normally lived in single men's quarters, in compounds or hostels.[4] Long-term urban residents, on the other hand, had acquired rights in the towns. Between these two lay a third category, comprised of migrants who had no urban residence rights but who (until 1948) hoped to acquire them, or who (after 1948) remained in the towns illegally.

Urban anthropologists working in the 1950s attached much importance to the third group of migrants and the relation between the towns and the rural areas they had left. They hoped to illuminate the urbanizing process by tracing the stages which individuals followed on their way to becoming townsmen. Mayer, for example, studying East London, distinguished 'School' migrants (who were willing to assimilate and recognized the advantages of Western education) from 'Red' migrants, who remained loyal to traditional rural values, were suspicious of town life and planned to return to their places of origin.[5] Working in Cape Town, Wilson and Mafeje likewise found differences between several kinds of 'Home Boys' — the name referring to the rural places of origin with which migrants identified themselves.[6]

These categories are relevant when it comes to sport, because modern sports were adopted first by the educated elite, in towns, where the population was dense, facilities more numerous and contact with Europeans and Coloured sportsmen possible; secondly, by long-stay migrants, who were assimilated into urban life; and finally, to a much smaller degree, by short-term contract workers confined to the mining compounds or isolated on farms. There is, therefore, a very close correspondence between the social structure and history of sport and the cleavages between permanent townspeople and African migrant workers.

All commentators at the time identify education and the urban environment as crucial to the adoption of modern sport in all three black communities. The administration of sport remained in the hands of educated and relatively prosperous elites, almost all of which were recruited from families with a long urban tradition.

> [Coloured] clubs with a specialized recreational purpose seem to be as yet restricted to the upper and middle classes . . . . Coloured recreational clubs are the answer to European social exclusiveness and are usually connected with some sport. From small local beginnings, clubs connected with the major sports have achieved national organizations, to which all local Coloured clubs are affiliated. The minimum requirements of equipment, training and leisure still confine these activities for the most part to better off individuals.[7]

> [Indian] sports organizers and managers are elected to prominent positions on sporting organizations by virtue of their pre-eminence in some other field of social life, such as politics, business or education . . . . Focusing more sharply on Indian participants in different sports, a selective process (based on economic class distinction), is evident, though the training ground in most cases has been the school which draws pupils from all levels. Soccer, football and boxing are played mainly by the working class, cricket and tennis mainly by the wealthy, the professional and intellectual elite.[8]

> In the [African] football clubs there are also the wealthy men, no longer players, who are elected to the unions and boards, and who are viewed with some suspicion by young players from the country. Their power derives from their position as townsmen (not country cousins), from their wealth — they subscribe to club funds — and their offers of transport when required . . . . It is said that 'higher-class people — townsmen — carry much more weight in the 'Rugby Union' than the representatives from the country boys' clubs.' The rugby clubs also invite as 'patrons' [the English word is used] middle-class people such as an advocate living in Langa, or a minister of religion. Responsibility, honesty and education are looked for in leaders in sport as in other things. The most respected sportsman in Langa, Ben Malamba, was not only an excellent rugby player and cricketer, and a table tennis champion, but he was also matriculated and a senior clerk in the administrative office. Even the leader of a team or choir of countrymen is expected to have at least as good an education as anyone else in the group.[9]

For African migrants, playing sport had a definite social significance in relation to the town and to town values. Pauw, for example, observed that, in East London, 'Red' migrants rarely played sport, whereas 'Semi-Reds' sometimes watched matches or joined clubs and 'School' migrants participated in sporting activities as keenly as townsmen.[10] Mayer also noted that 'Red'

143

migrants avoided sport and sports clubs which 'School' migrants 'join in eagerly':

> I am particularly interested in all sports. It seems to me that sport forms part and parcel of life in town, and I usually spend my free time in town playing cricket, or watching rugby according to the season.
>
> To be an active sportsman, in town, means being a member of one of the many clubs. 'When in sport you have many friends; if you are good at it they all want you to join their own clubs. If you are out of work they all try to get you a job so that you should not think of leaving town.'[11]

Sport was therefore a link between town and country for those who wanted to urbanize. Among the groups of 'Home-boys' this process was completed in several stages and the individual would gradually transfer from teams composed of migrants from his rural area to teams of townsmen.

> Joining clubs or associations is one of the ways of becoming integrated in town but . . . a number of the sports clubs and music clubs have a home-boy basis so that a rugby player or jazz musician does not necessarily move immediately outside his home-boy group, but it will at least be a wider group than that from his own village . . . . The more educated a man is and the longer he spends in town, the more his associations depend upon like interest and personal friendship rather than upon coming from the same village, and he tends to move out of the home-boy club and join one in which the activity itself is the primary bond.[12]

Sporting relations also expressed the *tensions* which existed between town and country — between the new, economically powerful values of the city, soiled by their association with colonial occupation, and those of pre-colonial society, shaken by defeat; as well as the tensions between social classes. Sport both stimulated these tensions and at the same time provided a peaceful outlet for them. The tremendous competition between clubs, the complexity of associational alliances and the frequency of secessions (proof of the rapid increase in club membership) all reveal the *integrative* role played by sport and sports associations in black social life.

> Most of the African Busy Bees came from the King William's Town area. The Border was, in fact, the first area in which Africans began to be interested in rugby and cricket, doubtless because three large and famous boarding-schools, and the University College of Fort Hare, were established there. So the Busy Bees Club, unlike the Bantu, consisted of members from the same area, the Border; and it is still largely composed of home-boys..
>
> As the membership of the Busy Bees increased, those from King

William's Town and East London, who knew more about rugby than those from smaller centres such as Peddie, Mount Coke, and Alice, controlled the club, and when selecting players for the first XV, they tended to choose from among themselves and their friends, to the exclusion of 'the pagans' (*amaqaba*) from country villages 'who knew nothing about rugby'. When the group which felt itself discriminated against had enough members to form a club, it withdrew from the Busy Bees and formed the Harlequins. Most members of this club come from villages and country towns on the Border, and they live in Langa in the barracks and zones, whereas the majority of the Busy Bees come from the larger towns of King William's Town, East London and Grahamstown, and they live in Salt River, Woodstock and District Six, so rural-urban differences and home-boy loyalties are both expressed in these two clubs. The Busy Bees are townspeople (*abantu basedolophini*) and the Harlequins 'ignorant pagans' (*amaqaba angazinto*).

However, each group is, in a sense, one of home-boys to the other. When there are matches at Langa between various teams, the Busy Bees members always cheer the Harlequins, and the Harlequins reciprocate. If a fight breaks out, the boys from these two teams rally to each other's help, as happened when a fight broke out during a match between a Kensington team and the Harlequins. The Border Boys watching, some of them members of the Busy Bees, were the first to rush on to the field to help their home-boys. And a member of the Bantu Club, who also came from the Border, was restrained by his fellows on the ground that the fight did not concern him. He protested: 'You can't say that, those are my home-boys, those are my fellow small boys.'

As the number of home-boys increases, the more narrowly are areas defined. The King William's Town, East London, and Grahamstown boys would never have discriminated against the others had their numbers not been sufficient to form a reasonably large club. The process is continuous. As the Harlequins increased in numbers they too split, this time on the basis of reserve versus farm people, a cleavage which is old and familiar. The Red Lions who broke away from the Harlequins mostly came from the Fort Beaufort and Adelaide area. Though they knew more about rugby than the other Harlequin members, who came from villages in reserves, the villagers 'would not be commanded by squatters and vagrants (*amaranuga*) who had lost their traditional customs'. The *amaranuga*, for their part 'could not waste their time trying to teach unteachable sheep from the villages', and so the split occurred.

At first, the boys born and brought up in Cape Town did not have any particular club of their own. Either they were not interested in rugby or else they joined the Busy Bees or the Bantu. About 1947, when the first generation born and brought up in Langa was old enough to form and control a club, and when rugby had become popular, the

city-born boys asserted their difference from the migrants by forming
their own club called the Mother City. One of the conditions of membership is that the recruit should give evidence of having been in Cape
Town for a continuous period of at least five years. The aim was to
keep out people not permanently settled in town . . . . The team is
criticized by others for its foul play 'and yet when it comes to the
election of Western Province Rugby Board officials, and the selection
of the Western Province team, the Mother City carries most weight'.[13]

Not all sports were as divided on sectarian grounds as rugby.[14] A number
of clubs accepted players from different racial or ethnic groups;[15] the Durban
and District African Football Association imposed severe sanctions on clubs
which were guilty of racism[16] and some associations (the Indian Weight-
lifting Federation, the Durban and District African F.A., the Coloured Rugby
Football Board among others) had an open policy on membership in spite of
their racial title.

Nevertheless, membership of sports clubs did generally correspond very
precisely with class groupings or sub-groupings. This seems to have been particularly true of minority sports. Mayer tells us that East London tennis clubs
each had a different social clientele: the Highlanders attracted teachers, civil
servants, nurses, etc., whereas the Silver Star Club served workers and servants.
The Stone Breakers Rugby Club was proud of the fact that its membership
was confined to 'educated people'.[17] But South African sport is interesting
not merely because its organization reflects the social relations and processes
at work in black society — sporting activity was itself a force of considerable
influence on those social relations. This was true above all for the African
population, for whom associations provided almost the only opportunity for
individuals to acquire positions of responsibility and thereby express their
status and ambition.

It is therefore not surprising to find that anthropologists were struck by
the complexity of procedure, the scrupulous attention to protocol and the
fierce competition for position within black associations, already apparent in
Kimberley in the 1890s, where 'both the Duke of Wellington and the Eccentrics Cricket clubs had long lists of office bearers. Anybody who was anybody
sought to become involved in running the club even if they did not actually
play the game.'[18] Meetings of sports clubs or cultural associations gave rise to
prolonged debates, frequently in English, with carefully recorded minutes. It
has been suggested that the rigid formality of the meetings of the Durban and
District African F.A. in the 1950s reflected African respect for, and desire to
conform to, 'European' standards and values.

At meetings, the committee procedures often take on an independent
life and the work of the association is enmeshed in the most complex
and obdurate debate . . . . With the passage of time, the minutes become
businesslike, but there is still much sterile debate. This arises in part
from the desire to display procedural virtuosity and from a lack of

familiarity with the rules. But the emphasis on ritual also shows the importance attached to the organizational mysteries of the White man. Magubane describes the obsession with constitutional procedure as an overconformity, enabling Africans who are barred from assimilation to identify mentally with the practices and outlook of the dominant White group; and he refers to some of the judicial procedures as vicarious participation in the European social structure. From another point of view, it seems as though the symbols of power represented by the committee procedures of the White man become a substitute for the exercise of power and that political energy, denied other expression, is projected into the football association. Certainly there is much rivalry for position.[19]

In East London, according to Mayer, 'the sports club — like the church — provides a welcome outlet for the ambitions and rivalries of the location dwellers. Each club has its President, two or three vice-presidents, a secretary, a treasurer and four to six members,'[20] while in Cape Town:

Scope for leadership among Africans is very limited and office in almost any sort of organization is a source of social prestige. Whereas for a White man or woman, there are many alternative opportunities of exercising leadership in work, in politics, in local government, as well as in church or social clubs or sport, the opportunities for an African are few. To a White man the secretaryship of a rugby club may indeed be a burden, not willingly undertaken, but to most Africans office in almost any organization carries prestige . . . . 'People in Langa cling to positions as tenaciously as if they were careers.'[21]

Club management was often oligarchical, and officials held to their positions for years, even decades. Between 1923 and 1960 there were just six Presidents of the Durban and District African F.A., and over half the Associations' officials held office for over ten years. Changes were almost invariably accomplished by coup d'etats or secessions, and there were many of these in the history of sporting and cultural associations throughout this period. Another incident from the history of the Durban and District African F.A. illustrates the significance of distinctions in rank:

In 1932 there was a move for changes in the executive. A.J. Luthuli, the Vice-President was elected president, 'Telephone' Ngcobo, the former president, was elected treasurer; and A.R. Ntuli, vice-secretary. Luthuli declined office; because of his duties as a teacher, secretary of the Natal Native Football Association, and secretary and treasurer of the South African Football Association, he felt his hands were full. Ntuli declined: 'seeing that I have been elected Vice-Secretary, I feel that the meeting has indirectly trespassed on my name, hence I feel compelled to decline the offer.' Ngcobo said: 'In the same way of the inferiority of the office of treasurer compared with the office he holds with the Natal Native Football Association and the S.A. African Football Association he decided to decline the acceptance.'[22]

It must be remembered, however, that sports officials faced immense difficulties, due to lack of money, material equipment, grounds, and Government interference in their affairs. Some associations had solid finances and organization. The Durban and District African F.A. was one: with a budget in the 1950s of £12,000 a year, 256 clubs and 5,000 members, it was in a position to organize a tour of Rhodesia (Zimbabwe) costing £1,000 and buy 50 acres of land at Inanda for £7,800. This was exceptional. In general, overheads (transport costs in particular) absorbed a high proportion of club income, and this income was limited by the fact that it was normally impossible to charge gate money, since pitches could rarely be fenced off.[23] Players and teams also prided themselves in their appearance: 'Boots, jerseys and stockings are expensive in terms of African wages, and a player may be ordered off the field if he is not correctly dressed. Team members are commonly required to buy their own togs, but the club or in tournaments the union or board, must provide balls and referees' whistles and pay for the hire or upkeep of a field.'[24] There were certainly cases of dishonesty (sometimes concealed from the police)[25] but they appear to have been rare. On the whole, sports officials devoted themselves unstintingly to the associations they led. Through the professionally dry commentaries of the urban anthropologists glimpses of the vigorous associational life of the townships peep through, in, for instance, the brilliant names of the clubs, which ring out sharply against the dull and impoverished milieu from which they sprang: the Swallows, the Bushbucks, the Black Lions, the Winter Roses, the Stone Breakers, the Boiling Waters, the Busy Bees, the Gunpowder Soccer Club . . .

Proliferation of Clubs
Of all the weaknesses from which sports associations suffered during this period, the most important was their vulnerability to splits. The multiplication of clubs was due in the first place to increases in membership, as sports were adopted by the ever-growing number of migrants to the mining and industrial towns. According to the urban anthropologists, disputes over structure and organization were rarely the immediate causes. Rather they were brought about by personality clashes between officials,[26] or conflicts between two groups of members (as when 'Home-boys' from one region accused 'Home-boys' from another of discrimination). Professionally preoccupied by kinship, the anthropologist Leo Kuper interprets such splits in terms of lineage segmentation. Wilson and Mafeje, using Botto's figures, suggest instead that secessions reflected other lines of social cleavage, and occurred when organizations reached a critical size which was related to the number of players needed to compose teams with a reasonable standard of play.

It appears that the size of the group which coheres is directly related to

its function; if it grows larger than the efficient minimum then splits
are tolerated; if it grows larger than the efficient maximum then splits
are essential . . . . In the rugby clubs the minimum necessary for a team
is fifteen playing members . . . but if the members exceed more than
sixty then more than half the players cannot play in either first or
second teams, and have little chance of playing in matches. Commonly
they prefer to form another club of their own . . . . Father Botto's
investigations show that the rugby clubs ranged in size from 15 to 75
with an average of 37 members. Soccer clubs averaged 45 members,
and cricket clubs 80 . . . . Sports clubs in the White community in Cape
Town are often considerably larger than this — rugby clubs may have 5
to 8 teams and 150 members . . . . The enjoyment of a good game and
the prestige of belonging to a well-known club, outweigh the feeling
that a member should be in the first or second team and large and old-
established clubs enjoy the ownership of facilities which seceding
groups cannot hope to equal. A Langa club owns no property at all,
except a ball, or a cricket bat.[27]

Apparently sporting causes of splits thus concealed others that were essentially social. Amongst other things, this indicates that material handicaps —
lack of facilities and resources — were among the principal constraints on
achievement of high standards. Where secessions were rare, and stronger and
larger associations developed, it was for reasons incidental to the promotion
of sport: for instance, Durban Council refused to recognize more than one
African Football Association. Wilson and Mafeje argue that in Langa the size
of federations simply corresponded to the size of the client group they served.
The clubs which survived longest were those 'with strong Home-boy or local
urban loyalty, which unifies them *in opposition to* other like groups. Once
the identity of a group diminishes, its association is liable to disintegrate'.[28]

In fact, no organizational or structural barrier to subdivision existed at
this period — other than the determination of individual sports officials to
increase the size and importance of their organization. Splits were occasioned
by internal pressures of a non-structural kind or by external pressures which
often had only an indirect bearing on sport. No doubt the tendency to absorb
new players by multiplying the number of small, local associations, rather
than by creating larger units of organization reflected to some extent the
'tribalizing' impact of apartheid, and this is supported by the fact that until
the end of the 1950s secessions were much more prevalent among African
than Coloured or Indian associations. Nevertheless, the frequency of splits
cannot be explained only in these terms. The absence of a common integrative aim and the fragility of administration and organization undoubtedly
reduced the ability of black sports associations to defend the interests of
their members and raise the standards of play.

The oligarchical and personalized leadership of many of the associations,
rendered large-scale integration even more difficult. By the 1950s, many
sports officials, as Leo Kuper has pointed out, were already playing the role

of intermediaries between the interests of the white sports organizations and the Government and the contrary interests of the black membership which had elected them. Squeezed, such officials 'oscillated', in Kuper's words, between 'servile and belligerent states': the servants of both parties, they behaved in the contradictory fashion which has become the hallmark of black officials under apartheid.[29]

The opposite reaction to white discrimination also existed: some black associations refused to recognize any form of leadership or organization at all.

> In a community in which order is maintained by force, any exercise of authority tends to be resented; all authority is identified with power, and resisted as 'persecution' or 'discrimination' . . . . In the Langa context it is instructive to find that the Statelytes, a group of educated young men, refused to choose a leader 'though in fact it was obvious who their leader was'. They followed a pattern prevalent for a time at Fort Hare, when teams used to refuse to elect a captain.[30]

One of the most important contributions of the non-racial sports movement which began to emerge during the 1950s was simply to provide a universal non-sectarian principle of organization. In a very short time, black sports officials and sportsmen and women were able to establish national structures in most sports and to put their demands to the white sports establishment and the Government in a new and altogether more forceful manner. At the same time, more people had access to sport and sporting standards rose.

Race Relations in Sport

As we have seen, the first official declaration of Government sports policy dated from 1956, when the Minister of the Interior, Dr Dongs, banned inter-racial competition in sport.[31] Before this date, sports associations were free to organize as they wished. It would be quite wrong, however, to take this to mean that the Government created racial segregation in sport, for none of the white sports federations had ever accepted black players as equals or recognized black sports organizations. What is significant is the fact that the 1956 policy was introduced *because* black organizations were beginning successfully to contest the hegemony of white federations and to demand national and international recognition.

Virtually no contact took place between white federations and the players affiliated to black unions either before or after 1956. The handful of exceptions to this rule only illustrate more clearly the completeness of racial segregation. Llewlyn, the only black cricketer to represent South Africa, was persecuted by his team mates; Papwa Sewgolum was prevented from playing in the South African Open Golf championships after 1965 and excluded from the national team; the gifted Indian sportsman Baboollal Maharaj, who played rugby with a white Transvaal team in the 1920s, was only able to do so because he spoke perfect Afrikaans and had a pale skin;[32] the tennis player David Samaai played in Wimbledon in 1951 and 1954, but was never recognized by the official white association,[33] etc.

Unofficially, some informal contact did occur between black and white sportsmen. This was particularly true in cricket and in other games where, 'it is possible to maintain social distance'.[34] For some years Rhodes University played friendly matches with Fort Hare and occasional friendly games were also played by white and black footballers on the Rand in the 1920s and 1930s. Some white footballers appear to have played for the Durban and District African F.A. and, as we have seen, inter-racial contacts were promoted within the Joint Councils Movement. None of these, however, threatened the hegemony of the white federations, which in addition enjoyed exclusive recognition abroad. Challenged in the 1950s, the white federations at once reaffirmed their monopoly over the organization of sport and claimed the right to remain racially exclusive while denying the right of black federations to seek independent international recognition. The strategy is revealed clearly in the case of weight-lifting, where, as Chris de Broglio wrote, 'there have always been very good relations between active white and non-white weight-lifters, who often train together . . . and only have one enemy in common — gravity.'[35] After the War, a group of white lifters formed a racial federation which was recognized by the British (then world) ruling body. When the other lifters demanded recognition in their turn, therefore, they were told that the rules of the racial white federation 'as with all national sporting associations in South Africa, will not permit of mixed contests between white and coloured athletes. This is also a condition of the South African Olympic Council, therefore no coloured man could be chosen to represent South Africa in the international contests.'[36]

It can, therefore, be said that the direct interference of Government in sport after 1956 did not modify the policies of the official white sports bodies, but confirmed the status quo. At best, black sportsmen were good enough to sharpen up the white champions: David Samaai beat several of South Africa's best white players in training;[37] black boxers regularly sparred with, but could not fight, white champions;[38] Coloured cricketers were employed to give white players net practice.[39] In contrast, within the black sports associations, inter-racial contact became increasingly common, and Africans or Indians frequently played in Coloured teams and vice versa, in rugby, tennis, cricket and other sports.[40]

Nonetheless, until the 1950s the black sports federations were constituted on a racial basis, as a list compiled in 1950 shows clearly (Table 5). A number of these associations, like the Durban and District African F.A., the Indian Weight-lifting Association or the Coloured Rugby Board, did not exclude sportsmen from other racial groups; others applied racial criteria to the letter. In general, most major federations were organizing inter-racial (i.e. between Blacks) national and provincial championships by the late 1940s or early

Table 5
Black Sports Federations, circa 1948

Football

S.A. African F.A.	Transvaal, Griqualand West, Natal, O.F.S.
S.A. Bantu F.A.	Transvaal, Natal, O.F.S.
S.A. Indian F.A.	Transvaal, Natal, Eastern Province, Border, Griqualand West, Western Province.
S.A. Coloured Football Board	Transvaal, Western Province, Eastern Province, Natal, O.F.S., Griqualand West, Border.

Rugby

S.A. Bantu Rugby Union	Transvaal, Eastern Province, Western Province, Border, Midlands, Griqualand West.
S.A. Rugby Sports Board of Control	Transvaal, Northern Transvaal, Eastern Province, Western Province, Griqualand West, Border, Southwestern Districts, Boland, City & Suburban (Cape Town).

Cricket

S.A. Bantu Cricket Association	Transvaal (2 unions), Border, Eastern Province, Western Province, Griqualand West, Natal.
S.A. Indian Cricket Union	Transvaal, Natal, Eastern Province.
S.A. Coloured Cricket Association	Transvaal, Western Province, Eastern Province, Natal, Griqualand West, Border.

Tennis

S.A. Bantu Lawn Tennis Association	Transvaal, Eastern Province, Western Province, Natal, O.F.S.
S.A. Indian Lawn Tennis Association	Transvaal, Natal, Eastern Province, Western Province, Border.

Athletics
No national black association; frequent competitions.

Swimming
No national black association; very few facilities.

Hockey
No national black association; there was a Bantu and an African Coloured Johannesburg Women's Hockey Association.

Golf
No national black association; played by all black groups; no proper facilities.

Basketball
No national black association; played by schoolgirls.

Boxing

Non-European Amateur Boxing Association	Transvaal, Natal, Eastern Province, Western Province.

Table 5 (Continued)

Weightlifting

Indian Weightlifting   (No information available)
  Association

Table Tennis

S.A. Table Tennis Board   (No information available)

Gymnastics

No national black association; played in boys clubs.

Source: Completed from information in Jokl, in Hellmann, 1949, pp. 445-7.

1950s: rugby 'tests' were played every year from 1950 to 1959 by the Coloured and African rugby associations; representative teams from the different cricket boards played one another within the Inter-Race Boards and then the SACBOC championships; Inter-Race Boards also brought Indian, African and Coloured football teams together in the Transvaal, Kimberley, Bloemfontein and Durban. Indian and Coloured athletes competed against one another in inter-provincial competitions.[41]

In addition, each national federation organized its own national championships. Some of these were 'open': Jasmat Dhiraj, for example, won all three of the black tennis trophies and in the 1960s was at once the Indian, Coloured and African champion.[42]

It was nevertheless a most wasteful system. There were up to four national federations in each sport, each with an independent organizing body, separate finances and facilities and competitions. Administrative and financial costs were quadrupled while the level of competition was reduced by a similar factor. As a result, standards inevitably suffered, because the best players rarely, if ever, competed against each other. On top of this, secessions were frequent, and the facilities to which competitors had access varied from place to place, and even more from race to race.

Inevitably, the African sportsman, with the fewest resources and the worst facilities, suffered most; Indian and Coloured sportsmen fared somewhat better; and white sportsmen, with access to excellent facilities and international competition, prospered. In short, it was a system which, at the greatest cost to the black population, ensured that the advantages of the white sporting fraternity would be preserved. Indeed, for many years, the official justification advanced by white sports associations for refusing to change their racially discriminatory policies was that these maintained competitive standards . . . white standards.

When the Nationalists took power in 1948, therefore, black sport was already almost entirely separated from white (and therefore international) sport, and was further subdivided into black racial associations. Separate at the top, the latter were, however, increasingly experimenting with multi-racial competitions and organization. By this time, sport occupied a most important place in black society, and particularly in urban life, which explains why the influence of Indian and Coloured sportsmen was so much greater than their numbers in the population as a whole. Sports associations were generally led by educated people from the small black middle class, and were organized after the pattern of white associations, whose hegemony was rarely contested in public. At club and team level (and more especially in the major popular sports of rugby and football) players had the same class background or social origin, and sport expressed, and diverted, the competition between different social groups. Reflecting the character of a society in rapid transformation, the history of sport during this period of expansion is studded with splits and secessions, and there is ample evidence that an increasing and sometimes extraordinarily high proportion of the black population played or took an interest in one sport or another.

The first attempts to question the hegemony of white associations were made in 1946. The arrival of the Nationalists in power two years later provoked a political crisis which extended to the organization of sport. During the 1950s, a new non-racial sports movement took shape: it is the subject of the latter part of this book.

References

1. Wilson and Mafeje, 1963, pp. 113-4.
2. Unfortunately, we know very little about women's sport, either in the past or today: the absence of sources is itself evidence of the neglect from which it has suffered.
3. This survey, unpublished, was carried out by D.H. Reader: reference to it is made by Mayer, 1961, pp. 220-1.
4. Servants (most women migrants) lived in, but did not necessarily have urban rights.
5. Mayer, 1961.
6. Wilson and Mafeje, 1963.
7. Patterson, 1953, pp. 153 and 155.
8. H. Kuper, 1960, p. 75.
9. Wilson and Mafeje, 1963, p. 144.
10. Pauw, 1963, pp. 44-5.
11. From an interview cited in Mayer, 1961, p. 220.
12. Wilson and Mafeje, 1963, p. 30.
13. Wilson and Mafeje, 1963, pp. 115-7.
14. Pauw, 1963, p. 173.
15. Pauw, 1963, p. 173.
16. L. Kuper, 1965, p. 357.
17. Mayer, 1961, p. 221.
18. B. Willan, p. 14.
19. Kuper, 1965, p. 351: the reference is to Magubane, *Sport & Politics in an Urban African Community*.

20. Mayer, 1961, p. 220.
21. Wilson and Mafeje, 1963, p. 145.
22. L. Kuper, 1965, p. 353.
23. Wilson and Mafeje, 1963, pp. 119-20.
24. Wilson and Mafeje, 1963, pp. 119-20.
25. L. Kuper, 1965, p. 350 and 353.
26. See for example L. Kuper, 1965, pp. 354-6, for the dispute between 'Japanese' and 'Russians' within the Durban and District African F.A.
27. Wilson and Mafeje, 1963, p. 177.
28. Ibid.
29. L. Kuper, 1965, p. 318: see below pp. 200-1.
30. Wilson and Mafeje, 1961, p. 173.
31. See p. 46. The Government's first intervention occurred in 1951, to stop multi-racial boxing: see Lapchick, 1975, p. 21.
32. P.B. Singh, interview, London, 23 April 1980.
33. S. Patterson, 1953, pp. 130-1.
34. S. Patterson, 1953, p. 131, note 29.
35. Chris de Broglio, 1970, p. 25.
36. Letter from Mr Oscar State, Secretary of the British Empire Games Association, in de Broglio, 1970, p. 1.
37. J. Dhiraj, interview, London, 12 February 1980.
38. Isaiah Stein, interview, London, 11 February 1980.
39. S. Patterson, 1953, p. 134, note 37.
40. Interviews with Messrs Abbas, Dhiraj and Compton.
41. E. Jokl in E. Hellman, 1949.
42. J. Dhiraj, interview, London, 12 February 1980.

7.   Sport and Apartheid

In the previous chapters we have traced the evolution of sport within South African history as a whole, paying attention to the major games and the development of black sport. In this chapter we shall try to provide a factual description of contemporary South African sport as it is specifically organized and structured by apartheid. Without launching into a full-scale account of the apartheid system as a whole, we have confined our attention to the principal socio-economic factors and divisions: *urbanization*, whose influence on the spread of sport we have already seen; the *standard of living and quality of life; health and social welfare* conditions; *education* (school attendance in particular); *public spending and provision* on sport (including facilities, coaching programmes etc.); and the *institutions* created to promote, organize and co-ordinate sporting activity.

On each of these counts, South African society is extremely unequal. Apartheid is not merely a system of segregation, it also works to *widen* the inequalities between the minority of white citizens on the one hand and the majority of disenfranchised Blacks on the other. Within this major division of the population, the African majority is then itself separated from the other black minorities — the Indians and Coloureds, who are relatively better off. Africans are subject to harsher laws and to specific restrictions which handicap them alone.

In this chapter we shall briefly examine each of the factors listed above with the aid of the available statistics in order to demonstrate the attitudes of different groups to sport, and to indicate to what extent sport is accessible to different groups, how much it is encouraged, its cost, its popularity, etc. We have paid particular attention to the African population because Africans are both the majority group and the most disadvantaged.

Apartheid does not, as the Nationalist Party pretends, promote the 'separate development' of the country's various racial groups. It is *a system of racial exploitation and domination organized in such a way that class and race tend to coincide*. Members of the white minority take it for granted that a black person is not the equal of a white person, and that the existing racial hierarchy, descending from the white minority, which is above all Blacks, through the Indian and Coloured minorities, to the African, who stands below all other groups, should be respected at all times, and in all domains of life. In sport this view implies that the least competent white player in the lowest league is qualified to instruct the best players in the top African teams. A limited number of concessions are offered to the two black minorities (and to certain members of the African middle class) which, though keeping them in the camp of the 'non-Whites', also serve to separate their interests from those of the African majority. It is a policy designed to disarm and exploit the African majority; it serves too to divide — and rule — the black population as a whole.

The White Minority

In 1904 white South Africans represented 21.6% of the total population; today they account for only 16.2%. At the beginning of the century, half lived in rural areas; today over 86% are urban residents. Almost all English-speakers live in towns (95%), which means that virtually all farmers are Afrikaners. 70% of Afrikaners are also city-dwellers, however, an indication of the gradual blending of the white community whose political beliefs and standard of living are increasingly similar. The Nationalist Party has become far more acceptable to English-speakers since it took power in 1948, and the Afrikaner population has been able to bring its level of material life closer to that of the English-speaking population. Only Whites have political rights including the right to vote: as a result they control all political institutions from Parliament to the trade unions, and monopolize socio-economic wealth.

Table 6
Rural and Urban Population by Racial Groups, 1970

	Urban Areas	%	Rural Areas	%	Total
Africans	4,989,371	33.13	10,068,581	66.86	15,057,952[1]
Coloureds	1,494,490	74.04	523,963	25.96	2,018,453
Indians	535,536	86.73	81,900	13.27	617,436
Whites	3,257,805	86.34	493,523	13.16	3,751,328

1. 8,060,773 (53.53%) of Africans are in 'white' areas, of whom 54.6% are urbanized.

Indians

The level of urbanization among Indians has always been close to that of Whites. Almost all Indians live in Natal (83%); they speak English and five Indian languages. 73% are Hindu and 20% Muslim. The community has always claimed an individual identity and its religious and cultural beliefs have helped to keep it a relatively closed society. Indian immigration was stopped definitively in 1913.

From this date, until 1975, Indians were forbidden to leave their province for another. For many years they were considered to be foreigners and their rights of residence and property were severely restricted even before the Group Areas Act was introduced in 1950. They did not receive South African nationality until 1961. Only since 1974 has even half the Indian Representative Council been elected. The Department of Indian Affairs is entirely under white control. Under the new Constitution (1980), Indians are also represented on the Presidential Council which first met in February 1981, and which has White, Coloured and Indian (but no African) members.

Comparatively Indians have suffered materially from apartheid more than the other two major black communities. The Group Areas Act entailed the forcible displacement of a very high proportion of Indian families, and the collapse of Indian businesses in areas allotted to other (usually the white) groups. The sociologist, Fatima Meer, has said that before 1966 about 75% of the Indians in Durban owned their own houses and the land they stood upon; today about a dozen Indian groups own land. The rest is in the hands of the Department of Community Development and Durban Municipal Council, both all-white institutions.[1]

The Coloured Minority

This is historically and culturally the black group closest to the Whites: 85% of Coloureds speak Afrikaans, 94% are Christian. Nine out of ten Coloured people live in the Cape Province where, since 1951, they compose the majority of the population of Cape Town and its surrounding area.

Coloured people are theoretically free to travel and own property within the areas ascribed to them. They have nevertheless suffered greatly from the Group Areas Act which resulted in vast numbers of people being forcibly moved to unhealthy and undeveloped areas where many still wait to be rehoused while living in the most deplorable conditions. Because they share much of their cultural heritage and history with the Whites, and had many rights which segregation and apartheid have subsequently stripped from them, the Coloured population is particularly sensitive to that great misnomer — so-called 'petty' apartheid in all its many forms: Coloured people can no longer walk in the same parks, share the same buses, cinemas or ambulances as white people — even their dogs have to be buried in separate graveyards.

In 1968, apartheid finally deprived Coloured people of their last political rights in the Cape Province. Under Vorster, the South African Government refused to allow even indirect Coloured representation in Parliament. Until 1981, the Coloured population largely boycotted the Coloured Representative Council, which had purely advisory functions and to which Coloured voters were allowed to elect only 40% of the members. The new Constitution dissolved the Council in May 1980; nominated Coloured members now sit in the President's Council, which has replaced the previous Westminster-style second chamber.

Africans

For the African population, apartheid means 13% of the territory for 71% of the population; it means the migrant labour system, the absence of free movement, the obligation to carry a pass book,[2] the denial of South African citizenship, the refusal of all political rights (Africans are only entitled to vote in their supposed 'Homelands'), and the humiliation of racial discrimination at all levels. Apartheid deepens the divisions between the minority of township dwellers and the mass of temporary labour migrants, recruited in the bantustans on one- or two-year contracts, separated from their wives and children, lodged in compounds or single-men's hostels, and put to unskilled work in white farms, mines and industry. One-third of the African population lives in towns, but only a very small proportion of these people have the right to live permanently where they work. Residence laws have been so tightened that it has become virtually impossible for Africans to acquire urban rights, and even the minority who do possess them have no right to own property.[3] In the huge, artificial city of Soweto (the acronym for South Western Townships), which contains 6% of the entire African population (although it does not figure on maps of the country), an average of 14 people occupy every house. Tens of thousands more are on the waiting lists. Although wide swathes of this city have no electricity or even elementary services, around the perimeter towering electric pylons have been erected by the Government to illuminate the streets and facilitate riot control.

For all Africans, apartheid is the ever present threat of being arbitrarily expelled to the bantustans under one of the numerous laws governing their movements. A person may be expelled if officials decide he or she is inconvenient, or undesirable, unemployed, old or 'unproductive' (*sic*). Removal to the bantustans means consignment to a living death: overpopulated and undercapitalized, these territories cannot support the people who live in them. Yet Africans cannot legally leave their 'Homelands' (which frequently they have never seen) unless they accept the exploitative terms of contract labour.

Income and Socio-economic Conditions

White South Africans have an income comparable to that of North Americans. Their standard of living puts them on a par with the six richest nations on earth (though actual figures vary depending on the sources and bases of calculation): according to the *Financial Times*, in 1975 the average white income per capita was approximately $3,150 per annum. In comparison, Coloureds and Indians earned on average 9 times less (350 dollars) and Africans on average 18 times less (185 dollars). In the 1970s, it was generally considered that wage differentials between Whites and Africans were of the order of 1:20.

This high standard of living for Whites, garnished with numerous privileges, explains why white voters have accepted the very considerable restraints which the Nationalist Government have placed on freedom of expression, the press etc. The white electorate has consistently voted for the party which has promised most forcefully to guarantee its privileges. In sport, privilege is expressed in the wealth of facilities available to most white South Africans —

facilities which, it must be repeated, are financed by resources appropriated directly and indirectly from the resources of the whole population to serve the white population exclusively.[4]

The 20:1 average income differential mentioned above includes Africans living in both the urban areas and the bantustans. But this makes it a rather artificial calculation. Incomes in the 'Homelands', where over a third of the African population is obliged to live, are on average 40% lower than the *average* African income. In many cases, rural incomes are so far below subsistence level that the families of migrant workers could not survive if they did not receive wages remitted from the towns, thereby reinforcing the migrant labour system.

In contrast, in Dube (a select suburb of Soweto), a tiny minority of prosperous Africans have come into existence since the 1960s: nicknamed 'Dubenheimers' after the magnate Harry Oppenheimer, some of them, like George Thabe, have made their reputation and much of their money through sport or its promotion.

The Poverty Datum Line (P.D.L.) fixed by the Chamber of Commerce is designed to indicate the absolute minimum income required to feed, clothe and lodge a family of six. In 1976, the P.D.L. for Johannesburg was set at 122 rand, and in May 1979 at 172.72 rand a month.[5] It is an indication of the appallingly low incomes of many African workers that as many as 43% of Soweto families were estimated to be earning less than the P.D.L. in 1976.[6] In 1973 a survey found that 22.5% of Africans were living below the P.D.L.: at that time 1% of white employees were manual workers, compared with 7% of Indians, 24% of Coloureds and 60% of Africans.[7]

There are, therefore, enormous differences in income and living standards between the urban and rural populations. The majority of Africans live in 'white areas' (53.5% against 46.5% in the bantustans) but nearly as many Africans live in white rural areas as in towns. Poverty is particularly acute on the white-owned farms where in the 1970s wages stood at about 5 to 6 rand a month,[8] and where living conditions, schooling, housing, health facilities frequently remain deplorable. According to the F.A.O. more than three-quarters of the African families living in rural areas earn less than the P.D.L. Africans in both the rural white areas and in the bantustans are poor in comparison with the African population which has permanent urban residence rights, and depend upon migrant labour for about 70% of family income.

The gap between African and white wages varies in different sectors, according to Table 7, from 1:5 to 1:8. Following major strikes in 1973,[9] African wages have risen but so has the cost of living. According to one calculation, mine wages in 1966 were no higher (if indeed they were not lower) than they had been in 1911.[10]

Table 8 shows the extent to which African labour is concentrated in the primary sector and in unskilled work, and the degree to which the white labour force dominates the tertiary sector and skilled jobs. The small minority of Africans working in commerce and industry is essentially composed of urban Africans who have been able to acquire a better education and are

Table 7
Average Wages by Sector and Racial Group, 1975 (rand per month)

Sector	White	Indian	Coloured	African
Mining	590	221	163	79
Construction	539	299	215	115
Manufacturing	550	167	143	117
Public Services	398	298	166	111

Source: I.L.O., 1975.

Table 8
Distribution of the Economically Active Population, 1970 (%)

Sector	Whites	Coloureds & Indians	Africans	Total
Agriculture	6.5	14.2	35.9	28.0
Mining	4.2	0.9	10.7	8.7
Manufacturing	25.9	36.3	14.4	19.0
Trade, Transport, Services and Administration	60.8	40.3	27.9	35.2
Unemployed/Other	2.5	7.8	11.1	9.1

Source: Percentages established from the *Statistical Bulletin*, March 1975, paragraph 2.1 and 2.11, in U.N.O., 1978, p. 24

closer to urban opportunities. The African 'bourgeoisie' which is today promoted by some Nationalist circles (and opposed by others),[11] today contains a handful of businessmen. This settled urban elite demands South African citizenship and, since 1976, municipal autonomy for Soweto and other major townships. These concessions would effectively protect them from falling under legislation concerning the bantustans.

The employment structure of the Indian minority has been radically altered in the last 20 years. Many Indian traders were forced out of business by the Government and a majority of Indians now work in the professions, or in manufacturing companies (food, textiles) employing Indian labour. The proportion of traders has fallen from 22% in 1960 to 13% in 1970, while the proportion in manufacturing and the professions has risen during the same period from 26% to 45%. The Indian community is sharply divided between its independent business community, many of whose members were free immigrants to South Africa, and which controls most cultural activity, and a growing minority of Indians who suffer from extreme poverty (19% in 1971). On average, however, the Indian population is relatively prosperous compared with both Africans and Coloured people. Many are white collar workers. Their wages are on average between 30% and 50% higher than those of Africans, and between 15% and 25% higher than those of Coloureds; they are between 25% and 50% lower than those of white employees.

25% of the active Coloured population is employed in manufacturing and another 19% in domestic service and the hotel trade. A significant proportion (about 17%) are still agricultural workers, whose wages are governed by the archaic and grotesque custom of the 'tot', which dates back to Van Riebeeck, and by which workers are paid largely in wine. Most live in deplorable conditions of poverty and insecurity. There is a Coloured 'middle class' composed of traders, restaurant owners, skilled artisans and professional people. Like members of the Indian elite, this group is generally opposed to apartheid, but is also courted by the Government, in the hope that in time it can be separated from the mass of the black population.

Health and Nutrition

> The poverty datum line (P.D.L.), or poverty threshold, is often used as a base to establish earnings levels. The extremely low salaries keep black workers in permanent poverty and at the limits of hunger. The payments in kind which Blacks receive on white farms produce the same, or worse, results . . . . In the reserves, families do not produce as many food products as they need. They therefore depend upon money sent by migrant workers . . . . Food alone . . . costs an 'average' family (composed of 0.5 men, 1.5 women and 3 children) about 40 rands a month. An *umnqqushe* diet of maize and beans costs about 17 rands. Even that represents more than the sum a miner can send every month to his family.[12]

According to a survey published by the *Financial Mail* in January 1980, 75% of the children admitted to the KwaZulu hospital at Nguti suffered from malnutrition: 10% subsequently died. According to another report (in the *Sunday Tribune*, 27 June 1976), in 1976 three children were dying of malnutrition every hour in South Africa. 'Between 15,000 and 30,000 die every year of malnutrition, without counting the diseases like tuberculosis which it encourages.'[13] Recent statistics indicate that the rate of infant mortality among the white population (12 in 1,000) is lower than that in the United Kingdom.[14] By contrast:

> It is difficult to obtain statistics concerning infantile mortality among the African population and generally one has to be content with estimates. At all events, the level of infantile mortality is 5 times higher than among Whites and 3 times higher than among Asians. The figure

has also been put forward for Africans of 200 to 250 deaths per thousand children born alive. According to some experts, this estimate is exaggerated, although others believe the rate could reach 450 deaths per thousand children born alive. According to one study made in 1966 'half the children born in a typical African reserve in South Africa die before they reach 5 years of age' [the rate among whites is 7%].[15]

Table 9
Rates of Infant Mortality (Deaths per 1,000 Live Births)

Year	White	Indian	Coloured	African
1960	29.6	59.6	128.6	?
1970	21.6	36.4	132.6	100-110[1]
1972	21.1	45.7	128.3	
1977	n.a.	n.a.	n.a.	(220 minimum (320 maximum

1. This figure appears to be a definite underestimate.

Sources: *South Africa 1977, Official Year Book* (1977), completed by figures from U.N.O., 1978, p. 11, and for 1977 by S.A.I.R.R., 1979, p. 563.

'Malnutrition is worse in the rural areas . . . . But when there is malnutrition in the urban areas, it is more serious because the poor there do not have the family network which comes to their aid in the rural areas.'[16]

Table 10
Proportion of Undernourished Children between 0 and 5 years, Transvaal, 1973

Type of Malnourishment	White All Areas	Black Urban	Black Rural
Too fat and obese	17.6	7.4	0.4
Moderately or gravely underweight	6.0	21.0	65.6
Calorie or protein deficiency	0.0	0.6	7.0

Source: *South African Medical Journal*, 47, p. 688, 1973, in F.A.O., 1978, p. 36.

In contrast, many white South Africans suffer from overweight and over-eating. More men in South Africa suffer from coronaries between the ages of 25 and 45 than anywhere else in the world,[17] a fact which has stimulated debate in Parliament in favour of popular sports programmes and official publicity in favour of physical education.[18]

Table 11
Estimated Life Expectancy at Birth, 1969-71

White		African		Coloured		Indian	
Male	Female	Male	Female	Male	Female	Male	Female
64.5	72.3	51.2	58.9	48.8	56.1	59.3	63.9

Source: *South Africa 1977, Official Year Book*, 1977, p. 29.

Education

Education has been free and compulsory for white children since 1913. Sporting equipment and facilities have also been supplied free to Government schools from the same period. In contrast, African children must pay fees for their education, which is not compulsory; free compulsory education for the Indian and Coloured minorities was only introduced in 1973-74.

White children have among the best educational opportunities in the world, as South African officials are fond of pointing out. A higher proportion of white children receive a university education than in any other nation except the United States. Nearly 30% of the white male population aged between 25 and 64 has been through 12 years of schooling, and 7% of this age group possess a university degree.[19]

After the white minority, Indians have the best educational provision. The Indian community began very early to organize, at its own expense, the education of its children. From all points of view — from school attendance to the proportion of university students — Indians are incomparably better served than either Coloured people or Africans. There are proportionately four times as many Indian as Coloured students, and 17 times as many Indian as African students.

At present, about four out of five African children go to school, but 45% of these remain only for the first four primary years or less. 60% of Coloured children also leave before or at the end of four years, which means that according to accepted educational criteria over 56% of African and Coloured children remain illiterate.[20] Table 12 compares the proportion of children who had never been to school with the proportion of children who had passed Matriculation, as of 1970.[21]

Table 12
Educational Provision, 1970

Group	Had never been to school (%)	Had passed the Matriculation (%)
Africans	57	0.27
Coloureds	39	0.94
Indians	29	3.4
Whites	14.4	23.0

Only 5.5% of those Africans who had entered school in 1966 had gone on to advanced level at secondary school in 1977. Even fewer (0.2%) went to university (no more than 1,000 Africans a year).

Table 13
The University Student Population, 1977

Group	Total	% of Student Population	Estimated as % of Total Population
Africans	11,509	8.5	0.059
Coloureds	5,357	3.9	0.22
Indians	7,868	5.8	1.02
Whites	111,218	81.8	2.54
Total	135,952	100.0	

In 1977, therefore, it appears that the proportion of white students (in relation to the white population) was 43.3 times higher than the proportion of African students (to the African population) and 11 times higher than the proportion of Coloured to the Coloured population.

In the same year, the level of schooling of the different races was also grotesquely uneven, as Table 14 shows.

Table 15 shows that, in 1977, 13.5 times more was spent on educating a white child than on educating an African child; and three and four times more than on educating Coloured and Indian children respectively. Moreover, not only do African taxes provide more than 25% of the total education budget, Africans also pay large sums in addition to this amount which do not appear on official accounts: African parents contribute towards the construction costs of schools; they pay fees; unlike white children they have to pay for educational materials (pens, paper etc.), and they frequently pay teachers' salaries.

To combat malnutrition, in 1943 the authorities decided that one free meal would be provided in schools. The Nationalist Government reduced

Table 14
Percentage of Children in School by Level, 1977

Level of Schooling	Africans	Coloured	Indians	Whites
Primary				
Lower	62.2 %	55.5 %	43.3 %	37.3 %
Upper	24.6	28.0	29.4	26.4
Total	86.8	83.5	72.7	63.7
Secondary				
Junior	12.2 %	13.7 %	21.4 %	24.3 %
Senior	1.0	2.8	5.9	12.0
Total	13.2	16.5	27.3	36.3
	100.0 %	100.0 %	100.0 %	100.0 %

Table 15
The Education Budget, 1953-77 (rand per year per pupil)

	1953	1970	1977
Africans	17	17	48
Coloureds	n.a.	81	220
Indians	n.a.	73	157
Whites	128	282	654

the nutritional value of this meal and after 1956 it was abandoned altogether.

Four different kinds of school supply an education to African children: private mission schools;[22] state schools run by the Department of Bantu Education or the bantustan regimes; local schools which are administered and run by African communities, but which must conform in all respects to official educational policy; and farm schools, directed by the white employers.

Table 16
Numbers and Types of African Schools, 1977

Types of Schools	'White' Areas	Bantustans	Total
Schools under local control	1,448	5,041	6,489
Government schools	102	115	217
Farm schools	4,387	0	4,387
Private schools	84	48	132
Total (excl. Transkei)	6,021	5,204	11,225

Table 16 shows that in 1977 nearly three-quarters of the schools in the so-called white areas were farm schools, which provide an execrable standard of education. Only 3.1% of all schools were either state run or private ex-mission schools — the only schools in a position to provide a reasonable standard of sporting and general education. Moreover, the Nationalist Government is systematically building African secondary schools only in the bantustans, thereby obliging many adolescent children living in 'white' areas to leave their homes if they wish to continue their studies. In 1977 there were 1,121 African secondary schools in the bantustans (82% of the total number) and only 245 in 'white' areas (18%). According to the 1974 *Transkei Annual*, secondary pupils had to contribute one rand each term to pay for school activities and facilities, especially sports materials.[23]

Teaching conditions in African schools are generally alarming. In order to double the number of registered pupils without increasing costs, the Bantu Education Department introduced a 'double session' system, according to which one teacher gives the same three-hour lesson, morning and afternoon, to two different groups of children. (In 1977, 800,000 African children were on 'half-time' in this way, and the double session system was in practice in 55% of classes.) A similar economizing device, called the platoon system, is also operated: in this case, two teachers are employed, one for each group of pupils, but they share the same classroom — one group being taught in the morning, the other in the afternoon. In 1977 (excluding the Transkei), 100,500 African pupils, nearly 80,000 Coloured pupils and 11,777 Indian pupils were being taught in 'platoons'.

Sports Expenditure and Facilities

Whites and Blacks are not subject to the same tax system. In addition to the general tax paid by the whole population, Africans (until 1978) were subject to a fixed per capita tax, the poll tax. They continue to pay a tribal levy and a tax to the bantustans to which they have been attached by the Administration. The distribution of tax income is also inequitable, as we have seen in the case of education. According to the London *Times*, in 1971 only 5% of the South African national budget was devoted to spending on the African majority (then 75% of the population), although the latter contributed more than this amount in direct and indirect taxes.[24] Thus the tax system, like the rest of South Africa's political economy, has widened existing inequalities.

As far as investment in sport is concerned, public expenditure is shown in Table 17.

In 1974-75, according to Joan Brickhill,[25] only 7% of the African sports budget was provided from public funds: 93% came from the S.A. Bantu Trust, a separate organization created by the Government to finance the purchase of land for the bantustans and other official programmes affecting Africans. In contrast, the whole of the budget devoted to white sport was drawn from public funds; and in addition white sportsmen benefited from

Table 17
Public Expenditure on Sport (in rand)

Period	Whites	Africans	Coloureds	Indians
1965-1972	2,708,900	?	102,150	?
Per capita[1]	0.71	?	0.05	?
1974-1975	1,217,612	464,317	333,792	?
Per capita	0.29	0.029	0.014	?
1975-1976	1,417,609	415,439	449,112	20,300
Per capita	0.33	0.023	0.018	0.028
1977-1978	1,586,724	495,394	187,420	?
Per capita[2]	3.6	0.026	0.077	?

1. Estimated from the 1970 Census.
2. Estimated from official statistics published for 1977, the last year for which official figures of expenditure on sport are available.

the wealth of sports resources in private clubs, white schools etc. This is another prime example of the way in which the benefits which Africans receive from public expenditure do not reflect their contribution to the exchequer. Public money which is appropriated from the whole community is used to the exclusive advantage of white sport.

Since 1973, African sport has also been financed by the Bantu Sport and Recreation Fund, which was originally floated on money provided by major companies. In the year following its creation, over half a million rand were collected; interest then waned and in 1976 the Fund had fallen to only 69,000 rand.

Finally, as we have seen, the construction and maintenance of sports facilities in the townships continues to be financed from income accruing to the local authorities from their monopoly of liquor sales. Not only is money distributed inequitably between different groups but the finances to fund the sport of the African majority, who receive least, are derived directly from the profits from alcoholism. Mrs Fatima Meer, quoting from the *Post* of 25 August 1974, mentions that Durban City Council spent 5 million rand in 1973-74 on the Indian areas of Durban, and 750,000 rand on the Coloured areas. The same council spent 2.5 million rand to maintain the white beaches and another 2.4 million rand on the upkeep of public gardens to which Whites alone had access. As for sport, 2 million rand was devoted to white sport and 0.02 million to black sport — one hundred times less.[26]

The inequitable distribution of public and private funding of sporting activity has directly affected the density of sports facilities in black areas. Africans suffer, as they do in all spheres, more than any other group — particularly since they are prevented from owning or managing social and sporting facilities of their own and are therefore, unlike the Indian and Coloured minorities, entirely dependent upon white organizations and the white municipalities for all the facilities they use.

> There is only one 'national' stadium in Soweto . . . . It is the Orlando Stadium, whose maximum seating and standing capacity is 15,000. When big games are played — boxing is also popular — 30,000 sports fans are jam packed into the stadium. Scattered here and there are a few smaller football pitches, 9 small community halls and a number of dilapidated children's playgrounds. There are 2 swimming pools, one cinema, an amphitheatre, an undeveloped park, and a derelict golf course where golfers are allowed membership provided they produce a valid pass book to the W.R.A.B. officials. The former Transvaal Non-European Golf Union was ordered to disband by W.R.A.B. who took over control of the golf course.[27]

Survey work carried out in 1974 allows us to compare sporting facilities among the three population groups. At Soweto, in addition to the ground at Orlando, there were five rugby pitches (1 for every 200,000 people), 112 football pitches (1:8,929), 48 tennis courts (1:20,833), 6 swimming pools (1:166,667).[28] In comparison, Indian and Coloured people on the Reef appear to have been better off, even though the number and quality of sports facilities available to them were also far from adequate. In the same year, they had access to 4 rugby pitches (1:33,714, a ratio 6 times better), 57 football pitches (1:2,365, 4 times better), 32 tennis courts (1:4,214, 5 times better), 4 swimming pools (1:33,714, 5 times better), 3 netball courts, 22 cricket pitches, 3 athletics tracks and 4 hockey pitches.[29] The 200,000 Africans at Umlazi (Durban), in the same year, had access to 6 football pitches (1:33,333), 1 athletics track, and 6 tennis courts. At Guguletu (Cape Town), the African population of 52,800 had access to 5 football pitches (1:10,560), 2 rugby pitches (1:26,400) and 2 tennis courts.[30]

The official figures of sports facilities provided by the *1977 Year Book* — which do not take account of non-racial sport — give us some idea of the distribution of (official, recognized) sporting activity among the different racial groups.

Table 18 provides figures for membership and facilities in the major sports played by Africans and Coloureds; it also suggests the ratio of players to facilities. Table 19 shows the range of facilities available to each of the black populations, and suggests the ratio of facilities to each of these population groups as a whole. It should be remembered when reading these figures that no allowance has been made for their quality (although there are clearly wide disparities between turf and clay pitches, matting and grass wickets, etc.); and that many grounds are in multiple use (i.e. the same playing area has to serve footballers, rugby players, cricketers, etc. in turn).

Table 20, finally, provides a rough guide to the shortfall in facilities. These figures are calculated in relation to the *official* criteria set by the Standards Committee of the Indian and Coloured Departments of Community

Table 18
Estimated African and Coloured Membership of Official Sports Clubs, and Access to Facilities, 1977

Type of Sport	Africans						Coloureds			
	Membership	Clubs	Facilities				Membership	Clubs	Facilities	
			In 'White' Areas		In Bantustans	Total Ratio of Facilities to Players				
			Facilities Available	Ratio of Facilities to Players**	Facilities Available				Facilities Available	Ratio of Facilities to Players
Football	140,394	2,917	826	1:170	372	1:117	26,396	805	264	1:100
Netball*	29,155	251	517	1:56	29	1:53	5,670	273	257	1:22
Rugby	19,506	211	106	1:184	67	1:113	20,978	350	247	1:85
Athletics	12,051	37	53	1:227	8	1:197	1,030	31	10	1:103
Boxing	8,729	243	75	1:116	–	1:116	1,601	27	(local halls)	
Tennis	8,691	277	372	1:23	137	1:17	4,309	183	256	1:17
Basketball	6,815	57	131	1:52	–	1:52	–	–	–	–
Golf	3,478	85	32	1:109	8	1:87	1,341	36	4	1:335
Softball	2,876	78	37	1:78	1	1:76	986	30	10	1:99
Cricket	2,119	62	38	1:56	15	1:40	4,018	132	101	1:40
Swimming	1,537	14	28	1:55	6	1:45	2,010	26	24	1:84
Hockey	54	4	2	1:27	–	1:27	2,139	91	45	1:48
Gymnastics	20	5	–	–	–	–	4,470	62	(local halls)	
Table Tennis	–	–	–	–	–	–	4,309	183	256	1:17

* Netball is mainly played in schools.
**This is certainly the most important column: it shows the number of facilities available to African sportsmen and women living in 'white' areas (the number of club players being divided by the number of available facilities). Most African sportsmen live in 'white' areas.
Figures derived from South Africa 1977, Official Year Book.

Table 19
Official Sporting Facilities Available to the Three Black Communities

	Indians		Coloureds		Africans In 'White' Areas		Africans In Bantustans		Total	
Type of Sport	Facilities Available	Ratio of Facilities to Total Population	Facilities Available	Ratio of Facilities to Total Population	Facilities Available	Ratio of Facilities to Total Population	Facilities Available	Ratio of Facilities to Total Population	Facilities Available	Ratio of Facilities to Total Population
Football	100	1: 7,650	264	1: 9,212	826	1: 12,540	372	1: 24,201	1198	1: 16,161
Rugby	–		247	1: 9,846	106	1: 97,718	67	1: 134,371	173	1: 111,913
Tennis	24	1: 31,875	256	1: 9,500	372	1: 27,844	137	1: 65,714	509	1: 38,037
Netball	2	1:382,500	257	1: 9,463	517	1: 20,035	29	1: 310,443	546	1: 35,460
Swimming	7	1:109,286	24	1:101,333	28	1: 369,933	6	1:1,500,477	34	1: 569,441
Cricket	33	1: 23,182	101	1: 24,079	38	1: 272,582	15	1: 600,191	53	1: 365,302
Athletics	2	1:382,500	10	1:243,200	53	1: 195,436	8	1:1,125,358	61	1: 317,393
Hockey	3	1:255,000	45	1: 54,044	2	1:5,179,067	–		2	1:9,680,500
Boxing	–		?*		75	1: 138,108	–		75	1: 258,146
Basketball	–		–		131	1: 79,070	–		131	1: 147,794
Golf	–		4	1:608,000	32	1: 323,691	8	1:1,125,358	40	1: 484,025
Softball	–		10	1:243,200	37	1: 279,950	1	1:9,002,865	38	1: 509,500

* Local halls.

Figures derived from South Africa 1977, Official Year Book.

Table 20
Estimated Shortfall in Black Sports Facilities, 1977

Type of Sport	Official Standard Ratio of Facilities to Players *	Africans			Coloureds			Indians		
		Facilities which should be available	Shortfall	Shortfall in %	Facilities which should be available	Shortfall	Shortfall in %	Facilities which should be available	Shortfall	Shortfall in %
Football	1: 7,000	2,765	– 1,567	57	347	–101	29	109	– 7	6
Rugby	1:10,000	1,936	– 1,763	91	243	+ 4		76	– 76	100
Tennis	1: 2,000	96,805	–96,296	99	1,216	–960	78	382	–358	93
Swimming***	1:15,000	1,290	– 1,256	97	162	–138	85	51	– 44	86
	1:50,000	387	– 387	100	48	– 48	100	15	– 14	93
Hockey	1:10,000	1,936	– 1,934	99	243	–198	81	76	– 73	96

* In the case of football, one football pitch should be provided for every 7,000 in the population. Africans should therefore have access to at least 2,765 pitches, according to official standards. In fact there are 1,567 less than this, a shortfall of 57%.

**Two different official standards were put forward for swimming: the upper line of figures is based on the lower norm (one 20 metre pool for every 15,000 people), the second on a higher norm of one Olympic size pool (or one pool of 25 metres by 20 metres) for every 50,000 people. In fact, to our knowledge, not one Olympic size pool is open to black swimmers in South Africa.

Development, and made public on 8 February 1973.[31] (We have included Africans in this table, although it should be said that the sports authorities in South Africa apparently do not assume that their needs are the same as those of other groups!)

It appears from Table 18 that, among the black population, there is a better ratio of facilities for men in tennis, hockey (an almost exclusively Coloured game amongst Blacks) and netball (widely played at school); and the worst ratio for sportsmen from these groups in the major games of football, rugby, boxing and golf. Given the time needed to play a full game, there is also a serious shortage of cricket pitches.

Compared with Africans, Coloured sportsmen and women have the advantage in all the major sports: football, netball, rugby, tennis, cricket. In hockey, swimming, softball and golf (all of which, except the last, are minority sports for them), Africans have relatively more numerous facilities.[32]

This table should not be misinterpreted, however: it shows only the degree of advantage one community possesses over another. It takes no account either of the real need for facilities. (The number of sportsmen and women able to affiliate to clubs is inevitably limited by the quality and quantity of facilities.) It also gives no idea of the massive disparities between black and white sports facilities available as a whole, either in absolute terms or per capita.

Tables 18 and 19 allow us to conclude that the Coloured community has, on average, access to more facilities (in relation to its size) than either of the other two black groups: it leads the list in tennis, netball, hockey, rugby, and shares the advantage with the Indian population in swimming and cricket. The Coloured community is also better endowed with athletics facilities than the African population taken as a whole.

The Indian community, in addition to swimming and cricket, has the advantage in football, but has the worst provision in athletics and netball.

Finally, *the Africans are the worst off of all three groups in all sports* except athletics, where they head the list in 'white' areas and have more facilities than Indians over the country as a whole. In 'white' areas, Africans also have the advantage over Indians in tennis, though not in the country as a whole.

If the number of facilities available to the black population is judged according to the Government's own criteria (column 1, Table 20), however, it becomes clear that sufficient facilities are available in only two cases: in football for the Indian population and in rugby for the Coloureds. Re-examination of Table 18 reveals that even this is an illusion for, relative to the number of active players, rugby and football (particularly African football) are two of the sports for which facilities are most lacking. In effect, this simply indicates that the official standards are inadequate. They have nevertheless been employed for the calculations presented in Table 20 (limited to the five sports for which quantified comparison is possible). Once again, the most blatant shortfall is to be found among African facilities: in all sports except football (where the standards, as we have seen, are grossly inadequate) scarcely *half* the necessary facilities exist. Indians are seriously lacking in rugby, tennis and swimming facilities, and Coloured athletes in hockey and swimming.

Overall, in all three groups, there are more facilities for football than any other sport — although the need, given the game's mass following, far outstrips any advantage which this might suggest. Tennis and swimming (with hockey) are the sports in which provision is least adequate.

Aware of the ideological role sport can play in forming or maintaining group loyalties, the white authorities have taken care to spend considerable amounts of the budgets set aside for launching the bantustans towards 'independence' on sports facilities. Thus a sports stadium was constructed post-haste in Venda during 1979 with money from Pretoria and technical assistance from the Department of Sport.[33] Their efforts are complemented by foreign investors, like the United States Chamber of Commerce which, in 1980-81, at a cost of four million dollars, constructed a sports complex with stadium and swimming pool at Soweto.[34]

Active Participation in Sport

Table 21 shows that, in absolute terms, there are more white sportsmen than Africans, even though the latter are four times as numerous. This is still the case when only club membership of the principal sports is measured, for white players account for nearly half the membership of official clubs. In addition, thousands of whites take part in less organized sporting activity, through the 'Run for Your Life' and other campaigns, or in 'Trimsa' Parks, of which 30 have been opened since 1978 and 40 more are under construction.[35]

Table 21
Number of Officially Registered Sportsmen, 1977-78

Whites	*Africans*	*Coloureds*	*Indians*
690,391 (90 sports)	180,306	90,160 (30 sports)	?

Source: Hansard, 4 Q., col. 416; 2 Q., col. 55; 4 Q., col. 44 and S.A.I.R.R., 1979, pp. 586-7.

Within each group of the population, the proportion belonging to official (racial) sports clubs was as follows (Table 22):

174

Table 22
Membership of Official Clubs

	Whites	*Coloureds*	*Africans*	*Total*
Each community as percentage of total population	16.2%	9.0%	71.9%	97.1%
Sporting population in each community as a percentage	48.0*	9.8	42.9	100.0
of total sporting population	69.9	5.7	24.4	100.0
Percentage of sportsmen in	13.3*			
each community	33.0	5.5	2.9	

* The lower figure refers only to those who play the major sports; the higher figure includes those who play all leisure sports.

In Table 23 we have attempted to estimate the participation of different groups in the principal sports. It has not been possible to provide adequate figures of membership of the non-racial federations; these have generally opted to avoid claiming to be representative by virtue of size of membership, partly because the non-racial principle upon which their constitutions are based is not one which is justified by numbers, and partly because, owing to apartheid legislation and repression, it is very difficult, and sometimes impossible, for black sportsmen and women to affiliate to non-racial federations. Figures are therefore indicative. The shading suggests the degree to which a sport is popular in different communities; numbers are given only when they seem fairly dependable.

Table 24 suggests the relative hierarchy of sports within each community. For Coloureds and Africans, the hierarchy suggested is based on membership of official clubs: in the absence of other guides, the popularity of different sports among Indians is based on the density of facilities and the subjective evaluations of informants. As a whole, the list is intended to be indicative rather than formally precise. The white hierarchy takes account of school and university sport; some social sports, swimming and athletics in particular, should occupy a higher position. In general, statistics of white sport reflect the level of competitive activity and underestimate white participation in sport as a form of recreation. The opposite is true of black sport, and the figures for club membership reflect less the level of competitive sport than the level of (official) organized associational sporting activity.

Both Coloured and African sportsmen share the same top three sports, and football is the most popular game for all three black groups (and would be among white sportsmen if school sport was excluded). The principal differences between the Coloureds and Africans is that Africans are fonder of athletics and boxing, while Coloureds play (and Africans do not) hockey, gymnastics and softball.

Table 23
Estimated Participation in Sport, 1977

	Whites	Africans	Coloureds	Non-racial
Rugby				
Racial	37,000 members 750 clubs (180,000 schoolboys)	19,300 members 211 clubs	9,300 members	
Non-racial				26,610 members 421 clubs
Football				
Racial	40,273 members	140,394 members 2,917 clubs	29,396 members 805 clubs	
Non-racial				±50,000 members
Netball				
Racial	11,400 members 400 clubs	29,155 members 251 clubs	5,670 members 273 clubs	
Non-racial				Unknown
Cricket				
Racial	c. 15,000 members	2,119 members 62 clubs	4,018 members 132 clubs	
Non-racial				± 5,000 members
Tennis				
Racial	36,000 seniors 39,000 juniors c. 1,000 clubs	–	–	
Non-racial				±15,000 members
Athletics				
Racial	17,400 members 223 clubs	12,000 members 37 clubs	1,070 members 31 clubs	
Non-racial				± 8,000 members
Hockey				
Racial	43,590 members 491 clubs	54 members 4 clubs		
Non-racial				Unknown
Gymnastics				
Racial	10,000		4,470 members 27 clubs	
Non-racial				Few
Swimming				
Racial	14,000 members* (20,000 schoolboys)	1,537 members 14 clubs		
Non-racial				8,000 members
Golf				
Racial	12,000 members	3,478 members 85 clubs	1,341 members 36 clubs	
Non-racial				Unknown

Table 23 (*continued*)

	Whites	Africans	Coloureds	Non-racial
Cycling				
Racial	1,000 members	134 members 10 clubs	429 members 24 clubs	
Non-racial				Unknown
Boxing				
Racial	3,600 members	8,729 members 243 clubs	1,600 members 27 clubs	
Non-racial				Few
Basketball				
Racial	3,000 members 72 clubs	7,360 members 67 clubs		
Non-racial				Unknown
Softball				
Racial	3,500 members 81 clubs	2,876 members 78 clubs	986 members 30 clubs	
Non-racial				Unknown
Table Tennis				
Racial	6,500 members 200 clubs			
Non-racial				± 6,000 members
Bowls				
Racial	69,104 members 760 clubs	275 members 5 clubs	368 members 4 clubs	
Non-racial				Few
Billiards and Snooker				
Racial	75,000 members 490 clubs			
Non-racial				Few
Body Building and Weightlifting				
Racial	3,000 members 10 clubs	1,294 & 591 members 68 & 44 clubs	180 members 12 clubs	
Non-racial				± 2,000 members
Darts				
Racial	6,000 members 350 clubs	50 members 2 clubs		
Non-racial				Few

* Excluding social swimming.

** Figures for Indians are not available.

Table 24
The Relative Popularity of Different Sports in the Various Communities

	Whites **	Africans	Coloureds	Indians
Most Popular	Rugby	Football	Football	Football
	Tennis	Netball*	Rugby	Cricket
	Bowls	Rugby	Netball	Tennis
	Cricket	Athletics	Gymnastics	Swimming
	Hockey	Basketball(W)	Tennis	Hockey
	Football	Boxing	Cricket	Golf
	Swimming	Tennis	Hockey	Netball
		Golf	Swimming	
		Softball	Boxing	
		Cricket	Golf	
		Swimming	Table Tennis	
		Basketball(M)	Athletics	
		Bowls	Softball	
Least Popular		Cycling		

* A school sport.
**Taking into account school and university sport.
 (W) = Women; (M) = Men

Sports requiring more costly facilities (cricket, tennis, etc.) are more popular among Indians than Coloureds, and among Coloureds than Africans: only boxing (which requires few facilities) and netball (which is a girls' school sport) reverse this tendency.

Table 25
South African Sport: Who Plays What

	Africans	Whites	Coloureds	Indians	
Bowls		●			Least Popular
Swimming		●		●	
Gymnastics		●	●		
Basketball	●	●			
Athletics	●	●			
Boxing	●	●			
Hockey		●	●	●	
Tennis		●	●	●	
Cricket		●	●	●	
Netball	●	●	●	●	
Rugby	●	●	●	●	
Football	●	●	●	●	Most Popular

Table 25 provides, in schematic terms, a picture of South African sport, and of the popularity of different sports among different groups. The sports are approximately in order of popularity (the most popular at the bottom): it will be seen that (at this level of simplification and, need it be said, for socio-economic reasons) Africans tend to excel at non-technical sports in contrast to the Indians and Coloureds, whose preference is for games like tennis, cricket, hockey, gymnastics, etc.

The Official Organization of Sport in South Africa

White Sport

A number of official institutions represent or promote white sport. Of these, the most important are:

The S.A. Olympic and National Games Association (S.A.O.N.G.A.: known between 1908 and 1961 as the S.A. Olympic and Empire Games Association — S.A.O.E.G.A.). This body represented South Africa at Olympic level until the country was expelled from the Olympic Movement. Since 1971, the S.A.O.N.G.A. has become a 'multi-national' body, and three representatives from the S.A.O.N.G.F. — which represents the black sportsmen and women who are members of the official (racial) Indian, Coloured and African federations — sit on the supreme national council, also called S.A.O.N.G.A., like the white association which still controls a large majority of the votes.

Eleven associated members and 24 affiliated associations belong to the white S.A.O.N.G.A., which is responsible for organizing South Africa's national championships. The latter were held in 1959, 1964, 1969 (separate 'non-white' games were held in 1970) and 1973. They were 'all-white' until 1970, when South Africa was expelled from the Olympic Movement. The next 'open' games were due to take place in 1981.

The S.A. Association for Physical Education and Recreation was created in 1950 to improve co-ordination between the different organizations active in the field. The Association organizes conferences, invites foreign speakers and experts, and co-ordinates research. In 1970, there were 10 provincial associations, representing 500 white physical education teachers.

The S.A. Sports Federation was created in 1951 and today represents 90 national sports bodies, whose interests the Federation represents and promotes.

The Sports Foundation was created in 1964 by the Rembrandt Group, directed by *Broeder* millionaire Anton Rupert. The aim of the Foundation is to promote amateur sport through specialized training. The organization gives technical advice to sports associations and finances the employment of foreign specialists. The Foundation employs a black coaching director in athletics, alongside a white coach, and four other coaches for swimming, gymnastics, football and tennis.

In association with South African Airways, the Foundation offers an annual award — the South African Airways Trophy — to the sport which makes the greatest impact on international sport during the year. It claims that half those who enrol on its courses are black; in 1976, 41 of 223 training courses involved black athletes (18%).[36]

The Department of Sport and Recreation was created in 1966 to promote white sport and assist white sports federations to promote sport. In 1979, its services were extended to cover black sport as well. Since 1971, it has striven to apply and render credible the 'multi-national' sports policy which was introduced by the Government to counter South Africa's international isolation.

Two campaigns have recently been launched by the Department: 'Sport for All' (the title of which is self-explanatory if one bears in mind that 'All' means 'white'); and the 'National Fitness Campaign', rechristened the 'Trimsa' campaign, which was launched in 1970 to stimulate popular physical recreation in walking, jogging, swimming, gymnastics and cycling. Since 1979, the Department has extended its services to cover all four racial groups.

Mention should be made of the Springboks motif. It was first adopted in 1896, and first worn by an official national team in 1903. Persuasion has been needed in recent years before all the national white federations would agree to extend Springbok status to 'multi-national' sport; today any athlete who is chosen to represent South Africa has the right to Springbok colours.

The State President's Award is bestowed annually on teams or individual athletes for their performances at international level. Officially, the award may go to any athlete; in practice, no black athlete has ever received it. Black sportsmen receive 'silver' or 'bronze' medals instead, which are awarded at separate ceremonies.

African Sport
Until 1979, African sport fell under the responsibility of the Bantu Affairs Department. In 1973, a sports division was created within the ministry. In 1979, the Department of Sport and Recreation assumed partial responsibility for the organization and promotion of African sport.

Sport within the bantustans is organized by the 'national tribal authorities' concerned.

The Bantu Affairs Department organizes courses in athletics, netball, tennis and swimming and provides financial assistance, through its local offices, to the municipal bodies which administer African sporting facilities. Consultative Councils preserve the fiction that African opinion is represented in policy-making at local Bantu Affairs Department offices. Debate continues as to whether African representatives should be elected.

In 1973, a Bantu Sport and Recreation Fund was created to provide financial assistance, via the private sector, to African sport. All such aid is devoted exclusively to the promotion of official, recognized African sports federations organized on a racial basis.

Coloured Sport
Coloured sport is administered by the Coloured Affairs Department, which runs support services, and by the Department of Community Development,

which is responsible for financing the sports programme of local authorities.
A Culture and Recreation Council was created in 1967, which also had the
aim of promoting Coloured sport. 231 local offices, 141 provincial offices
and 29 national offices have been created to ensure that Coloured sport is co-
ordinated locally in accordance with official policy. The Department of Sport
and Recreation now awards a medal to Coloured sportsmen, coaches or
officials, for services they render to official sport.

Indian Sport
Indian sport is administered, as far as facilities are concerned, by local authorities. The Department of Sport and Recreation again provides some administrative back-up and training facilities to officially recognized (racial)
federations. For other needs, Indian sportsmen are serviced by the Department
of Indian Affairs.

In addition, important material and promotional support is provided by
sponsorship. Sports sponsorship has increased enormously since the 1960s.
We shall have occasion to make frequent reference to commercial influences
upon organized sport in the rest of this book. It suffices here to say that white
sport is by far the principal beneficiary of commercial sponsorship. Almost
all sponsorship, furthermore, is devoted to official (racially constituted)
associations; on the whole, sponsoring companies have provided unequivocal
support to the Government's 'multi-national' sports policy.

The Political Character of Sport in South Africa

All the information presented in this chapter indicates that the African
population suffers far more than any other group from the effects of apartheid. Racial legislation affects Africans most harshly and many laws have
been framed expressly to restrict their freedom. In sport, as in every area of
social life, Africans are the most deprived and oppressed, they suffer more
from discrimination and from the arbitrary authority of local and national
Government, they are penalized more cruelly for legal infractions, and they
are systematically confined within the impoverished environments of the
townships and bantustans. The Group Areas Act affects the playing of sport,
and relations between the black communities, more than any other. As we
have seen, it confines each racial group to a fixed area of residence, outside
which its social and economic activities are circumscribed or debarred. In
general, nevertheless Coloured and (to a lesser degree) Indian people are
relatively less constrained by the innumerable laws of apartheid than Africans,
whose freedom of movement is severely hampered by the pass laws. Africans
are *physically confined* to the townships and prevented at the same time
from meeting people from other racial groups unless the latter are prepared
to apply for passes to enter African areas.

Apartheid is a totalitarian philosophy. Since sport, like everything else, is
subject to apartheid laws and affected by the many discriminating contradictions

they create, sport in South Africa is necessarily a part of political life. The Government, if not all foreign commentators, certainly recognizes that it raises political choices and problems. The authorities use sport as one way of maintaining their political ascendancy.

Segregation politicizes sport by imposing a prohibition on black-white relations except where these involve economic production, and by inhibiting, frustrating or rendering antagonistic, contacts between black people (i.e. between Indians and Coloureds and Africans, and between migrant and urban Africans etc.).

Sport is thus transformed into an activity with political content. In reaction, black sportsmen and women and their communities may unite to defend themselves against the oppression and deprivation from which all, unequally, suffer; alternatively, their resistance may take the fragmented form of an assertion of separate cultural identity. By denying the reasonable aspirations of Blacks, and reinforcing inequality, apartheid widens the gap, in sport as elsewhere, between aspirations and the hope of satisfaction. Political consciousness is increased by frustration and the links between specific injustices and the organized injustice of the apartheid system become clear.

By invariably suppressing all forms of political and non-political organization which express black opposition to apartheid, the white regime informs *all* cultural expression with a seditious character — including sport. For the powerless, condemned to silence, sport, with its overtly apolitical ideology, provides an accessible (sometimes unique) opportunity to prove in daily life the existence of an alternative to segregation and racial humiliation. The principles of non-racial organization are in flagrant contradiction with apartheid; the non-racial sports movement is, as a result, political in character.

This conclusion must not, however, be confused with the accusation frequently levelled by the white political and sporting establishments against non-racial sports associations. They suggest that these associations have been created *in order to* achieve political ends, thus implying that non-racial sportsmen and women are not really sportsmen and women at all, but politicians in disguise. This absurd accusation really does not merit discussion, for, as we have seen, the policies of apartheid have themselves 'politicized' sport, and all social activities, including sport, have some political content simply because they are subject to class and other social pressures. In the case of South Africa, furthermore, apartheid affects social life in a way that turns sport into a favourable terrain for political action. For all these reasons, the 'plot' theory is unworthy of consideration.

Moreover, it conceals one useful insight. For it is true that taking part in sport under apartheid entails *choosing the terms and conditions under which it is played* (racial/non-racial, with or without permits etc.). It is illegal to play mixed sport in South Africa without a permit; it is illegal for Indian or Coloured players even to enter African areas without a permit, etc. Those who play, and still more those who administer sport, therefore take decisions which have an explicitly political content. And because sport is assumed to influence ideas and promote community organization, administrators are very conscious that they have a responsibility to defend and promote the sporting *and ancillary* interests of their associations and communities. The dispute between 'official' and 'non-racial' black sports administrators arises over the *definition* of those interests. And it is because this is so, that the evolution of contemporary South African sport can be described in terms of 'political' strategies which are in opposition to the regime or in alliance with it. Indeed, in our view, such an analysis provides the best means of understanding the recent history of South African sport.[37]

This can be seen most clearly in the Government's use of sport to divide the black population. Apartheid confronts the most enterprising and/or privileged black minorities with the choice between collaborating with the white establishment, or refusing to do so. In many instances, it may be in the immediate interest of Indian and Coloured South Africans — whose influence on black sport is, as we have seen, considerable — to collaborate in return for the elimination of so-called 'petty' apartheid. Unlike Africans, Indians and most Coloureds have the right to urban residence, are South African citizens, have certain commercial rights and limited political representation. Moreover the Nationalist Government has promised to improve their status. For the vast majority of Africans, however, white rule means further despoliation of their elementary human rights and their legal transformation into racially inferior helots. Collaboration is realistic only for a minute number of businessmen and officials who staff the institutions of 'separate development' in the bantustans and townships. Even for these men, the choice is stark indeed, for collaboration entails assisting the white minority to enslave their countrymen.

The white Government has made considerable efforts to drive a wedge between the African majority and the two black minorities, by playing on these interests. In general, the two black minorities have nevertheless continued to identify their long-term interests with those of the black population as a whole, whose oppression they share and whose experience reveals the futility of the half-solutions and second-rate citizenship they have been offered by the white community. The black population continues to unite over the demand for real freedom.

In saying this, we have arrived, in political terms, at the heart of the issue of non-racial sport.

References

1. In M. Cornevin, 1977, p. 155.
2. 120,000 Africans were arrested in 1979 under the pass laws (*Rand Daily Mail*, March 1980). 'In 1975-76 one in every four blacks was arrested every year for technical infringements of laws applicable to blacks only.' Callinicos and Rogers, 1976, p. 161, quoting the *Financial Times*, 15 October, 1975.

3. Among other conditions, it is necessary to have worked for 15 years without interruption for the same employer, or to have lived in an urban area *without the slightest interruption* for 10 years. Following the 1976 riots, Soweto residents – and only Soweto residents – were given the right to buy their house (but not the ground on which it stands), at prices so high they effectively debarred the vast majority of residents.
4. Until 1980, the Government made regular provision for white sport out of national tax income. No such provision was made for black sport, which was financed by monies acquired directly from Blacks through direct and indirect taxes (liquor profits, etc.).
5. In 1974 it was 90.8 rand a month (S.A.I.R.R., 1975, p. 230). In 1975 it was set at 113 rand a month in Johannesburg, 110 in Durban, 80 in the bantustans. The needs upon which the P.D.L. is based are set so low – taking no account of health costs, for example – that a Household Effective Level has been calculated, which simply adds 50% on to the P.D.L.
6. *Financial Mail*, January 1980.
7. In M. Cornevin, 1977, pp. 115 and 152. Others estimate the percentage earning less than P.D.L. at 30%. The figures for manual workers almost certainly underestimate the reality.
8. Department of Statistics, Pretoria; in UNO, 1978, p. 24.
9. See B. Lachartre, 1977, passim.
10. In A. Hepple, 1973, p. 57.
11. The 1979 Riekert Commission recommended, for example, that a small minority of urban Africans should be accorded limited civil and commercial rights – while the movement of migrants should be further restricted and controlled.
12. F.A.O., 1978 (translated from the French).
13. F.A.O., 1978, p. 35 (translated from the French). Other diseases enhanced by malnutrition include: meningitis, intestinal infections, kwashiorkor, pellagra, rickets, pneumonia, measles.
14. F.A.O., 1978, p. 35.
15. In UNO, 1978, p. 11 (translated from the French).
16. F.A.O., 1978, p. 36 (translated from the French).
17. R.R. Miller, member of the South African Parliament. Hansard, 29 May 1979, column 6955.
18. Ibid., column 6957.
19. *South Africa Official Year Book, 1977*, p. 4.
20. It is internationally agreed that an individual does not become literate until he or she has accomplished more than four years' schooling. The figures employed in this section are taken from *Apartheid Non! Du Cote Noir du Tableau*, 1980, except where stated. See also Hirson, 1980, passim.
21. In M. Cornevin, 1977, p. 153.
22. I.e. schools run by certain Churches: see pp. 26-29 and 49 above.
23. *Transkei Annual*, 1974, p. 54.
24. *Times*, 27 April 1971, in U.N.O., 1978, p. 28.
25. Joan Brickhill, 1976, p. 71.
26. In M. Cornevin, 1977, pp. 155-6.

27. J. Sikakane, 1977, p. 53.
28. J. Brickhill, 1976, p. 70.
29. Survey by Jane Norman, S.A.I.R.R., April 1974, passim. In 1974, the Coloured and Indian population together amounted to 134,859 inhabitants.
30. J. Brickhill, 1976, p. 70.
31. See J. Norman, 1974, pp. 3-4, and J. Brickhill, 1976, pp. 69-70.
32. Athletics has been excluded, because the available information is difficult to evaluate.
33. Report of the Department of Sport, 1978.
34. Agence-France-Presse, 3 October 1979.
35. *Annual Report of the Department of Sport and Recreation, 1979.*
36. *South Africa Official Year Book, 1977*, p. 810.
37. See Chapter 11.

8.   From Black to Non-Racial Sport

As long ago as February 1947, the S.A. Table Tennis Board, a body whose black membership was organized on non-racial principles, was admitted as a provisional affiliate of the International Table Tennis Federation, which had refused to recognize the S.A. Table Tennis Union (all-white) because of its racially discriminatory policies.[1] Following this decision, a tour which had been arranged for two British players was cancelled, owing to the difficulties their black hosts would face because of segregation.

The Nationalist paper *Die Burger* devoted two columns to the incident. In March 1950, the President of the S.A. Union proclaimed in a newspaper that South Africa had no colour bar but a 'social bar' which foreigners found difficult to understand. Ignoring the ban, one of the British players, Bergmann, visited South Africa at the request of the white Union and was fined by the British table tennis federation. In the press, a white sports official remarked that the International Table Tennis Federation's decision was the thin end of the wedge and would affect all the Olympic sports and lead eventually to the suspension of other South African sports associations.[2]

This was the first formal victory won by non-racial black sportsmen in South Africa against segregation in sport and the hegemony of the white sports establishment. The incident contained in miniature many of the features — the absurd, the irresponsible, the hypocritical — which were to mark white resistance to the demands of the non-racial sports movement.

There had already been other expressions of protest among black sportsmen. By the early 1950s spectators were beginning systematically to applaud visiting sides and boo the Springboks or their local white teams. In 1949-50, an attempt was made by black spectators to boycott the football stadiums, and in Durban, where the racecourse was segregated in 1950, 'pamphlets were distributed in the city urging a non-European boycott of the races, but apparently without result'.[3] From 1946, the black federations in football, boxing, weight-lifting and later cricket and rugby, applied to join the official white federations on non-racial terms, and when this was refused, demanded recognition from their international bodies. Nevertheless, for nearly ten years, table tennis remained an isolated success. In this chapter we shall see why.

Towards Non-Racialism

Between 1945 and 1960, black sportsmen had to overcome legal, political and organizational difficulties in their attempts to win recognition and end segregation in sport. As a result, it was not until the end of the decade that a national non-racial sports movement took shape. Their demand for recognition on terms of equality with other (white) sportsmen was contrary to Government policy, threatened the power of the white federations and embarrassed the international sports bodies. Abroad, furthermore, few were aware (at the end of the colonial period) that organized sport was played by black South Africans, and the black organizations themselves were divided into racially constituted bodies. The fact that most of these difficulties had been overcome by 1960 is a measure of the determination and force of the non-racial movement among sportsmen and women.

It was no simple matter politically for the black federations to establish relations with international bodies many of which had long-standing colonial links with South Africa and close ties with the white, official South African associations. Furthermore, South Africa had frequently been a founder member of the international sports bodies and as a result was all the more difficult to dislodge. Finally, voting distribution in several international bodies was heavily weighted in favour of European or ex-British Empire members, whose relations with South Africa were traditionally close.

Legally, the white sports federations also had the advantage, for they were already recognized whereas black associations were in the position of pretenders. This advantage was further increased by the fact that the constitutions of international bodies exclude the possibility of recognizing more than one affiliate from each country.

Black sports associations, therefore, had to turn the white associations out of office. Their argument was based on an appeal to the non-racial principle of the Olympic Charter. It was relatively easy for the black federations to demonstrate that white associations were guilty of racial discrimination and could not claim to represent the South African people (both the International Table Tennis Federation in 1949 and F.I.F.A. in 1955 recognized these facts).[4] But it proved a very difficult argument to drive home because the black federations could not claim themselves to be non-racial or representative. They were not non-racial because apartheid laws prevented the playing of truly non-racial sport in South Africa, and they were not representative because very few Whites (who composed the absolute majority of sportsmen in a number of disciplines) were affiliated to them. During the 1950s, the black federations therefore stopped asking to be recognized in place of the white federations and were forced by the political conditions imposed by apartheid to limit themselves to the *negative* demand for exclusion of the white bodies. The white associations had no such scruples and lobbied vigorously for maintenance of the status quo and full white affiliation.

During the 1950s, the international federations' general response to the problems raised by black South African sportsmen was evasive:

> On application to the world body [the non-racial federations] were told that this was a matter for the International Olympic Committee and then on application to the International Olympic Committee they were told that this was a matter for the South African Olympic Committee. This body recognized, when approached, that its affiliates . . . have racially exclusive constitutions, but explained that it was powerless to act — either because it was 'traditional' to have a racial policy, or later because it was the law of the land.[5]

The S.A. Olympic Committee assembled the most varied and labyrinthine arguments to defend itself from criticism. In 1959, non-racial sportsmen catalogued some of them: (1) the S.A.O.E.G.A. had no colour bar, but their affiliated units did, this was not their fault, but dictated by conditions in the country; (2) S.A.O.E.G.A. was willing to help non-white sportsmen who would be able to affiliate to white bodies once they had formed united non-white bodies; (3) Non-Whites had never been *excluded* from national teams; they had simply never reached national standards; (4) The non-whites were disunited and divided; (5) Non-whites would be considered for selection in national teams for South Africa if they belonged to an affiliated organization; (6) Mixed sport was against the traditions and laws of the country; (7) Mixed sport would lead to racial friction and even bloodshed; (8) Sportsmen seeking international recognition were inspired by political motives.[6]

An even greater problem was the fact that, paradoxically, it was difficult for black federations to prove the existence of formal segregation in sport. White associations were able to omit racially exclusive clauses from their constitutions without mitigating the effects of apartheid or changing their actual membership; and most did so in the 1950s, particularly after 1958, when international pressure began to mount.[7] Nor was there a formal law or regulation which expressly extended apartheid to sport, or legally obliged sport to be segregated. The South African Government has never passed legislation forbidding mixed matches between teams of different race or between multiracial teams.

This point is important. A test case was brought before the courts in 1962-63 when two White, five Coloured and two Indian footballers belonging to the multi-racial Lincoln City team were accused of violating the Group Areas Act by playing in a multi-racial match in an Indian group area in October 1961. The Durban Supreme Court acquitted the accused on appeal, on the grounds that the Group Areas Act prohibited matches between *individuals* of different race who spontaneously formed a team, but not matches involving players of different race who belonged to a formally constituted association. The players were found innocent, because they had not consorted or drunk together afterwards. The Durban Sports Association, which administered the pitch on which the match had taken place, was also declared innocent, being considered to be a group of clubs and not individuals. The match itself was therefore legal. This judgement has never been reversed.[8]

The absence of identifiable legislation expressly enforcing segregation at team level in sport and the suppression of racially exclusive clauses in the constitutions of white associations greatly complicated the task of the black federations. For the apartheid legislation nevertheless made it impossible in practical terms to play sport in truly non-racial fashion, and the political and sporting authorities saw to it that these laws were respected and apartheid upheld in sport as elsewhere. To argue their case, the non-racial sportsmen were therefore forced back upon more general, and apparently more complex arguments, which questioned South African legislation as a whole. In doing so, their demands necessarily echoed the call of all Blacks for their civil and political rights. Yet was it not over-ambitious to seek to overturn the country's entire legislation in the name of sport?

At the same time, both the Government and the white sports establishment were able to claim that racial segregation had not been *imposed* on sport. Each sought to blame the other for the discrimination which undoubtedly existed. The white associations proclaimed that they were opposed to apartheid but prevented from integrating by Government pressure, while the Government declared that sports associations remained loyal to a tradition of separate organization and that the Nationalist Party would defend vigorously their right to autonomy. The sophisticated hypocrisy of these arguments has since become the hallmark of a regime whose propaganda is a triumph of double think.[9] During the 1950s, the white authorities certainly had some success in fending off the claims of black sports federations and confusing international opinion.

That the arguments were false, however, is undeniable. The white sporting associations were entirely responsible for the segregation which existed in the 1950s, and made no attempt to eliminate it. Their passivity contrasts with the attempts of other organizations to delay, if they could not resist, the application of apartheid: scientific associations, for example, refused to modify their constitutions to prevent mixed membership.[10] One looks in vain for any comparable reaction from any of the sports associations.

As for the Government's mask of innocence, this was removed whenever it was felt necessary to reimpose order. In 1951, the black South African boxer, Jake N'tuli, won the British Empire flyweight title in London, thereby overturning one of the principal arguments against integration used by white associations, namely the claim that Blacks were simply never good enough to compete on equal terms with white sportsmen. Dr Donges, the Minister of the Interior, intervened to state that foreign black boxers would no longer be permitted to box in South Africa against black South African boxers.[11] When, in 1956, a number of black federations (in football, cricket, weightlifting and rugby) applied to affiliate to the relevant international bodies, Dr Donges intervened again, this time to outline publicly for the first time the policy of his Government in sport (see above p. 46). The substance of that declaration has remained largely unchanged as far as domestic sport is concerned.

Donges' interventions projected sport and the issue of non-racial sport into the overtly political domain. This was indeed his intention. No longer could the problem be resolved through purely 'sporting' or 'non-political' channels. But once Government itself took a direct interest, foreign countries and international sports associations predictably did so too, and the prospect of an international boycott became imaginable.

If, in retrospect, it seems that Government interference probably accelerated the progress of the non-racial sports movement — and its campaign for South Africa's isolation — it should not be forgotten that at the time Donges' policy greatly increased the difficulties — the threats, harrassment and at times simple violence — which black sportsmen had to encounter. The successes of their international campaign and their ability to unify across racial lines within the country forced Government and the white sports establishment to create new racial black federations, with or without membership, to undermine the national non-racial bodies and discredit their claims abroad to be representative of black sportsmen. At the same time, the Government attempted to isolate them from international contact. In 1959, Donges carried out his 1956 threat to withdraw passports from sportsmen whose 'intentions were subversive' by preventing the S.A. Table Tennis Board from attending the world championships in West Germany, and denying travel facilities to representatives of the non-racial S.A. Soccer Federation and the non-racial boxing association.[12]

The interference of the Government, which from then on was to co-ordinate and support the white sport establishment's opposition to non-racialism, had one positive effect, nonetheless. It made unification of the black sports associations, and their reorganization on non-racial lines, indispensable to the future progress — and survival — of an independent black sports movement. We have seen that the sheer number of black sports associations and their racial principles of organization were two of the principal weaknesses of black sport in the 1950s.[13] Some progress had already been made before 1956, in football, boxing, cricket and weight-lifting, for example; and other sports were beginning to establish the basis for non-racial organization (rugby, tennis). Nevertheless, the process of combining several vertically organized national bodies into one, without creating tension between them — which would inevitably put at risk the non-racial principles which inspired the initiative — was by no means a simple operation, and most bodies chose in the first instance to form a confederation, the members of which subsequently amalgamated after a trial period lasting for several seasons — punctuated, in a number of cases, by secessions.[14]

By the end of the 1950s, unification was sufficiently advanced to allow the black federations to form the first national inter-sport associations. The Co-ordinating Committee for International Recognition in Sport (1956) soon collapsed,[15] but in 1958, the South African Sports Association (SASA) was formed with the backing of 70,000 black sportsmen and women from athletics, cycling, cricket, football, weight-lifting, tennis, table tennis, softball, netball and baseball. Its aims were:

> To co-ordinate non-white sport, to advance the cause of sport and the standard of sport among non-white sportsmen, to see that they and their organizations secure proper recognition [in South Africa] and abroad, and to do this on a non-racial basis.[16]

The non-racial sports movement in South Africa dates from the creation of the South African Sports Association. Inspired by its staff and in particular by its Executive Secretary Dennis Brutus,[17] SASA greatly accelerated the movement towards unification of the national bodies upon which its influence depended. Above all, however, its creation was to permit black sportsmen to surmount the sectarian tendencies and fragmentation which had inhibited unity. SASA proved that the majority of black sportsmen were opposed to racialism in sport, and permitted black sportsmen and women to support the struggle against apartheid while advancing the interests and progress of black sport in purely sporting terms.

This said, the S.A. Sports Association was not initially non-racial in the modern sense, for it did not demand complete integration with the white bodies, within single national associations. It merely demanded recognition and the right of black sportsmen to be selected for national (Springbok) sides on equal terms with white sportsmen. In other words, at least until the creation of the South African Non-Racial Olympic Committee (SAN-ROC) in 1963, SASA was not campaigning for true non-racialism in sport but for 'international participation for black sportsmen within the framework of segregation in national sport'.[18]

SASA and SAN-ROC: Success and Repression

SASA's efforts from 1958 were principally directed towards strengthening the administration of black sport and, by lobbying the I.O.C. and other international bodies, forcing white associations and the S.A. Olympic Committee to adopt a more reasonable stance. Inside South Africa, SASA also organized protests against discrimination and campaigns against sporting contacts with foreign countries.

SASA had some success internationally. A cricket tour planned by an all-black West Indian side to play all-black South African (Cricket Board of Control) teams was cancelled, as was a football match with a Brazilian touring side.[19] In 1961, after years of hesitation, FIFA suspended the white Football Association of South Africa (FASA). In June 1962, following a letter from SASA demanding the expulsion of the S.A. Olympic Committee because it was in contravention of the first principle of the Olympic Charter, (banning racial discrimination in sport), the I.O.C. threatened for the first time to suspend South Africa 'if the policy of racial discrimination enforced by the Government is not changed before the October 1963 session'. This letter opened the way to international isolation of South African sport, and South Africa's expulsion from the Olympic Movement in 1970.

Within South Africa, however, SASA was less successful. 'Hundreds of letters were written. Petitions were organized. Representations were made. But there was very little response.'[20] In 1961, SASA launched Operation SONREIS (Support Only Non-Racial Events in Sport), a boycott of all racial sporting events which earned Dennis Brutus a banning order. The police had kept the organization under close surveillance from its beginning (detectives were in fact present at the founding meeting in October 1958), and in April 1960 its offices were raided and all its archives seized. The documents taken included signatures to a petition which had been organized by the African National Congress (A.N.C.) and SASA to protest against the exclusion of Maoris from the New Zealand All-Black rugby team which was to tour South Africa. Although their activities were perfectly legal, SASA officials were forced by police harassment to work in semi-clandestinity.

The degree of surveillance is not surprising. SASA's campaigns had the effect of extending black resistance to apartheid into sport. The tactics of civil disobedience adopted by sportsmen were also those used by the A.N.C. and continued a long tradition of boycotts in the Cape. Furthermore, because it was played by the petty bourgeoisie and by urban workers, and because of its non-discriminatory and apolitical ideology, sport offered particularly favourable ground upon which to attack apartheid. It is, therefore, not surprising to find the A.N.C. supporting a SASA campaign against an All-Black tour without Maoris, or to read that 'the A.N.C. Youth League is said to have gained control of the Gompo Rugby Union in 1953 before turning its attention to the more recognized organs of local government'.[21] As we have seen, apartheid is a totalitarian ideology, which has totalitarian effects, and one consequence is that legal protest tends to find a common platform, whether it is for political or economic or social (sporting) rights.

Furthermore, SASA was operating within the charged and violent period of repression which preceded and followed Sharpeville in 1960. In due course, repression had the effect of leaving sports protesters in virtual isolation, for almost all other organizations, working on issues which were more central to the society, were banned or destroyed. It is all the more significant, therefore, that it was precisely at this time, in 1963, the year that the A.N.C. leadership was arrested at Rivonia, that SASA created the S.A. Non-Racial Olympic Committee (SAN-ROC) — an organization 'completely non-racial [which] will choose representatives purely on merit'[22] — whose task was to direct the campaign to expel the white S.A. Olympic Committee from the Olympic Movement. The creation of SAN-ROC marked the end of attempts to negotiate with white associations and the opening of a full-blooded campaign to destroy the racial structures in South African sport and to replace them by a system based on merit alone, in line with Olympic principles.

Given the context, the courage of SASA's officials should not be underestimated. SAN-ROC first raised its voice at a moment when black South Africans were suffering more than at almost any other time from overt repression; and unequivocally, again for the first time, it called for an international boycott of South African sport, in the name of non-racial principles with which all black people could identify. SAN-ROC demanded the expulsion of South Africa from the Olympic Movement, the expulsion of racist South African associations from the international sports bodies, and declared itself ready 'to expose and fight racial discrimination wherever it exists in sport.'[23] Its activities were not only to change the balance of power between black and white sportsmen but would severely damage white South Africa's image abroad.

As Dennis Brutus has recalled somewhat phlegmatically, 'SAN-ROC had a relatively short run in South Africa'.[24] Those who were associated in its creation were well aware that they were inviting violence from a regime armed with a formidable array of repressive laws. At the time, they were all but isolated inside a country in which most other black organizations were banned or destroyed, and virtually unknown outside it, for the international movement of support which continues to be the non-racial sports movement's best guarantee against repression had yet to form.

Within two years, so many leading members of SAN-ROC and SASA had been 'rendered harmless' that SASA suspended its activities and SAN-ROC was forced into exile. Its President, Mr Rathinsamy, lost his passport;[25] Mr Reg Hlongwane, its Secretary, had to flee abroad to avoid being banned;[26] Chris de Broglio, who was to be SAN-ROC's Secretary in London, also had to leave when the Government harassed his employers;[27] Mr George Singh,[28] who had already been detained for two months in 1960, was banned and put under house arrest after the white Football Association of S.A. was suspended by FIFA. Finally, Dennis Brutus, banned in 1961, was arrested in 1963 in the offices of the S.A. Olympic Games Association in the company of a Swiss journalist.[29] Before his trial, Brutus attempted to reach Switzerland for a meeting of the I.O.C.: although he had a British passport, he was arrested by the Portuguese police in Mozambique in defiance of international law and handed back to the South African security services. To attract attention, for his friends, family and colleagues were not aware of his plight, Brutus leapt from the car in which he was being escorted through Johannesburg. A policeman shot him in the stomach. When finally an ambulance arrived, it was discovered to be 'white', and Brutus had to wait, bleeding on the pavement, until a 'coloured' ambulance could be found to escort him to hospital.[30] He exchanged hospital for a prison cell on Robben Island; and when he was released, he was again banned.

Mr John Harris, a white Johannesburg teacher, became SAN-ROC's President after Brutus' arrest. His fate was personally tragic. In July 1964 he was arrested for sabotage, having planted a bomb. Although a psychiatrist testified at his trial that at the time he had been technically insane, in 1965 he was sentenced to death and hanged.

Yet it was exactly at this dark period in its history that SAN-ROC scored its first major victory. In 1964, the I.O.C. (which had failed to implement any of its earlier threats) suspended South Africa and for the first time prevented South African athletes from participating in the Olympic Games. According to Peter Hain, 'SAN-ROC members were in fact extremely surprised by their

decision and put it down to a combination of shock at the shooting of Dennis
Brutus and worry by the I.O.C. establishment of the growing strength of the
African countries.'[31] Repression nevertheless prevented SAN-ROC
from continuing. When Brutus left South Africa for London in 1966, he
joined de Broglio and Reg Hlongwane: together they re-established the
organization in exile. In the late 1960s and during the 1970s they and SAN-
ROC were to chalk up a long series of successes against white South Africa,
by co-ordinating an international boycott of South African sport which was
backed diplomatically by the African countries and won wide popular support
(especially at the end of the 1960s) all over the world.

1960-70: The War of Attrition

During the 1960s the non-racial federations within South Africa were not
only deprived of a national organization to represent them. They had to
resist a campaign waged against them by the white associations and co-
ordinated by the Government, with the support of the municipalities. Until
1963, the struggle against apartheid in sport had been led from within the
country, and international bodies including the I.O.C. had persisted in arguing
that South Africa's problems should be resolved internally, by the S.A.
Olympic and National Games Association. With the creation of SAN-ROC
the lead was now taken by the international movement, directed by SAN-
ROC from London. Inside South Africa the primary task of black associations
was simply to try to survive.

In the next chapter we shall examine the reasons why the Nationalist
Government attached such importance to upholding apartheid in sport. The
intensity of 'official' white feeling can be judged by this editorial from *Die
Transvaler*, written the day after Verwoerd's Loskop Dam speech in September 1965, which reiterated Government racial policy:

> It must be ascribed to one particular factor that the white race has
> hitherto maintained itself in the Southern part of Africa. That there
> has been no miscegenation . . . no social mixing between whites and
> non-whites . . . . In South Africa the races do not mix on the sports
> field. If they mix first on the sports field, then the road to other forms
> of social mixing is wide open . . . . With an eye to upholding the white
> race and its civilization not one single compromise can be entered
> into.[32]

To undermine the non-racial sports movement, apartheid planners evolved
during the 1960s a strategy which informs to this day the 'multi-national'
sports policy inaugurated in 1971 and finalized in 1976. It has three main
axes: (1) *to break up the unified sports federations and create separate
Indian, Coloured and African associations;* (2) *to create new racial federations
where it proves impossible to provoke a division;* (3) *to finance and promote*

*the emergence of a new sporting elite among Blacks whose sporting and
political interests will lead them to support the status quo and the official
policies of the regime*, while effectively depriving the non-racial sports associations of finance and facilities.

Politically, the first of these aims proved the most successful because dis-
integration of a multi-racial body into its racial constituents not only reinforced
and confirmed apartheid principles but drove a wedge between the Indian and
Coloured minorities, on the one side, and the African majority on the other.
We have already seen that the former, being more urbanized, a little more
prosperous and less victimized by apartheid, are proportionately over-
represented within the non-racial movement, and among black sportsmen
generally. Separating Indian and Coloured sportsmen from the African would
effectively decapitate the non-racial movement and render harmless one of
the few national organizations publicly opposed to apartheid. Alone, Indian
and Coloured sportsmen, whatever their principles, could not claim to represent — even potentially — black opinion or South African sport. For their
part, Africans would also be unable to re-establish a meaningful non-racial
movement without the other black minorities: subject to a system designed
to reduce them to powerlessness, confined physically to their townships and
bantustans, deprived of the basic legal and political freedom to organize, they
would be unable to put non-racial principles to practical use. Isolating the
African majority and forcing the non-racial movement into illegality would
be one and the same thing.

By looking at examples from several sports we can see the difficulties
which non-racial sportsmen faced in their attempt to create sporting structures able to serve the interests of the black community as a whole. They
also show why the non-racial associations have concluded that, under conditions of apartheid, they cannot play truly non-racial sport.

The Example of Football, 1961-63[33]
Football offers a particularly good illustration of the campaign waged against
the non-racial associations. It is the most popular sport in the country (except
in the Cape). It is played by large numbers of Africans. It was also one of the
first sports to unify across the three black communities, under the S.A.
Soccer Federation. Finally, it is a major professional and spectator sport
with considerable capital committed to it. All of these factors have bearing
on its history.

The S.A. Soccer Federation was formed in 1951, when three black racial
organizations, representing Indian, Coloured and African footballers, whose
association dated from the Inter-Race Boards of the 1940s, decided to feder-
ate. They amalgamated on non-racial terms between 1958 and 1962, having
created a professional wing in 1959 (the S.A. Soccer Federation Professional
League — S.A.S.F. - P.L.). This movement towards unification provoked an
immediate response from the white body. First of all, in 1959, the white
Football Association of South Africa created its own professional league, the
National Football League; in the same year, it allowed the S.A. Bantu Football

Association (which did not represent the majority of African footballers at this time) to affiliate to it.

Then, in September 1961, the Football Association of South Africa was suspended by FIFA for its racial policies and as a result became ineligible to play in the World Cup or international competitions. This decision effectively isolated F.A.S.A. from contact with foreign teams. From that moment events moved even more rapidly. In November 1961, the African association created the National Professional Soccer League (N.P.S.L.) with white financial and technical assistance. In early 1962, the F.A.S.A. gave its African associate a seat and a vote on its executive and created a co-ordinating committee on which football representatives from each race were to sit and discuss their relations. Inter-racial matches between professional teams were also organized, abroad: 9,000 spectators watched a game between the Germiston Callies and Black Pirates in Basutoland. This initiative led the Government to warn the F.A.S.A. that inter-racial matches involving South Africans were as unaccept-able abroad as at home; several footballers were prosecuted and the white Association ordered mixed matches to cease.

Finally, in April 1962, on the eve of a meeting with FIFA, the white Football Association, with its African affiliate and their two professional leagues, called a meeting with the S.A. Soccer Federation and S.A.S.F.-P.L., at which it proposed the creation of a single federal structure within which each football body would organize its affairs independently (i.e. on racial lines), under an executive committee with powers to co-ordinate general policy and harmonize relations between the different members. FIFA never-theless confirmed the suspension of the white Association, but announced that a commission of inquiry would shortly be sent to South Africa. At this point, supported by the Government, the white Association even went so far as to offer, by way of concession, to send alternatively to the World Cup a black team (1966), then a white team (1970)! The S.A. Soccer Federation refused to entertain this extraordinary concept.

This bald summary of events provides an excellent illustration of the effect-iveness of international isolation. Initially the white federation gave way to foreign pressure; it was then brought up short by the Government, when it made concessions which begin to weaken apartheid, and proceeded, as the gap widened between the demands of apartheid and those of the international authorities, to concoct increasingly bizarre and implausible negotiating posi-tions. Such diplomatic wrangles, which preoccupied the attention of inter-national observes, were only one aspect of the struggle for recognition between racial and non-racial sports bodies, however. Of far more immediate impact for the participants was the war of attrition waged against the facilities, spectators and finances of the non-racial footballers by the white body and officialdom.

On the initiative of the manager of the National Football League, Mr Granger, the white Association appealed to all the municipal authorities to close the grounds to Soccer Federation teams, making them available only to teams from the S.A. Bantu Football Association — that is, to F.A.S.A. Since every football pitch within African areas was owned and administered by the municipalities, this had the effect of strangling the Soccer Federation and, more particularly, prevented Africans belonging to the non-racial Federation from playing altogether. At the same time, it undermined the non-racial Federation's finances and gave the white and African professional leagues an opportunity to tout for the S.A.S.F.-P.L.'s specators.

The strategy was very successful. In May 1962, the Durban and District African F.A. joined the African Association, with 130 clubs and 3,000 players. Its President declared in substance that 'this affiliation would hold many advantages for African soccer and was in its best interests, particularly in the fight for grounds to play on.'[34] A short while later, a team affiliated to the Soccer Federation, the Moroka Swallows, agreed to play the best N.P.S.L. side, the Black Pirates, at Orlando Stadium, which had been closed to non-racial sides by Johannesburg City Council. Moroka Swallows had been virtually bankrupted and the only pitch which remained open to its players, at Natalspruit, had been closed for maintenance. In protest, a non-racial 'counter-match' was organized on the same day but had to be cancelled because police pulled out the goalposts.

In December 1962, the white Association announced the creation of a new Indian football federation, which would seek associate affiliation. The following year a new Coloured association was born, which also sought sub-ordinate association with the white body. 'The stage has now been set,' declared the Top-Level Committee of the Football Association, 'when F.A.S.A. does not recognize the S.A. Federation, which is now, in its opinion, a non-existent body. We will have no more negotiations with them.'[35] Indeed, deprived on paper of its players and in reality of its facilities, and with George Singh, its energetic Secretary, banned, the future of the non-racial Federation was difficult to foresee. The occasion was ripe for the arrival of the FIFA delegation, led by Sir Stanley Rous, in January 1963. The S.A. Bantu F.A., which had claimed to represent 47,000 players in 1961-62, affirmed to the FIFA delegation that it now possessed 285,000 members. Welcomed with generous hospitality by the Football Association, warmly greeted by repre-sentatives of the new Indian Federation and the S.A. Bantu F.A., who declared themselves 'perfectly happy to be affiliated to F.A.S.A.'[36] reassured by meetings with the S.A. Olympic and National Games Association and the South Africa Foundation (a propaganda organ set up by business interests), the delegation set off again for Europe convinced that the white Football Association was doing all it could for the well-being of South African football, and intended to seek reform of Government policy. In contrast, representa-tives of the S.A. Soccer Federation had seemed resentful and bitter, their attitude had been 'one of destruction, not construction', and they had been irresponsibly critical of government policy.[37] FIFA announced in January 1963 that its suspension of the white Football Association was to be lifted, thereby demonstrating the harm that such international commissions can do, in 10 days of lightning 'inquiry' which rarely leave the issues less confused than they had been beforehand.[38] On hearing that the suspension had been lifted (it was reimposed the following year), Mr Granger declared to the press that the decision was 'a defeat for communism'. South Africans, he said, 'were obliged to practise apartheid in sport because it is the policy of the government and traditional, but we must ensure in future that it is a Christian apartheid.'[39]

After three years of harassment and isolation, the Soccer Federation's Professional League had lost its grounds, many of its supporters, a good proportion of its clubs (including most of the African affiliates), and the heart of its income. In contrast, the white Association and the Government had strengthened white control over this strategic sport, had broken the unity of the non-racial union, had moderated criticism abroad, and had separated all but a minority of African footballers from the Indian and Coloured clubs. A tidy score.[40]

Cricket, Boxing, Tennis

In Chapter 3 we left black cricket at the point in 1957 when the S.A. Cricket Board of Control (SACBOC) was created, following a decision taken in 1947. A decade later, the Board's four constituent bodies[41] decided unanimously to transform SACBOC into a fully non-racial national cricket body, a decision which was effectively implemented in 1961. During the period of amalgamation, however, the Bantu (renamed African) Cricket Board elected to withdraw, on the grounds that the terms of unification did not serve the interests of African cricketers.[42] Forming an independent association, they were isolated from national (and international) competition during the 1960s and their organization, membership and finances collapsed. Some of the best African players, like Ben Malamba, continued to play within SACBOC leagues.

As a result, when the M.C.C. cancelled its 1969 tour following the d'Oliveira Affair, the white S.A. Cricket Association did not have far to look in its search for a black ally. It had already offered money and technical assistance to SACBOC, which had refused it. It now offered similar terms (50,000 rand) to the African Cricket Board, in return for an agreement to affiliate with subordinate status to the white Association. At a meeting to arrange the deal, Mr Mlonzi, a representative of the African Board, stated the position of his organization in the following manner: 'The African people support the stand of Mr Howa's organization [SACBOC] in principle. It would be stupid for anyone who is not white to dismiss the demands made by Mr Howa's Board . . . . The only difference between Mr Howa's group and ours is that we cannot afford to wait . . . and say that we will not play cricket until the laws of the land are changed.'[43]

There was a good deal of truth in these remarks. More than anything else, political vulnerability and geographical isolation (exacerbated perhaps by some insensitivity and lack of flexibility among its partners within SACBOC) drove the African Board into the arms of the white Cricket Association, when this body found it convenient to lay hands on an ally which could defend it from international accusations of racism.

Turning to boxing, the international status of the white S.A. Amateur Boxing Association (S.A.A.B.A.) was first endangered in 1961, when South

Africa was criticized at a meeting of the International Amateur Boxing Association. Mr Frank Braun, president of S.A.A.B.A. and member of the S.A. Olympic and National Games Association, reacted at once by seeking to recruit black boxers. At the time, several black federations existed, two of which were sympathetic to the non-racial positions of the S.A. Sports Association. The first was the S.A. Boxing Association, based in Durban, which had joined SASA before 1960, but broke up as a serious organization when it attempted to amalgamate with the S.A. Non-European Amateur Boxing Association (S.A.N.E.A.B.A.) from Cape Town. The second was the S.A. Boxing Union with strong membership in the Transvaal and Orange Free State, which, recommended by SASA, applied for international recognition in 1960.

In 1961, the white Association opened negotiations with S.A.N.E.A.B.A. and the latter agreed to affiliate to the white body on terms which guaranteed the latter's pre-eminence and respected the dogma of 'separate development'.[44] In 1961 and 1962, the S.A. Amateur Boxing Association organized tours for black and white boxers in Rhodesia (now Zimbabwe) and the United States, and instructed referees and white officials to cease to recognize, or take part in, all competitions organized by the S.A. Boxing Union, which at the time claimed to represent the majority of black boxers. Deprived of competition and tempted by foreign tours, many of the Union's best boxers joined S.A.N.E.A.B.A., thereby weakening the Union and non-racial boxing to such an extent that non-racial boxers in South Africa have not succeeded in setting up a non-racial boxing association to this day.[45]

In tennis, finally, the black federations began to prepare amalgamation and the creation of a non-racial union as early as 1957, and finally achieved their aim in 1962, when the Southern Africa Lawn Tennis Union (SALTU) became fully non-racial. Two years later, it asked to be recognized by the International Lawn Tennis Federation (I.L.T.F.), thereby threatening the status and authority of the all-white S.A. Lawn Tennis Union.

The white tennis association immediately offered SALTU associate status, which the latter refused. With the support of the Government, the official white body then threatened to close all the courts under municipal control to African players, if they continued to play with Coloured and Indian tennis players. This ultimatum was sweetened with offers of technical assistance and financial aid if the African players would agree to form a separate association affiliated to the white body. Mr Reggie Ngcobo accepted these terms, took over the defunct S.A. National Lawn Tennis Union (African) and travelled abroad to defend the white Association's policies before the I.L.T.F. In so doing, he put back the creation of a non-racial union for all black tennis players by 15 years. It was not until 1976 that the African Tennis Union ended its association with the white body and rejoined SALTU to form a new non-racial body in 1978, the Tennis Association of South Africa (TASA), which today represents all but a handful of black tennis players (see Chapter 11).

Black Collaboration

Ngcobo's case illustrates the predicament of many sports officials, particularly African, whose associations are financially weak and vulnerable to harassment. Tempted by private advantage and menaced by official sanctions, many officials have been persuaded to ally with the white associations, at the expense of the long-term interests of their players, who have little choice between giving up their sport (facilities being shut to them) and playing under the impoverished conditions imposed by apartheid. The support of a small number of black collaborators has been essential to the strategy and credibility of the white sports associations, if they are to divide black sportsmen and at the same time uphold official policy.

Reggie Ngcobo was also one of the founders and Vice-president of the S.A. Soccer Federation until it was discovered that he was negotiating with the S.A. African (previously Bantu) Football Association, whose original defection had made it possible for the white Football Association to maintain its political supremacy. In 1966-67, he was expelled from S.A.S.F., and soon afterwards from the non-racial Tennis Union.

The behaviour of such officials is inevitably contradictory, for they are caught between their career allegiance to the white bodies and their duties towards the associations whose interests they theoretically represent. Leo Kuper characterized this predicament with insight, writing at just this period when white associations were busy recruiting allies among the black sports officials:

> The associations officially structured for Africans are paternalist, racially exclusive — under white control — and conservative with respect to social change, or if they involve social change, then it is in a direction determined by Whites. The goals are externally defined by official policies. This has a number of consequences. The associations tend to be rigid. In situations of protest or challenge, they are maintained by repression and change of personnel. The responsibility accorded Africans is limited, and deliberations may be unrealistic, since the major decisions are taken outside the Association by white executives. Contact between White and African is on a basis of inequality, thus reinforcing the system of racial stratification. The leaders may appear to be representative, even elected, but by and large leadership is determined or controlled officially. Acceptance by African leaders of positions in the associations involves the acceptance of a subordinate status, and a loss of initiative as a result of the commitment to externally defined goals. An aspect of the personality of the leader is as it were detached, and utilized under the direction of others. The leader may be alienated from himself in the same way as the worker from his labour. This is perhaps an element in the oscillation sometimes observed between servility and belligerence.
>
> The intercalary position of the leader may have the same consequences. The leader is suspended between two worlds, that of his own people

and that of the Whites. He has a responsibility towards, and no doubt an identification with, Africans, but he can do very little to help them. As tensions rise under acute racial conflict, his position becomes increasingly ambiguous, since he is rewarded by white patronage, and may be an instrument for executing the hated policies. In consequence he is threatened with rejection by his own people. He is therefore obliged to manipulate two different systems.

He must maintain his affiliation to the Whites and abide by the rules of the game (or give up his position) and at the same time, he must ensure his acceptance within the African community. This ambivalence can be partly resolved by playing along with Whites in all essential respects necessary for continued membership, and yet displaying hostility towards them within carefully defined limits inside the asso-ciation, but with less restraint outside. Here again is a source of oscillation between the servile and belligerent states.[46]

If the majority of collaborating officials of this kind have been African (for the reasons we have described) a number were not. Kuper's description fits the behaviour of Mr Cuthbert Loriston, for example, President of the Coloured S.A. Rugby Federation, which separated, under his leadership, from the non-racial S.A. Rugby Union in the 1950s, and which today is a member of the 'multi-national' confederation led by the white S.A. Rugby Board. Mr Loriston is himself a member of the executive of the Rugby Board (since 1980) and of the S.A. Olympic and National Games Federation.[47] In 1976, he accepted the Sports Merit Award for his services to Coloured sport and to the S.A.O.N.G.F. He is known for his frequent outbursts in South Africa against the inequality and lack of recognition from which his organization suffers within the S.A. Rugby Board — and for his readiness to patch up relations with white rugby and testify on all occasions when he is abroad, that multi-racialism is on the verge of realization.

Mr Reggie Baynes has also received the Sports Merit Award for his services to Coloured sport and to the S.A.O.N.G.F. During the 1970s, he was President of the S.A. Coloured Football Association which, like the Indian F.A., repre-sents an insignificant number of footballers, but has provided useful support to the white Football Association when the latter travels abroad to defend its record. In 1973 Mr Baynes was responsible for creating a still smaller organi-zation, the S.A. Amateur Swimming Association (Coloured), which appeared shortly after the white S.A. Amateur Swimming Union had been suspended by FINA. The creation of this Coloured Association enabled the white Union to claim that it had formed a multi-racial co-ordinating body, the Amateur Aquatics Federation of South Africa, although at the time the 'national' Association which Mr Baynes led had use of one pool and was apparently composed of four swimmers including two of Mr Baynes' own nephews!

The Napoleon among this group of collaborators, however, is to be found in football, in the person of Mr George Thabe, President of the powerful S.A. National Football Association. Sports official and businessman, Thabe represents the new African petty bourgeoisie which the Government has been trying to promote during the 1970s. Between 1976 and 1980, during a major crisis in football, Thabe's organization succeeded in breaking the power of the S.A. Soccer Federation again, and eliminating the influence which the United Party had enjoyed over football since the war. The victors in this struggle were Dr Koornhof, Minister of Sport, the Nationalist Party, and Thabe himself (one of Koornhof's proteges), who greatly consolidated his power.[48]

Thus the white federations, in collusion with the Government and municipal authorities, have consistently attempted to dismantle the non-racial sports movement, by encouraging splits, creating fictitious or semi-fictitious racial black associations, and by mixing offers (of money, travel, technical assistance) and threats (closure of facilities). Some of the most powerful and organized bodies were seriously weakened during the early 1960s and, like the S.A. Soccer Federation, took several years to recover; others were virtually destroyed, like the S.A. Boxing Union. Many, however, survived the period with minimal damage and were able to profit from the experience of other non-racial bodies to emerge with new strength in the 1970s. In particular, the S.A. Amateur Swimming Federation (non-racial, formed in 1964), the Southern Africa Lawn Tennis Union and the S.A. Rugby Union succeeded in maintaining a vigorous line during the 1960s and re-emerged in the 1970s with good organization and increased membership.

It would be an error, in fact, to assume, because harassment was so severe during the 1960s, that the non-racial movement did not make progress. Certainly, individual federations and particular areas suffered, lost members or collapsed; but, throughout the decade, increasing numbers of clubs affiliated to the non-racial federations, whose survival was itself a sign of strength. One major weakness remained, nonetheless: the Government and white sports establishment succeeded almost everywhere in separating the African associations from their Coloured and Indian counterparts. They did so by violence, but the consequences were nevertheless profound. Perhaps the most important of the achievements of the non-racial movement in the 1970s was to reverse this tendency — albeit partially and only in certain sports.

References

1. For details, see M. Draper, 1963, pp. 72-3.
2. S. Patterson, 1953, p. 155.
3. S. Patterson, 1953, p. 155, n. 51, p. 131, n. 40, 41.
4. Lapchick, 1975, pp. 22-4; de Broglio, 1971, p. 23.
5. D. Brutus, 1972, p. 155.
6. From a Memorandum from the S.A.S.A. to the I.O.C. in May 1959; quoted by de Broglio, 1971, pp. 3-4.
7. J. Brickhill, 1976, p. 46.

8. M. Draper, 1963, pp. 3-5; R. Lapchick, 1975, p. 43; Brickhill, 1976, p. 46; de Broglio, 1970, p. 7. This was by no means the only multi-racial match to take place at this period. Others involved the Durban Coasters, the Germiston Collies and Black Pirates. The frequency of these matches no doubt caused the Government to intervene — successfully, because such matches generally ceased after 1963, under pressure from the white F.A.S.A.

9. The astonishing linguistic jugglery of the regime is captured by J. Slovo (1976, p. 112) who lists some of the laws passed during this period: 'Limited Indian representation in Parliament (provided for in a 1946 statute but never implemented) was abolished by the *Indian Representative Act* of 1948. The pass laws were extended to women and to some previously exempted men in the Cape Province by the *Abolition of Passes Act* in 1952 (under this act the annual rate of pass law arrests reached new heights). The meagre indirect representation of Africans (by 3 Whites) in the central Parliament was ended by the *Promotion of Bantu Self-Government Act* in 1959. In the same year the right of Blacks to attend White universities was ended by the *Extension of University Education Act*. And joint political organization across the colour line was interfered with by the *Prohibition of Political Interference Act*, 1968,' [Author's italics].

10. UNESCO, 1972, p. 111.

11. R. Lapchick, 1975, p. 22.

12. M. Draper, 1963, pp. 76-7; R. Lapchick, 1975, p. 31; J. Brickhill, 1976, p. 9. The S.A. Table Tennis Board has not travelled abroad since.

13. See de Broglio, 1971, p. 2.

14. Many of these secessions were not 'natural'; see pp. 194-9.

15. R. Lapchick, 1975, p. 25.

16. Speech of Alan Paton at the opening ceremony of the S.A. Sports Association, 10 January 1959, quoted in de Broglio, 1970, p. 3. See also M. Draper, 1963, p. 96 and R. Lapchick, 1975, pp. 27-8.

17. Poet, teacher, President of SAN-ROC at its creation in 1963, banned then arrested for his sporting activities; spent 3 months on Robben Island before seeking exile in London. There became President of SAN-ROC again, and led the organization for several years. Today is Honorary President of SAN-ROC, President of ICARIS. Lives in U.S.A.

18. De Broglio, 1970, p. 4; also P. Hain, 1971, p. 53.

19. Lapchick, 1975, p. 30.

20. P. Hain, 1971, p. 53.

21. Mayer, 1961, p. 212. This does *not*, of course, mean, as official propaganda tends to suggest, that Gompo Union members played rugby to make a political point!

22. M. Draper, 1963, p. 104, citing a non-racial spokesman at the press conference to launch SAN-ROC.

23. Ibid.

24. D. Brutus, 1972, p. 156.

25. First President of SAN-ROC, headmaster of Lenitia High School (Indian) until 1975, President of the Senior Schools Sports Association; member of Transvaal Council on Sport. Played cricket and football in the Transvaal.

26. Weight-lifter; with Brutus and de Broglio, reorganized SAN-ROC in exile from London, in 1966.
27. President of the white weight-lifting association, South African weight-lifting champion 1953-62, left the white federation to rejoin the non-racial movement; current Secretary of SAN-ROC in London.
28. Solicitor; Secretary then President of the non-racial S.A. Soccer Federation; today, Patron of the S.A. Council on Sport and honorary life Vice-President of the S.A. Soccer Federation.
29. Brutus was banned under the Suppression of Communism Act (1950), which made it illegal for him to belong to associations, teach, write, be quoted in public. He contravened his banning order by being present at a meeting of more than two people.
30. P. Hain, 1971, p. 57; J-C. Ganga, 1979, pp. 190-1; R. Lapchick, 1975, p. 50.
31. R. Lapchick, 1975, pp. 63-4.
32. 7 September 1965. Verwoerd himself was even more explicit: 'Reduced to its simplest form the problem is nothing else than this: we want to keep South Africa white .... "Keeping it white" can only mean one thing, namely white domination, not "leadership", not "guidance", but "control", "supremacy". If we agreed that it is the desire of the people that the white man should be able to protect himself by retaining white domination . . . we say that it can be achieved by white domination.' (S.A. Parliament, January 1963.)
33. Most of the information upon which this summary is based is to be found in M. Draper, 1963, pp. 40-67.
34. M. Draper, 1963, p. 53.
35. Statement of Top-Level Committee, 4 December 1962 in M. Draper, 1963, p. 55.
36. Report of the FIFA delegation's inquiry in South Africa to the FIFA executive, January 1963, in *Star*, 24 January 1963, quoted by Draper, 1963, p. 59.
37. Ibid.
38. The quotation marks are not mere irony: it is impossible to take seriously the quality of research carried out by such delegations — like those sent out by the French Parliament in January 1980, called the Marie Commission after its president, or by the British Sports Council, led by Mr Jeeps, in February 1980. They spend most of their short visit in official interviews, cocktail parties and tourist trips, and recognize only verbally the restrictions on movement and freedom of expression of members of the non-racial 'dissident' bodies.
39. M. Draper, 1963, p. 60.
40. M. Draper, 1963; R. Lapchick, 1975, pp. 105-6 and the S.A.I.R.R. Surveys of 1963 and 1964 (pp. 292-3 and 339-41) provide further details of the 'ground war' practised against S.A.S.F. by F.A.S.A.
41. The S.A. Independent Coloured Cricket Board; the S.A. Bantu Cricket Board; the S.A. Indian Cricket Union; the S.A. Malay Board (ex-Coloured Cricket Board).
42. Apartheid forbade Indians and Malays from living in the Orange Free State. Yet the statutes of the new Board stipulated that provincial units would only be recognized if at least 3 of the member associations were

represented. The African Cricket Board judged that, since many African members lived in the O.F.S., the Transkei and the Midlands (where the same restrictions were enforced) its interests could not be properly represented. See the argument put forward by Mlonzi in Odendaal, 1977, p. 315.

43. A. Odendaal, 1977, p. 316.
44. R. Lapchick, 1975, p. 38; M. Draper, 1963, pp. 82-3.
45. For details of this period, see M. Draper, 1963, pp. 82-90 and R. Lapchick, 1975, pp. 38 and 54.
46. L. Kuper, 1965, pp. 317-8.
47. The black body affiliated to the S.A. Olympic and National Games Association, which has a white membership.
48. See below, Chapter 11. Thabe is President of the Football Council of S.A., President of SANFA, a public relations employee of S.A. Breweries (the country's major sports sponsor, directly involved in the township beer-hall business), ex-President of the Vaal Triangle Community Council (under the authority of the Department of Co-operation and Development), member of the official International Liaison Committee, member of S.A.O.N.F., etc.

9. The Crisis of 1970 and the 'Multi-National' Policy

1970 was the year when the nightmare of white South African sportsmen came true, for quite suddenly they found themselves widely ostracized and under attack from all directions. They had already been excluded from many international federations and competitions — table tennis, football, basketball, volleyball, swimming, fishing, sea fishing, fencing, cycling, amateur boxing — and in 1969 were expelled or suspended from netball, cross-country, pentathlon, gymnastics, judo and weight-lifting. In 1970, they were suspended from international tennis and no fewer than nine major tours were cancelled, in sports including cricket, hockey (with Germany), athletics (tour to New Zealand). Only rugby among the major sports remained intact — but at what a cost! The 1969-70 tour of Britain had made headlines throughout the world; each match had been harassed by protests which had involved tens of thousands of people from all political backgrounds — and the Springboks had even been beaten![1] The All-Blacks Tour of South Africa the following year was scarcely less embarrassing: wherever they went, the visitors were applauded and the home side booed by black spectators, to such effect that the police had to intervene on several occasions to restore order among white fans. And again the Springboks lost, this time at home!

Excluded from the Olympic Games in 1968 as in 1964, the S.A. Olympic and National Games Association organized two series of Mini-Games — one for white athletes (1969), another for Blacks (1972). The first was remarkable for the absence of foreign guests and for an astonishing attempt to exclude even black spectators.[2] The second was distinguished by the resounding success of a boycott by non-racial sportsmen and women, so effective that at certain football matches the players outnumbered the spectators.

Finally, South Africa became in 1970 the first country in the history of the Olympic Movement to be expelled. Year of the boycott, of massive demonstrations in Britain, Ireland, Australia, New Zealand. Year of judgement, when one after another the United Nations, the I.O.C., the Commonwealth, the Supreme Council of Sport in Africa condemned apartheid and sports apartheid. Year of humiliation, when South Africa was expelled or suspended from the international federations of wrestling and amateur athletics, when the Sports Minister himself was hissed publicly at the South African tennis championships. Members of the Government attempted, like

Viljoen, to blame the catastrophe on the 'communists' or argued, like Vorster, that a choice had to be made between sport and the South African Way of Life: it was nonetheless evident that the white sports establishment had been thrown into profound disarray. White federations even began to initiate talks and offer new terms to the black sports bodies: in cricket, athletics, tennis and weight-lifting, they offered to select national teams on merit; a 'non-white' Olympic Committee (the S.A.O.N.G.F.) was established and invited to send observers to the deliberations of the white authority; in November 1970 the white S.A. Rugby Board invited the black rugby associations to form a national confederation under white authority; and the S.A. Cricket Association agreed to aid African cricket financially and technically in return for political co-operation. Officials like Dave Marais of the white Football Association and Frank Braun of the Boxing Association and S.A.O.N.G.A., appealed to the Government to reconsider its policies in the light of the international political situation.

After prolonged secret debate, wrangling and negotiation, the Government finally laid an egg: South African sport became 'multi-national'. A new minister, Dr P.G.H. Koornhof, was given responsibility for establishing the new policy, which eventually took final shape in 1976, having been tested against South African and international opinion. To understand its sense and appreciate its linguistic niceties, we need to retrace the background to multinationalism within the wider political context of apartheid in the 1970s and 1980s.[3]

The Other Name of Apartheid

> In the railway station the Blacks used to have to take a different entrance and walk a very long way round to the platform. Well, they say they have changed that and now Blacks can go the short way. But the notices are still there. Whites Only. And if you have a third-class ticket you cannot go the short way — only if you have a second class ticket can you go through. I suppose your money makes you White.[4]

The dependence of tne South African economy on a plentiful supply of black, and especially African labour in the urban areas, has been a major issue since the 1940s. For employers the surplus of cheap labour has meant that wages may be depressed, guaranteeing a profitable rate of exploitation — though at the concealed cost of exacerbating the shortage of skilled labour.[5] On the other hand, the influx of workers into the towns raises the question of their civil and economic rights and, by extension, threatens white authority. Apartheid, the Nationalist solution, has addressed itself almost entirely to the political aspect of the problem, for little economic development of the reserves has been undertaken, and black workers have been systematically under-trained. Instead, all Africans have been transformed into migrant workers and artificially attached to eight 'national homelands' and to 'tribal' structures which were already failing to ensure the reproduction of labour power before they were called upon to finance and supply the maintenance costs (health, education, insurance, sanitation, etc.) of the African population, in place of the White Government.

> In the light of the country's multi-national and historical realities, the majority of Whites are convinced that relations between the White nation of the R.S.A. and the various Black peoples within the borders of present-day South Africa cannot be satisfactorily regulated in a single integrated superstate, but rather on the historically tried basis of separate nation states, i.e. a system of political interdependence. This policy — evolved from a philosophy forged and determined by the realities of more than three centuries — has in both official and common parlance become known as separate or multi-national development.⁶

The concept of 'multi-nationalism' arose out of official attempts to resolve this issue. In 1963, when the Transkei became a separate territory, with its own cabinet and council, 'separate development' became a political and legal reality; in 1970, when Prime Minister Vorster announced that black 'states' were now free to seek 'independence', he was giving form to the government's 'multi-nationalist' policy which would serve both to maintain racial oppression and to conceal its existence.

As it stood, however, 'multi-nationalism' provided no answer to the issues raised by black sportsmen and women within South Africa or by the international sports boycott. The multi-national theory of 'separate development' had been evolved to resolve the fundamental problem created for the white minority by the contradiction between the requirements of apartheid dogma and the needs of the economy for African labour. As it stood, 'multi-nationalism' did not reduce but rather increased the level of racial discrimination, in sport as elsewhere. Moreover, it left undetermined the status and future of the two black minorities — styled, in multi-national language, the Coloured and Indian 'nations'. As we have seen, it was precisely these two groups which were in the best position to provide articulate opposition to discrimination in sport, from within the non-racial movement.

If, however, 'multi-nationalism' had little effect on the political structure, the concept of 'separate development' proved to be of the greatest value *ideologically*, both within the country and internationally. 'National differences' rather than racial superiority became the justification for segregation, and South Africa was defined as a 'multi-national' society, a form of words which interpreted racial oppression as an honourable recognition of traditional social practices. As the policy was introduced earlier, and has been carried further in sport than in most other areas, it has been used by the South African Government as a paradigm for the introduction of 'multi-nationalism' more generally.

The policy of multi-national development for the disparate peoples of

South Africa envisages a number of politically independent peoples, each of which will order its own affairs without interference from any other. It does not envisage the Westernization or 'integration' of individuals, but the full development of distinctive peoples, each with its own language, culture, traditions and mores.

This policy encompasses all spheres of human development for each of these peoples: political, economic and social, including, naturally, sporting activities. Blacks, Coloureds, Indians and Whites have always administered and practised their sports separately at all levels of competition.[7]

The policy has been relatively successful for the regime because of its ambiguity. The Minister of Sport reassured the white electorate in 1973 that: 'Announcements in respect of certain points of departure relating to sport should therefore be seen as adjustments, development and progress without sacrifice of principles.'[8] At the same time, he could argue abroad that the new policy was 'normalizing' sport, and even fudged the issue to the point of replacing the word 'multi-national' by 'multi-racial'.

The 'multi-national' policy also enabled the Government, without alienating white opinion, to license the playing, under strictly controlled conditions, of matches between teams or players of different race — a vital step if the white sports federations were to rejoin international sport. Such games, introduced gradually over several seasons, became 'multi-national competitions'. The sports establishment was thereby given room to manoeuvre ideologically between the demands of its membership and the requirements of the international community, *without, in any substantial way, upsetting the status quo or weakening existing segregation in sport.* As Koornhof himself avowed: 'The interpretation of the sports policy should constantly be consistent with the country's fundamental policy of separate development. If this is not done, it is not only erroneous and meaningless, but also causes confusion.'[9]

The Evolution of Sports Policy, 1971-76

On 11 April 1971, Prime Minister Vorster delivered a speech which has since been frequently quoted, for the circumlocution of its prose and perhaps for its significance:

I want to make it quite clear that from South Africa's point of view no mixed sport between Whites and non-Whites will be practised locally, irrespective of the standard of proficiency of the participants . . . . Our policy has nothing to do with proficiency or lack of proficiency. If any person, either locally or abroad, adopts the attitude that he will enter into relations with us only if we are prepared to jettison the separate practising of sport prevailing among our own people in South Africa, then I want to make it quite clear that, no matter how important these sport relations are in my view, I am not prepared to pay that price. On that score I want no misunderstanding whatsoever. I also want to say in advance that if, after I have said on these matters what I still have to say, anybody should see in this either the thin edge of the wedge or a surrender of principles, or that it is a step in the direction of diverging from this basic principle, he would simply be mistaken. Because, in respect of this principle we are not prepared to compromise, we are not prepared to negotiate, and we are not prepared to make any concessions.[10]

Essentially Vorster was reiterating the policies in force ever since Dr Donges' 1956 declaration. Nevertheless, he had become convinced that the official policy would need to be adjusted. In 1968, he had attempted to secure permission for the Maoris to tour South Africa with the All-Blacks and, in an effort to prevent South Africa's expulsion, had made it known that his government would permit a racially mixed (but separately selected) team to represent South Africa at the Mexico Olympic Games. His purpose was *to separate the question of international sporting relations from sporting relations within South Africa.* Although they did not secure South Africa's participation in the Games, these decisions had raised a storm of right-wing protest which divided the Nationalist Party and the *Broederbond*. Obliged to temporize, Vorster vetoed Basil d'Oliveira's inclusion in the M.C.C. team to tour South Africa in 1968. But he persisted in working for change and, faced by a choice between policy reform and complete international isolation, the majority of the *Broederbond* and the Nationalist Party finally reconciled themselves to making certain concessions. In October 1968 Vorster dropped the conservative leader Hertzog from his Cabinet and drove the '*verkramptes*' ('hardliners') into outright opposition. In a vote of confidence taken at the Transvaal Nationalist Party Conference in 1969, sport was identified as one of the four areas of policy upon which Vorster asked for a mandate for reform.[11]

This was unacceptable to the *verkramptes* who, by forming the *Herstigte Nasionale Party*, offered Vorster his opportunity to call an election, in which the sports question was a major issue, and which the Nationalist Party won by a crushing majority. Secure in power, Vorster authorized an All-Black tour including Maoris and prevailed upon the *Broederbond* to draw up guidelines for a new sports policy. A committee of *Broeders* was appointed to examine alternatives, chaired by Dr Andries Treurnicht, an eminent right-winger (nicknamed 'Dr No' for his intransigence) who had not followed Hertzog into opposition.

The committee was asked to find a formula which would permit the Government to satisfy both foreign opinion and the policy of separate development — an impossible task. Not surprisingly, the solution which emerged was merely a novel form of wording; the 'multi-national' policy was gradually divulged to *Broeders* and Nationalist circles, who were given time to get used to it,[12] and then, on 25 April 1971, revealed, by Vorster himself, to the world.

The policy, as put forward, had three main strands:

1) Mixed teams from countries which had traditional links with South Africa (the United Kingdom, New Zealand, Australia, etc.) would be permitted to tour South Africa and to play, separately, against white teams and 'non-white' teams;

2) Black sportsmen affiliated to white federations would be permitted to take part, as individuals, in 'multi-national' competitions; within South Africa these would be strictly 'national' (race against race), but internationally (in the Davis Cup or the Olympic Games etc.) might take a relatively 'open' form;

3) No racial mixing would be permitted at provincial or club level.

A former Secretary of the *Broederbond* and an ally of Vorster, Dr Piet Koornhof, who had helped to introduce the new policy inside the Nationalist Party, was appointed Minister of Sport. His knowledge of, and standing in, the *Broederbond* fitted him well for the delicate task of introducing a policy without real substance but in need of popularization. By semantic artifice Koornhof was to dress up the policy as radical and conservative by turns. Initially, the danger was from the Right, for the fears of Afrikaner nationalists were far from appeased by Vorster's declarations and the most ambiguous diplomacy was required. The *Broederbond* executive had insisted that 'multi-nationalism' should respect the dogma of 'separate development', and recommended avoidance of the term 'mixed sport'. *Broeders* were asked to take an active role in sports associations, in order to ensure that the policy would be applied correctly.[13] By these concessions, Koornhof neutralized Treurnicht and the Nationalist press, while forcing through amendments in his favour on the grounds of urgency.

The task was not easy. A questionnaire circulated among *Broeders* in 1974 revealed that 92.7% were opposed to the inclusion of black athletes in a South African Olympic team, except as a transitional measure, and that 92.1% were against the principle of extending racial mixing to other sports like rugby, cricket and football. Yet in 1975, Koornhof succeeded in winning acceptance for the idea of mixed representative teams for international matches, including rugby and cricket. He did so despite the fact that the theory of 'multi-nationalism' logically suggested that representative teams ought not to be mixed but divided into as many teams as there were 'nations' within South Africa. Racial integration had in fact to be justified as an *ad hoc* measure which would last only until the bantustans became independent:

> The selection of a single black team from the African people is an interim measure. The consequence of multi-nationalism is that there will eventually be eight separate national black bodies, each representing a different ethnic group. These groups must establish relations with other countries through their own bodies.[14]

Secondly, 'multi-nationalism' made no allowance for the Indian and Coloured minorities, which were not usually defined as 'nations', but which

were not 'white' either. No territory had been set aside for them and, if the
African population could be balkanized, their future was embarrassingly
vague, and remains today a very large, unresolved contradiction in the theory
of apartheid and 'multi-national sport'.

Alarmed by the changes which had been introduced, a number of *Broeders*
called for legislation to prohibit racial mixing at club level. Such a law would
have been fatal to the international credibility of the policy and Koornhof
resisted it. In 1976, in fact, after the riots of Soweto, he extended 'multi-
nationalism' to provincial and club level. In a series of contradictory assertions,
he let it be understood that clubs would not be permitted to allow mixed
membership, or mixed teams, but that no legislation would be passed to
enforce the rule; the Government laid great emphasis upon the autonomy of
sports organizations, and affirmed that individual cases would be examined
on their merits. Problems raised by the new policy, it was declared, would be
resolved by persuasion.[15]

After considerable experiment and evaluation, in September 1976 Vorster's
Government, convinced that both the Nationalist Party and international
opinion were ready to accept its package, gave definitive form to the multi-
national sports policy which has governed official thinking until today (see
Appendix 1). All of Koornhof's successors — de Klerk (1978-79), Punt
Janson (1979-80), Viljoen (since 1980) — have reaffirmed the principles
established in 1976. The only novelty has been the slow and difficult introduction of token 'multi-nationalism' into school sport. Significantly,
Koornhof himself has since taken up the key post of Minister of Development
and Co-operation (previously the Ministry of Bantu Affairs).

Five years of bargaining were necessary before details of the 'multi-
national' policy could be made public. The complexity and bitterness of the
negotiations indicate the degree of ideological and political significance which
the white establishment attached, and still attaches, to sport. Let us therefore
turn to public attitudes during the same period, to see the extent to which
they reflected, or were influenced by, the preoccupations of the Nationalist
Party and the white establishment.

Multi-Racialism and White Attitudes

For most white South Africans, it is self-evident that sport is a social activity
which they will practise with other Whites. Segregation is taken for granted,
it is the normal pattern of life, without political significance. As a result conflicting statements about sporting practice can be made without any sense of
embarrassment or contradiction. A Member of Parliament can declare in the
same speech that 'The sportsman in this country is denied nothing. There is
no discrimination on grounds of colour or race'; and that 'almost all our
people prefer to practise their regular sport on club level within an ethnic
context and even within certain social strata as far as certain forms of sport
are concerned . . . . Mutual participation in sport within the club context is

to a large extent on the same level as ordinary social discourse.'[16]

Yet, for exactly the same reasons, apartheid inevitably causes sport to become an area of political significance, influenced by the values of apartheid, or by the values of those who oppose it.

> The fact of the matter is that South African society has become so politicized as a result of its racial composition and the nations of which it is composed, in the international world as well as locally, that one can hardly imagine a practical politician being able to discuss sport today without, at some stage or other, dealing with the essential reality of peaceful co-existence, of potential conflict and national relations . . . . All the deficiencies with regard to peaceful co-existence inherent in society also appear in many respects in the world of sport.[17]

The fact that during the 1960s black South Africans themselves appear to have measured improvement in race relations partly in terms of the development of inter-racial sport is itself evidence of the association South Africans make between politics and sport and between the latter and the spread of egalitarian and non-racial values. According to Donald Woods, even Steve Biko was a partisan of sport's 'snowballing' effect — a theme dear to sporting ideology and to many of the 'bridge-builders' who have argued that sporting contact naturally improves understanding and racial relations.[18]

In contrast, Whites apparently did not believe in 1970 that sport was likely to improve Anglo-Afrikaner relations[19] — an indication of the fact that the cultural division between them is less profound, and that *physical* contact is not the issue which it is in black/white social relations. As far as the latter are concerned, one can say that technical sports lend themselves more to specialized skills and to professionalism, both of which facilitate integration; and that racial mixing causes increasing tension (among Whites) as sports become more social and local, where teams are involved, and where the game entails physical contact. Rugby is a prime example, for it is a mass sport, a team sport and a contact sport. For the white population, familiar with segregation and conditioned to certain racial stereotypes, mixed sport raises first and foremost the question of bodily contact, with all its complicities, conflicts and sensations; only at a later and different stage do political perceptions and rationalizations become relevant.

In apartheid society, sport is therefore considered to have political significance and is treated accordingly. The existence of a specific political policy concerning sport is one proof of this; widespread resistance to the introduction of multi-racialism — and the fact that official policy has had to accommodate and nurse the feelings of *Broeders* and Nationalists — is another. The number of occasions on which the Government has interfered in sport reveals the extent to which the sports issue is antipathetic to the Nationalist philosophy. Indeed many Afrikaners seem to feel that the least concession in this area threatens their cultural identity and the nature of Afrikanerdom, which is preserved by racial separation:

> The slightest deviation from strict Afrikaner norms can jeopardise membership . . . . Scores of otherwise eminently eligible Afrikaners have been rejected because they married English-speaking women. Others have been turned down because they were sent to English-medium schools; others, again, because they belonged to sports clubs whose members were mainly English-speaking.[20]

An internal *Broederbond* circular (4 April 1971) mentioned that:

> Members draw attention to the need to maintain our language through the singing of sporting and school songs. It is noticed that many Afrikaans schools sing English songs at sports meetings. Members in the educational field should use their influence to accord our language its rightful place. [21]

Indeed, regular participation in sporting activity on Sundays is one of the eight reasons for which membership of the *Broederbond* may be terminated.[22] The *Broederbond* executive, which contested the influence of non-Afrikaners in the administration of certain sports, like rugby, defined the aim of official sports policy as 'the maintenance of the white population in South Africa through and within the policy of separate development'. When questioned, local *Broeder* branches showed concern that concessions in sport would 'dilute' apartheid, would be the 'thin end of the wedge' and argued that 'Vigilance must be strong against mixing after sports games, mixed audiences, integration, conditioning of whites towards integration'.[23]

The behaviour of the electorate also reveals the political dimension of sport. There was evident resistance to the idea of multi-racialism, but over time, as the 'multi-national' policy was introduced, white opinion shifted. Three polls, held in 1964, 1970 and 1976, illustrate this progression clearly.[24] The first (1964)[25] showed that three out of four white voters were hostile to multi-racial sport. Another poll conducted at the same time by M. Schlemmer confirmed this finding, although the level of opposition was lower: 24% of English-speakers and 61% of Afrikaans-speakers rejected mixed sport. The very high political tension which reigned at this period no doubt helped to raise the figures.

The most recent poll we have been able to examine was carried out in October 1976 by the *Rapport* newspaper.[26] White electors were asked, soon after Koornhof had revealed the new sports policy, which of several changes they would, or would not, accept. These reforms included abolition of the ban on mixed marriages (57.1% against, 30.5% for, 11.7% uncertain) and abolition of the Immorality Act (50.2% against, 36.2% for, 12.6% uncertain). Among the reforms towards which there was least resistance were abolition of passes, (74.9% for, 13.1% against, 11% uncertain) and the introduction of mixed sport, to which respondents answered as follows:[27]

Table 26
White Attitudes to Mixed Sport, 1976 (%)

Response	Nationalist Party Supporters	United Party Supporters	Progressive Party Supporters	Average
Yes	56.4	81.8	97.0	65.6
No	29.5	12.3	0.0	22.8
Don't know	13.2	6.0	1.9	10.5

In 1976, therefore, the majority of white South Africans — including a majority of Nationalist Party supporters — were in favour of mixed sport up to club level. The high proportion of Don't Knows within the Nationalist Party is significant, for it suggests that by this time only about 30% of Nationalist Party members were firmly opposed to 'multi-nationalism'.

An earlier poll (1970), carried out by another paper *Dagbreek,*[28] asked many more questions and provides much more information. Respondents were asked three questions:
1) 'Are you for or against the admission into South Africa of players with Maori blood who may be included in a visiting All-Blacks team?'
2) 'Are you for or against the inclusion of non-Whites in sports teams which represent South Africa overseas?'
3) 'Are you for or against competition between Whites and non-Whites at athletic meetings in South Africa?'
The responses were as follows:

Table 27
White Attitudes to Mixed Sport, 1970 (%)

	Nationalist Party	United Party	Progressive Party	Herstigte Nasionale Party	Total
1st Question					
For	51.1	75.1	93.1	17.4	59.6
Against	25.2	6.6	0.0	76.0	19.8
Indifferent	15.2	14.7	6.5	5.0	14.1
Don't Know/ No Reply	8.5	3.6	0.4	1.6	6.5
2nd Question					
For	27.8	64.3	95.4	12.4	42.9
Against	58.2	21.2	1.1	74.4	43.0
Indifferent	8.9	10.0	2.7	7.4	9.3
Don't Know/ No Reply	5.1	4.5	0.8	5.8	4.8

Table 27 *(Continued)*

	Nationalist Party	United Party	Progressive Party	Herstigte Nasionale Party	Total
3rd Question					
For	12.6	42.2	87.4	0.8	26.6
Against	75.6	36.0	3.5	89.2	58.5
Indifferent	6.2	12.4	6.9	5.0	8.5
Don't Know/ No Reply	5.6	9.4	2.2	5.0	6.4

The respondents' answers clearly reveal that they were replying to a *political* (and not moral) question. Firstly, opposition to multi-racial sport increased with each question — that is to say, as multi-racialism was extended to sport *within* South Africa (Question 3) opposition rose from 19.8% to 43%, then to 58.5%. The majority of replies were favourable to the first reform, divided about the second, and frankly opposed to the third. The fact that the first question had been much debated since the 1960s, that the second was familiar to South Africans, and the third a new and untested suggestion (provoked by the S.A. Mini-Games of 1969-70) almost certainly influenced respondents' attitudes.

The second point that must be made is that apparently public debate of the issue also influenced the replies of different political groupings. For example, H.N.P. followers appear to have been less opposed to the inclusion of Blacks in a Springbok team than to the presence of Maoris among the New Zealand tourists (the number of Don't Knows increasing sharply as one passes from the first to the second question): this may well have been largely a result of the debate between the N.P. and H.N.P. over whether or not Maoris should have been allowed to play in South Africa. While the H.N.P. was firmly opposed, the N.P. was far more divided, which explains why many N.P. respondents were undecided or unwilling to reply.

These apparent distortions (more Progressive Party voters also appear to have supported the inclusion of Blacks in representative South African sides than Maoris in an All-Black side) should nonetheless not conceal the fact that, overall, hostility to the three propositions increased progressively within all political parties. This implies that all sectors of white political opinion viewed the issue in the same terms and attached the same relative importance to the changes advocated in the questions. This shows both the degree to which electoral opinion was homogeneous, and suggests that all white South Africans consider sport to be a social activity primarily for Whites. (Even Question 3, the most radical, only suggested that multi-racial sport should take place at senior competitive level.)

Finally, the sharp cleavage between the H.N.P. and N.P. on the one hand (most opposed to multi-racial sport), and P.P. and U.P. on the other (U.P.

electors being less decisively in favour of mixed sport than P.P. — and highly uncertain about the last question), indicates that sport divided political opinion along the same lines as other, overtly political questions, from H.N.P., through N.P. and U.P., to P.P. This once again suggests that sport was perceived to be a political issue.

It also suggests that Afrikaners and English-speakers divided (in traditional terms) over the issue, a hypothesis supported by two other polls taken at about the same time. The first, run by Ben Vosloo and J. Lever in Stellenbosch University,[29] showed clearly that English-speakers had more liberal views about racially mixed sport. To the question 'Do you think that the Government ban on mixed sport in South Africa should remain, or should it be changed?', replies were as follows:

Table 28
Afrikaans- and English-Speakers' Attitudes to Mixed Sport (Stellenbosch, 1)

	Afrikaans-Speakers	*English*	*Bilingual*
Ban should remain	61%	19%	23%
Ban should be changed	38	81	77

Another poll was carried out in 1968.[30] It showed a correlation between political attitudes and first languages of respondents, who were asked: 'Do you or do you not agree that overseas non-white sportsmen should be allowed to compete against white sportsmen in South Africa?'

Table 29
Afrikaans- and English-Speakers' Attitudes to Mixed Sport (Stellenbosch, 2)

	Afrikaans/Bilingual	*English/Other Languages*
Agree	19%	49%
Disagree	74	45
Don't Know	7	6

The level of disagreement of the English-speaking electorate is revealing. It helps to explain the weakness of political opposition to racism in sport, and in other domains, and why the Nationalist Party, committed to a strong and identifiable moral doctrine, has found it so easy to erode white opposition to its policies.

Finally, a poll which was carried out before the 1971 All-Blacks Tour further reinforces the view that white South Africans not only perceive sport as a political issue but attach surprising significance to it. Asked to suggest the disadvantages of apartheid in order of importance, sport came as high as third on the list: 6.1% of respondents mentioned it compared with international hostility (11.5%), and inefficient use of the labour force (7.7%).[31]

In conclusion, we should distinguish three levels of white political opinion, each of which are in constant interaction: the doctrines and theories which underpin the decisions made by the different political forces involved; official policy as defined and implemented by the Government; and public opinion, which appears to follow the evolution of, and be moulded by, the latter, and which political parties certainly seek to manipulate. As Henry Lever remarks with reference to the 1976 sports poll, the fact that even within the Nationalist Party there is a majority in favour of mixed sport down to club level, suggests that Government decisions are influenced at least as much by the opinions of factions within and on the fringes of the Nationalist Party as by the movement of electoral opinion. Indeed, we have seen the extent to which the *Broederbond* can influence Government and public attitudes alike. Nationalist factions are engaged in perpetual internal debate which inhibits the introduction of change. It is not just a matter of the gap between Government policy and white opinion but between Government policy and the Nationalist ideology which officially inspires it. At all levels, however, the sports question is perceived and treated as an issue which is intrinsically political in character, incorporated within an overall political programme. The *Broederbond* therefore had relatively little difficulty in persuading its members that sport reform were necessary because of sport's *political* significance:

> We have always believed that sport should not be mixed with politics, and politics must be kept out of sport. Throughout the world, however, the importance of sport in international affairs, for the prestige of countries and the promotion of a cause, has come strongly to the forefront and politics are drawn more and more into sport.
>
> That the two issues can no longer be separated is obvious from recent developments . . . . It is very clear that our enemies have gained much courage from their success [in isolating South Africa] . . . . A total of 500 million people participate in sport . . . and sport has indeed become a world power.[32]

Rule by Confusion

The political interest aroused by the sports issue, both within political circles and among the white electorate helps us to appreciate the complexity of demands on the Government. The latter was forced to coin an artificial vocabulary, a double language, which replaced 'separate development' first by 'multi-nationalism' and then by 'pluralism', all to avoid the word 'apartheid'. In November 1979, Mr Punt Janson, Sports Minister at the time, even declared that the word 'apartheid' should be suppressed.[33] Moreover, all these words were given one meaning abroad and another within South Africa, thereby providing the Government with room to manoeuvre between its various, irreconcilable commitments. The white, and particularly Afrikaner, public, trapped between traditional faith in its leadership and alarm at the evidence of change, was visibly manipulated. In fact, one could describe official sports policy — a body of directives without force of law — as a *double* double language; in the 1970s, official sporting relations became infected with Kafkaesque uneasiness, and interpretation of Governmental and Ministerial declarations becomes as hazardous as it is indispensable.

The most prickly problems are raised by club sport. Was it legal to set up multi-racial clubs? If so, was it acceptable? For a considerable time after 1976, this question dominated Government thinking. Koornhof's declarations suggest that initially the Government intended to interpret the 'multi-national policy' (see Appendix 1) literally. It was not, therefore, as was suggested abroad, a multi-racial policy — even if, in practice, the Government was unable, or, for political reasons, unwilling to enforce the policy at all times. A short extract from a speech by Dr Koornhof illustrates both the delicacy of the issue of club sport and the duality of Government thinking. Speaking in May 1977 of his September 1976 statement, Koornhof stated that:

> This first principle upholds the premise of separate development, namely that instead of mixed clubs, each population group belongs to its own club and that every club arranges and controls its own affairs within its own sphere . . . .
>
> The third principle of the policy is probably the most important development in the whole policy, and one which our friends and enemies here and abroad do not fully realize. Where multi-national sport was previously allowed only at the highest level, that is at national or international level, it is now permissible to arrange multi-national sport right down to club level if the controlling bodies so desire.[34]

The 'multi-national' policy assumes, in fact, that clubs are to be organized on racially exclusive lines. Nevertheless the authorities were caught in a dilemma. If clubs were denied the right to recruit a multi-racial membership, 'multi-nationalism' would be discredited abroad and the Government once again accused of interfering in the autonomy of sports clubs. Yet if multi-racial clubs were tolerated, this would not merely infringe the laws of apartheid and distort the sports policy, but unleash ferocious reaction from the right wing of the Party. Moreover, if clubs did choose to become multi-racial in membership, how was sport to be separated from the rest of society? A dangerous precedent would have been set. Political discourse became, as a result of this dilemma, extraordinarily dextrous: mixed clubs were neither forbidden, nor authorized, and policy declarations were constructed around double negatives that held together logically contradictory statements. Although the whole performance was ridiculed by Opposition members in Parliament, the Government was thereby enabled, crabwise, to pursue its policy without quite alienating either Nationalist opinion, or international observers. Boiled down to its essential practice, in fact, 'multi-nationalism' is a policy which, by prohibiting without banning, and tolerating without authorizing, is calculated to satisfy the irreconcilable demands of its critics at home and abroad. The latter are encouraged to believe that sport has been 'normalized', and the former assured that the status quo will be respected.

The Government's hypocrisy is revealed nowhere more clearly than in its refusal to legislate against mixed sport. Instead, the complexion of sporting activity is rigorously controlled through pass law legislation and the permit system, which requires organizers of matches involving racial mixing to apply for permission from the authorities. Permits are given, suspended or withdrawn entirely at the discretion of local officials and the Minister; there is no appeal. The permit system gives the Government the power to suffocate all mixed sport of which it disapproves, and to promote 'multi-national' sport which conforms to official policy.[35]

The policy has certain disadvantages for the Government, nevertheless. Its obscurity, the absence of defined limits and specific constraints, gave nonracial sportsmen and women, supported by international opinion, room to exploit its contradictions. Many white sportsmen, understandably confused by the plethora of conditional clauses and double negatives, were also slow to respond to a policy which continued to give directions to white sportsmen but claimed at the same time to be offering sports associations complete autonomy. Here again, the Government was trapped in its own contradictions. On the one hand, it felt the need to define an official sports policy that would accord with the general policy of 'separate development' and permit the Government to exercise control over sports associations. On the other, it realized that South African sport would never be readmitted to the world community while the Government openly interfered with the policies of the sports associations. As early as April 1967, Vorster had declared: 'Above all, I want to request that the matter [of sport] would not be dragged into politics,' only to state, a few lines on, that since 'separate development' was the country's official policy, it 'therefore applies also to the field of sport'.[36] This conflict of attitude was to remain unresolved throughout the 1970s, while the need for a credible sports policy became increasingly pressing as the international sports boycott tightened and popular resentment increased within the country — not least among the white electorate.

Even the executive of the *Broederbond* came to accept that mixed representative teams were necessary because 'international sporting ties, especially in rugby and cricket, have serious implications at this critical stage for our country, regarding international trade, national trade, military relationships and armaments, and strategic industrial development.'[37] When concessions were made to international pressure, Ministers interpreted them as political initiatives to defend the State. The same reasoning was largely responsible for the creation of a number of organizations to promote the interests of South African sport (particularly black racial sport) abroad. Three of these should be mentioned.

The S.A. Sports Foundation was created in 1964 to 'promote sport among all racial groups', by Anton Rupert, a *Broeder* businessman and chairman of several major companies. The Foundation finances black sportsmen and associations affiliated to white federations. In 1968, the Foundation offered Basil d'Oliveira a large sum to train black cricketers on condition that he agree to stand down from the M.C.C. tour to South Africa. The Committee for Fairness in Sport was created in 1973 to encourage international participation in South African sport and promote the sports reforms introduced after 1970. Among its founders were the millionaire Louis Luyt (a friend of Dr Koornhof), and the President of S.A. Breweries, Dick Goss. The Committee organized an international publicity campaign to promote the interests of South African sport, through advertisements in newspapers all over the world, and promotional tours. Several Blacks took part, among whom the best known is Leslie Sehume, at one time the Committee's Secretary: Sehume toured Britain in March 1974 to promote the Lions' tour, and New Zealand in 1975 to weaken the boycott there. Finally, the Bantu Sport and Recreation Fund was also created in 1973 with the support of Rupert and the Rembrandt Group.

Many other examples could be found of the exploitation of sport by South Africa for political ends. One came to light during the Muldergate scandal, in which at least 73 million dollars were made available from a secret slush fund controlled by the S.A. Department of Information to persuade Western newspapers, journalists, trade unionists and businessmen to support South Africa. The project involved Gary Player, who was given 30,000 dollars to invite managing directors of major companies (Chrysler, Ford, Boeing, the Bank of America . . .) to play golf with him in South Africa, and thereby weaken the American campaign against investments in South Africa. (When taxed about his role, Player declared that he was 'proud' to have been 'useful' to his country and would do the same again.)

Sport is clearly not separable from politics under these conditions. Yet, politically, it needed to be separated. Here again, the Government — and white South Africa as a whole — is caught in a dilemma. The official South African press continues to lament the fate of sportsmen 'victimized' by political manipulation abroad; 'sport is no longer merely an affair of sport,' protests *Panorama*, de Coubertin's Olympic ideals have become mere 'dreams'.[38] Yet it is clearly apartheid which has injected political significance into sport, and divorced its practice from the principles and ideals which are internationally recognized by sportsmen and women — and by white South African sportsmen: equality, selection on merit, fraternal competition, etc.

The credibility of Government propaganda depends upon four particular, disingenuous claims:

1) That the racial divisions between South Africans are a *natural product* of the South African situation: 'Ethnicity forms part of the reality in South Africa. We did not create it. Nor did we forcibly impose it on sport. It forms part of the historic foundation on which sport in South Africa has been built . . . . It is something that manifests itself, something we cannot talk our way round.'[39]

2) That sporting associations are autonomous bodies whose independence the

Government will defend at all costs. (Even here, the Government derives political advantage by its own peculiarly circuitous logic: 'The percentage of the total budget allocated to sport in South Africa . . . is among the lowest in the entire Western World,' declared the Minister of Sport, de Klerk, in 1979, deducing that: 'Therefore, when we say that we recognize the autonomy of sports bodies, it is a meaningful statement.') [40]

3) That the laws restricting the freedoms of sportsmen and women are all general laws, necessary to security and to peaceful co-existence in the country:

> There is not a word about sport as such in the general laws of the land. Surely the Group Areas Act and the Liquor Act are not sport laws. They are laws that apply generally. They apply to all sections of society. [41] . . . . In South Africa one needs a permit to enter a Black residential area but one does not need a permit to play sport. One needs a permit to enter a Black residential area for two reasons. The first is one's own safety . . . . The second is so that the authorities can know who is entering those Black residential areas, because we in South Africa are faced with various problems, including matters such as urban terrorism, and a form of control for the sake of the security of everyone in South Africa, Black, Brown and White, is required. That permit that Cheeky Watson, or I, or the Hon. Member, requires when one of us wants to enter a Black residential area, has nothing whatsoever to do with sport. [42] [The autonomy of sports associations is therefore accorded] on condition that good order does not suffer and that the general laws of the land are recognized. [43]

4) That it is South Africa's internal and external enemies, in sport and in politics, who use the sports issue as a political weapon and are responsible for confusing one with the other:

> Autonomy of sports bodies carries with it a heavy responsibility . . . . If a situation of racial friction should develop, or if individuals, newspapers or pressure groups should misuse sport as a vehicle for political change in South Africa, then sport will move into the political arena, with the logical consequences attached thereto. [44] . . . . I want to tell SACOS and its leaders this afternoon: in South Africa's sports dispensation, there is no place for political activists. [45]

The Advantages of a Liberal Opposition[46]

In the context of these arguments a word should be said about the sports policies of the main opposition party. The P.F.P. accuses the Government of introducing politics into sport and contests the first three of the propositions above. It regards 'ethnicity' as a socio-political institution, maintained by law and extended over all areas of life; and it points out that normal sport is impossible because of apartheid legislation and the permit system. It also argues that 'If one looks at the various types of sport in South Africa, that have made the most progress towards change and "normalization", a word initiated by the previous Hon. Minister, one finds them to have been those sports which have deviated the most from Government policy.'[47]

The P.F.P. summarized its attitude to sport in 1979 as follows:

(1)   We are opposed to all forms of political interference in the areas of sport, whether these are external, as in the case of sports boycotts against South Africa, or internal, as in the Government's past interference with the autonomy of sportsmen.[48]

(2)   We stand for an open society . . . a society which is free from all forms of statutory or administrative discrimination . . . . When we use the term 'non-racial sport', this implies a move away from what the Hon. Minister described earlier as being one of the principles of the N.P. policy, a move away from ethnic considerations in sport . . .[49]

(3)   We believe that the decision about whether or not to participate in sport, as well as what sport to participate in, and most important, with whom one is going to play is, above everything else, a private decision and one that should be above political or governmental interference.[50]

So legalistic an approach, although it permits the P.F.P. to reveal and attack the contradictions in Government policy, is nevertheless wholly inadequate. It is as incapable of satisfying the expectations and needs of sportsmen and women — and black sportsmen and women in particular — as it is of seriously upsetting Nationalist policy-makers. Brave protests in favour of individual liberties sound somewhat flippant when they overlook the weight of racial legislation and social discrimination which prevent black sportsmen and women from realizing their potential or freely joining the sports clubs of their choice. The shortcomings of the liberal opposition's policy — which are turned to good use by the Government — are most cruelly revealed by its attacks on all forms of boycott and on the non-racial sportsmen regrouped within the S.A. Council on Sport: 'We do not go along with the pressure they [SACOS] have brought to bear on sport and the politicking they have engaged in,' declared Mr Widman in Parliament in 1979.[51]

Ironically, the consensus between the P.F.P. and Nationalists transforms the former into ideal propagandists for the Government and white sport. P.F.P. liberals have greatly assisted the South African lobby, both within South Africa (at meetings with Commissions of Inquiry) and internationally, for on several occasions they have formally criticized SACOS (to whose non-racial principles many of them were sympathetic in the past). Dalling himself in 1979, for example, asserted that SACOS should admit 'that non-racial sport is fast becoming a fact', and that its slogan 'No normal sport in an abnormal society' was 'a recipe for conflict, for bitterness, for isolation, for frustration.'[52] In the 1979 parliamentary debate on sport, the P.F.P. blamed SACOS for refusing to negotiate, and accused its leaders of perpetuating attitudes which, both internally and internationally, were 'counter-productive'. It should have come as no surprise that at the end of the debate the Minister of Sport had handsome praise for the official opposition:

> I want to conclude on a friendly note to the Hon. Member [Mr Dalling] and thank him for his positive co-operation with regard to SACOS. I think that in this regard he advanced balanced arguments and I want to thank him for the fact that we are absolutely unanimous in regard to that important matter — because SACOS is doing us tremendous harm abroad.[53]

References

1. Peter Hain, one of the campaign's main organizers, has written a full description of the Stop The Seventy Tour in P. Hain, 1971, pp. 113-95.
2. Cf. J. Brickhill, 1976, p. 13. The effort was scarcely necessary, for during the first three weeks of the games, only 485 Blacks attempted to buy tickets.
3. For a good short summary of the general situation today, see Catholic Institute of International Relations, 1980.
4. Interview with a Coloured woman, London, February 1980.
5. See Catholic Institute of International Relations, 1980, pp. 9-10, 16.
6. *South Africa 1977 Official Year Book*, 1977, p. 203.
7. *South Africa Official Year Book, 1977*, p. 807.
8. Dr Koornhof, *Hansard*, 25 May 1973 in Ramsamy, *Racial Discrimination*, p. 14.
9. Dr Koornhof, Minister of Sport, *Hansard*, 18 May 1977.
10. *Hansard*, 11 April 1967, in J. Brickhill, 1976, pp. 21-2.
11. Vorster called upon the Party to: i) Reinforce the white minority by improving co-operation between English-speakers and Afrikaners; ii) Reinforce the white minority by encouraging immigration; iii) Improve relations with African States ('dialogue'); iv) Accept, under certain conditions, tours in South Africa by racially mixed teams from abroad.
12. For example, a newsletter was sent out to *Broeders* on 1 April 1971: '*Sport and the present onslaught against South Africa:* A study document on this subject is hereby sent to divisions. It has been made available by the Sport Committee. You are requested to consider how its contents can be made public in your area. A talk by school principals or teachers in primary and high schools, a talk to *Rapportryers* or other public bodies (youth organizations, sports clubs, etc.) are methods that can be used. You should not mention the study document. The contents can be rephrased and given as the speaker's own thoughts. Please do not read the document in public. (It will seem very strange if people all over the country suddenly appear in public with the same document!) (in Wilkins and Strydom, 1979, p. 243. Their chapter on sport contains much information, which we have used here.)
13. Hannes Botha became President of the S.A. Amateur Athletics Union;

Jannie le Roux took over the presidency of the Transvaal Rugby Union. Attempts to dislodge Danie Craven from the S.A. Rugby Union and Morne du Plessis (then Captain of the Springboks) failed. Wilkins and Strydom, 1979, p. 245.

14. Dr Koornhof, interview in *Topsport*, in Odendaal, 1977, p. 123.
15. In September 1977, for example, Koornhof intervened at the Nationalist Party Congress at Pretoria, to oppose a call for legislation, on the grounds it might damage South Africa's interests at home and abroad (A.F.P., 14 September 1977).
16. Mr J.N. van der Westhuysen (N.P.), in Parliament, 21 May 1979, *Hansard*, columns 6960-1.
17. Mr Nothnagel, 21 May 1979, *Hansard*, columns 6935-6.
18. D. Woods, 1979, p. 205. According to surveys, after Sharpeville the majority of Africans believed that race relations were deteriorating. Another sample, in 1970, indicated that most thought relations were improving slightly. In 1976 opinions were pessimistic once more. The reason given most frequently by Africans who believed, according to the surveys, that social relations were improving, was none other than 'mixed sport'. H. Lever (1978, p. 204) does not suggest that Africans believed mixed sport might of itself produce change in the social order, but that they believed it might favourably influence social attitudes. Apparently, Biko went further than this: Asked at his trial why he believed pressure could be exerted on the South African government through sport, Biko answered "The importance of groups like the South African Rugby Union, the South African Cricket Board of Control, and various sporting groups within the black spheres that control sport have grown tremendously influential over the years . . . I think it is simply because this is one sphere where the end is imminent . . .

    I think unless white people in this country are illogical, if you are going to mix on the sports field and mix fully, as is eventually going to happen, then you have to think about other areas of your activity, you have to think about cinemas, you have to think about shows and dancing and so on, you have to think about political rights. It is a snowball effect . . ." (in Woods, 1979, p. 205).
19. Among factors likely to improve relations between the two white communities sport was considered important by only 2.5% of Whites, as against 3.8% in favour of bilingual schools and 19.4% for social mixing (*Argus* poll, 1970, in H. Lever, 1978, p. 174). Sport scored much the same among all political parties.
20. Wilkins and Strydom, 1980, p. 373.
21. Ibid., p. 148.
22. Ibid., p. 398.
23. Ibid., p. 246.
24. Polls were rare in South Africa before 1970, and in general do not have the socio-political standing they have acquired in Europe, and to an even greater degree in the U.S.A.
25. Hudson et al., cited without details by H. Lever, 1978, p. 172.
26. Mark en Meningopnames, *Meningspeil vir Rapport*, Cape Town: M & M, October 1978, in H. Lever, 1978, pp. 170-1 (2,300 respondents).
27. The question asked was apparently ambiguous: respondents were asked

to give their reaction to 'the introduction of mixed sport up to club level'. 'Mixed sport' can be understood to mean 'multi-national' or multi-racial sport; and 'up to' club level can be interpreted as exclusive or inclusive of clubs. The definition of 'multi-nationalism' and the high level of positive response suggest that the question was interpreted as asking whether those questioned were in favour of extending 'multi-national' relations to relations *between* clubs.

28. In H. Lever, 1978, p. 173; the size of the sample is not given.
29. In J. Barber, 1973, p. 223.
30. Public Opinion Survey, Nov.-Dec. 1968: Market Research Africa (Pty) Ltd, Johannesburg, in J. Barber, 1973, pp. 223-4.
31. *Argus* poll, 1970, in H. Lever, 1978, p. 163.
32. *Broederbond* Newsletter, 1 April 1971, in Wilkins and Strydom, 1979, p. 243.
33. *Muslim News*, 2 November 1979.
34. Speech to Stellenbosch University, April 1977 in A. Odendaal, 1977, pp. 126-7. (See Appendix 2).
35. Permits are necessary to suspend apartheid laws, such as the Group Areas Act, for the duration of matches. It has recently become possible to apply for an annual permit, even to make an application by telephone. This in no way removes the legal obligation upon sports organizers, or reduces the power of Government to refuse permits to players of whom it disapproves. Nevertheless, these concessions have satisfied some foreign observers, including two Commissions of Inquiry, sent out by the French Parliament and by the British Sports Council, in 1980. Both were assured by white associations and by the Government that legislation requiring permits had fallen out of use. Mr Marie, leader of the French Commission, had not even *heard* of the 'multi-national' policy when he returned to France! Government figures are more reliable: according to Dr Koornhof himself, speaking in 1977, 99.9956% of organized sport respected the Government's segregated sports policy (Parliament, 10 October 1977). In 1980, the proportion was officially held to be   %.
36. In Barber, 1973, p. 300.
37. Wilkins and Strydom, 1980, p. 250.
38. *Panorama*, magazine published by the South African Government, June 1979.
39. De Klerk, Minister of Sport, in Parliament, 21 May 1979, *Hansard*, column 6983.
40. Ibid., column 6978.
41. Ibid., column 6987-8.
42. Ibid., column 6992-3.
43. Ibid., column 6900-1.
44. Ibid., column 6902.
45. Ibid., column 6905.
46. The so-called liberalism of English-speaking South Africans deserves critical examination. A study carried out by the Association of Sociologists of Southern Africa concluded that, although Afrikaans- and English-speakers within the Nationalist and United Parties were distributed in roughly the same proportions (80% of Afrikaners were

Nationalists, against 8% of English-speakers; 82% of United Party followers were English-speakers, and only 7% Afrikaners): '1) The English elite was dispersed between the U.P. (36%) and the 'progressive' parties (29%), while the Afrikaner elite confined its vote almost exclusively to the Nationalist Party (83%), giving only 4% to the U.P. and Progressive Parties; 2) The 'liberals' among the English-speaking elite were quite unrepresentative of the English-speaking electorate in general. Only 3% of voters in the 1970 elections voted for the 'progressive' parties, but 18% of the elite did so; in contrast, the United Party received generally less support from the elite than from the population in general.' (A.S.S.A., 1973, pp. 198-9, 277-8).

47. Dalling (P.F.P. spokesman on sport), *Hansard*, 21 May 1979, columns 6908-9.
48. Dalling, ibid.
49. Dalling, ibid.
50. Dalling, ibid.
51. Mr Widman, ibid., column 6943-4.
52. Mr Dalling, ibid., column 6919. To do credit, Mr Dalling was recently rather more critical of Government policy in a recent television interview with Cl. Salviac (Antenne 2, France).
53. De Klerk, Parliament, 21 May 1979, *Hansard*, column 6989.

10. The Non-Racial Movement under SACOS

1970 was not only the year in which white South African sport was effectively isolated: the non-racial movement inside the country also reorganized itself and took the first steps towards establishing a new national organization to represent non-racial sportsmen. In September 1970, eight non-racial federations met in Durban and set up the S.A. Non-Racial Sports Organization (SASPO), which three years later was to create the S.A. Council on Sport (SACOS).

It was a favourable time for taking such an initiative. International support was at a peak, providing some guarantee against repression. The boycott of South African sport had weakened the bargaining position of both the white sports associations and the Government. And finally, a new political climate, which found expression in the rise of the Black Consciousness Movement, raised the level of resistance to apartheid throughout the country.

SASPO's initial platform was moderate. 'Multi-nationalism' was rejected and denounced in the name of non-racialism, but the organization stated that it was prepared to negotiate with white sportsmen over their differences — a significant concession, for at the same period the Black Consciousness Movement was ending relations with white liberalism and insisting upon the need to re-establish black identity as a first stage of struggle.

A completely non-racial sports structure from school level upwards, adequate facilities for sportsmen and women of all races, and realization of the non-racial principle of equality at all levels were also among SASPO's 12 stated aims, which included a declaration condemning the permit system and the unequal distribution of commercial sponsorship.

At the first signs of improvement in their international relations, however, the white associations and the Government hardened their bargaining positions and withdrew the various concessions that had been held out to the non-racial organizations.[1] White tennis players who had complained about official policy in 1971 ceased to do so when South Africa was readmitted (temporarily) to the Davis Cup in 1972. Frank Braun, senior member of the white Olympic Committee, met SASPO but subsequently arranged meetings only with racial black sports federations. The S.A. Rugby Board was to do likewise. In 1971, segregation was maintained among spectators when black golfers were permitted to take part in competitions, and in the first 'multi-national' athletics competition (1971) black and white athletes were even sent to separate hotels. The Government made it known that those who persisted in playing multi-racial matches on private grounds (which did not need permits) were simply advancing the day when they would be banned by law.[2]

In short, the limitations of 'multi-nationalism' soon became apparent, and when the non-racial federations met on 13 March 1973 to form the South African Council on Sport (SACOS), their mood was more aggressive. Indeed, the intransigence of some SACOS policies has caused concern even among its members, many of whom fear that, under the artificial and totalitarian conditions created by apartheid, the inflexible application of radical policies may sever the movement from its base, and in particular from the mass of African sportsmen and women. The name of SACOS has nevertheless become so closely associated with the struggle for non-racial sport, both within South Africa and outside it, that the two have almost become confounded. In this chapter we shall examine SACOS's aims, organization and policies, and in the next chapter its impact upon sport and sporting politics since 1973.

The Aims of SACOS

SACOS recognizes the international principles of the Olympic Charter, the I.O.C. and international federations (see Appendix 1). It claims that its affiliates are the only sports associations in South Africa to do so. However, it has not sought official recognition from the I.O.C., nor do its members seek to affiliate to their respective international bodies, because they believe that under the laws of apartheid sport cannot be organized in a non-racial fashion, and that no organization can therefore claim to fulfil the twin requirements of representativity and non-racialism.[3] SACOS members nevertheless claim that, unlike the racial federations, they are actively working towards a non-racial future for sport, and that when apartheid legislation has been repealed and the country freed from racial exploitation, their affiliates will legitimately be able to claim recognition. A number of international organizations agree with this argument. SACOS is an associate member of the Supreme Council for Sport in Africa.

The number of SACOS affiliates grew rapidly between 1973 and 1980, from 8 initially to 13 (1975), 22 (1979) and finally 26 (1980: see Appendix 4). All affiliates are bound by a common commitment to non-racial principles and SACOS reserves the right to expel any which contravene them. (It has expelled several, including the powerful S.A. Soccer Federation in 1977-79.) Essentially, however, SACOS is a representative body created to promote the interests of non-racial sport, which has no formal right to intervene in the internal affairs of its affiliates. Policy decisions are taken at biennial conferences, or by the Executive Committee of SACOS, which is composed of the permanent officials — President, Vice-president, Secretary, Treasurer and Patron[4]) — and representatives of each affiliate. The executive committee meets every month and an interim conference is held annually.

SACOS's role is essentially to co-ordinate and unify the non-racial move-ment, to act as a forum for its members and as a spokesman for non-racialism in sport. As a result, and because it has no formal authority over its affiliates, its influence depends upon the degree to which it truly represents their wishes and speaks for the majority of black sportsmen and women. The organization is financed by the contributions of member associations and by private fund-raising activities. Unlike sports associations recognized by the Government, which receive many important financial subsidies, neither SACOS nor its affiliates receive official grants of any kind.

School Sports Associations and Provincial Councils

Two other kinds of association, in addition to national sports federations, belong to SACOS.

The two school sports associations — the S.A. Primary Schools Sports Association (SAPSSA) and the S.A. Secondary Schools Sports Association (SASSSA) — make a considerable contribution to the non-racial movement. Primarily, of course, they bring schoolchildren into contact with non-racial ways of thinking. They also represent a considerable number of players — around 200,000 all over the country — and, being multi-sport associations, promote inter-sport contact between sportsmen. They play a crucial role in forming the next generation of sportsmen and women and provide the most solid guarantee of the survival of non-racial values.

Unfortunately, very few African schools are affiliated to SAPSSA and SASSSA. This is principally because African education is extremely segrega-ted and tightly controlled, and very little contact is possible between African and Indian or Coloured schools. No African school sports association has been formed, despite — or because of — Government attempts to do so. African teachers are well aware that a new sports association for African children would at once be taken over by the authorities and used to reinforce apartheid.

SACOS has no official relations with student bodies in the black 'tribal' universities, for these are organized on racial lines. Affiliates are encouraged not to use these university facilities, although it is very often difficult for non-racial clubs to find sports grounds. On the other hand, some associations, like the S.A. Rugby Union, do permit student unions to affiliate, and students are certainly very active in the non-racial movement. The candidature of SABIC, a national association representing black students, was under exam-ination by SACOS in 1979.[5]

The role of the provincial Councils of Sport is more controversial. They were originally created to increase public awareness of, and support for, SACOS and the non-racial movement.[6] Since 1977, however, the Councils of Sport have been represented on the SACOS Executive Council, on which they have a vote even though they have no responsibility for the organization of sport and no formal relationship to the sports associations in each province. Their influence has increased sharply, for they fulfil a number of important roles. They reinforce local organization in the provinces; they help individual clubs and sportsmen resist intimidation and harassment from racial federations and from municipal authorities; they can encourage the formation of new clubs, particularly in sports for which national federations have not yet been created (clubs can affiliate via provincial councils to SACOS); and they provide a line of communication between the central body and individual sportsmen. Between 1977 and 1980, seven provincial Councils of Sport were admitted to SACOS, each having proved that it represented five different sports; provincial associations have been encouraged to affiliate to their local Councils of Sport by the SACOS executive.

The difficulties are caused by the conflict in mandate between members of the national sports associations, which have responsibility for and duties towards their members, and provincial Councils, which are not normally beholden to any elected body, and whose mandate is therefore less well defined. The growing influence of the Councils of Sport has been contested on the grounds that their authority within the provinces is both unaccountable and in competition with the authority of national associations; and there is no doubt that, on occasion, and claiming to represent non-racial sportsmen throughout the province, these Councils have intervened to criticize the policies of particular federations, thus effectively questioning their autonomy, which theoretically is guaranteed and preserved by the structure of SACOS.

Potentially serious disputes relating to these Councils have arisen particularly frequently around the Double Standards Resolution, which was intended to prevent SACOS members from joining racial and non-racial associations at the same time. According to this rule, members of non-racial clubs may not play for or against racial clubs either in their own or in another sport. According to more extreme interpretations, the rule also forbids sportsmen and women to seek employment in, or even frequent establishments which respect apartheid regulations.

A number of non-racial officials and players find it unnecessary or distasteful to enforce this rule universally on all their members; they argue that it is not always clear at a given time whether or not a club is racial or not, and that it is unrealistic to require non-racial sportsmen to isolate themselves completely, in sport or in other areas of their lives, from the apartheid environment which surrounds them. For a considerable time, provincial affiliates of the non-racial S.A. Rugby Union, which is particularly jealous of its autonomy, refused to join the provincial Councils of Sport because of the potential conflict of interest which might result.

The difficulties can be exaggerated, however: members of the Councils have some mandate from the provincial sports associations which have affiliated to them, and in a country as large as South Africa, a degree of decentralization is probably essential. They may also help to counteract the centralizing tendencies of a national multi-sport organization like SACOS, whose central principle is liable to variable interpretation. On the whole, the integration of the Councils within SACOS has radicalized the language of the organization, but not necessarily its practice, and strengthened, at some risk to the movement as a whole,[7] the most intransigent national administrators.

The Importance of International Backing

International solidarity with the non-racial sports movement has consistently provided the non-racial movement with the best security against repression. SACOS has been able to advance its non-racial standpoint more explicitly than has previously been possible precisely because international support for its activities has been better organized and more extensive than during the 1950s and 1960s. Nonetheless, its officials are still refused passports and travel visas, and SACOS is therefore represented internationally by SAN-ROC, and by its president Mr Samba Ramsamy.[8]

The Council is an associate member of the Supreme Council for Sport in Africa, the official representative of national African sports bodies, and is therefore implicitly recognized by the Organization of African Unity, and the United Nations, and indirectly by the I.O.C. SACOS has the support of a number of foreign national sports associations, like the Indian Golf Union, the All-Indian Football Federation, the French Federation Sportive et Gymnique du Travail. On a more political level, the struggle of SACOS to promote non-racial sport is recognized and supported by the U.N. Centre Against Apartheid (Department of Political and Security Council Affairs), by anti-apartheid movements and other organizations devoted to resisting racism and apartheid in sport, by church bodies, university staff, trade unions, students, etc., particularly in countries which have traditional ties with South Africa, and by the official sports bodies in communist countries.

SACOS Policies

Permits

From its inception, SACOS declared its firm and undivided opposition to the 'multi-national' policy (see Appendix 1). As part of this policy of non-recognition, SACOS members refuse to apply for permits for their fixtures. The permit system was introduced by the Government to facilitate the introduction of 'multi-nationalism' while continuing to prevent non-racial sportsmen and women from organizing truly multi-racial games. SACOS players are regularly questioned by the police and not infrequently arrested. The most notorious case of such legal harassment involved 'Cheeky' Watson and his brother Valence, members of the S.A. Rugby Union, arrested and found guilty on appeal of playing rugby in an African area without a permit to do so. Both are white: their cases attracted the attention of the press. Alongside them, tens or hundreds of anonymous black sportsmen have been similarly intimidated, detained or arrested for the same 'misdemeanour'.

In 1978, SACOS distributed a pamphlet explaining its stand over permits. The campaign illustrates how the sports movement can have a broad impact on public opinion because of sport's particular status in South Africa:

> People who live in houses where they require permits, or people who work under permit or have children educated under permit have no

option but to do so. There are laws governing these things — although we detest them. But sportsmen and others who play and attend sport under permit are not forced to do so. They do it from free choice, voluntarily. In other words, they are collaborating in their own humiliation . . . . Sportsmen should refuse to play sport or watch it under permit because it . . . injures their human dignity and it deprives them of their right as South Africans.

There is only one way to equality and that is to abolish all laws which militate against the playing of sport in a truly non-racial manner in a democratic society.[9]

By defending their own interests — which they were able to do because of the particular status of sport — sportsmen drew attention to a problem of general human rights, concerning all South Africans. The effects of this highly successful campaign were, however, revealingly double-edged, for the Government — stung by the unfavourable publicity the permit system was attracting abroad, and unwilling to further damage its reputation by repressing the campaign against it — proceeded in stages to 'liberalize' the granting of permits, until in 1980 it was claiming quite falsely to have done away with the system altogether. Initially, grounds were allowed to acquire annual permits (on 'multi-national' conditions); then tickets sold in advance were held to stand in lieu of permits; and finally, when embarrassing cases of segregation continued to recur, the Department of Sport issued a special phone number, which organizers could call at all hours if they required permits at short notice. Official spokesmen of both the Government and the sports establishment affect to believe that permits have become a simple formality, a tiresome relic of bureaucracy. However, as non-racial sportsmen point out, permits are still legally necessary for all multi-racial matches, can be refused by the authorities without appeal or explanation, and *are* refused, on occasion, to non-racial sports organizers.

The campaign against permits illustrates the predicament of non-racial associations. Originally an act of resistance to racial legislation, the campaign was manipulated by the racial federations and the Government to advance their own causes. Racial federations have frequently claimed recently that, since they no longer ask for permits, this proves they are non-racial; and the Government dismisses critics with the argument that it no longer implements the permit legislation. The permit campaign undeniably damaged the credibility of the Government's 'multi-national' policy. It identified a criterion against which the 'non-racial' performance of sports bodies could be judged, but when the official sports establishment recognized this it turned the situation to its own advantage by skilful use of misinformation. The struggle to occupy what may be called the 'non-racial space' that is created within apartheid sport by the existence and activities of SACOS is a central theme running through the history of South African sport during the 1970s. Its outcome will determine not only whether 'multi-nationalism' will be accepted abroad, but whether the non-racial sports associations will be able to win the *public* support of black, and in particular African sportsmen, despite apartheid and in competition with the promoters of professional and racial black sport.

Another, quite different effect illustrates the complexity of relations within the non-racial movement, which has to combat racialist attitudes rooted in South African social life since the colony was first created. In the report of the provincial Councils of Sport for 1979, it was noted that certain clubs had used the permit campaign 'as a pretext for racial prejudice', arguing that since it was not possible to play in African areas without permits, African fixtures should be cancelled. Rules which had been laid down to reduce segregation were thus being employed to reinforce it. We shall have occasion to return to the problem of relations between African sportsmen and the black minorities: this example indicates how much flexibility in the application of principles is required if the separation which apartheid has created between them is to be narrowed.

These two examples relating to the permits campaign both bring us to the central issue raised by SACOS's existence and non-racial activities. Is it possible for an organization to respect and represent non-racial principles at all under apartheid? And if it is not, what should non-racial organizations seek to achieve? If it is admitted that, given the constraints on liberty imposed by racial legislation, no organizations can function without making concessions to racialism, by what criteria, what right, can they claim to be more 'principled', less 'racial' than other organizations? How is 'true' non-racialism to be distinguished from 'false' non-racialism? While he was President of the S.A. Cricket Board of Control. Hassan Howa admitted the contradictions with his usual bluntness: 'If we were non-racial purists we should stop playing cricket altogether. I have said this before: at a school debate where children said we were racialist. We are. We are forced to be racialists by the laws of the country.'[10]

The difficulties are enormously increased because SACOS, like other non-racial associations, cannot identify its principles in political terms, in relation to apartheid. This would mean sacrificing the unique advantage of sport's politically neutral status. Yet without 'non-sporting' criteria by which to define 'non-racialism', the quest for legitimacy easily dissolves into squabbles about personalities, charges of hypocrisy, ambition, intolerance or racist views.

This predicament is not caused by SACOS and its affiliates of course. It is a direct consequence of apartheid which politicizes all areas of life while at the same time outlawing political debate. Though it has failed so far to resolve these contradictions, the history of SACOS since 1976 (when the 'multi-national' policy was defined and the Soweto riots took place) is largely a story of its attempts to do so. Its most consistent approach has been to promote practical solidarity between all non-racial sportsmen — players, officials, trainers, spectators. The principal instrument of this policy is the so-called Double Standards Resolution, which is probably the most controversial of SACOS initiatives to date.

The Double Standards Resolution

The first statement against double standards was issued in 1977 by the SACOS executive, in the context of a serious dispute within the S.A. Cricket Board of Control over its relations with the white Association. (For this statement and subsequent SACOS policy declarations, see Appendix 3.) Its purpose was clear: to reinforce the non-racial movement against splits and secessions by stating that non-racial sportsmen would be defined as all those, and only those, who agreed to break their ties with officially recognized sports bodies.

Clarity was necessary not only because Koornhof's 'multi-national' policy was creating serious divisions of opinion among black sportsmen. SACOS sports officials themselves differed over the correct response to 'multi-nationalism'. While all wished to advance non-racial principles, they by no means shared the same political beliefs or agreed over the best means of achieving their ends, as is shown by the case of SACOS's first President, Mr Norman Middleton, President of the powerful S.A. Soccer Federation and a longstanding campaigner for non-racial sport. The clauses of the 1979 Double Standards Resolution almost identified him by name, for he was also Vice-President of the Coloured Labour Party and a member of the Coloured Representative Council. In 1977 he was forced to resign as President of SACOS; and in 1978, his continued presidency of the Soccer Federation was undoubtedly one of the reasons for their expulsion from the Council in 1977-78.

The original statement was reformulated by the interim conference in October 1978. While the 1977 statement declared that sportsmen were not to entertain relations with racial or multi-national *sports* bodies, the terms of the 1978 declaration were much vaguer. On the other hand, while the 1977 resolution provided no criterion by which to determine which organizations were 'multi-national' or 'racial', the 1978 declaration declared that SACOS, and SACOS alone, should determine whether a given club or affiliate was non-racial.

At the third biennial conference of SACOS, in 1979, the Double Standards Resolution was further amended. The *moral* responsibility of SACOS members to abjure contact with official institutions was re-established; but the criteria by which SACOS members were to judge whether a given body was 'non-racial' or not, were not clarified. The terms of reference remained unlimited — and were indeed extended to cover by name *all* official institutions, whether sporting or not, which 'supported or promoted' apartheid and racial discrimination.

As a result, since 1979 not just sport but associational life in general — and theoretically, relations with all official institutions — falls under the Double Standards Resolution; and the arbiter of its application remains SACOS. This requirement on players is undoubtedly at odds with SACOS's insistence that it is not possible to live non-racially under apartheid; concessions have to be made, some contact with official bodies (outside, if not in sport) is inevitable. In this respect SACOS has consistently recognized that it is the *quality* and *character* of contacts which determine whether non-racial principles are being furthered or not.

However flawed, the Double Standards Resolution did fulfil its original intention, which was to provide a simple guideline for non-racial sportsmen and women confused by the appearance of several 'multi-national' confederations all claiming to be 'non-racial'. By dividing an essentially shady world into clearly opposed camps, it offered an unambiguous guide to allegiance.

Defining the non-racial standing of a player or a sports association by reference to his or its relations with organizations which were recognized by the State, has had a number of implications. The criterion is non-sporting in character; nor does it give a positive content to the idea of 'non-racialism', merely defining it in terms of its opposite. One effect of this has been that, in general, SACOS affiliates have made no attempt to judge their own or rival associations by the *number* of black players among their members, or by the number of black officials on the executive, as many 'multi-national' bodies do. In the final analysis, any organization was judged 'racial' by SACOS if it collaborated with Government policy (which is unquestionably racist), yet this position side-stepped the real problem of whether an association *could* 'refuse' to collaborate. The clarity and apparent rigour of this approach highlighted SACOS's combativity, however, and increased its audience in two directions.

First, it brought the non-racial movement into line with the general struggle against apartheid in the 1970s. The riots in Soweto and elsewhere emphasized black autonomy and there was widespread refusal to collaborate with municipal councils, the police, school authorities, the bantustans, and official bodies of all kinds. The Double Standards Resolution could be seen as the extension of this strategy to sport. Secondly, the Double Standards Resolution enabled SACOS affiliates to adopt a coherent line of conduct, thus sharpening their public image and increasing their audience both abroad and inside the country. By contrast rival black federations which accepted 'multi-national' relations rarely proved their independence and their leaders were frequently shown to be venal or indecisive. Public opinion was also irritated and confused by the concepts of 'multi-nationalism' and by the baffling and wearisome 'unity' negotiations in which 'multi-national' white and black federations became bogged down in the 1970s. SACOS and SACOS affiliates offered a firm, if flawed, public policy in relation to 'multi-national' sport, and required their representatives to honour the principles which had been established and prove their financial and political independence.

Within SACOS, the Double Standards Resolution has greatly strengthened the hand of the more radical wing of the movement, and the increasing use of the Resolution reflects their growing influence in comparison with those who have reservations about the Double Standards Resolution, especially for non-sporting relations. However, both groups support its application to sporting relations, because it throws the non-racial principle into sharp focus, and clearly separates those who will not accommodate segregation from those — like many white liberals, the P.F.P., and a proportion of the black sporting elite — who will. More than any other of SACOS's polices, the Double Standards Resolution has been attacked by the sporting and political establishment for its 'political' and 'dictatorial' character. For many non-racial sportsmen, this reaction is a good measure of its effectiveness.

Nonetheless those who query the extension of the Double Standards rule beyond sporting relations have a point and it is the reason why a number of senior non-racial administrators in national sports bodies are concerned to ensure that the application of the Resolution is very carefully monitored and flexibly interpreted. Essentially the resolution requires faultless and uniform behaviour from SACOS affiliates, although they are under intense political pressure and although wide social, educational and material differences exist among their members and between affiliates. Many feel that it is not only difficult but unwise for federations to apply a single uniform rule. If they do so, without reference to the very different means, membership, or quality of administration of their members then the unilateral application of a rule which was formulated to *unify* the non-racial movement behind SACOS may in fact undermine its authority and divide the national sports federations from each other. When the particular situation of African sportsmen and women is taken into account, the implications are even more dangerous. For, while apartheid exists, they will in all likelihood never be able to side unambiguously with the non-racial movement. The vast majority of Africans, confined by law in their compounds and townships, and in the rural areas, are not *legally* in a position to satisfy the Double Standards Resolution. If the Resolution were to be formally and strictly enforced, hardly any Africans could join SACOS.

On Sponsorship

The question of commercial sponsorship is also a delicate and political issue. Non-racial federations have declared themselves in favour of an alternative sports structure which, without devaluing competitive standards, will raise and uphold the range and quality of *amateur* sport. Commercial sponsorship necessarily works in the opposite direction, promoting commercially viable, professional and spectator sports, often at the expense of amateur competition. In South Africa, this tendency has been accentuated by isolation, for large commercial companies have been called upon to bail out the white sports federations, who claim that the losses from cancelled foreign tours threaten their viability. The major sponsors, glutted by profits from the gold boom of 1978-81, responded by granting very large sums of money.[11]

Moreover, SACOS is pledged to combat the system of apartheid; yet the companies which sponsor sport derive their profits from, and support, this system.

Sponsorship is also distributed unequally, on racial and on political grounds. White associations receive the largest amounts, racial black federations a much smaller share, and non-racial federations virtually no sponsorship at all.[12] In certain cases, discrimination is explicit or flagrant: in 1979, SACOS ran a successful boycott of *Simba Chips* products, because the company had refused to sponsor a SACBOC schools cricket tournament for 3,000 rand when it had just announced it was to sponsor the S.A. Grand Prix for 100,000 rand.[13]

SACOS therefore has political and sporting reasons for opposing sponsorship. Yet its members simply cannot afford to do so. Should the non-racial associations, representing the oppressed in sport, be forced by their poverty to accept financial dependence upon the system which oppresses them? There is no simple solution to this problem. A report on sponsorship compiled by the provincial Councils of Sport illustrates the mixture of anger and pragmatism which characterizes SACOS policy over the issue:

> a)   Sponsorship is a product of the race-ridden society with the big business houses obtaining their wealth through the system. In considering the awarding of sponsorship to non-racial organizations the maintenance of the apartheid system is their prime concern.
> b)   A late development in the awarding of sponsorship to non-racial organizations by the large organizations such as S.A. Breweries, U.T.C. etc. is that such sponsorship is cleared by the Dept. of Sport, alternately sponsorship by these companies are directed through organizations such as the Urban Foundation and the South African Sport Foundation.
> c)   In considering the application for such sponsorship, non-racial organizations should establish that no conditions are attached . . . .
> e)   It is generally accepted that in order to exist, non-racial organizations do need sponsorship. However organizations should not become so dependent on sponsorship that sponsors are in a position to eventually dictate to them.[14]

SACOS resolutions have been even less assertive, confined for the most part to criticizing the unjust distribution of sponsorship, and asking members to consult before signing contracts.[15] Discreetly, SACOS affiliates have continued to appeal for funds from commercial companies.

Nevertheless, non-racial officials would like to establish unequivocal conditions for the acceptance of sponsorship. They have been pushed in this direction by players, who, in this as in other areas, have often proved more uncompromising than the leadership. On one occasion, an athletic contest in 1979, the Western Province College Union invited the *Rapport* newspaper group to provide sponsorship. A SACOS official was consulted and cleared the request. The athletes, however, demonstrated their distaste at this decision by returning all the track suits to the sponsors. Council officials then decided that in future they would be more careful about sponsorship from institutions eager to make political propaganda out of it.[16]

The incident reveals the vulnerability of non-racial sports and SACOS officials, who must hold the balance between general policy — which must remain firmly in line with non-racial principles but supple enough to avoid political repression — and the expectations of their members, many of whom are young and impatient, and find the pragmatism of their leadership difficult to tolerate. To yield to this intransigent line would certainly increase political harassment and probably make it more difficult for Africans to rejoin the movement; to ignore it would alienate a section of the membership and exacerbate tensions within the non-racial federations. The sponsors have themselves forced SACOS towards adopting a harder line. The 1979 meeting of the provincial Councils asked affiliates to refuse sponsorship from all official organizations or organizations associated with the Government. It is only another step to ending contact with private companies which finance official sport. It remains to be seen whether it will be taken.

The Moratorium

A summary of this kind cannot do justice to the intense activity of consolidation which has marked SACOS's first years of existence, nor give due weight to the range and variety of opinion represented within the organization. In 1981, it could nevertheless be said that SACOS had fulfilled its initial purpose. It had brought together the non-racial associations and had provided the non-racial movement with coherence and confidence at a time when the movement in favour of non-racial sport was threatened by the 'multi-national' policy. Over the decade, non-racial federations generally increased their membership, reinforced their organization and agreed upon a common policy. This is a considerable achievement given the internal and external pressures dividing non-racial sportsmen. Furthermore, SACOS has secured a wide international audience, and for the first time non-racial federations have been making their voices heard within South Africa, in defiance of the white sports establishment.

On the other hand, 'multi-nationalism' did not have a bad decade either. The policy certainly created confusion abroad, and foreign observers — whose objectivity was on occasion more than doubtful — reported that certain South African sports were 'integrated' or were making significant strides towards full integration.[17] Some of the black racial federations also succeeded in occupying 'non-racial ground', after forming 'multi-national' confederations with white unions. Because some Blacks hold executive offices or play in senior teams, the official sports establishment could plausibly claim that their confederations were multi-racial — although, in fact, Blacks are out-voted in every case on the executive of 'multi-national' confederations and very rarely play in mixed teams except at professional and representative level. These arguments were particularly effective for official football and cricket. In these sports George Thabe and Rashid Varachia were respective Presidents of their 'multi-national' confederations, but were in a clear minority in their executives, while black participation was confined to the powerful professional sector in both sports.

The Double Standards Resolution was designed to clarify the distinction between non-racial and official sports bodies, which had been obscured by the 'multi-national' policy. Another SACOS policy, as fundamental and more ancient, has the same effect; and unlike the Double Standards Resolution, it has the complete support of all SACOS affiliates and of all tendencies within the non-racial movement. The call for a moratorium on international sporting relations with South Africa until apartheid is abolished has strengthened the non-racial movement and weakened sport apartheid more than any other form of sanction or action. The commitment of non-racial sportsmen and women to this demand is highlighted by SACOS resolutions, which ban *all* tours, by non-racial as well as racial associations,[18] because SACOS members believe that it is impossible to play truly non-racial sport under apartheid. An incident involving the S.A. Table Tennis Board illustrates their attitude. Because it is recognized by the International Table Tennis Federation, the S.A.T.T.B. was invited to take part in the 1975 world championships in Calcutta. When the South African Government unexpectedly decided to grant passports and travel facilities to the team, however, the Indian Government refused to allow the South Africans to enter the country. S.A.T.T.B. protested, on the grounds that it was a non-racial federation recognized by both the International Table Tennis Federation and SACOS, but SACOS supported the decision of the Indian Government. 'India's decision to debar the S.A. Table Tennis Board can be likened to the decisions on trade sanctions, which is also in terms of United Nations Resolutions. Once taken there can be no concession on grounds of compassion or sentiment.'[19] In 1977, when S.A.T.T.B. was again invited to the world championships, held in Britain, the Board declined because 'Propaganda can be made of the fact that "special permission", under the new sports policy, has been obtained for participation in these championships . . . . Participation . . . under the present conditions in South Africa will do irreparable harm to the S.A.T.T.B.'s long established, widely known and much respected policy of complete non-racialism.'[20]

The present moratorium therefore covers all team tours without exception. Two related questions were still under discussion in 1981. Should individuals be allowed to pursue training abroad? And should foreign coaches, invited to train sportsmen in South Africa, be included in the moratorium? While these two issues remain under discussion, SACOS will certainly support the United Nations ban on individual sportsmen who play in South Africa, and on contacts with individual South Africans who seek to play abroad. SACOS has given its approval to the initiative of the U.N. Special Committee against Apartheid, which began in 1981 to compile a boycott list of sportsmen who, as members of teams or individuals, have chosen to break the moratorium.[21]

It is not surprising that the moratorium commands universal support among non-racial sportsmen and women. Experience has convinced them that isolation is the key to change, the only non-violent weapon which they possess and the best guarantee against eventual repression. From the beginning, non-racial strategy has been based upon this belief, and white sports officials themselves now admit that the disruptive effect of isolation on white sports associations and on official thinking during the late 1960s and early 1970s was the principal force encouraging them to introduce the 'reforms' incorporated in the 'multi-national' policy.

Question: Is it not true that international pressure and expulsions from international sporting bodies have been mainly responsible for the changes which have been brought about to normalize sport in South Africa?
Answer: It can hardly be denied that such pressures must indeed have

been a factor. The credibility, motives and intentions of those behind the unabated witch-hunt on South African sport, however, come under serious suspicion . . . .

Question: If punitive action at the international level is admitted to have been a factor to bring about change, should it not continue?

Answer: If a given strategy is unduly prolonged it invariably becomes less effective. Many sports are becoming acclimatized to isolation . . .[22]

If one is to believe the statements of Mr B.K. de W. Hoek, Secretary for Sport, in the Department's *Annual Report* for 1979, isolation continues to have major effects — although, as usual, one must read between the lines to discover their sense. Mr Hoek declared that South Africa was defeating the boycott, and that 'during 1978 more sportsmen proceeded abroad and more foreign sportsmen came to South Africa than at any other stage during the past decade'; moreover, standards were being maintained, since a very high number of athletes (18) had qualified for the President's Award (the top athletic prize).[23] Characteristically, Mr Hoek avoided mentioning the standing of these contacts, however, and on inspection these are shown to be rather less imposing than suggested. Tables 30-32 show that, in contrast to the years 1966-72, almost all the President's Awards between 1974 and 1978 were given to minority or marginal sports. The number of awards has also suffered severely from inflation, no doubt to conceal this fact! In 1978 only 3 of the 18 awards went to 'popular' sports, while 15 went to aerial or water sports which are virtually inaccessible to black sportsmen and women. The list of world championships hosted by South Africa since 1974 reinforces this impression: no major popular sport is represented except boxing, which is a special case.[24] All the others are either technical (thereby excluding Blacks) or wholly marginal in relation to world sport (like model boating). When the rhetoric is shaved away, it becomes apparent that South African isolation in sport has continued to increase.

Table 30
The State President's Awards in Sport, 1966-77

*1966-72**		*1973*		*1974-77***			
Rugby	4	Boxing	1	Gliding	3	Water Skiing	1
Cricket	3	Athletics	1	Life-saving	2	Model Boating	1
Athletics	3	Equestrianism	1	Surf-riding	2	Powerboat Angling	1
Tennis	2	Fishing	1	Tennis	2	Hockey	1
Golf	2			Motor Racing	1	Bowls	1
Hockey	1			Athletics	1	Canoeing	1
Swimming	1			Model Aeroplane		Smallbore Rifle	
Sailing	1			Flying	1	Shooting	1
				Motor Cycling	1	Air Sports	1
				Parachuting	1	Yachting	1
				Model Powerboat			
				Sport	1		

*   An annual average of 2 awards spread over 8 leading sports.
** An annual average of 6 awards spread over 21 sports.

Table 31
The State President's Awards in Sport, 1978*

Major Sports	*Minor/Technical Sports*
Motor Cycling	Parachuting
Tennis (2)	Sky Diving (2)
	Surf-riding
	Water Skiing
	Model Powerboat Sport
	Canoeing (2)
	Powerboat Angling
	Life-saving
	Yachting (2)

* A new 'high' of 15 awards in a single year!

Table 32
World Sporting Championships Hosted by South Africa, 1974-79

1974	*1975*	*1976*	*1977*
Parachuting	Fishing	Parachuting	?
Trampoline	Bodybuilding	Snooker	
Water Skiing		Bowls (men)	
		Gymkhana	
		Model Boating	
		Power Boating	
		Tug of War	

1978	*1979*
Surf-riding	Boxing
Model Yachting	Yachting
	Pistol Shooting
	Radio-controlled
	Model Aerobatics

References

1. See above. p. 207. See also J. Brickhill, 1976, pp. 18-21.
2. J. Brickhill, 1976, p. 20.
3. SACOS does not in fact fulfil the technical requirements for recognition by the I.O.C. in particular the requirement that national Olympic Committees have at least 5 affiliates in Olympic sports that are themselves recognized by their international bodies. Only two SACOS affiliates are recognized internationally — the S.A. Table Tennis Board and the S.A. Darts Board of Control — and neither are Olympic sports.
4. In 1981, the permanent officials were: President: Morgan Naidoo, President of the S.A. Amateur Swimming Federation, patron of CARDS — of Durban Provincial Council on Sport; Vice-President: Frank van der Horst, President of the S.A. Hockey Board and of the Cape Provincial Council on Sport; Secretary and Treasurer: M.N. Pather, estate agent, Vice-President of the S.A. Sports Association in 1958, Secretary until 1975 of the S.A. Weight-lifting Federation, Secretary since the 1940s of the S.A. Lawn Tennis Union and now of the Tennis Association of S.A., member of the executive of the S.A. Soccer Federation until 1977; Patron: Mr George Singh. None of the permanent officials are paid.
5. Western Province C.O.S., 1979, p. 6; S.A.I.R.R. Survey, 1979, pp. 588-9.
6. The Natal Council on Sport, for example, circulated a petition demanding better sports facilities in the black townships, which in October 1978 had attracted over 10,000 signatures. A press campaign was organized at the same time.
7. See below pp. 235-7; and 313-15.
8. The latest case concerns Mr Pather, who was permitted, on the eve of visits by two Commissions of Inquiry into Sport at the beginning of 1980, to testify before the United Nations in Spring 1980. His passport was withdrawn on his return. Mr Abbas and Mr Patel of the S.A. Rugby Union were permitted to represent their association at a television debate in Ireland, in January 1981; three members of the racial federations were also present. Mr Ramsay, 41 years old teacher of physical education, trained in Natal, London, East Germany, was President of the Natal SASSSA, member of the S.A. Amateur Athletics Association executive, national trainer of the S.A. Amateur Swimming Federation. Exiled since 1972 in London.
9. S. Ramsamy, *Racial Discrimination* . . ., p. 21.
10. A. Odendaal, 1977, p. 277.
11. In 1977 total sponsorship was estimated to be of the order of 7 million rand. Exact amounts are rarely divulged, however, so no precise or complete figures of sponsorship can be compiled. In 1978-79 the S.A. Rugby Board received 1.25 million rand spread over 5 years; cricket was relaunched in 1980 with a new sponsorship programme; Thabe, President of the S.A. National Football Association reported in 1980 that football had more money than it needed. Large sums are also invested in golf, motor-racing, boxing, tennis, swimming; and in a number of growth sports — squash, surfing, bowls, snooker etc. Commercially, in fact, sponsorship is booming.

12. See below p. 276.
13. *Financial Mail*, 8 June 1979.
14. Western Province C.O.S., 1979, p. 22.
15. Resolution (f) of the 1977 biennial conference reads: 'SACOS calls on all sponsors to positively support non-racial sport as against sports played on a multi-national or racialist basis. SACOS calls on all affiliates to consult with SACOS Executive to scrutinize the terms of any sponsorship before its acceptance.' (in SACOS, Report of Third Conference, p. 16).
16. Western Province Council on Sport, 1979, p. 14.
17. Dick Jeeps, Chairman of the British Sports Council, who led the latter's fact-finding mission there in 1980, found in favour of athletics, judo, football; M. Bernard Marie, leader of a Commission of French parliamentarians (1980), declared that fencing, football and cricket were 'integrated'; Mr Walter Hadlee, member of the Australian Cricket Association, declared in June 1980, after visiting South Africa, that 'multi-national' cricket there was entirely integrated etc. See Chapter 11.
18. 'SACOS in a declaration of its solidarity with the Supreme Council for Sport in Africa . . . accepts a complete moratorium on all sports tours to and from South Africa until all the laws and institutions of apartheid have been removed from South African sport.' (SACOS, Minutes of Third Biennial Conference, resolution (2), 1979, p. 18).
19. SACOS, 1975, p. 64.
20. SACOS, 1977, p. 108.
21. The list is compiled principally by SAN-ROC in London, and published every quarter by the United Nations.
22. S.A. Olympic and National Games Association, 1981, pp. 9-10 (also in Sports Council of Great Britain, 1980, p. 149). The reader will note that the SAONGA does not answer directly even those questions which it asks of itself.
23. Department of Sport and Recreation, Annual Report, 1978.
24. One of the two world bodies which administer professional boxing, the W.B.C., observes the boycott; the other, the W.B.A., is, it so happens, largely staffed by South Africans. See below pp. 287-8.

11.   The State of Play, 1971-81

For the present, SACOS sportsmen and women are not in a position to compete properly with white athletes, whose standards are generally superior in all sports except football and middle distance running (where African athletes have the advantage of the superb facilities on the mines). Many individuals have reached a high standard, however, and it is this sporting elite which the Government has tried to attract into the 'multi-national' confederations with promises of multi-racial competition at professional and representative level. The Government's success has been only partial, as we shall see in this chapter, which describes and analyses the confrontation in several key sports between non-racial and 'multi-national' federations during the 1970s. Table 33 gathers some of the variables which significantly affect the balance of

Table 33
Factors Affecting the Struggle between Racial and Non-Racial Sports
Federations

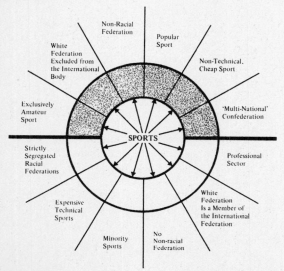

power between the racial and non-racial federations in most sports. Two of the axes are evaluative (minority/popular; technical-expensive/non-technical-cheap); the others are descriptive or 'political'. Most sports belong in one of the two 'hemispheres', although it is rarely the case that a sport satisfies all the variables in one, and none in the other hemisphere. Rugby, for example, is amateur, popular, non-technical and has both a non-racial federation and a 'multi-national' confederation, but it is not excluded from its international body. Equally, in a few minority sports which are technical with a professional sector, there is a non-racial federation.

We shall refer to twelve representative sports. Eight of them only (for reasons of space) will then be examined individually. All are described from the point of view of the black, rather than white sports associations, partly to redress the lack of information about them, but chiefly because it is really the allegiance of black sportsmen which is at stake in the confrontation between the federations attached to SACOS and those grouped within 'multi-national' confederations. A white federation exists in each of the twelve sports we shall be referring to.

Table 34
Registered Black Club Membership, by Sport

A	Football	400,000+
B	Rugby Netball	up to 50,000
C	Athletics Tennis Boxing Cricket Golf	up to 20,000
D	Swimming Karate	
E	Table Tennis Bowls	under 5,000

We have listed the black federations in five groups. Football stands on its own, for it dwarfs all other sports by sheer number of participants. It is followed by rugby, and by netball (played principally by schoolgirls). These three sports are the major black sports by number of players. The five sports below them all have a sizeable following, are well organized and have been played for many years among the black population; all except athletics (and boxing) are technical, and all except athletics have a professional sector (like football). Swimming and karate have been grouped separately, less because of their size than because they are rapid growth sports, recently adopted by black sportsmen. Swimming, like golf, has been inhibited by a lack of basic facilities. Table tennis and bowls, finally, are marginal or minority sports, selected because bowls is dominated by whites and very racialist, while table tennis is one of the two sports in which a non-racial federation has won international recognition.

Tables 32 and 33 enable us to make several generalizations about the influences of different factors upon the political evolution of different sports.

The five most popular sports are neither technical nor expensive to play, whereas the following seven, although they can certainly be played for leisure, involve material or technical investment. (The exceptions are swimming and perhaps table tennis; the former merits the title of 'technical' sport only because in South Africa the authorities have refused to provide most of the population with pools or adequate beaches.)

The sports with a black professional sector are all to be found in the major- and medium-sized sports (groups A, B, C): in these groups, only athletics, rugby and netball are exclusively amateur.

A non-racial federation exists in all the major and traditional sports (groups A, B, C), except in boxing; in contrast, one has been formed in only two of the four minority sports. (The proportion is in fact artificially high; very few non-racial players, or black players are to be found in minority sports.)

'Multi-national' federations have been created in six of the top nine sports. The exceptions are significant: in golf and netball, the non-racial federations have been created very recently (netball is also primarily a school sport among Blacks); and tennis is the only sport (with table tennis) in which the non-racial federation has succeeded in uniting all black sportsmen within a single association, thereby depriving the white body of black associates.

In all cases, the non-racial body was formed before the 'multi-national' confederation came into being. This suggests that 'multi-national' federations are created primarily in response to the presence of a well-organized non-racial federation.

The most turbulent disputes, involving major secessions, have all taken place in sports with a professional sector (football, cricket, tennis). Rugby is the only exclusively amateur sport in which considerable movement of players and clubs has occurred, although there has been no formal organizational secession. This supports the view that the professional sector plays a significant role in secessions and major disputes.

In two of the three sports which have suffered secessions (football and cricket), the white federation had been excluded from international sport by the world body, and had subsequently created a 'multi-national' confederation. The third sport, tennis, was a special case, as we have seen: the racial African tennis body, which had been associated with the white federation, left it to join the non-racial Union.

Where white federations are recognized by their international bodies, this undoubtedly hinders the process of change. This may be seen in golf, where no 'multi-national' golf confederation has been created; in boxing, where the white association has colonized one of the two world professional bodies, and continues to promote a large number of fights in South Africa; and in rugby, where the S.A. Rugby Board has been challenged by the powerful S.A. Rugby Union but has continued to tour because it has had exceptionally active backing from the International Rugby Board.

Table 35 represents the balance of power between 12 of the official and non-racial federations. It should be read horizontally and vertically. Occupation of space towards the right of the figure increases advantage for both sides: e.g. in rugby, the situation is very much to the political advantage of the racial associations, whereas in tennis advantage lies rather with the non-racial Tennis Association. The exception to this rule is the secession column (far left). A secession in favour of one of the racial federations outweighs other advantages: this can be seen in football and cricket, where the balance in other respects appears to be almost equal, but is not so, because both the non-racial federations were seriously weakened by secessions in 1977 and 1978. Such 'rogue' advantage occurs for the non-racial federations when, like the Table Tennis Board, they are recognized by the world body.

Vertically, the chart indicates the balance of advantage. (It should be remembered that the chart does not take account of the weight of apartheid. In no instance is a non-racial federation truly on equal terms with the white federations; the chart is intended to reflect the relative movement of influence.) From top to bottom, the advantage moves progressively towards the non-racial federations, of which the most favourably placed is the Table Tennis Board. The white bowls and karate federations head the list because there is no non-racial federation in either of these sports, which are played by relatively few black South Africans.

It can be seen from Table 34 that rugby is the major sport in which the non-racial federation has most difficulty in challenging the hegemony of the white association. It is also the only exclusively amateur sport where the advantage clearly lies with white sportsmen. We have already seen the causes for this situation.

All the major sports with a professional sector follow rugby — except tennis, the most social, and the only major sport to have achieved a formal secession in favour of non-racial sportsmen. If this secession had not occurred, tennis would also conform to the pattern of other sports with a professional sector, in which the advantage lies with white associations. Unsurprisingly, given the role of money in this sport, boxing heads the list (the triangle marks its exceptional international position, with two competing world bodies, one of which recognizes South Africa (W.B.A.), the other of which does not (W.B.C.)). Football, with cricket, was the only major sport in which the balance of political advantage was more or less equal — until the recent crises whose histories in many respects lie at the heart of the entire sports issue, as we shall see.

After the professional sports appear the major amateur sports, in which the political balance is generally less favourable to white interests. Athletics is, however, dominated by the African runners promoted by the mines; and netball is something of a special case because it is played principally by

Table 35
The Relative Strength of Racial and Non-Racial Sports Federations

	SPORTS	Factors favouring racial federations					Factors favouring non-racial federations			
		Split in racial federation	No non-racial federation	White federation member of international federation	Black racial federation exists	Multi-national federation exists	Non-racial federation exists	White federation excluded from international federation	Split in non-racial federation	Non-racial federation recognised abroad
Minority sports	BOWLS (E)*		●	●						
	KARATE (D)		●	●						
Amateur	RUGBY (B)			●	●	●	●			
Sports with professional sector	BOXING (C)			●	●	●	●	●		
	FOOTBALL (A)	●			●	●	●	●		
	CRICKET (C)	●			●	●	●	●		
	GOLF (C)			●	●		●			
Mainly amateur sports	ATHLETICS (C)					●	●	●		
	SWIMMING (D)					●	●	●		
	NETBALL (B)				●		●	●		
	TENNIS (C)			●			●		●	
Minority sports	TABLE TENNIS (E)	●					●	●		●

Strong racial federations ←——————→ Strong non-racial federations

Direction of greater advantage →

* Letters indicate popularity of sport (A = most popular etc)

schoolchildren, and also because its non-racial federation is very young and in a minority. Swimming, as we have seen, is the sport which has suffered more than any other from lack of facilities for Blacks.

Non-racial federations are in the strongest position in tennis and table tennis, in the former because of the secession in its favour, in the latter because it is recognized by the world body and also represents the quasi-totality of black table tennis players.

Finally (if tennis and netball, as special cases, are exempted), there is a perhaps significant symmetrical relationship between the groups of sports, which, in descending order, read:

$$E : D : B : C : A : C : B : D : E$$

This probably indicates that in general the conflict between non-racial and 'multi-national' federations intensifies as sports become more *popular* on the one hand (minority sports are all to be found at the extremes), and on the other, as they acquire a *professional* sector (groups A and C, minus athletics).

Football: Who Profits from the People's Sport?

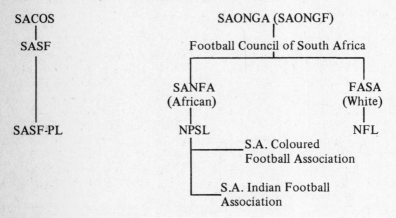

International Status
The (white) *Football Association of South Africa (F.A.S.A.)* was suspended by FIFA in 1962 and again in 1964; it was expelled in 1976.

Organization
A.   Non-Racial:
The *S.A. Soccer Federation (S.A.S.F.)*, formed in 1951, became formally non-racial in 1959-61. About 45,000-75,000 players (in secession). President: Mr Norman Middleton. Suspended, then excluded by SACOS in 1978-79; provisionally readmitted in 1979.
The *S.A. Soccer Federation Professional League (S.A.S.F.-P.L.)*, created in

1959, in 1980 ran 12 1st Division teams. President: Mr R.K. Naidoo. Suspended, then excluded by SACOS in 1978-79; provisionally readmitted in 1979.

B.   Official Federations:

'Multi-national' Confederation: the *Football Council of S.A.*, formed in 1976-77, following the expulsion of the (white) Football Association from FIFA. President: Mr George Thabe.

The S.A. National Football Association (S.A.N.F.A.), re-formed in 1959; 'African', today 'integrated'. President: George Thabe. 400,000 members.

The National Professional Soccer League (N.P.S.L.), formed in 1961-62; 'African', today 'integrated'. Director (1980): Kgomotso Modise.

The Football Association of S.A. (F.A.S.A.), 'white', formed in 1892. President (1980): Dave Marais. 60,000 members.

The National Football League (N.F.L.): the 'white' professional body; created in 1959, dissolved in 1978. Ex-director: Mr Vivien Granger.

The S.A. Football Association (Coloured), formed in 1962-63; marginal. 30,000 members, officially.

The S.A. Soccer Association (Indian), formed in 1963, marginal. 10,000 members, officially.

Football is by far the most popular sport in South Africa, and with half a million adherents, it lies at the heart of the Government's 'multi-national' strategy. It is crucial to the future of non-racialism, for it is played above all by Africans. As we have seen, it passed through a crisis in the early 1960s (see Chapter 8), from which the white Football Association emerged victorious, with a flourishing professional sector and no less than three subservient black federations grouped under it within a 'Top-Level Committee' which pre-figured the 'multi-national' confederations of the 1970s. Following the introduction of the new sports policy in 1971, and the white Association's exclusion from FIFA in 1976, football ran into a second crisis from which the 'African' National Football Association emerged on top, backed by the Department of Sport. In the 1970s as in the 1960s, the non-racial S.A. Soccer Federation was the main loser: its professional affiliate was seriously weakened and S.A.S.F. itself was suspended, then excluded from SACOS for collaborating with 'multi-nationalism'.

The crisis involved a tortuous series of deals, negotiations and reprisals which cannot be detailed here. We have isolated three major themes: first of all, the crisis undermined the power of the white Football Association and eventually caused the white professional league to collapse altogether; secondly, the crisis reinforced the power of the professional clubs, which re-organized South African football to satisfy their own commercial and technical interests, and those of the sponsors who finance them, although they represent only about 2% of African footballers (many of whom are only part-time professionals); thirdly, the crisis revealed a structural rift between the coast — where most of the non-racial clubs and Coloured and Indian players are to be found — and the interior, dominated by the Witwatersrand and the clubs of the 'African' SANFA.

These three factors largely explain why this crisis evolved as it did — causing the most severe internal dispute SACOS has so far had to overcome, and generating major political consequences for the future of South African sport. They also explain (if they do not justify) the decisions of the Soccer Federation's executive, which made the political error of trying to compete for supremacy against SANFA, although its organization was smaller, poorer and relatively isolated in the less populous (and less profitable) coastal zone. Initially, the Soccer Federation succeeded in draining players, spectators and clubs from the weakest of the three major associations, the white Football League; but it was then itself engulfed. Its experience has confirmed the view of other non-racial federations that it is misjudged, if not politically suicidal, to compete directly with racial federations which are protected by apartheid and the State.

'Multi-nationalism' versus White Football

In 1976, the hegemony of the white federation was vulnerable in several respects. It controlled fewer players than either the Soccer Federation or SANFA; it had just been expelled from FIFA; and, because its executive was traditionally close to the United Party, it could expect little sympathy from the Government, which dearly wished to extend its influence over this strategic sport.

Its principal weakness, however, was economic. As we have seen, in the 1960s the Football Association had built up a following among black as well as white spectators. When black spectators were excluded from many white stadiums after 1965 by Proclamation 228, however, many moved to SANFA, the white federation's 'African' associate, which had exclusive access to the 'African' grounds. SANFA membership grew rapidly and so did the following and prosperity of its professional league (N.P.S.L.).

While the revenues of the black professional leagues began to rise, those of the white National Football League fell. By the beginning of the 1970s, the number of professional clubs had far outstripped the number of grounds, particularly black grounds, and the different professional leagues began competing with each other for spectators. The white federation, which controlled the best grounds, continued to hold the advantage while their stadiums were closed to all but Whites, who could afford higher prices. 'Multi-nationalism', however, made it possible to organize matches before mixed audiences — a most attractive commercial opportunity, because of the vast untapped market represented by black spectators. In 1976, therefore, SANFA officials demanded more and better facilities, and public money to build them, while the white Association called for re-organization of the professional leagues and the creation of a single 'super-league' (a solution which would have protected FASA, which ran the largest grounds); as for the Soccer Federation, smaller than SANFA but short of grounds, it called for better facilities *and* fewer professional teams.

There followed a prolonged war of attrition, whose first victim was the white National Football League. When permission was given, in 1974-75, to organize mixed matches under the terms of the 'multi-national' policy, S.A.S.F. and SANFA clubs had an opportunity to prove the quality of their play: they attracted many spectators away from the all-white League, while the invasion of the white clubs' stands by black spectators caused some Whites to give up watching football altogether.[1] Many of the best white clubs saw that there was no future in a small white league and opened nego- tiations with black clubs. When Durban City F.C. affiliated to the Soccer Federation in 1977, for example, its director, Mr Elliot, declared: 'I'm gamb- ling by joining Federation, I'm hoping the crowds will improve by our taking this step'.[2] In this way, the 'multi-national' principle of weakening the weak and strengthening the strong worked, for once, against the interests of the white federation: in 1977 the National Football League was bankrupt and the power of its parent body, the Football Association, was in evident decline. As early as 1975, the African SANFA was openly criticizing the slow pace of 'integration', and the Presidents of the minority Indian and Coloured Football associations, Messrs Peffer and Meer, joined George Thabe in demanding more justice for black footballers.[3] Thabe himself refused to accompany the white Association's delegation to the FIFA conference in Montreal in 1976: he did not intend, he said, to defend the Whites before the international body. Soon after the Association's expulsion at that meeting, the Football Council of S.A. was created, with George Thabe as President. In 1978, the National Football League clubs were divided between the National Professional Soccer League and the S.A.S.F. Professional League. And in 1980, several long-standing members of the Football Association's executive resigned, including the President, Dave Marais (a United Party M.P. from Johannesburg) and the Vice-president, Issie Kramer (President of the white Swimming Union), who declared:

> I'm thoroughly disillusioned with soccer. The set-up in South Africa is nothing short of stupid, and I'm sick and tired of all the infighting and personality clashes. We've got the Football Council, SANFA, FASA, the Federation, NFL, TCL and heaven knows how many other bodies. These bodies should not be autonomous. There should be only one body with total autonomy. And that should be the Football Council, I firmly believe that until all the other groups fall under the Council we are wasting our time.[4]

His remarks betray the bitterness of white officials who had become victims of a struggle they had themselves promoted. Their defeat was the more galling because it implied a transfer of power from the United to the Nationalist Party.

The Power of Money

The fall of the National Football League was also caused by the pressure of sponsorship. The creation of the first all-professional 'super-leagues' in 1974 stimulated both political and commercial interest in football. During the

1970s, certain newspapers depended for their survival on the sale of black 'extras'. The Government also began to take a hand in the League's affairs, knowing that between 40,000 and 60,000 black spectators would flock to watch major games even though not a single ground in black areas was capable of seating them properly.

Above all, companies lined up to sponsor the game. 'We have too much money!' declared Thabe in 1980, and Bhamjee, then an official of the S.A. Soccer Federation, stated in 1978 that 'There are always 6 or 8 companies waiting in line.'[5] They were attracted by the size of the audiences, the drawing power of the top players, and by the possibility of television transmissions. 'There's a definite spin-off from black consumers,' declared the publicity director of *Mainstay*, one of the earliest sponsors of South African football. 'They identify your product with the game and support it. Football's helped us to retain our market share in a competititve industry.'[6]

Access to such financial backing rapidly transformed relations within the football federations. Few of the professional clubs made a profit from ticket sales alone and most came to depend upon their sponsors to cover costs. The national associations relied upon the financial contributions of the professional affiliates, which in turn derived their income from the contributions of league clubs. At the same time, it was in the interest of clubs to reduce their obligations to their controlling bodies. As a result of this dependence on sponsorship, amateur football tended to be seen simply as a charge which had to be supported by the national associations and professional clubs.

If the racial associations took this process furthest, the Soccer Federation did not escape it. The Soccer Federation's Professional League made a large contribution to its parent body, and both were major donors to SACOS. In 1977, the S.A.S.F. Professional League was accused by supporters of non-racialism of having attempted to co-ordinate a sponsorship programme with the white Football Association.

When the opportunity presented itself in 1975-76, the professional clubs therefore began to assert their independence from their administering bodies by establishing lateral contacts with each other. Officials found it very difficult to prevent them from doing so, for their own commercial interests were being served and it was evident to all that power would eventually come to the white, African or non-racial federation which succeeded in attracting the best players from the other two, and therefore the most spectators, and therefore the highest sponsorship. As it turned out, the two smaller associations — the white National Football League and the Soccer Federation — attempted to combine against the African federation, by far the largest. When this attempt failed, the Federation created a new league. Nevertheless, the National Professional Soccer League continued to grow, and increased its power from 1976 onwards until by 1978-79 it controlled the majority of the best professional teams in the Transvaal and Orange Free State, and by 1979-80 many of the best sides in the Cape and even Natal.[7]

Professional 'Non-racialism'

The authority which officials of the professional federations exercised over their players and clubs was scarcely more secure than that of the national federations over them. In 1975-76, N.F.L. clubs began to poach players from the N.P.S.L., and S.A.S.F.-P.L. clubs to poach players from the white league. Almost as soon as multi-racial matches were authorized by the Government, the players themselves began to criticize the authoritarian control exercised by SANFA over their policies and finance. In 1976, a team refused to play a 'mixed' match against Argentinian tourists, because, in the words of Kaiser Motaung, 'he and a lot of other soccer players were opposed to the multi-nationalist sports policy and would only be satisfied when non-racialism was introduced at club level. He said that he regarded multi-nationalism in sport as a modification of the apartheid policy in South Africa.'[8]

The 1979 boycott of the Rand Stadium illustrates this conflict of interests. The Johannesburg Municipality had refused to grant a permit to allow two black teams, championship finalists, to play off against one another in the white-controlled Rand Stadium. The black professional clubs therefore organized a boycott, supported by the white clubs who agreed to play their matches at the (black-controlled) Orlando Stadium 'despite the fact that it is smaller and they may lose revenue'.[9] It was also supported by the National Professional Soccer League, which had been radicalized by its players, whose 'non-racialism' coincided with their professional interests as players.

In contrast, SANFA, the parent body, overwhelmingly amateur, defended 'multi-nationalism' and opposed the boycott. Thus, a cleavage was created between the professional elite and amateur footballers — exactly the cleavage which the 'multi-national' policy was designed to achieve. One month later, at an executive meeting of the N.P.S.L., Thabe reimposed order: he stripped the director of the professional league, Modise, of some of his powers, fired two white executives, denied votes to two ex-S.A.S.F. clubs which had recently registered, and expelled two other delegates from the meeting.[10] A new executive was elected, amenable to SANFA policy, and the Rand Stadium boycott was terminated even though the majority of African spectators were in favour of it. The incident certainly increased Thabe's reputation as a firm, aggressive President; his handling of affairs appealed to the 'nationalism' of many Africans who would like to see all non-Africans excluded from 'African' organizations. But his efficiency and high-handed leadership concealed the fact that his policy played entirely into the hands of the Government. Far more combative because of their dependence upon sponsorship, and their financial independence from the SANFA, the professional clubs were brought to heel.

The same line of cleavage between amateurs and professionals, commercial and non-commercial sport, split the S.A. Soccer Federation, but politically the roles were reversed. It was now the amateurs who defended non-racialism. Swept up in the war of attrition between the professional leagues, the S.A.S.F.-P.L. sought an understanding with its rivals, and from 1975-76 began to recruit white players without requiring them to resign beforehand from their own (racial or 'multi-national') clubs. In 1977, the non-racial Professional League began to allow clubs which were still affiliated to the F.A.S.A./N.F.L. to play in its leagues. Joint sponsorship was discussed. These initiatives corresponded to the interests of the players, who wanted better grounds, pay and playing conditions, and the right to free movement between clubs. However, the Soccer Federation at once found itself torn between the interests of its professional affiliate and the non-racial principles to which it was committed as a member of SACOS.

When the professional league of S.A.S.F. was eventually disciplined, it was criticized on virtually the opposite grounds to those which had led the SANFA to discipline the N.P.S.L. Supported by the provincial Councils of Sport, between 1975 and 1978 the organization CARDS[11] ran a campaign to denounce the collusion between the non-racial Federation and official soccer. In complete contrast to Thabe's and SANFA's attitudes to the issue, the Councils and CARDS asserted the rights of amateur footballers, which they claimed were being overlooked, although amateurs constitute more than 98% of South African footballers. Sponsorship was blamed for corrupting non-racial principles, and white clubs were accused of joining the Soccer Federation simply to make money and to rejoin international sport. Both S.A.S.F. and its Professional League were condemned for double standards and threatened with suspension. In a series of leaflets, CARDS pointed out that, although professional football was mixed, nowhere in South Africa were amateur footballers playing together. CARDS attacked the Professional League for having 'completely and totally ignored amateur soccer and soccer in schools — the very nursery on which our soccer depends so much'[12] and called upon 'each and every individual in the South African Soccer Federation to reject any moves at so-called "unity" until conditions of genuine non-racial sport exist.'[13] The S.A. Soccer Federation and its Professional League were finally expelled from SACOS in the summer of 1979: affiliates were instructed to have no contacts of any kind with S.A.S.F. clubs.

Divided and weakened, both organizations were provisionally readmitted, at their request, during the third biennial conference later in the same year. Stringent conditions were attached:

> SACOS emphasized to the Federation that the cause of non-racialism was not dependent on quantity, but rather the quality of the convictions of its affiliates. In this regard it was clear that certain persons inside the S.A.S.F. had by reason of their support for racist institutions and ideas no place inside SACOS .... No further concessions of any kind would be tolerated. SACOS made it abundantly clear that it was prepared to accept the application (of S.A.S.F.) on the specific understanding that all SACOS Resolutions be fully honoured. That SACOS are providing the S.A.S.F. with a platform from which it can regain dignity, status and recognition within the fold of the fraternity of non-racialism.[14]

The implication was clear enough: rather than exclude its most powerful and oldest affiliate, with all its members, SACOS would have preferred to reform the leadership. But since the S.A.S.F. President, Norman Middleton — principal target of criticism, for his role as Vice-President of the Coloured Labour Party and member of the Coloured Representative Council — had just been re-elected by the S.A. Soccer Federation, this was not possible. The status of the Soccer Federation within SACOS therefore remains provisional.

The Geographical Factor

South Africa is a very large country. As a result, the coastal clubs, further from the heartland of football on the Witwatersrand, bear particularly high transport costs.[15] This geographical disparity played a part in the crisis, for most of the white or African clubs which joined the Soccer Federation after 1975 were based in the Cape or Durban, where the non-racial federation was strongest, whereas those which moved to the N.P.S.L. were almost all from the Transvaal or Orange Free State. Subsequently, when the supremacy of the N.P.S.L. and SANFA became evident, and the S.A.S.F. coastal league less attractive, several of the best coastal clubs left the non-racial federation to join the multi-national league — a recognition of economic and political advantage which made it even more difficult for S.A.S.F.-P.L. to balance its books and provide an attractive programme of fixtures across the 1,500 kilometres which separate Durban from Cape Town.

The facts of geography should not be allowed to mask the social and political consequences to which they gave rise, however. Since the great majority of Indian and Coloured footballers are to be found in the coastal provinces, the cleavage between S.A.S.F. and SANFA also coincides with the racial divide between Indians and Coloured on the one hand and Africans on the other, which the multi-national policy and the Government sought to promote. This suggests at least one reason why the Government and those who prosecute its policies were willing to allow the crisis to develop as far as it did. Only when the professional leagues had sorted out their differences to the advantage of the N.P.S.L., did Thabe intervene to re-establish the status quo and deliver football to the multi-national policy.

The Cost to S.A.S.F. and the Non-Racial Movement

In the 1980s, the Soccer Federation has to again re-establish itself as in the 1960s. Its amateur clubs have been virtually unaffected by the crisis — multi-nationalism tending to ignore the non-elite sector to which most players belong — but the professional league is no longer competitive in size or quality with its official rivals in the National Soccer League. In effect, this means that the non-racial body has suffered *political* rather than structural damage: doubt has been cast on the non-racial character of the organization, and particularly of its leadership; and worse, the failure and opportunism of its policies have allowed the multi-national confederation to occupy much of the 'non-racial space' won by the Federation during the 1960s and early 1970s. This is a loss to SACOS and to the non-racial movement as a whole, for soccer is a sport of such strategic importance that the pre-eminence of the multi-national confederation has effectively widened the rift between Africans and the Indian and Coloured minorities. To this extent the multi-national Government policy has been successful in its objective.

The unity and reputation of the non-racial movement have also been weakened by the crisis which the soccer dispute provoked within SACOS. Added to the secession of one segment of the S.A. Cricket Board of Control to the white Union, the debate over the Soccer Federation's performance undoubtedly caused the SACOS executive to look more closely at the behaviour of its affiliates and to draw up clearer and more rigorous guidelines. It may be that, in exacting too much discipline, SACOS has partly defeated its purpose: in their widest applications, the Double Standards Resolutions of 1978 and 1979, for example, appear to exclude the possibility of recognizing any intermediate position between absolute adherence to non-racial practice and outright collusion with multi-nationalism. The rule was created to prevent non-racial sportsmen from sliding imperceptibly into the arms of racial federations; it may have the effect of preventing members of racial federations from feeling their way gradually towards affiliation to the non-racial movement.

Moreover, this restriction will above all affect the African sportsmen and women, so much more severely handicapped by apartheid, particularly in football, which is dominated by 'African' federations. Many non-racial sportsmen who believed strongly that some ruling against double standards was necessary were disquieted by the fact that its rigorous application in football would actually reduce the number of African footballers in the non-racial movement.

Thabe, politically the most redoubtable black sports official working for multi-nationalism, was not slow to press home this advantage. Meeting members of the British Sports Council delegation which visited South Africa in 1980, his testimony is in the purest style of black apologists:

> We have done everything that is required. Were we to send a team overseas, it would be under one manager, they would live and eat in the same hotels. What more are we expected to do? They say we must integrate in such a way that every white club must have black members. In that way we would be practising integration in reverse because we would be enforcing it.[16]

The Soccer Federation, he proclaimed, represented no more than 3% of South African footballers — a straightforward falsehood, for even opponents of the Federation allow that it administers at least 45,000 members. Whereas he, Thabe, was opposed to apartheid, SACOS and its affiliates were politically motivated: 'Mr Thabe said that, if he were Hassan Howa, he might want to talk politics. Hassan Howa's people were better off than the blacks: they could trade and live in an area where the white man was ready to trade. In Soweto it was different.'[17]

Thabe's confidence is proof of the relative weakness of the Soccer Federation, following the crisis of 1976-79. Like the French Parliamentary Commission a few days earlier, the British delegation faithfully recorded these opinions and returned to Europe to declare that racism was virtually eliminated from South African football.

'Normal' or 'Abnormal'? Cricket after Soweto

			SAONGA ↓
1960-72	SACBOC	SAACB	SACA
1972-77	SACOS ↓ SACBOC		SAONGA ↓ SACC ↓
			SAACB SACU
1977	SACOS ↓ SACB*		SAONGA ↓ SACU**

* Re-constituted out of the former SACBOC.
** Formed from SACC (SACU and SAACB) and from SACBOC.

International Status
South Africa is no longer a member of the International Cricket Conference (I.C.C.) which administers world cricket.
Organization
Non-Racial:
The S.A. Cricket Board (SACB) was created in 1978, after the dissolution of the *S.A. Cricket Board of Control.* President: Mr Hassan Howa. Membership: 4,000 to 6,000.
Official Federation:
The S.A. Cricket Union (SACU), founded in September 1977. President: Mr Rashid Varachia, ex-president of SACBOC. SACU is not a 'multi-national' confederation in the true sense, for its constituent organizations were formally dissolved at its creation. These were: the *S.A. Cricket Association* (SACA), 'white', with 15,000 members; the *S.A. African Cricket Board* (SAACB), 'African', membership unknown; and a proportion of ex-SACBOC members. The total membership of SACU was about 16,500 in 1980.

A second major crisis for SACOS followed the introduction of multi-nationalism into cricket. It was marked by a formal split within the non-racial S.A. Cricket Board of Control, and by the creation of a new 'integrated' official Cricket Union which, in contrast to all others of its kind, was not a multi-national confederation, because the constituent racial bodies dissolved themselves when they created it. This justified the claims of white cricketers to have achieved a more integrated structure than any of the other major sports. But the result has not been that cricket is practised non-racially — or that it is likely to be, while apartheid exists.

Most of the factors underlying the crisis in football reappear in the secession within SACBOC — including sponsorship, the split between the professional elite and the amateur majority, the geographical divide, etc. — even though the social organization and character of the two games are so markedly different. However, whereas in one case, the non-racial body was drawn into a struggle for political supremacy which it lost rather humiliatingly, in the other — despite, or perhaps because of the formal secession of part of the membership — the non-racial body emerged smaller but without having suffered serious damage to its non-racial reputation.

In 1972, the S.A. Cricket Association and the S.A. African Cricket Board, then grouped within the Cricket Council of S.A., began to negotiate with the non-racial S.A. Cricket Board of Control to form a single national cricket body. The white Association and SACBOC were unable to agree over the terms of the non-racial clause upon which SACBOC insisted, but in 1976, nevertheless, SACBOC agreed to the creation of a joint steering committee representing all three associations, which was assigned the task of establishing the terms under which integration might eventually take place. This agreement was at first welcomed; but it proved difficult to resolve the differences between the Association and SACBOC, and the decision of the non-racial body to sit on the Committee provoked serious disagreement among its members and within SACOS. Hassan Howa had resigned from the Presidency of SACBOC in 1975, in favour of Vice-President Rashid Varachia, because his negotiations with the white Association had come under criticism. But Varachia pursued the dialogue himself, and in 1977 he because the first President of a new 'integrated' national cricket body, the S.A. Cricket Union.

SACBOC, like the Cricket Association and the S.A. African Cricket Board. was dissolved on the formation of the Union, but only some of the non-racial cricketers were prepared to join the new body: most objected to its multi-racial character and, under Hassan Howa, formed a new non-racial body, the S.A. Cricket Board. A war of attrition followed this declaration of hostilities, very similar to that which occurred in football during the same period. Players moved from one federation to the other, and for much the same reasons. Only the best black players or teams moved into white associations or clubs; few white players joined black SACU clubs, and generally did so out of personal interest, or to coach; a very small number of white clubs elected to join the non-racial Cricket Board.[18] Three broad tendencies may be distinguished: 1) A pro-unification group: composed of most of the best national cricketers (including many of the best black players); a minority of the SACBOC executive, led by Rashid Varachia; and a majority of non-racial cricketers in the Transvaal (where Varachia was president); 2) A group opposed to unification: composed of the majority of SACBOC members (most of the executive and almost all players in the Western Cape and Natal, and many in Eastern Cape); this group had the support of SACOS which had at first followed the negotiations with reserve, but had finally decided to oppose the merger; 3) A third 'pro-multi-national' group: composed of the majority of white club cricketers and white officials, who were in a clear majority within SACU and favoured a 'multi-national' solution which would not offend against the laws or social practice of apartheid; this third group had the support of the government and the Department of Sport — a fact which persuaded many SACBOC members that unification was neither possible nor desirable.[19]

As in football, the professional elite were strongly in favour of unification, which served their professional interests. However, many of the best non-racial cricketers who had joined SACU in its first full season left again to rejoin the S.A.C.B. in 1978-79, because they had not found the playing opportunities they had expected and were revolted by the racism they had encountered.[20] Professional, top class cricket was promoted by the creation of new multi-racial leagues, as in football, and this had the same effect of diminishing the status of, and attention paid to amateur cricket. S.A. Breweries and Datsun both increased their sponsorship of the Currie Cup and the Limited Overs Championship: between 1979 and 1980, commercial sponsorship doubled, to reach an official figure of 300,000 rand per annum.[21] Stars like Barry Richards, one of the best batsmen in the world in the 1970s, went into print to appeal for more sponsorship to stimulate top-class cricket. 'The future belongs to the era of sponsorship, advertising, colour and gimmicks on the cricket field,' he wrote. 'Cricket cannot afford to lag behind in accepting the demands of the modern age'.[22] Commercial logic and the social and technical character of cricket combined to make it possible for only a handful of the most gifted and privileged black cricketers to join top-class teams.[23] This problem lies at the heart of the bitter differences between the S.A. Board and the SACU executive.

Behind the legal wrangles (in 1979, SACU tried to sue the non-racial Board for using SACBOC's name and for denying that SACU was non-racial) and the personal animosity Mr Varachia and Mr Howa felt for each other, [24] lies a different understanding of the principle of non-racialism. Is it enough to proclaim a non-racial constitution or show evidence of good intentions? The Union's executive claims, with reason, that SACU is the only official body to have dissolved its constituent racial associations and created in their place a single, unified national body. Even its opponents recognize this to be true [25] and do not condemn SACU as violently as the multi-national confederations in rugby, athletics and other sports, which are far from achieving SACU's formal non-racialism.

It is precisely this formalism, however, that SACU's opponents find objectionable: they argue that in practice SACU is still multi-national. Virtually no white clubs have accepted black members, virtually no club teams are mixed and only a handful of black players reach top class cricket.

The Impact of Soweto

Above all, SACU's detractors accuse it of ignoring the interests of amateur and school cricketers, who are particularly important in a sport like cricket which takes so long to learn. Inevitably, the issue of school sport also became politically charged following the Soweto riots of 1976 and the Government's refusal to allow racial mixing in school teams, even on multi-national terms. The Soweto riots appear to have strongly influenced Hassan Howa himself. His subsequent statements, both as President of the SACB and of SACOS, revealed a new preoccupation with youth sport. In 1980, for example, when asked by *The Times* what needed to change before SACOS would compromise with the government, he declared that 'the most important thing would be a guarantee over the next ten years that non-white children would be given a chance to develop their full potential in sport, education and other matters relevant to their job and their future. It is too late for their parents but it had to be done for the children.'[26] Soon after the riots, in an interview in 1977, he admitted that the school protests had forced him to reconsider his attitudes: 'How can I play [multi-national sport] under these circumstances? Our children have given us a clear mandate not to co-operate these last six months. We cannot ignore them.'[27]

The influence on SACOS of the demonstrations and of the repression which followed can also be detected in the Double Standards Resolution (1977), which gave the younger generation the unequivocal response to 'multi-nationalism' which they expected. The arguments and language employed by the non-racial federations became more intransigent; officials stressed that financial interests and professional support must give way to the over-riding needs of the amateur majority and of schoolchildren. It was no accident that the crisis in football and cricket took form in 1977 – or that the famous slogan 'No Normal Sport in an Abnormal Society', with which the name and reputation of SACOS have become identified, was first coined in the same year.

The interview given by Rashid Varachia to the British Sports Council delegation to South Africa in 1980 shows how much the criticisms of SACB and SACOS preoccupy the SACU executive – although once again the meaning must be inferred from what is left unsaid. During the interview (at least that part of it reproduced in the Sports Council's Report) Mr Varachia made no reference to first league cricket, to competitions, or to white clubs or players. Instead, he dealt with the need to develop school cricket, to promote African cricket, and to provide equipment and training facilities for black players. Yet, when only 15% of SACU players are black, and when no Africans sit upon the Union's executive of ten (which includes two black members, Varachia himself and a Coloured representative), how is such a policy to be carried through? It is very difficult to believe that white cricketers – 85% of the membership, 80% of the executive – are behind such an expensive and expansionist policy, which directly affects their pockets and their interests. It is even more difficult to believe in the realism of Mr Varachia's remarks when the power of commercial sponsorship and the professional game is taken into account, along with the fact that 'multi-nationalism' is imposed in its most rigorous and segregative form in school sport.

It is evident, in fact, that Varachia was implicitly replying to the non-racial sportsmen of SACOS and S.A.C.B., who accuse him of downgrading amateur and schools cricket, and black — especially African — cricketers, in favour of a small, black professional elite.

The irony is that the *abstract* non-racialism promoted by SACU has the effect of perpetuating and reproducing the inequalities which divide white from black cricket. Merit selection is meaningless if players do not have an equal opportunity to learn and practise their skills: it simply cages existing inequalities behind a facade of good intention. This indeed is the lesson Hassan Howa learnt from the younger generation. If the non-racial philosophy is to contain more than legal form, if it is not simply to provide cover for an immoral system which breeds racial inequality, then its implementation must involve the reduction of inequalities at all levels in sport, from school and amateur sport upwards. 'I cannot agree that the South African Cricket Union has the same non-racial principles as ours,' Hassan Howa has said. 'If they succeed in their efforts, they will still not be normal, they will be multi-national.'[28]

The challenge thrown down by SACU cannot simply be dismissed, however. It is up to the Cricket Board to prove that it can put its non-racial principles into practice, and produce better cricket for its members. Finally, cricketers will vote for one or the other with their feet.

Until then, SACU officials travel the world in search of support and international recognition, while representatives of the Cricket Board continue to be deprived of passports. Various South African and foreign personalities have lent support to the rehabilitation of South African cricket.[29] In 1977 a delegation from the I.C.C. met both sides and recommended that South Africa should again be recognized. However, international resistance to such a proposition has remained strong, within and outside the I.C.C. — and India, Pakistan, the West Indies and Sri Lanka can be relied upon to vote against readmission of South Africa in the forseeable future.[30]

Rugby: The Force of Conviction?

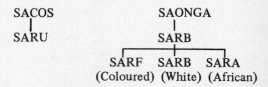

International Status
The S.A. Rugby Board is a member of the I.R.B., whose affiliates organize regular tours to and from South Africa. South Africa is not a member of the International Federation of Amateur Rugby.

Organization

Non-Racial:

The S.A. Rugby Union (SARU), formed in 1964, has been a member of SACOS since 1978, and has always supported its policies. President: Mr Abbas; secretary, Mr Patel. Has 26 provincial affiliates, and about 26,000 players.

'Multi-national' Confederation:

The S.A. Rugby Board (SARB), formed in 1978. President, Dr Danie Craven. Runs two national leagues, which play for the Currie and Pienaar Cups. Its central committee is composed of representatives of the three following organizations:

The S.A. Rugby Board (SARB), 'white': runs 22 provincial federations, all with votes in the council of the 'multi-national' confederation. Supplies all but two of the teams in the first and second leagues. President: Danie Craven. 37,000 members; 180,000 school players.

The S.A. Rugby Federation (SARF), 'Coloured'. President: Mr Cuthbert Loriston, who sits since 1980 on the SARB executive. The Federation has a vote on the Council of the 'multi-national' confederation. Has one representative team in the second league. Official membership: 9,000.

The S.A. Rugby Association (SARA), ex-*S.A. African Rugby Board* (SAARB) President: Mr Curnick Mdyesha. The Federation has a vote on the Council of the 'multi-national' confederation. Has one representative team in the second league. Official membership: 19,000 (contested).

Rugby provides the most 'classic' confrontation between official and non-racial federations. On one side, the white Rugby Board is invested with enormous authority by virtue of the importance of rugby to the white population; on the other, it is confronted by one of the most confident and vigorous members of SACOS. White rugby has never reformed any of its racial structures in advance of Government policy; changes have occurred only under the threat of isolation, and they have been limited to the most strict reading of multi-nationalism. More than any other official federation, the white Rugby Board is subject to the pressure of Akrikaner and Nationalist opinion. The Presidency of Dr Danie Craven, considered a liberal, has helped to conceal the innate conservatism of the Board and the poor prospects of change; deceptively, for Dr Craven has not hesitated to discipline players who step out of line, and has argued consistently in favour of laws like the Group Areas Act.

In addition, white rugby has been actively supported abroad by the members of the International Rugby Board: Wales, France, Ireland, England, Scotland, New Zealand, Australia. Here again, Dr Craven's personal influence has been important. Hassan Howa has said: 'Among the white administrators there is no individual with the quality and charisma of Danie Craven . . . I am quite certain . . . that when Dr. Craven goes, then South Africa's international rugby contacts will also be broken.'[31] Alone of the major sports bodies, 'multi-national' rugby has continued to entertain and be entertained by major touring sides. Indeed, since 1979, the S.A.R.B. has engaged in a concerted campaign to loosen the rugby boycott, and has organized tours in rapid succession in or with Britain, Argentina, France, Ireland, New Zealand and the USA.[32]

In the 1960s black rugby had some difficulty in establishing a solid non-racial platform. The sheer weight of white ideology in this sport was one impediment — for Whites were unwilling to see Blacks play 'their' sport, and Blacks were often unwilling to play a game so directly associated with oppression. Rugby is also unevenly distributed throughout the country. It is very popular among Coloureds in the Western Cape and among Africans in the Eastern Cape, but few Africans play it anywhere else and hardly any Indians play it at all.

Nevertheless, black rugby has old and solid roots, especially in the Western and Eastern Cape (see Chapter 2). In spite of this, unification proved particularly difficult, and it was not until the early 1970s that the non-racial S.A. Rugby Union really began to make an impact on the non-racial movement.

In 1960 there were three black unions: The S.A. Coloured Rugby Board (1896), which regrouped the majority of Coloured players and had a tradi-tionally 'open' policy towards African players; the (Coloured) S.A. Rugby Federation, which C. Loriston created 1959 around his own club (which he had taken out of the S.A.C.R.B. in 1955) in the rural parts of Western Province; and the S. A. African Rugby Board, which had been created, in 1935, following a secession of African players from the SACRB (See Chapter 2). During the 1950s, teams from the S.A.C.R.B. and from the African Board played annual 'tests' against one another.

Attempts were made to unify on non-racial lines from the end of the 1950s, and negotiations also appear to have taken place with a view to associating with the white Rugby Board. The chronology and interpretation of these events is somewhat confusing, however. M. Draper [32] affirms that SARF policies at this time were close to those of the non-racial S.A. Sports Association, and that Loriston attempted to encourage unity on non-racial lines — behaviour which, if true, does not square with his previous or sub-sequent attitudes. She also asserts that in April 1962, the S.A. Coloured Rugby Board 'did in fact vote (9-8) in favour of affiliating to the White controlling body. This decision was, however, unanimously rescinded at a meeting held in June 1962, i.e. a couple of months later. The following day, a joint conference was held between representatives of the African and Coloured Boards when it was decided to amalgamate on a non-racial basis.'[34] This initial attempt appears to have collapsed when Eastern Province affiliates refused to collaborate with the African clubs. This description does not square altogether with the recollections of Mr Abdullah Abbas, President of the S.A. Rugby Union and an official of the S.A.C.R.B. at this time. He contests that the SARF had always been close to SASA and affirms that SARU came into being after a conference was arranged in 1964, at which Loriston proposed the formation of a single national body, which he sub-

sequently refused to join.[35] A recent article in *Work in Progress* further
suggests that SARU was not created until the City and Suburban Union
(affiliated to SARF) refused to eject its non-Coloured members (as SARF
demanded) 'and opened negotiations with SACRU, stipulating that the word
"coloured" be dropped. Thus was SARU born.'[36]

At all events, from its creation, SARU recognized non-racial principles
and, during the 1960s, distanced itself from the two other black federations,
which proved unable to break out of their sectarian and essentially provincial
traditions. SARF has remained a strictly Coloured body confined to the rural
areas of South-Western Cape and the African Rugby Board was increasingly
troubled by financial mismanagement and the general administrative shortcomings we have described in Chapter 6.[37]

A True 'Multi-nationalism'

Following its catastrophic tour to Britain in 1969-70, the white Rugby Board
realized it was in great danger of being isolated internationally. It therefore
took representatives of all the black federations to London, where they were
told by the International Rugby Board that they could not affiliate to international rugby without passing through the S.A. Rugby Board. A 'National
Rugby Advisory Council' was therefore set up to co-ordinate relations
between the four federations; no multi-racial matches were arranged.

In the same year, a much more important event passed almost unnoticed
at the time. In June 1971, in protest at the mismanagement and multi-
nationalist policies of the Port Elizabeth African R.B., a group of African
clubs seceded and formed the Kwazakhele Rugby Union (KWARU), which
defended non-racial principles and affiliated to SARU.[38] Between 1971 and
1975, others followed suit and numerous African clubs which were dissatisfied with the racially-compromised policies of the African Board formed
similar associations: among them were the SEDRU (South Eastern Districts
R.U.) in Grahamstown, the KADRU in King Williams Town, the VEDRU
(Victorian East) around Fort Hare, the MDARU at Mdantsane. Like KWARU,
these predominantly African associations seceded because of dissatisfaction
with the racial and administrative policies of the African Board; they were
isolated by the African Board and the municipal authorities, and subsequently
moved from mere sympathy with the stand of SARU to the point of
affiliating to the non-racial Union. All of them have a sense of independence,
however, and it was essentially by virtue of its relatively decentralized and
non-authoritarian structure that SARU became, in the 1970s, one of the few
non-racial federations with a high African membership. In 1975, SARU,
which had withdrawn earlier from the 'National Advisory Council', joined
SACOS for the first time.

During the same period, the Rugby Board promoted the first 'international' games between touring sides and 'representative' racial teams from
the S.A. Rugby Federation (*Proteas*) and the African Rugby Board (*Leopards*).
Such matches were organized on the occasion of every tour between 1972 and
1976, and the S.A. Rugby Board also organized tours abroad for 'African' and

'Coloured' teams. After 1975, occasional 'multi-racial' sides were also selected, composed of African and Coloured players and, subsequently, white players as well. All these teams played *only* against foreign sides.

In 1975, the S.A. Rugby Union was invited by the white Rugby Board to provide players for one of their 'mixed' matches, against a French side. The Union refused. Representatives of the White Board and the African Board then summoned three associations affiliated to the Union — Western Province Rugby Board, KWARU and SEDRU — and invited them to propose players for selection. The meeting was attended by the Minister of Sport Dr Koornhof, and a representative from the Ministry of Bantu Affairs, Mr Punt Janson (later to succeed Koornhof as Minister of Sport). When all refused, in line with SARU policy, the white Board and the Department of Sport fell back on a form of intimidation which had been successful in both tennis and football during the 1960s: the black associations were informed that access to municipal and bantustan facilities would be closed to them while their teams remained 'mixed'. The aim of this approach will by now be evident: to sever contact between the Coloured and African players.[39]

The reaction of the victimized associations and of the S.A. Rugby Union reveals how far the non-racial movement had travelled since the early 1960s. Officially supported by the S.A. Rugby Union, KWARU and SEDRU continued to play their matches, with multi-racial teams, on patches of wasteland and improvised pitches. Mr Patel, Secretary of the S.A. Rugby Union, declared that 'Both units confirmed that they would play the remaining South African Cup matches on open fields rather than join up with SARB . . . . The Government now has its grounds and we have the right to believe in non-racial sport.'[40] In August 1975, SARU organized a match in Johannesburg between Tygerburg (Cape Town) and KWARU, its top teams, on the same day as the *Proteas* (SARF) were due to play the *Leopards* (SAARB), also in Johannesburg. 3,000 came to the non-racial game, comfortably outnumbering the 600 spectators at the official 'multi-national' match. At the end of the year, 20,000 spectators, black and white, turned up at a patch of rough ground to watch the final of the South Africa Cup, while 5 stadiums in Port Elizabeth remained virtually empty.[41]

Throughout 1975 and 1976, associations affiliated to SARU continued to attract players and clubs from the S.A. African Rugby Board, in spite of the fact that the municipal authorities and bantustans kept facilities closed to them.[42] At the beginning of 1977, the SAARB suppressed its racial title in favour of the S.A. Rugby Association (SARA), but this had little effect: it lost to SARU 29 'national' caps, 12 East London clubs and 3 clubs from Port Elizabeth. Only two SARA affiliates remained in the Transvaal. In the same year, 11 white players also joined SARU, including the Watson brothers: 'Cheeky' Watson, who had been a candidate for a Springbok cap, was subsequently arrested, along with his brother Valence, for playing without a permit. The case provided SARU with wide publicity.

Nevertheless, in April 1977, the white Board, the Federation, the African Association and SARU met to negotiate terms for the creation of one single

267

controlling body for South African rugby. The four associations might have reached the same sort of provisional agreement which, at the same period, provoked crises in the non-racial cricket and football federations. Under pressure from the Western Province Rugby Board, SACOS and other SARU affiliates, however, Mr Abbas withdrew from the talks at an early stage because it seemed to the SARU executive that unification would be impossible while the laws of apartheid remained in force. SARU's participation in the talks nevertheless aroused much criticism, and Mr Abbas even offered to resign.

The three other federations pursued talks and concluded an agreement in November, whereby a new ruling body was to be created, bearing the same name as the white association. Within it, each 'national' body was to retain its 'national' identity; but, whereas each of the 22 affiliates of the white Board were to have two representatives on the Council of the new Rugby Board, SARA and SARF were only to have three representatives each – a voting arrangement which guaranteed a huge majority of white votes. Fusion of the three bodies and full integration on equal terms was to occur only when it was accepted by provincial white unions that black clubs had reached the same standard as white clubs.[43] In short, it was a 'multi-national confederation' of the first water.

The first mixed national trial were held at the end of the year. No black player was selected for either the first or reserve sides. SARU expelled three players who had agreed to take part. Multi-national confederation in the bag, the S.A. Rugby Board welcomed a delegation from the International Rugby Board, which did not deign to meet the non-racial Union: 'We are here to talk sport, not politics,' declared summarily the I.R.B. spokesman, Mr. Lord.[44] Although the presidents of both SARB's black associates complained that the reforms which SARB had introduced were inadequate, Dr. Craven declared that rugby was 'open'. Black teams played for the first time in the white leagues: two (national) black sides, one 'African', the other 'Coloured', were entered for the Pienaar Cup, the second division club championship. A handful of the best black players were selected for white teams. Several SARU clubs joined the S.A. Rugby Board, a larger number of Federation clubs crossed over to SARU, and African clubs continued to leave the dwindling SARA to join the non-racial movement.

In 1979, the S.A. Rugby Board, in collusion with members of the I.R.B. attempted to blow open the boycott by organizing a series of tours in close sequence, which would reinforce each other and complicate the task of anti-apartheid movements. The first was planned for France in 1979; it was cancelled. The second went to Britain (Barbarians, 1979); the third went to Latin America (1980); the fourth and fifth were in South Africa (British Lions and French Tricolors, 1980). In May 1981, despite intense opposition, an Irish XV went to South Africa, and, later in the same year a Springbok team toured New Zealand (see the next Chapter). In 1980, 1,250,000 rands of commercial sponsorship was provided over five years by S.A. Breweries – a colossal sum for an amateur sport.

SARF and SARA have continued to turn around their mighty partner, their black presidents bleating for better conditions, SARF continued to attract a limited number of players, if only because its teams in the Coloured Armed Services and police force are forbidden to join SARU,[45] the African Association is today almost non-existent:

> Undoubtedly the best kept secret of the 1980 Lions tour was the struggle of SARA to find fifteen 'African' rugby players willing to participate in the token match . . . In the event, SARA could find only eight black players to pit against the Lions, although they could easily have fielded an army of administrators.[46]

SARU has continued to grow steadily, and efforts are being made to raise standards of play and organization. Nevertheless, it is in no position to compete directly with the powerful white body. In the short term, the latter is threatened more by dissension within its own ranks, where there is a very powerful conservative lobby unwilling to accept even the slow introduction of limited reform. In 1980, the presence for the first time of an invited Coloured school team in the Craven Week — premier championship of white schools, sponsored by Toyota and dominated by Afrikaner teams — provoked a major scandal, and the competition was almost boycotted by a group of administrators and schools. Weeks of patient negotiation were required to persuade the hardliners to accept this precedent, at the end of which the Week went ahead . . . with the announcement that in 1981 an African side was to be invited ! . . .

SARU's Contribution to the Non-Racial Movement

SARU is the non-racial federation which, after tennis, has the highest proportion of Africans in its membership. Since 1971, a steady flow of clubs and players has continued to join it. Since 1977, a small number of white players have also affiliated, enabling the organization to prove, like the S.A. Cricket Board, that it does not practise racism in reverse. Given the political and ideological status of rugby to white South Africans, these are considerable achievements.

As a result, during the 1970s, the non-racial Union began to threaten the public reputation of the white Rugby Board, and to prove a thorn in the flesh of the 'multi-national' policy. Perhaps overconfidently, the Rugby Union's executive agreed to dialogue with the racial associations within a 'multi-national' context, but because, unlike the S.A. Soccer Federation and the S.A. Cricket Board of Control, it withdrew swiftly, it was compromised very little and suffered no internal dispute of the kind which led to schisms in the other two major sports. On the contrary, their resistance to multi-nationalism helped to provoke a serious collapse in the administration of the African Board (SARA), and an extensive movement of players and clubs towards non-racial rugby. In this, SARU was fortunate, for at the time of the talks many still believed that negotiations might be of value, and that 'multi-nationalism' was not a mere paper reform. The decision to dialogue cannot, in this case, be blamed on the weakness or lack of non-racial commitment of the SARU executive, for in Mr Abbas and Mr Patel the organization possesses two particularly hardened and experienced administrators, whose position within SACOS has always been both independent and clear — and, certainly in relation to the Soccer Federation, radical. In 1976, SARU resigned from the Council in protest against Norman Middleton, then its president, and in 1978-9, the Union was among the SACOS affiliates which demanded exemplary penalties against the Soccer Federation and its Professional League. (In 1978 SARU rejoined the Council and campaigned for the provisional reacceptance of S.A.S.F. and S.A.S.F.-P.L. provided stringent conditions regarding its non-racial policy were satisfied.)

It is probably SARU's decentralized structure and tradition of autonomy which best explain its attractions to African rugby players as well as the firmness of its policy on non-racialism. Unlike some other federations, the SARU executive has left general responsibility for local affairs to the provincial Unions, which therefore enjoyed considerable autonomy, provided they adhered to non-racial principles. Far from weakening executive control, this had the effect of increasing the executive's accountability and making local clubs and unions more self-reliant. The modern S.A. Rugby Union is in fact largely the product of a coalition between the old S.A. Coloured Rugby Board and the new, predominantly African, rugby unions. Both support SARU policy, but are not always ready to let SARU officials speak for them. SARU's democratic organization and its willingness to encourage regional self-reliance require flexible and sensitive handling by the executive, particularly when dealing with the relations between primarily Coloured clubs or associations and primarily African clubs or associations, rendered difficult by apartheid. It is SARU's achievement to have succeeded in this task during the 1970s, in a way which would probably have been impossible for the Soccer Federation, the hierarchy of which is far more authoritarian and centralized. KWARU, SEDRU, KADRU and the other new rugby unions give public emphasis to the voluntary character of their affiliation to SARU, underlining their autonomy of decision. The unions which have a majority of African players are subject to particularly strong political harassment — exclusion from grounds, arrest for playing without permits, seizure of 'squatted' pitches, etc.[47] — all designed to force them back into an 'African' association. Though their support may be unconditional, neither the SARU executive nor Coloured rugby players (who suffer much less harassment) can — precisely because of apartheid — struggle directly for their colleagues' interests, or struggle beside them. 'Abbas and Patel cannot speak for us against Mdyesha [president of SARA] because they are from Indian and Coloured townships and they haven't the problems we have as Africans'.[48] This fact of political life in South Africa is itself a strong argument in favour of the self-reliance and relatively decentralized structure promoted within SARU.

The same spirit of autonomy is to be found in SARU's relations with SACOS. The Rugby Union has been at once one of SACOS's most respected and most critical affiliates. SARU's view has always been that SACOS is the representative organ of South Africa's non-racial sports bodies, created to provide a single voice for non-racial sportsmen. It has no mandate and no right to interfere with the internal affairs of its affiliates. 'SARU was affiliated to SACOS but the Union claimed complete autonomy. SACOS was made up of a number of autonomous bodies and the Union did not feel bound by SACOS decisions. They were affiliated to that organisation so that there was unison of thinking. SARU reserved the right to make their own decisions and act independently of SACOS which remained a consultative or advisory agent with no constitutional right to interfere with its members.' [49] It is most important to understand this position, which does *not* constitute a criticism of SACOS, but reflects SARU's approach to the problems of running a multi-racial organization under conditions of racial oppression. A democratically accountable executive with a firm general policy based on non-racial principles, complements a high degree of responsibility and autonomy at provincial and local level.

This is why SARU has opposed the Provincial Councils' tendency to intervene in the affairs of provincial affilates of national associations. In SARU terms, the officials of Provincial Councils of Sport are neither democratically elected by, nor answerable to a defined body of members; nor do they have any more right than SACOS to interfere with the internal affairs of affiliates. If they do so, they create a conflict of interest within the national sports bodies which can only decrease their efficiency and unity. In SARU's view, if the national policy of a given sports body is wrong, then the membership should reform its executive; if local policy is wrong, it is the job of the national executive to discipline it. For a considerable time, SARU refused to implement a SACOS directive asking members to instruct their affiliates to join their Provincial Council. SARU also expressed considerable reserve about the effects of the Double Standards Resolution, which also tended to reduce the autonomy of national sports bodies and imposed an inflexible rule of conduct upon conditions of play which were anything but identical in different federations and in different areas. 'There are players who would watch cricket or play in a league associated with Mr Varachia,' Mr. Patel has said. 'SARU had never felt it necessary to victimize in any way. The constitution covered the situation where a participant was a member in any other code or any other type of code — where this was interpreted *as prejudicial to the objectives of SARU*, only then would a player be dropped ... If you look after the rights of players, you will get the right reaction.'[50]

In short, SARU has attempted to promote non-racialism by policies which are less directive and more sensitive to members' feelings than those of many of the other non-racial bodies. By choice or because of the particular character of the Union's membership — perhaps also because rugby is also exclusively amateur — the executive has permitted itself few liberties. Its respect for members' interests had helped it to become in 1980 one of the strongest non-racial federations in South Africa, with a high reputation for loyalty to non-racial principles and one of the largest African memberships.

Although white rugby appears to have lost none of its arrogance, it is threatened in the long term by SARU, which has already virtually destroyed the African federation and would no doubt have further weakened the Coloured SARF if military and police teams were permitted to play for the Union. Internationally, the present strength of the white Board — and of the multi-national confederation which it runs — is largely due to Dr. Craven's close ties with the IRB. When Dr Craven finally takes the retirement he announced in 1980, the white Board will almost certainly become visibly more reactionary, and its international relations are likely to suffer in consequence. At such a time, SARU is likely to have to resist increased harassment and a concerted campaign to subvert its African membership.

Tennis: The Numbers Game

```
SACOS              SAONGA
  |                  |
TASA               SATU
```

International Status
The S.A. Tennis Union (white) remains a member of the International Tennis Federation (ITF). The South African championship is one of five recognized by the I.T.F. South Africa is suspended from the Davis Cup (men) and the Federation Cup (women).

Organization
Non-Racial:
The Tennis Association of South Africa (TASA), formed in 1979 by the *Southern Africa Lawn Tennis Union* (SALTU), non-racial and a member of SACOS, and the *S.A. National Lawn Tennis Union* (S.A.N.L.T.U.), 'African'. TASA is affiliated to SACOS and represents about 14,000 black tennis players. President: Mr Fortuin; Vice-President: Mr D. Kali.
'Multi-national':
The S.A. Tennis Union (SATU, previously the *S.A. Lawn Tennis Union)*, 'white'. Represents about 39,000 adult and 36,000 school players. President: Mr Justice Blen Franklin.

Tennis is the only sport in which, during the last 20 years, a formal secession has occurred to the advantage of the non-racial federation.[51] At the time of writing, all but a handful of black tennis players belonged to the non-racial S.A. Tennis Association which was created following a merger between the previous non-racial Tennis Union and the African S.A.N.L.T.U., which had brought its association with the white Union to an end in 1977.

Non-racial tennis has not conquered its problems, however. Whereas black rugby players and footballers outnumber or have parity with the white federations, white tennis players have a comfortable majority over black. An expensive and technical game, tennis is an essentially middle-class sport and consequently beyond the reach of the majority of the black population.

Furthermore, when the game turned professional in the 1960s, it became one of the most commercial and competitive of sports, played in the public eye by 'stars' travelling the championship circuit. The depreciation of amateur tennis and the traditional 'national' competitions (Davis Cup etc.) greatly reduced the pressure which the non-racial federation and its supporters abroad could exert upon the white Union and the International Tennis Federation. The latter's evasive and inadequate reaction to the accusations of racism made against the white Union reflected its weakness, as well as more than a little irresponsibility.

At its creation in 1962 the non-racial SALTU represented all black tennis players. Soon afterwards, in 1963, as we have seen, it lost its African membership to the white Union, which had recruited the services of Reggie Ngcobo. SALTU's history ended with the return of these players. The period in between is a story of the white Union's timid moves towards multi-nationalism and of feeble interventions by the I.T.F. The African association remained merely an associate member of its powerful 'patron', and the non-racial Union remained impoverished but independent.

The white Union's participation in the Davis and Federation's Cups was increasingly criticized within the I.T.F. towards the end of the 1960s, although South Africa was safe from expulsion owing to the loaded voting system which heavily favoured European countries. In 1969, Basil Reay, then President of the I.T.F., visited South Africa to inquire into the situation. To the non-racial Union he made a proposition which he himself admitted was neither attractive nor in accordance with international tennis law: affiliation to the white association with federal status. SALTU refused on the grounds that 'it's not administration we're after. We want to play with them [whites] '[52] The white Union offered a vote to its African affiliate and, when Arthur Ashe was refused a visa to play in South Africa, announced that black players would henceforward qualify for selection to South Africa's Davis Cup team. International pressure continued to grow, however, and when Arthur Ashe was refused a visa a second time, in 1970, South Africa was suspended from the Davis Cup.[53] The South African professional players protested against the Government's decision, and the white Union appeared to be on the point of giving ground.

It was at this point that the white Union made attempts to recruit the non-racial Union's best players. Jasmat Dhiraj was among them. For several years he had been SALTU champion and during the Arthur Ashe dispute he wrote an open letter to the press, titled: 'If Ashe Can Play, Why Can't I?' With the aid of a journalist, Marshall Lee, a private match was arranged with Cliff Drysdale, who then declared publicly that Dhiraj was good enough to go 'open'. At a secret meeting, officials of the white Union invited Dhiraj to resign from SALTU and apply to join their Union: Dhiraj refused, and in 1971 was obliged to seek exile when he was informed that the police were interested in the date of his return from Britain, where he was playing in a tournament.[54]

The following year, the white Union organized mixed trials — in camera — for the Federation Cup. An all-white team was selected, which won the competition, contested that year in South Africa. Two black players took part in the national championships, which black spectators were permitted (literally) to watch. Having made these spectacular innovations, the white Union asked to be reinstated by the I.T.F., which agreed.

The white Union then suggested that a multi-national confederation should be formed, in which the non-racial Union would have the status of a provincial association, with one starting vote and one additional vote for every 2,000 members. (The African S.A.N.L.T.U., which had fewer members than SALTU, had been offered 11 votes, presumably for loyalty.) The non-racial body was also offered technical aid and training facilities, the opportunity to play in SATU's 'multi-national' tournaments, and seats on the selection board. A joint committee would meet to study racial problems in tennis.

This was the recipe for a classical multi-national confederation: SALTU refused the offer, arguing that its members knew more than enough about racial problems and were opposed to all 'multi-national' solutions. That year South Africa won the Davis Cup by default, when India refused to contest the final against her. From 1974-76, South Africa's participation was strongly contested by non-aligned countries in the Third World, and defended by the United States and other Western members of the I.T.F. Peter Lamb, a young black tennis player, was selected for the Davis Cup, and the white Union changed its name to SATU.

The turning point came in 1976, when Mr. Reggie Ngcobo, who had led the African Union since 1963, was voted out of office by the membership, which accused him of pandering to SATU. The African players dropped out of the white Union's multi-national competitions and in December 1977 ended their association with it. The new president, Don Kali, met representatives of the non-racial Union in January 1978, and the two associations opened talks with a view to creating a single non-racial association.

The time was ripe: an I.T.F. delegation, conducted by its president Philippe Chatrier, arrived in South Africa. It met all three parties concerned. The non-racial SALTU remained adamant that as proof of sincerity the white SATU should resign from the ITF, so that discussions could proceed on equal terms, and should accept a moratorium on all international competition until a new non-racial body had been properly established. The delegation recommended that South Africa be suspended from both the Davis and Federation Cups, and asked all three associations to settle their differences and form a single ruling body. It refused to agree to a moratorium, because I.T.F. rules stated that it was illegal to suspend any of the five major tournaments this would breach the contracts of professionals who had agreed to play in them.

Understandably, the press claimed that the report was favourable to SATU, for the I.T.F. had not criticised Government policy but, on the contrary, accepted at face value a letter containing one of Dr Koornhof's most majestic non sequiturs.[55] Strengthened by this support, the white Union advanced new proposals for unification, which for once, since numerical advantage lay with the white sportsmen, were impeccably democratic. The number of votes enjoyed by each organization, SATU suggested, should depend upon the number of members they possessed. Undeterred, the two black federations pursued their discussions and in May 1978 formed an interim committee. Another I.T.F. delegation visited South Africa and confirmed that no change had taken place. TASA was formed in September, representing all black tennis players with the exception of a handful who, like Peter Lamb, saved appearances at SATU's multi-national competitions.

This short history demonstrates the impact of socio-economic inequality on sport. Numerical advantage permitted the white Union, when it lost the support of its African associate and was confronted by a united and firm non-racial federation, to fall back upon force of numbers to defend its privileges. In adopting this tactic, the Union found an ally, as it always had done, in the I.T.F., whose several forays into the thickets of apartheid have contrived, voluntarily or not, to confuse the issues and entrench the white Union.

In a sense, this history is also the story of world tennis, because during this period the International Tennis Federation lost control over the game, which fell largely into the hands of the professional associations. This development 'overtook' the struggle which the non-racial tennis players were waging against the racial policies of the white Union, and rendered their progress worthless, for in the meantime tennis had been transformed into a sponsor's dream, with its individualism and 'stardom', its glamour and skill, in scale and audience perfectly adapted to television. SATU was able to finance its best juniors to travel abroad, while S.A. professionals were as independent of material constraints on their movements as golfers and other sportsmen in individualist, highly commercialized sports. Championship tennis is dependent on the players, who tour the circuit in quest of fees and prize money. A boycott of South African tennis made no sense to I.T.F. officials, who believed it to be 'impractical' and 'illegal'.[56]

In 1979, Standard Bank announced it would sponsor a three-day Davis Cup-type tennis tie for 60,000 rand. According to group marketing division PR manager John Pank, this 'is no altruistic exercise. We went into this sponsorship with our eyes open. It's a definite business proposition, a good visible thing to do. We've deliberately involved ourselves in showing social responsibility for the game in view of South Africa's exclusion from a lot of international competition.'[57]

A list of tennis sponsorships (see Table 36) reveals more clearly than words the political impact of prosperity. The figures cover the years 1977-79; they are complete for TASA/SALTU; the white SATU may well have received money from other sources in addition to those cited here. The latter are compiled from various references, not all of which it was possible to verify.

Table 36
Commercial Sponsorship 1977-79

TASA		SATU	
Coca Cola Bottling Company	R 8,000 p.a.	Telefunken	R 30,000
		SA Breweries	R 70,000
		Philips SA	R 75,000
		Peugeot	R 25,000
		SA Sugar Assoc	R 48,000
		African Eagle	R 48,000
		Standard Bank	R 60,000
		Sarie Marais (Pers)	R 40,000
		Sustagen	R 40,000
		Stellenbosch Farmers' Winery	R 25,000
		Bata, Syfrets, Makro	unknown

Figures from various sources, not all verifiable.

As a result, the exclusion of South Africa from the Davis and Federation Cups, which was finally achieved in 1972, was in fact a relatively insignificant event because the 'national' team championships under I.T.F. control were already seriously devalued compared with the championships on the professional circuit. The top players even refused to play in them on occasion, so low were prize money and prestige; it therefore mattered little if South African players were excluded. At most it was a small matter of pride.

The emergence of TASA will therefore have little immediate impact on the future of white tennis, for the I.T.F. has neither the will nor the power to exclude players affiliated to the white Union from international contests. While it is assured of its majority within the country and of competition where it matters, abroad, the white Union has little to fear from a competitor impoverished by lack of courts and sponsorship. Moreover, it is highly unlikely that the white Union will continue indefinitely to lack the black players it needs to justify the formation of a 'multi-national confederation'. 'It was all very frustrating to the Tennis Union,' admitted Justice Franklin, SATU's president, to the British Sports Council in 1980, 'because they saw black tennis withering and dying in South Africa.' Justice Franklin bewailed the fact that since 1976 'there had not been one black or coloured player in the South African Tennis Union national championships'.[58] If this was an admission of SATU's *political* defeat, the non-racial players belonging to TASA should draw little comfort from it. Money, as they know too well is all too likely to attract young black players into the orbit of the white Union, which will have the additional effect of lowering the standard of play of the non-racial Association, as it has in football. Although the TASA has the advantage of a particularly principled and experienced executive, much must happen before the political and sporting advantage is likely to swing in its favour — although it must be said that if professional tennis players are seriously inhibited from playing in South Africa, or against South Africans, by the sanctions introduced by the United Nations in 1981 (through the so-called Boycott list), much of SATU's complacency will evaporate.

Athletics: The Role of the Mines

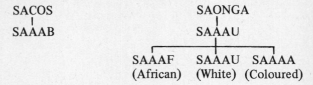

International Status
The white *S.A. Amateur Athletics Union* was expelled from the International Amateur Athletics Federation (I.A.A.F.) in 1976.

Organization
Non-racial:
The S.A. Amateur Athletics Board (S.A.A.A.B.) has between 9,000 and 12,000 members; until 1977 was also responsible for cycling.

'Multi-national' Confederation:
The S.A. Amateur Athletics Union (S.A.A.A.U.) created in 1977. President: Professor Nieuwoudt. Is composed of the following three racial federations:
The S.A. Amateur Athletics Union (S.A.A.A.U.), 'white', created in 1894. President: Professor Nieuwoudt. Membership: 17,400 in 1977. Organised cycling until 1957.
The S.A. Amateur Athletics Federation (S.A.A.A.F.), ex-S.A. African Amateur Athletics Association, (S.A.A.A.A.A.), 'African'. President: Mr Setshedi.
The S.A. Amateur Athletics Association (S.A.A.A.A.), 'Coloured', created in 1974.
The two black associations have the same status within the 'multi-national' confederation S.A.A.A.U. as a provincial affiliate of the white S.A.A.A.U.

The importance of athletics does not need to be stressed: it embodies the ethos of amateurism (or what remains of it), and it is the cornerstone of the Olympic Games. For this reason, it was natural that the first reaction of the S.A. Olympic and National Games Association, upon its expulsion from the Olympic Games, was to organize, in 1964 and again in 1968, a South African mini-Games. The importance of athletics is such that, if South Africa was to be readmitted to the I.O.C. and to the I.A.A.F., it would signal the end of the country's international isolation.

The strategic place occupied by athletics is no doubt one reason why the white Union has been dominated, certainly at executive level, by Afrikaners. The multi-national confederation created in 1977 took very much the same form as the S.A. Rugby Board, which, as we have seen, perfectly protects white interests. Unlike rugby players, however; black and white athletes have trained together for a number of years and, since the multi-national policy was announced, run regularly against one another. The fact that athletics is an individual sport, without physical contact, in which performances can be measured very precisely, makes this possible.

This is not the only reason, however. Most of the best athletics facilities belong to the mines and to the armed forces, which administer them as part of their social and recreation policies. They were opened to athletes of all racial groups in the 1960s, although athletes rarely ran 'mixed' until a decade later.

The apparent liberalism of this policy is deceptive. The mining companies, and *a fortiori* the armed forces, have always followed official sports policy to the letter, and black runners have been permitted to use their athletics facilities only if they respect official rules. Even before 1959, when the African Athletics Association affiliated to the white Union, it was firmly under white control. 'The chairman and secretary are White officials in the employ of mining companies, as are some of the members of the Committee.'[59] The very high standards some black athletes were achieving were also due to the technical services provided by their employers.

> As mentioned, the membership of the S.A.A.A. and C.A. is drawn largely from Africans in the employ of the gold mining companies in the Transvaal. As part of their recreational schemes for employees, mining groups have provided tracks, expert coaching and other facilities. According to a Press report (*Star*, 6 May 1963), every major gold mine has an international standard track and several also have Olympic-standard cycling tracks . . . . All recent performances of any note in the field of Non-White athletics have been from amongst the ranks of S.A.A.A. and C.A., almost all of whom have been Africans employed by mining companies.[60]

As a result, the 'multi-national' confederation has had a considerable advantage over the non-racial federation, which has about the same black membership but disposes of few facilities of mediocre quality, quite inadequate to permit its athletes to reach modern standards of performance. As a result, all the black athletes of international or national standing have belonged to the racial black federations. In addition, the mines have considerable powers as employers to inhibit their athletes from joining non-racial associations and to prevent non-racial associations from entering the mine compounds to run against African athletes. Members of the armed forces are officially barred from playing for or against teams associated with the non-racial movement. This means, once again, that African athletes are effectively separated from Coloured and Indian athletes, very few of whom are to be found on the mines. The 'Coloured' S.A.A. Association, formed in 1977, recruits almost exclusively among Coloured members of the armed forces.

Finally, it is worth pointing out that promotion of athletics by the mines and armed services is not entirely disinterested: a work force in the peak of condition is more productive, while fit and physically alert soldiers fight better. Both institutions, but particularly the mines, have shown interest in research programmes to test physical performance and resistance to stress; and athletes have provided, in South Africa as elsewhere in the world, excellent subjects of study.[61]

Such political, technical and financial assistance has to a great extent protected the white S.A.A.A. Union from the effects of isolation. It has also been helped by the amateur status of the sport which has prevented its athletes from falling under the influence of sponsors. The crisis of 1970 did not spare South African athletics altogether, however. Several attempts made to promote professional competitions — accompanied by a breath of corruption — suggested that the market forces which transformed South African sport during the 1970s were also at work within this most ancient and purest of sports.[62]

'Multi-national' gaffes

As a result of appeals from the S.A. Sports Association at the end of the 1950s, the I.O.C. instructed the S.A. Olympic Committee to eradicate racial discrimination from sport within the country. The Committee replied that it had no power to do so, but would seek to attenuate the effects of apartheid. When, in 1963, the I.O.C. issued its first serious threat of suspension, the Committee promised (although it was not admissible under Olympic rules) to organize separate national trials from which separate teams of black and white athletes would be picked for the South African Olympic team: this, the committee claimed, was as far as they could go.[63]

Under pressure, they nevertheless made further concessions, although in a manner calculated to produce anything but a good impression. In 1962, it was announced that a multi-racial team would take part in a triangular competition between South Africa, Portugal and the Central African Federation, in Mozambique. Separate trials were held, in Queenstown for the Whites, and a week later in Welkom for the Blacks: two athletes were to be selected for each event, on the basis of their performance. Two Africans duly qualified, Makgamathe in the 3 miles and Khosi in the half mile; but they were not selected. When inquiries were made, it was argued that a white athlete had run faster than Makgamathe on the same day on another track, and that Khosi's performances were not consistent.[64] The truth, however, emerged a few days later: the selectors *had* nominated the two black runners, but their names had been vetoed by the S.A.A.A.U. executive. The President of the Western Transvaal Union expressed the view of most of the Union's members when he roundly declared that 'It is not necessary to send combined teams . . . We are looking for trouble if we go against the policy of the Government . . . Recreation for the non-Whites does not depend upon competition with the Whites. When the Bantustans are developed, they will get all the competition they want.'[65] These attitudes were rarely ruffled during the 1960s, while repression prevented non-racial sportsmen from expressing

279

their views: 'We are one of the strongest bodies in the country,' asserted
Colonel Vissier (a S.A.A.A.U. official) in 1966. 'We must make it clear that
there can be no deviating from Government policy.'[66]

With the approach of the 1968 Olympics, however, pressure on the white
Union once more increased. With Vorster's permission, the white Olympic
Committee proposed to send a single representative South African team,
selected by a multi-racial committee, to the Mexico Games. The decision to
accept South Africa on these terms provoked a threat of boycott from all the
African and non-aligned countries, and the invitation was rescinded. In 1970,
South Africa was expelled from the Olympic Movement.

In compensation, the South African Olympic Committee organized its
own 'mini-Games' — which were separated not merely racially but by an
interval of one year. From 1968 onwards, South Africa was very effectively
isolated from world athletics, because the Supreme Council for Sport in
Africa saw to it that this was so. The voting system within the I.A.A.F.
remains weighted in favour of European members, who have generally given
South Africa a more than sympathetic hearing, but the number of top class
black athletes made it unthinkable to organize international tournaments
in their absence.

There was a catch to the ban, however, for it applied to team rather than
individual participation, and many South Africans arranged to go to the
United States or Europe, where they ran under club or even other national
colours. Nor did isolation stimulate the white Union's taste for change. The
latter continued to accumulate grotesque incidents, and must be accounted
the most literal-minded of the white sports associations. 'Athletics,' declared
the Official Year Book in 1977, 'was one of the first sports in which multi-
nationalism was introduced with success.' [67] This satisfecit was no doubt
delivered in recognition of the Union's astonishingly bureaucratic and formal
implementation of the policy. In 1974, to take one example, the Comrades
Marathon (a celebrated race in Natal initiated by veterans of the First World
War) was declared 'open' and 'multi-national': black athletes were instructed
that they could take part if they had permits and if at least two foreign
athletes had registered to run. Even this formula proved too liberal, however,
and the event had to be closed again: 'All participants in our events must be
registered in clubs in the S.A. Amateur Athletics Union,' explained an
official, with almost endearing gravitas. 'Black runners simply are not!' [68]
The following year another attempt was made: black athletes were admitted,
but had to wear tribal armbands!

> It is reported that there were not enough tags, and the Zulus had to
> wear Xhosa tags. The Minister of Sport, Dr. Piet Koornhof in Parlia-
> ment on 17th June 1975 when asked by Mr. Radclyffe Cadman (UP
> Umhlatuzana) 'Would the Minister run with a tag around his neck
> indicating he was an Englishman?' He answered 'If I was an English-
> man I suppose I wouldn't mind.' [69]

In 1976, the I.A.A.F. extended the ban to include individual athletes and excluded South Africa altogether. No South African was thereafter able to compete in contests recognized by the I.A.A.F. except by subterfuge. The Masters' Athletics Association proved to be particularly adept at such tricks. In 1977, no less than 40 competed in the United States, concealed, in defiance of their age, as American College students. [70] In 1980, with the same panache, they contrived to supply an entire team to the World championships (in New Zealand) with forged passports. [71] At home, the S.A.A.A.U. continues to furbish its less brilliant image. In 1977, the Northern Transvaal white Union organized a 'multi-national' competition at the end of which even the finishing line was racially separated! [72]

A 'multi-national confederation' was inaugurated in the same year: it was blessed with the same name as the white Union, and was composed of 18 provincial white Unions, each with a vote, and two national black unions, each with a vote. White officials continued to sit on the African Federation's executive, but one African, Mr Setshedi, was nominated Vice-President of the new confederation. In the opinion of SAN-ROC 'This person is an employee of the mining consortium and he never dares defy the wishes of the White Union for fear of losing his job.' [73]

The new confederation is financed by the traditional sponsors of official athletics — the government and mining houses — and by companies such as Dalrymple, S.A. Breweries, Colgate, Holiday Inns and SASOL. In the late 1970s, no doubt stimulated by the Fun-Run and Trimsa campaigns, athletics became widely popular. Up to 10,000 runners competed in major events. At the same time, in 1979 and 1980, attempts were made to introduce professional track racing at cricket matches in the Transvaal. The initiative was vetoed by the S.A.A.A.U. with imposing logic, on the grounds that 'cricket is cricket and athletics is athletics' [74] but reports continued to circulate that top athletes were nevertheless accepting fees. [75]

Some black runners have earned themselves an international reputation. A number, like Sidney Maree, have accepted scholarships to train abroad. The publicity given to their performances and advancement is good propaganda for multi-nationalism, but black athletes continue to suffer from the effects of discrimination and inequality, the terms on which they are given access to the mines' marvellous facilities. (One of the most recent cases involved Moshwarateu, a promising middle-distance runner who was refused a visa to the United States in 1980 because he was registered as 'Tswana' — a citizen of Bophuthatswana whose 'independence' is recognized by no country in the world outside South Africa). As for the non-racial athletes, barred from mining and many municipal facilities, they have little opportunity to raise their standards or to spread non-racialism among the majority of African runners. In the foreseeable future, it is unlikely that they will be able to narrow the political, material and sporting lead enjoyed by the multi-national confederation.

Swimming: A Case of Organized Poverty

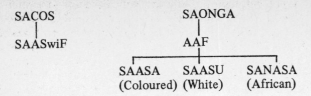

International Status
South Africa was excluded in 1973 from the Federation International de Natation Amateur (FINA); the decision was ratified in 1976.

Organization
Non-Racial:
The S.A. Amateur Swimming Federation (SAAwiF), was created in 1966. President: Morgan Naidoo. In 1978, represented 7,000 members, excluding school swimmers affiliated to SASSSA.

'Multi-national' Confederation:
The Amateur Aquatics Federation, formed in 1975 by the white S.A. Amateur Swimming Union, which dominates it administratively and by the size of its membership. It is composed of:

The S.A. Amateur Swimming Union (SAASU), 'white', created in 1899. President: Issie Kramer. Represents 14,000 adult and 20,000 school swimmers
The S.A. Amateur Swimming Association (SAASA), 'Coloured', created in 1973. President: Reggie Baynes. Small membership.
The S.A. National Swimming Association (SANASA), 'African', formed in 1977. President: Monnathebe Senokoanyane.

The non-racial Swimming Federation occupies a central position in SACOS by virtue of its proven commitment to non-racial principles and the energy of its executive, and above all of the president, Morgan Naidoo. SAASwiF is also one of the fastest-growing federations within the non-racial movement, having increased its membership between 1973 and 1978 from 4,000 to 7,000 in spite of a crippling shortage of facilities.

Since swimming is a mass sport which provokes particularly intense racial feelings among white South Africans, it is not surprising that most of the black swimmers have been excluded from public baths as well as from the vast majority of private pools in South Africa. As a result, unlike the white Union, the non-racial Federation takes responsibility for the organization of social as well as competitive swimming. To make matters more difficult, even the best black swimmers lack the means and opportunities to undertake the intense and consistent training which modern swimmers require to reach competitive standards. As a result, the level of competitive swimming attained by the non-racial Federation has been, and remains lower than that of the white Union, which exists to administer and promote the competitive swimming of a white community which has easy access to excellent facilities throughout the country.

On the other hand, the Federation has established good relations with the international body, and represents the great majority of black swimmers in the country. In this sense, the political advantage lies with SAASwiF.

When Morgan Naidoo became President in 1969, five provincial units were affiliated to the non-racial body. At this period, the white Union was in a golden age, with world champions like Karen Muir and Anne Fairlie taking nine gold medals between them between 1964 and 1969. Soon afterwards, in 1970-71, the non-racial and official associations met to negotiate, as in so many other sports at the same time, the creation of a single national body. Discussions were as fruitless: the Union agreed in principle to a non-racial constitution, only to argue that Government policy had to be respected. It also asserted that since SAASU was the senior association recognized by FINA it was only natural that the Swimming Federation should seek affiliation to it. In January 1972, at the Federation's biennial conference, SAASwiF resolved to apply directly for recognition to FINA.

One month later, the white Union announced that a 'Coloured' organization, SAASA, led by Mr Reggie Baynes, had affiliated to it. In March of the same year, a FINA delegation visited South Africa to investigate swimming. On the basis of its findings, the world body expelled the S.A. Swimming Union, in August 1973. A few months later, Morgan Naidoo was banned for five years under the Suppression of Communism Act. The following year, a 'multi-national confederation' was created; the Coloured Association participated in the white Union's 'multi-national' tournaments, when it could muster enough swimmers to make up a team.[76] The tale is familiar.

As characteristically, when the white Union felt itself to be threatened politically by SAASwiF, the central and municipal authorities intervened to close swimming facilities to 'mixed' groups of Federation swimmers. In Durban, black swimmers had no pool of international standard in which to swim, whereas Whites had access to 16. Nevertheless, in 1975 the municipal council refused to finance the building of an Olympic-sized pool for 'Coloured' swimmers.

Talks were reopened in 1976-77, after the white Union's expulsion from FINA was ratified, but the Federation continued to refuse to negotiate the non-racial principle, and demanded free and equal access to pools for all swimmers. In 1978, Morgan Naidoo's 5-year banning order was not renewed, largely owing to FINA's refusal even to reconsider the status of South African swimming while the SAASwiF president remained in detention. In 1979, the Federation was persuaded, against its better judgement, to meet the white Union again; but when no progress was made, FINA cancelled a planned visit of inquiry, and shelved reconsideration of South Africa's expulsion. Federation officials also met representatives of the 'African' National Swimming Association, formed in 1977, a body which, without seeking to identify with the non-racial movement, appeared to wish to decrease its dependence on the white Union.

At the end of the decade, the Union's position was not satisfactory. First

283

of all, there was little likelihood that FINA would restore its international
status, at least until the Union could prove it administered a substantial
black membership. For this reason, in 1980 a very public campaign was
launched to promote black swimming, with financial support from the
government (which recognized that swimming would not attract commercial
sponsorship because of its amateur status).[77] The timing of this promotion
drive was probably influenced by the talks between the African Association
and the Federation, which must have reminded observers of the secession of
black tennis players from the white Union in 1977. (Relations between the
non-racial federations in these two sports are particularly close.) Like the
official cricket body, SACU, which launched a spectacular drive to recruit
young African cricketers in Soweto (because it had none), since 1979 the
white Swimming Union has organized training sessions for young swimmers
in Soweto, Coronationville and other black townships.

Secondly, however, the state of white swimming was also a cause of
concern to the Union, which claimed that both the standards and keenness
of young white swimmers were falling. In 1979-80, the Union appealed for
aid from the Government and municipal authorities. Durban Council
authorized the construction of yet another new international pool for white
swimmers in 1980-81, and the Government agreed to pay the salary of a
national coach detached from the Department of Sport and to provide grants
to provincial swimming unions.

In short, SAASwiF has the 'political' advantage over the white Union and
its multi-national confederation, both internationally and inside the country;
but it is paralysed in practical terms by lack of facilities and the particularly
cruel weight of racial discrimination in swimming. Mr Issie Kramer's arrogant
dismissal of the quality of Federation swimming is probably factually correct
'The limited training given to young people in the Swimming Federation was
evidenced by their latest results which, compared with the Union's results,
were very poor. No child from the Federation would qualify for the Union's
National Championships.'[78] The statement is unforgiveable because, as
President of the multi-national Union, Mr Kramer must have known that the
deprivation from which Federation swimmers suffer is a direct result of his
Union's policy and the policy of the white government and municipalities.

This can virtually be proved in the case of swimming, where the Municipality of Durban has consistently refused to build or open additional swimming facilities for black swimmers, in the face of expressed public demand,
petitions and newspaper campaigns. While 500,000 rands were being spent in
1979 on a new international pool for Whites, the Council refused to build a
pool for Coloured swimmers or to open existing pools to 'non-Whites'.

The effects of this policy can be seen in the SAASwiF membership figures
between 1973 and 1978. (Table 37).

It is noticeable that the increase in the number of swimmers registered in
Natal was markedly lower than in any other region. The rapid growth of
membership in an area like the Transvaal can perhaps be explained by the fact
that non-racial swimming was not well-established in this province in 1973;

Table 37
SASSwiF Membership (Swimming), 1973-78

Provincial Affiliates	End of 1973		February 1978		Percentage Increase
Transvaal	278	6%	870	12%	312%
Griqualand West	602	14	941	13	156
East Cape	873	21	1314	19	150
Western Cape	992	24	1833	26	184
Natal	1324	32	1622	23	122
Boland	—	—	414		—
TOTAL	4069	100	6994	100	171

but the same cannot be said of the Western Cape, where the increase was equally spectacular. Natal, the traditional centre of non-racial swimming, increased in size less than any other region. Is it likely that the demand of Natalians for swimming has been satisfied? The repeated public demands for more swimming facilities prove that this is not the case. The relative decline in growth in Natal is surely attributable to the racially exclusive policies of Natal Council and the Swimming Union.

Finally, a word must be said about the role of the African Association. In numbers, facilities and standards, Africans lag further behind in swimming than in any other major sport, but, as elsewhere, they hold the key to the future. The Federation cannot claim to be a representative non-racial body until it has the support of African swimmers; similarly, the white Union will never recover its international status until it convinces FINA that the African Association both represents the majority of African swimmers and is willingly federated to the Union. In consequence, despite its insignificant size, the National Association has an opportunity to play a broker's role in South African swimming. This is all the more true because the number of African swimmers is certain to increase. In 1979, the Association's president had already declared that all three bodies should unite in a single federation and that until they did so 'the SANASA would continue as a racial body and would not liaise with SAASU or SAASwiF'.[79] From the Federation, Mr Senokoanyane demanded 'political' concessions, and from the white Union material aid. The latter appeal may certainly prove fruitful, for the Union will surely be willing to buy into a partnership; but SANASA's apparent desire for independence, if confirmed by events, can only give white swimming officials cause for disquiet.

Golf: A New Weak Link in the Non-Racial Sports Movement

SACOS		SAONGA	
SANRAGA		SAGU	SAGA
		SAPPGU	SAPPGA
		(White)	(Black)

International Status
The white *S.A. Golf Union* is a member of the World Amateur Golf Council.
Organization
A. Non-Racial:
The *S.A. Non-Racial Golf Association* (SANRAGA) was created in August
1979. President: Dr R.R. Human. The *Durban Golf Club* (1928) had
previously represented golf within SACOS as an associate member.
B. Official Federations:
The *S.A. Golf Union* (SAGU), (white), controls South African golf. It has a
professional affiliate, the *S.A. Professional Players Golf Union.*
The *S.A. Golf Association* (SAGA), (black), represents black golfers who
play within the official framework. It has a professional affiliate, the *S.A.*
Professional Players Golf Association.

As we have seen, golf — like weight-lifting, cricket, boxing and athletics —
is among the sports in which black players have reached international standards of excellence in spite of very great handicaps. Sewgolum's example
has been followed by players like Tshabalala, winner of the French Open in
1976. Nonetheless, black golfers in general remain highly disadvantaged.
The social role and status of golf explains why segregation has been maintained strictly and why material facilities are so unequally distributed among
the different racial categories: after decades of promises, in 1980 there was
still not a single reputable 18-hole golf course upon which Blacks could
play in the whole of South Africa. To make matters worse, the best course
that existed, the 9-hole course leased by the Durban Golf Club, was requisi-
tioned in 1979 by S.A. Railways.[80]
   Given the nature of the sport — traditionally elitist, individualist, highly
commercialized and international — it is not surprising that South African
professional golfers have suffered little, in the past, from isolation. Pressure
to exclude South Africa has nevertheless been growing, and the publication
of the United Nations 'boycott list', which has featured numerous foreign
golfers, may prove a turning point. The latter are likely to be deterred from
playing in South African tournaments if they are subsequently barred from
playing throughout the Third World, in Japan etc. In due course, the pressure
brought to bear on the white golfing establishment may also hamper the
proselytizing activities of individuals like Gary Player.[81]
   If the new non-racial SANRAGA, created in 1979, succeeds in establishing
itself, this will also weaken the national and international standing of official
golf. Until 1979, the tradition of non-racial golf had been preserved in Natal
by the Durban Golf Club, but no national association had been formed.
Under favourable circumstances, SANRAGA might begin to attract black
golfers from the official black association, thereby weakening its authority,
and indirectly that of the white Union itself. If this was to occur, the white
Union would be obliged to promote racial — particularly professional — black

golf on 'multi-national' terms, by offering material incentives to players
like Tshabalala, or intimidating them by withdrawing facilities. There were
signs in 1980-81 that, for these or other reasons, some professionals, including
Tshabalala himself, were willing to escalate their public criticisms of the
white Union.

It must be said, however, that non-racial golf cannot become competitive
– even in political terms – while players remain deprived of facilities to the
degree they are today. A handful of gifted individuals may continue to reach
professional standard, much as they do in tennis; in doing so, they will not
improve the opportunities for the mass of black golfers without facilities, but
merely refurbish the white Union's palling reputation.

Boxing: 'We'll Make No Money out of It'

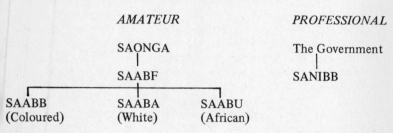

International Status:
The white federation has been excluded from the International Amateur
Boxing Association (I.A.B.A.) since 1968. The professional body, the *S.A.
National Boxing Board,* is recognized by the World Boxing Association
(W.B.A.), but not by the World Boxing Council (W.B.C.).
Organization
There is no non-racial boxing association.
'Multi-national' Confederation: The S.A. Amateur Boxing Federation
(S.A.A.B.F.), which is composed of:
The S.A. Amateur Boxing Association (S.A.A.B.A.), 'white';
The S.A. Amateur Boxing Board (S.A.A.B.B.), 'Coloured';
The S.A. African Amateur Boxing Union (S.A.A.B.U.).
Professional boxing is organized by the *S.A. National Boxing Board*
(S.A.N.B.B.), which is directly responsible to the Department of Sport.

Amateur boxing is almost entirely in the hands of the white Boxing Association. There are very few non-racial clubs, and non-racial boxers have failed,
since their first attempts in the early 1960s, to form a national association.[82]
Most boxers are affiliated to the multi-national Federation which is one of
the multi-national confederations which do not even claim to be integrated
at club level. Only national and provincial championships are 'mixed'. Most
black boxers are African, and therefore members of the Union. The Boxing

Board is a minority organization; there are so few Indian and Coloured boxers in Natal, for example, that some have affiliated to the provincial African body (NABU). In 1979, racial categories were abolished for the first time at championship level, and instead of three or four champions at each weight (Indian, African, White, etc.), there is now one national champion. One step forward . . . ? The eliminating bouts remain segregated.

Professional boxing occupies, in contrast, a crucial position in the Government's sporting (and political) strategy. The role of money in professional boxing and the conflict between the W.B.A. and W.B.C. gave South Africa a rare opportunity to influence events in their interests, and both the National Boxing Board and the Government have actively promoted prestige bouts in South Africa. In October 1979, the black American John Tate boxed the white South African champion C. Coetzee for the W.B.A. heavyweight world title, in Johannesburg before world television and a de-segregated audience. South Africa's investment is not just financial, however: no less than four senior executive positions in the World Boxing Association are held by South Africans, including the Vice Presidency (Mr Justice Klopper) and the Presidency of the Rankings Committee (Mr Mortimer).[83] The American media and American promoters have shown great eagerness to mount or show the various title fights staged in South Africa, because profits there are guaranteed by the terms of contract. Bob Arum, eminence grise of the W.B.A., arranged the Tate/Coetzee bout and the preliminary eliminators, and numerous black American boxers are tempted to swallow their pride and moral doubts by the very high purses they can expect to receive. While the Government and white boxing federations find political advantage in the promotion of such contests, and the media and promoters make considerable profits from television rights etc., only the ordinary black boxer loses out consistently. Use has even been made of boxing to legitimize the bantustans, for several major bouts have been organized by Holiday Inns (Southern Suns Hotels) in their leisure resort in Bophuthatswana. The organization, which was accused of receiving laundered money during the 'information scandal', is alleged to have invested one million dollars in the Tate/Coetzee fight: Southern Suns has argued that the investment was legitimate, intended to promote its tourism interests. The publicity and sponsorship director of Holiday Inns even declared to the *Financial Mail* (27 April 1979) that his aim was to put Bophuthatswana (which is not, of course, recognised by any State outside South Africa) on the tourist map. 'We'll make no money out of it', he said.

References

1. *Financial Mail,* 1 September 1978.
2. *Mercury,* 1 September 1977; in 1979 Mr Elliot transferred his club to the SANFA.
3. *Black Review*, 1974, p. 201.

4.   *Star*, 23 February 1980.
5.   Thabe in British Sports Council, 1980, p. 140; Bhamjee in *Financial Mail*, 1 September 1978.
6.   *Financial Mail*, 1 September 1978.
7.   In 1979-80, the two N.P.S.L. leagues (31 clubs) included at least seven which had belonged to the N.F.L., and at least two from the S.A.S.F.-P.L. In that year, five more clubs left the S.A.S.F.-P.L. for the N.P.S.L., of which two were ex-N.F.L. clubs, that had joined the non-racial league after 1975.
8.   *Black Review*, 1975-76, p. 177.
9.   Modise in *Financial Mail*, 16 March 1979.
10.   *Financial Mail*, 13 April 1979.
11.   Committee Against Racial Discrimination, created in 1973 to inform the public about the principles and aims of non-racial sport, and oppose the 'multi-national' policy. Its patrons were Hassan Howa, Morgan Naidoo and M.N. Pather, all officials of SACOS or SACOS federations.
12.   CARDS Newsletter, n.d. (1978?).
13.   CARDS Statement, October 1977.
14.   Extract from SACOS press release, in SACOS, Minutes of the Third Biennial Conference, 1979, p. 19.
15.   It has been calculated that it cost Cape Town City and Hellenic more than half a million rand in additional travel costs when they joined the N.P.S.L. from S.A.S.F. The Durban City President has stated: 'Our costs are far greater than those incurred by the Transvaal clubs. If the excess was borne equally, or if the Transvaal clubs could step up their payments a little it would make things easier.' *Star*, 8 April 1978, 23 February 1980.
16.   British Sports Council, 1980, p. 138.
17.   Ibid., p. 137.
18.   The best known of these is probably the Aurora C.C. Created in 1973 as a multi-racial club, Aurora selected the first mixed side to play in one of the white leagues. When the initiative did not produce effects, a majority of the players voted to join S.A.C.B. in 1977, soon after the ruling against Double Standards was introduced. See M. Hickson, 1979.
19.   The interventions of the Department of Sport, and of Dr Koornhof in particular, were frankly provocative in this respect; their verbal ambiguity and sense of strategic hesitation ensured the demise of any serious attempt at truly multi-racial unification, if this had in fact ever been desired by the white Association. For a ball-by-ball commentary, see A. Odendaal, 1977, pp. 50-61.
20.   In the first season of SACU cricket, only three members of the Western Province first team remained with the non-racial body. One of the best SACBOC cricketers, Yacoob Omar, played for Natal in 1977 and declared that he would stay with SACU if a secession occurred. In 1978-79, Omar and most of the ex-SACBOC stars were back in non-racial cricket, playing for SACB teams.
21.   *Star*, 16 February 1980.
22.   B. Richards in A. Odendaal, 1977, pp. 249-55. He also called for Sunday cricket — outrageous heresy for Afrikaner purists — on the grounds that it 'has the potential to draw vast crowds. It will bolster

the gates and encourage sponsorship and advertising.'
23. 'Only a handful [of black cricketers] have made their mark in Open cricket.' *Star*, 28 January 1978.
24. Varachia and the SACU executive accused Howa and the S.A. Cricket Board (in front of the British Sports Council Delegation, 1980, pp. 74-6) of shifting their ground whenever an issue was negotiated, of wasting (official) resources which were made available to them, of administrative inefficiency and of exerting political pressure on children. Howa and the S.A.C.B. reproached Varachia and SACU for opportunism, for falsely claiming to be non-racial, and for depriving S.A.C.B. players of municipal facilities.
25. 'Fundamentally, I cannot fault SACU's principles, but certainly their modus operandi can be faulted. At the same time that they are shouting out their principles, they are very actively engaged in breaking those same principles. They state one thing and do another.' Hassan Howa in A. Odendaal, 1977, p. 277.
26. *The Times*, 17 January 1980.
27. In A. Odendaal, 1977, p. 67.
28. Hassan Howa, in A. Odendaal, 1977, p. 277.
29. See A. Odendaal, 1977, pp. 51 and 77.
30. These countries refused to join the I.C.C. delegation to South Africa in 1977, which was composed of representatives from England, Australia and New Zealand.
31. Odendaal, 1977, p. 272.
32. See pp. 294-5.
33. Draper, 1963, p. 68.
34. Ibid., pp. 67-8.
35. Private communication.
36. *Work in Progress*, 1981, p. 3.
37. For details, see ibid.
38. According to *Work in Progress* (1981, pp. 203) 'The KWARU secession was primarily motivated not by political considerations, but by the desire of the clubs to escape the corruption and maladministration of the P.E.A.R.B. [Port Elizabeth African Rugby Board]. In the initial stages of the breakaway, the KWARU executive did not contemplate abandoning the S.A.A.R.B. which was still committed to the official government policy of multi-nationalism in sport. They applied to the Eastern Province Rugby Board . . . for recognition as a separate union, but were turned down. They then appealed to the S.A.A.R.B. but this decided (under pressure from the P.E.A.R.B.) that it was bound by a 1965 resolution prohibiting the recognition of 'mushroom' unions. The cream of Khosa rugby was left without anyone to play against. On the advice of Eastern Province, their Coloured sister Union, they applied to the South African Rugby Union (SARU).'
39. *Black Review*, 1974-75, p. 205.
40. *Cape Herald*, 14 June 1975.
41. For this paragraph: *Black Review*, 1975-76, pp. 181-3; J. Brickhill, 1976, p. 37; *Black Review*, 1974-75, p. 205.
42. The Ciskei Government, for example, which included several ex-players or officials of the S.A. African R.B., closed its facilities to

MDARU teams while these included Coloured players. (*Black Review*, 1975-76, pp. 184-5.)

43. Needless to say, the terms of the agreement are both vague and complicated. We have no room to describe them here, but a summary of them, and the process of integration as foreseen officially by the white Rugby Board, is to be found on pp. 40-46 of British Sports Council, 1980.

44. *Cape Herald*, 10 September 1977. The Confederation was officially inaugurated in March 1978.

45. Thus in 1978, for example, Kimberley policemen playing for the Red Eagles (SARU) were barred from doing so by the Police Commissioner.

46. *Work in Progress*, 1981, p. 5. This is something of an exaggeration.

47. KWARU recently prepared a pitch and stand, at its own expense (20,000 rand), in New Brighton: the municipal authorities are attempting now to expropriate this, and make it available to SARA (British Sports Council, 1980, p. 52.)

48. KWARU statement in British Sports Council, 1980, p. 52.

49. Testimony of Messrs Abbas and Patel in British Sports Council, 1980, p. 55.

50. Testimony of Mr Patel in British Sports Council, 1981, pp. 55-6 (author's italics).

51. The diversions of rugby and football were at the expense of the non-racial bodies; the movement of Africans into non-racial rugby took the form of defections from SARA, and the creation of new associations which then affiliated to SARU.

52. Lapchick, 1975, p. 146.

53. Ashe was not finally to receive a visa until 1973.

54. Interview, London, February 1980.

55. In a letter of 'clarification and a confirmation of the normalisation of sport on a non-racial basis in South Africa' (February 1978), Dr Koornhof declared to the I.T.F. delegation that no rules or orders hindered the free association of tennis players *and* that the system of permits was to be maintained.

56. Testimony of Justice Blen Franklin to British Sports Council, 1980, p. 107.

57. *Financial Mail*, 27 April 1979.

58. Testimony of Franklin to British Sports Council, 1980, p. 108.

59. M. Draper, 1963, p. 11.

60. Ibid., pp. 16-17.

61. In 1978, the annual conference of the International Committee for Physical Fitness Research was held at the Rand Afrikaans University, with 48 delegates from 7 countries. In the same year, sponsored by the Ministry of Sport, a new research journal for *Sport, Physical Fitness and Recreation* was launched by university researchers (Annual Report of the Department of Sport, 1978). In 1979, 'The Department received twice as many applications for research grants as in the previous year ... Research in sport continues to centre around sport physiology, but there are various other projects that border on the sociological, psychological, motor-perceptual, bio-mechanical and anthropometrical fields. Agencies that undertake work for the Department are the

Universities of Pretoria, the Orange Free State, Port Elizabeth, Stellenbosch and Potchefstroom, Rhodes University and the Department of Industrial Hygiene at the Chamber of Mines. In all, 45 projects are at present being financed by the Department.' (*Annual Report,* 1979, p. 17.)

62. *Star,* 28 January 1978.
63. Even this statement of their position is a simplification. The Committee offered to hold mixed selection trials *outside* the country . . . knowing that neither the Government nor the I.O.C. would be likely to entertain such a bizarre proposition. The Government's position was clear: the *number* of teams did not matter to them; only the white athletes, however, would represent South Africa. The Blacks would run for their own people or their region. It must be said that, at this stage, the I.O.C. was astonishingly receptive to these eccentric propositions.
64. These justifications, of course, were in clear breach of the selection procedures; but, in addition, they were highly questionable. Makgamathe had run much faster himself on other occasions, and subsequently beat the Zimbabwean athlete who won the 3 miles in Mozambique. As for Khosi, it was in relation to his case that Matt Mare made his celebrated retort, when asked why Khosi had not been picked, although his time had been 0.1 secs faster than the selected white runner: '0.1 second does not really count.' *Star*, 30 April 1962, in R. Lapchick, 1975, p. 46.
65. *Star,* 2 May 1962, in M. Draper, 1963, p. 15.
66. Colonel Visser, *Daily News,* 8 February 1966, in R. Lapchick, 1975, pp. 73-4. (This statement caused British athletes to vote against competing in South Africa while discrimination continued.)
67. The 'first' 'multi-national' event referred to in this quotation took place in the Cape in 1971.
68. *Black Review,* 1974-75, pp. 207-8.
69. SACOS, 1975, p. 25.
70. *Sun Express,* 14 August 1977, in SACOS, 1977, p. 30.
71. See p. 296 below.
72. S.A.I.R.R. Survey, 1977, p. 567.
73. S. Ramsamy, p. 24.
74. *Star,* 16 February 1980.
75. *Star,* 28 February 1980.
76. In February 1975, for example, five non-racial swimmers of the Federation were surprised to discover that their names had been included in an Association team.
77. 'The government . . . have agreed to give a . . . grant amounting to 2,000 rand for each province affiliated to SAASU: this money will be allocated entirely to the training of non-white swimmers.' Issie Kramer in British Sports Council, 1980, p. 135.
78. Testimony of Issie Kramer to British Sports Council, 1980, p. 134.
79. S.A.I.R.R. Survey 1979, p. 599.
80. The cost of erecting new facilities (estimated at 363,000 rand) and buying the land (625,000 rand) for a new course, amounted in 1980 to over one million rand. In that year, Durban City Council had still not declared whether or not it would guarantee financial support to the Durban Golf Club, nor even whether it would give its agreement to the

acquisition of a new site. The cause for delay was given as . . . administrative procedure. Durban Golf Club is a non-racial association (SACOS, Third Biennial Conference, 1979, pp. 85-6).
81. Cf. p. 221 above.
82. A S.A. Amateur Boxing Council claimed in 1979 to be non-racial but its application to join SACOS was rejected because the president of SAABC had been involved with 'multi-national' organizations. (SACOS, Third Biennial Conference, 1979, pp. 7 and 11.)
83. Government of South Africa, Annual Report of the Department of Sport, 1978.

12. International Responsibility: Lessons of the 1981 New Zealand Tour

One thing is certain after the 1981 Springbok tour of New Zealand: the sport issue still has fire in its belly. The strength and extent of public opposition in New Zealand — and in Ireland six months earlier — has probably put an end to any concerted South African attempt to break out of its isolation, using rugby to do so. For two months, New Zealand was virtually in a state of siege. The entire police force was mobilised, and the army held in reserve, to guard rugby stadiums and prevent demonstrators from repeating their exploits at Hamilton, where the second match of the team was stopped by police after demonstrators had broken down a fence and occupied the pitch under the astounded gaze, not just of New Zealanders but a huge television audience in South Africa, which was receiving the programme live by satellite.

South African Attempts to Breach the International Sports Boycott

There is some evidence that the South African government and sports federations, led by the South African Rugby Board, did anticipate some breakdown of the boycott, at least in rugby. The South African Rugby Board alone organised some eight tours between 1979 and 1981, and more are scheduled: a Springbok tour of the United Kingdom, scheduled for 1982, had not been cancelled at the beginning of the year. After 1976, the South African Rugby Board had played no matches with any of the major rugby-playing countries in the I.R.B., although it had continued to play teams from Latin America (Argentina, Paraguay, Uruguay, Chile) and the United States. Then, almost without notice, in the autumn of 1979, a South African Barbarians team played a short tour of the United Kingdom. Composed of 8 white, 8 coloured and 8 African players, it was presented as a 'multi-racial' team, and passed off uneventfully, because anti-apartheid organisations were unable to mount a concerted campaign of opposition in the short time available. In the same year, the French Rugby Federation was only prevented from organising a short Springbok tour when the French government decided to require visas of South African visitors and made it known that these would be refused to the South African team.

In 1980, two more tours were arranged with I.R.B. sides. The British Lions tour was followed shortly afterwards by a short French tour. The fact that the Olympic Games took place in the same year meant that the issue of South Africa's isolation was confused by the desire of a number of Western governments, including Mrs Thatcher's government in Britain, to impose sanctions against the U.S.S.R. Britain withdrew its official approval from athletes who chose to compete in the Moscow Olympics and put pressure on the British Olympic Committee to withdraw altogether. In contrast, though observing the letter of the Gleneagles Agreement (which supports isolation of South African sport), the government made relatively little fuss about the Lions tour. By inviting I.R.B. teams to South Africa, the South African Rugby Board was also able to take advantage of the refusal of all European governments to deny travel facilities to their nationals travelling abroad on private business.

The following year, in May 1981, the Irish Rugby Union also took a team to South Africa. It did so in the face of intense opposition in Ireland. Led by the government, most of the Republic's institutions, from trade unions to churches, appealed to the players to withdraw — and several did so. Public demonstrations were the biggest ever seen in Ireland on this issue. The level of public disapproval was such that, had a Springbok team been visiting Ireland, the opposition would probably have been as great as it was in New Zealand six months later.

A number of other issues and initiatives surfaced at the same time to reinforce the impression that South Africa's isolation was decreasing. In January 1980, The British Sports Council unilaterally sent a delegation to South Africa, under its Chairman Mr Dickie Jeeps, 'for the purpose of examining and establishing independently, progress made, at all levels, with multiracial integration in sport.'[1] The report, which has been criticised elsewhere in this book, abstained from drawing any formal conclusions, but a number of delegates, notably Mr Jeeps himself, afterwards commented on the visit in a manner which suggested that certain sports had been effectively integrated. Mr Jeeps was subsequently reported to have been criticised by the British Minister of Sport, Mr Howell, for exceeding his authority.[2] Other sports officials, including Mr Bill Hicks of the Sports Council and Mr Walter Hadlee, an Australian cricket official, visited South Africa on holiday and also made public statements following their visits in which they argued that sporting contacts ought to be reopened because of the progress that had been made.

Other South African sporting federations were active as well. During 1981, South Africa made a serious attempt to rejoin both the International Athletics Federation and the International Cricket Conference, using the argument that progress had been made towards integration; both applications were refused. In other sports, the S.A. National Football Association offered over $100,000 to a team of First Division English footballers to tour South Africa, but the tour was cancelled following intervention by FIFA. In Biarritz, a South African surfing team attempted to compete in the world championships; on this occasion visas were refused by the French government.

A scratch South African hockey side, composed of the members of the
national team, secretly toured Germany, Luxemburg, France and Holland
in September 1980, and so on. Individual boxers, golfers, cricketers and many
other Western sportsmen, with or without the approval of the international
bodies concerned, also continued to play in South Africa for substantial fees.
A full team of South Africans even arranged to compete in the World Veteran
Athletes championships — held, significantly, in New Zealand — by supplying
each competitor with a Dutch passport!

The New Zealand Tour

These incidents exemplify the constant skirmishing and subterfuges which are
part of the modern South African game. But the real battle has been in rugby —
and the crucial battlefield in Zew Zealand. It had been clear from the beginning
that the New Zealand tour was to be the test case of South Africa's capacity
to tour abroad in the face of international disapproval. It was a full tour, it
was to be played abroad, and New Zealanders had been given warning of its
coming. If the tour was successfully completed, it would certainly affect the
credibility of the international sports boycott campaign.

On all levels, the New Zealand government and the New Zealand Rugby
Union have played a unique role in the development of the international
campaign to isolate South African sport. Maoris have frequently been members
of the All Blacks national side, and from the 1920s were the subjects of controversy whenever tours were played with South Africa. During the 1960s, the
South African Government was acutely embarrassed by the issue because,
although their presence subverted the official sports policy, the prospect of
banning rugby tours with the world's top rugby-playing nation was in-
tolerable to white opinion; as we have seen, the 'multi-national' policy in
sport was formulated partly to resolve this ideological and political difficulty.
In one sense, therefore, tours with New Zealand were a traditional touchstone
for white South Africans of the acceptability of their rugby internationally,
and more generally of their sport.

Secondly, it was the New Zealand Rugby Union's decision to tour South
Africa in 1976 which had led directly to the boycott by African nations of
the 1976 Olympic Games — and accelerated the process which ended in
South Africa's expulsion from the Olympic Movement in 1980. International
sports federations have ever since been exceptionally sensitive to sporting
contacts, particularly in rugby, between New Zealand and South Africa.

Thirdly, the record of the New Zealand Government on the issue has been
one of the principal subjects of dispute in recent years within the Commonwealth. The history of this question cannot be dealt with here,[3] but the
reluctance of the New Zealand Government to make specific commitments
over sporting contacts with South Africa was one of the factors which led
African leaders to urge the Commonwealth Heads of State to sign the
Gleneagles Agreement in 1976. Since then, New Zealand has been sharply

criticised for its cavalier approach to enforcement of the Agreement, and Prime Minister Robert Muldoon's refusal to summon representatives of the New Zealand Rugby Union or ask them formally to cancel the 1981 tour convinced many observers, inside New Zealand and abroad, that he had no intention of severing New Zealand's sporting contacts with South Africa.

More important in many ways than all these considerations, however, was the impact of the sports issue on domestic politics in New Zealand. It was very clear after 1976 that a Springbok tour to New Zealand would provoke massive public opposition, and inflame the political situation. Therefore, when Mr. Muldoon refused to withhold visas from the South African touring side and the New Zealand R.F.U. refused to cancel the tour in the face of public protest, they were knowingly provoking a confrontation in the country. New Zealand has had a relatively tranquil history. It is nevertheless a country which was occupied by Europeans at the expense of the original inhabitants, the Maoris, following the colonial expansion of Britain in the 19th Century, and, although there is a fairly liberal tradition compared with Australia, the Maoris are clearly underprivileged. This has become increasingly apparent to the Maoris themselves, and the question of Maori rights is correspondingly sensitive. As a result, sporting contacts with South Africa naturally touch political nerve ends in New Zealand.

In contrast, rugby has the same popular appeal in New Zealand that it has in South Africa: it is the national sport, the sport New Zealanders play supremely well, and particularly for the New Zealand working class, it has become a symbol of national culture.

Predictably, therefore, the tour divided New Zealanders along both class and racial lines which, in the relative calm of normal political debate, usually remain concealed. The sports issue in the last resort has no middle ground; there can only be two reactions, in practice, to a decision to invite a South African touring team. At the same time, both proponents and opponents of the tour claimed to be defending their rights — the right of New Zealanders to play rugby without interference, against the right of people in South Africa to play sport without discrimination. This conflict of belief and interest, cutting across issues of both race and class, generated intense feeling. On one side was ranged the government, the New Zealand Rugby Football Union, all those who stood for law and order at all costs, and the majority of working-class New Zealanders for whom rugby is a symbol of their culture; on the other, the anti-apartheid organisations, the churches, all those attached to New Zealand's liberal tradition, the great majority of the middle class, and the Maoris. Quite predictably, although perhaps to an unexpected degree, popular attitudes polarized *not* just in relation to the Springbok tour, but in relation to New Zealand culture and society as a whole. Enormous demonstrations were organised and violence escalated sharply.[4] Protestors were appalled to discover the ferocity of fellow New Zealanders when, after the Hamilton match, these devotees of the sport realized their rugby was threatened. Men and women were beaten, attacked with bottles, kicked ui the ground; and the police themselves used aggressive riot techniques and were increasingly guilty of unjustified physical violence. On the other side, the spectacle of mass demonstrations and civil disobedience against law and order shook the deeply conservative assumptions of a large section of the population which could foresee nothing but anarchy emerging from such behaviour.

It is not the place here to assess the ripple effects of the tour on New Zealand's political life. Undoubtedly, however, the tour sharpened political tensions within New Zealand society — particularly over the rights of the Maoris and the powers and actions of the State. The tour also probably won Mr Muldoon a new term of office, for he won a general election in November 1981 by a narrow majority, based mainly on his support in small towns and country areas which, in general, coincided with the areas of strongest opposition to anti-tour demonstrations. In the urban areas, Muldoon's National Party won scarcely a seat. However, what effect did the tour have on South Africa's isolation?

Prospects for South Africa's Continued Isolation in World Sport

At one level, the answer is: very little. South Africa is today isolated in most major sports, primarily because the constitutions of the IOC and many other international federations ban racial discrimination. This has meant that sports officials have voted to exclude South African affiliates because they are in breach of their international constitutional commitments. This is, in fact, the crucial issue on which SASA and later SAN-ROC have campaigned, for South African sports associations are provably guilty of racial discrimination, simply by virtue of their adherence to apartheid law and practice. Whatever sympathy may exist among some Western affiliates of international sporting bodies (in some instances considerable) and however weighted the voting system may be in their favour, if there is an anti-racial clause in their constitution, the case against South Africa is unanswerable.

Other factors of course play a role. Since the Communist countries and Third World and African nations are committed to the isolation of South African sport, the latter is excluded from most of the sports in which these countries are influential or pre-eminent. Many sports officials are also personally opposed to apartheid.

Nevertheless, it follows that, for sporting bodies, the exclusion of South is not essentially a political decision, but reflects the commitment national sporting institutions to their own sporting values (which th African sports federations also claim to share). To be reinstated, an affiliates must simply prove (which, under apartheid, they discrimination is no longer present in sport.

international institutions like the United Nations, governments mental institutions base their stand on *general* moral and . The Gleneagles Agreement justifies sanctions against

297

South African sport by reference to the 'end of apartheid':

> Mindful of these and other considerations, they accepted it as the urgent duty of each of their Governments vigorously to combat the evil of apartheid by withholding any form of support for, and by taking every practical step to discourage contact or competition by their nationals with sporting organisations, teams or sportsmen from South Africa or from any other country where sports are organised on the basis of race, colour or ethnic origin.
>
> They fully acknowledged that it was for each Government to determine in accordance with its laws the methods by which it might best discharge these commitments. But they recognised that the effective fulfilment of their commitments was essential to the harmonious development of Commonwealth sport hereafter.

The South African Catholic Bishops Conference justified its opposition to the New Zealand Springbok tour in similar terms, saying that: 'A situation of great inequality exists between Black and White citizens in South Africa. This is evident in sport *as in other aspects of South African life.* We wish to encourage *all* attempts to bring about real change in South Africa by non-violent means. Sports boycotts are an effective means of applying pressure for change.' (Our italics).[5]

These and other organisations are not seeking to defend universal sporting values as such: they support the isolation of South African sport because doing so will, in their view, strengthen the movement inside the country towards change, and promote the political demands for democracy, social and economic justice, and equality before the law. The difference becomes clear if we say that, whereas the declarations of non-sporting bodies in favour of South Africa's isolation would remain coherent so long as the general laws of apartheid remain in force, sporting associations would be bound to reconsider the applications of South African federations if they were convinced that racial discrimination had been removed from sport (whatever laws and practices still existed elsewhere in the society).

It is this which permits official South African sports federations to apply regularly for readmittance to their international bodies and which encourages the South African Government and SAONGA to pursue the 'multi-national' sports policy of minimising the application of apartheid laws to particular sporting events. The approach reached its logical conclusion with the 1981 report of the Human Sciences Research Council which recommended that apartheid legislation should be completely suspended in the field of sport. This aim is, in practice, wholly unrealistic, of course, for no sporting event can be isolated from the social context in which it occurs; but it undoubtedly has a certain appeal for many European and American sports officials, and is clearly intended to facilitate South Africa's re-entry into international sport.

Popular opposition to sporting contacts with South Africa is the third level of international support for South Africa's non-racial sports movement.

Arguably both sports federations and governments depend upon the existence of this opposition to be effective. The massive campaigns in New Zealand and Ireland, like the British Stop the 70s Tour in 1969-70, directly influenced national policy.

Since 1970, the British Government has sought to avoid provoking public demonstrations of hostility to sporting contacts by acting to reduce them, even though it is unwilling, because of its strategic and economic interests, to support general sanctions against South Africa. Since the Irish tour in 1980, it is equally unlikely that the Irish Government will permit future tours in Ireland of major South African teams. Even in New Zealand, where Mr Robert Muldoon's National Party used the crisis provoked by the tour to reinforce its electoral position, any future government will find it very difficult, if not impossible, to license the visit of another Springbok team.

Popular opposition to apartheid sport also influences the credibility of the campaign to isolate South Africa in indirect, but equally important ways. It discredits, first of all, the suggestion that governments and international institutions have no mandate to isolate apartheid sport. The diplomatic commitments of Commonwealth leaders, the votes in favour or sanctions in the United Nations, and the political demands to extend sanctions to cover individuals and other countries which play sport with South Africa have all been given more force by the demonstrations in New Zealand. At the same time, they oblige sports officials and players to consider carefully before associating themselves with South Africa.

An interesting illustration of this is provided by the so-called sports boycott list, which was originally compiled by SAN-ROC and later recognised by the United Nations Centre Against Apartheid. It named the adult sportsmen and women who have played against South African teams and sports officials who had encouraged or organised such contacts during the previous three months. Regularly updated, its publication led directly to the cancellation of a test match in Guyana with an MCC touring side which included several players who had visited South Africa, and it also caused several British players to be banned from competing in tournaments in Africa. As a result, a number of prominent sportsmen renounced plans to visit South Africa.

Predictably, the issue aroused considerable controversy in the British and South African press. SAN-ROC was accused of using blackmail, although the list did no more than apply to individuals the same principles that had been applied to team sports for well over a decade. There is, after all, no *prima facie* reason why tennis players, golfers, boxers and other players of individual sports should be permitted to compete with South Africa when players of team sports are not — and no reason why cricketers who are banned from touring as a team should be allowed to play in South Africa as individuals. The list was, in effect, an answer to the attempts of South Africa's sports establishment to subvert the boycott by concentrating on individualistic and minority sports (golf, tennis, yachting, parachuting, motorboat racing etc.) which are out of the public eye and less easy to monitor. The list brought these exchanges to public notice and made individual players accountable for their decisions to play with South Africa — not only to governments and international sports associations, but to the public at large. In another sense, too, it gave a voice to individual sportsmen like Graham Mouie (the All Black captain) who refused to put their names forward for selection for the All Blacks team to play the Springboks in New Zealand because of their opposition to apartheid.

Finally, the personal sacrifices and the efforts made by New Zealanders to stop the Springbok tour of New Zealand were an outstanding statement of solidarity with the non-racial sports movement in South Africa. The nations of the Commonwealth may decide to exclude New Zealand from the Commonwealth Games which are to be held in Australia in 1981. In time, the member nations of the United Nations may also vote to extend sporting sanctions to cover all countries which continue to play sport with South Africa. These would be important political contributions, and greatly increase the real isolation of South African official sporting bodies. Initiatives at this level of political action are essential to force changes in South Africa. But they are abstract: the decisions reached emerge by institutionalised processes which have no obvious connection with the daily discrimination and exploitation experienced by black South Africans. Nothing could surely convey a simpler or stronger sense of international sympathy and commitment to their cause than the anger and frustration of the thousands of New Zealanders who demonstrated against the Springbok tour. It is difficult from abroad to have any idea of how much non-racial sportsmen and women in South Africa were heartened by the sight of demonstrators swarming onto that rugby pitch at Hamilton and bringing the match to a halt. It means they are not alone.

References

1 British Sports Council, 1980, p. 2.
2. *Guardian*, 3 April 1981.
3. For a summary, see Luke Traynor, 'The Primacy of Internal Policy: National Sport and External Relations 1975-78', in *Political Science*, University of Canterbury, Vol. 30, No. 2, pp. 63-78.
4. For a pictorial description of the tour, see Tom Newnham, 1981.
5. South African Catholic Bishops' Conference, press release, 1 May 1981.

13. Conclusions

South Africa is unusual and perhaps unique in that sport has become the object of civic struggle in the name of social justice, involving not just players, but the whole population; the full weight of State institutions has been brought into play, as if the survival of the social system was in question, and all sportsmen and women inevitably on one side or the other of a racial and political divide imposed by apartheid; sport is, both rightly and wrongly, held up as a mirror to society. It is for the reader to make up his or her mind about where to stand in relation to the issue. In this closing chapter, we will attempt to evaluate the issues involved and examine the likelihood of future change.

How well does the strategy of the non-racial movement under SACOS meet the challenge of Government policies and the white or 'multi-national' sports federations? Or, put another way, what contribution does the non-racial sports movement make to South African sport and to the aims of South African sportsmen and women? Or to the liberation of the South African people from apartheid? The questions are political; preceding chapter have shown that 'sporting' and 'political' questions join early in South Africa. We have judged apartheid; how do the decisions and actions taken by SACOS and the non-racial sports movement stand up to critical examination?

We cannot answer this last question without first estimating what sort of contribution sport *can* make. All but the most fanatical sportsmen would probably agree that sport is not central to South African politics, or to the liberation of the country from apartheid. But this does not render it marginal Sport certainly influences the regime's international relations. The State promotes sport to reduce the country's political isolation, with hard cash and sales methods on a scale first revealed during the Muldergate scandal. Reintegration into world sport is a priority for the Government as well as for official sports federations.

Sport is also part of the 'South African Way of Life'. The ruling Nationalist Party seeks to satisfy the expectations of its all-white electorate; and since these conflict with the interests of the black majority, sport has naturally become a domestic political issue. Moreover, because the central issue of the sports dispute is the central issue of apartheid, it has been difficult to suppress it. It is no coincidence that the two principal parties to the dispute, the Nationalist Party and SACOS, both agree that the future of sport cannot be separated from the culture of South African society as a whole. Indeed, it is partly because they share this belief that they *are* the principals.

Nevertheless, the relation is neither direct nor immediately apparent. The sports issue is bound up with the fundamental issues of apartheid society only for those whose policies make claims on the future of sport. Sport and sporting policy *is* marginal in that relatively few Africans play sport, which means that even if sport were completely 'integrated' under apartheid, it would have little effect upon the well-being of the majority, who would still be confined to the compounds, townships and bantustans. The links between sporting rights and other social rights become evident in everyday terms, in fact, only in a system as totalitarian, as encompassing, as apartheid. The socio-economic and political assumptions which make sport an inherently political problem only become apparent when the sports issue is seen as part of a socio-political credo, of an anti-apartheid or non-racial programme. It is in these terms that sport has become an issue of relative significance.

(handwritten: NOT POSSIBLE)

The present Government's sports strategy can be summarized under three headings:

(1) Pursuit of the Bantustan Policy: The 'multi-national' policy is designed to create a South Africa composed of nine 'nations'. Eight of these are to be 'African', the population of each is to be smaller than that of the ninth — 'white' — nation. These African 'states' are to be provided with a basic sporting infrastructure, which will theoretically be managed autonomously but in practice will remain under white control. In all the 'independent' bantustans the sports stadium has been one of the first public buildings to be constructed; indeed it has frequently been almost the only one, apart from the President's residence. Upon 'independence', matches against teams from other parts of South Africa become, by a stroke of the pen, 'international'.

(2) Resolution of the Problem of Urban Blacks: A high proportion of the African population will nevertheless continue to work or reside in white areas, alongside the black minorities. Recognizing the importance of sport for this population, the 'multi-national' sports policy authorizes matches between races, subject to permit, and presents them abroad as 'multi-racial'. In addition the policy seeks to:

(a) Improve sports facilities but reserve them for use by black associations which respect official policy. Officially promoted sport is intended to reduce political tension among Blacks in the cities and at the same time isolate dissident sportsmen and women in the non-racial movement. The provision of better facilities will also improve the status and authority of black sports officials working in the 'multi-national' federations.

(b) Create federated structures ('multi-national confederations') of separate 'national' White, Indian, Coloured and African sports federations, whose representatives sit together on a single executive board. The 'independent' sports associations of the bantustans will not of course be included on these bodies. Black federations have until now generally been affiliated on the same

303

footing as provincial white associations, thereby preserving white authority. Abroad, these confederations are said to be fully integrated.

(c) Encourage the development of a small black sporting elite, active in top class or professional sport, which will be exempt from segregation. Like the black political and business elite, black stars and sports administrators will provide favourable publicity abroad for the Government, and weaken the non-racial movement at home. At the same time, promotion of a black elite will accelerate professionalism, commercial sponsorship, media coverage of sport, etc.

(3) Efface Government Interference in Sport: To convince international opinion that South African sport is prepared to integrate racially, the autonomy of sports bodies has been 'guaranteed' by the Government, which claims that it will not interfere with sport except to maintain public order and uphold overall policy (i.e. apartheid). Associations of different races may therefore establish links with one another, provided they respect the laws regarding segregation and the permit system (which suspends those laws for the duration of approved 'mixed' matches).

'Reforms' and all, the sports policy is wholly compatible with the general policy of the regime. Under P.W. Botha, who acceded to power in 1978, 'separate development' — bantustanization or apartheid — remains the key principle; it has simply been sweetened for public consumption. According to Botha's Government, in fact, the sports issue no longer exists, for the terms of 'multi-nationalism' have resolved it once and for all. The rest is futile agitation. [1] The sports policy is designed to efface 'petty' apartheid, without undermining the efficient, organized exploitation and repression of the black majority by the white minority, through the reserves, the so-called 'national states'. It is necessary to restate this point because the South African Government's recent propaganda argues that apartheid is disappearing — and that the organization of mixed sports competitions is proof of its demise. Nothing could be further from the truth: where purely social features of apartheid are being suppressed, it is precisely in order to reinforce the system as a whole.

Moreover, the degree of change, even in social activities like sport, is admitted to be strictly limited. This can be seen clearly in the programme of the official opposition party, the P.F.P., which would accord certain civil rights to Indians, Coloureds and the urban African elite, but would continue to keep the great majority of Africans in the reserves. Bantustans would no longer be pseudo-independent, they would be associated with the white State in a federal structure: but they would nonetheless remain in existence. The African proletariat would have South African citizenship, would be able to own property and join a trade union; but they would not all have a vote, which would be subject to property qualifications. Both these reforms and the policies of Botha's Government display a willingness to consider the rights of a small minority of skilled African workers and to alleviate the humiliation of 'petty' apartheid. They differ over 'multi-nationalism' and the bantustans, for here the Nationalist Party remains intransigent. As P.W.

Botha has repeated: 'A government formed by the National Party and with myself [as head] will never admit a unitary State with a vote for all. . . . We reject it, for that would lead to confrontation and a struggle for power and end in a black dictatorship . . . . I am not in favour of models based on consensus or on federations.' [2] The principal effect of the liberal policies of the P.F.P. would be to accentuate class differences within the oppressed majority. This in turn would weaken resistance to apartheid and make it easier to exploit the black work-force. As for the reforms of the present Nationalist Government, sometimes presented as the beginning of the end of apartheid, they promote the development, within strictly defined limits, of a small black middle class. This group is to be awarded certain privileges, in the hope that it will dissociate itself from the mass of African workers, who are to be subjected to an ever greater degree of control and restrictions. The Wiehahn and Riekert Reports (1980) on trade unionism and black city dwellers respectively, have clearly indicated the sort of 'mix' which is intended. Neither the Nationalist Party nor the P.F.P. are prepared to countenance a democratic solution affording all South Africans the same rights.

As for sport, nowhere has the Nationalist Party argued that sporting activity should be organized on fully non-racial lines. The permit system may be adjusted, 'petty' segregation reduced (thereby widening the gap between Indians and Coloureds and a small African elite, and the mass of the African population) but the rules according to which sport is to be organized are to remain 'multi-national', in other words based upon the concept of 'separate development'. P.F.P. alternatives, founded upon the principle of sporting autonomy, would provide little redress for Black sportsmen suffering from discrimination, and might, as we have seen, actually disadvantage them further in the long term.

Government policy and the actions of official sports bodies tend to divide black sportsmen and women in terms of *race* — through the 'multi-national' policy — and in terms of *class*, by promotion of a small sporting elite drawn from the black urban petty bourgeoisie. Official policy assumes that this elite will, to an increasing extent, share the management of federated sports structures which will remain separate at local level, although top-class games and certain national administrative services will be integrated. South African sport will show its 'multi-racial' face to the outside world, while at home private segregated clubs will be free to organize 'as they choose'; in this way the pre-eminence of white associations will be guaranteed, and the laws of 'separate development' respected.

The task facing SACOS is therefore by no means easy, particularly because in certain countries (notably in the West) and in certain sports (notably rugby), the official federations have partially succeeded in making headway against international criticism. Nevertheless, SACOS has undoubtedly had some international success. It opposes the interference of racial criteria in sport, and the discrimination in services which results, in the name of the rights of taxpayers to equal access to public services, and the rights of the individual to equal opportunity and equality before the law. As a sporting body, however,

SACOS also benefits specifically from the flagrant contradiction between the principles of world sport — the *idea* of sport as it is understood all over the world — and the ideology of apartheid. However sympathetic to white South Africa, no sports body or international forum can afford to express sympathy for sports apartheid.

SACO's principal weapon, however, continues to be the international boycott of South African sport, and the widespread indignation which sports apartheid arouses throughout the world. The boycott has proved to be the major, and many would say the only, influence for change which has had any effect upon the white sports establishment. This has been admitted even by those who most strenuously opposed it in the past, as well as by white sports officials. There is little doubt that the non-racial movement's ability to contest Government policy largely depends upon the level of international support and the maintenance and reinforcement of South Africa's isolation.

Wishing to create a sport free from all forms of racism including the racism inherent in 'multi-nationalism', concerned to defend the interests of the majority of sportsmen and women and potential sportsmen and women, particularly the young, SACOS has refused to separate sport from society as a whole, and rejected unconditionally the official sports policy. Its weaknesses however, have not been overlooked by the Government and the white sports establishment. They have made every attempt to prise Indian and Coloured sportsmen, who are in a position to defend their interests, from the mass of Africans, who in general are not. The future of SACOS, and its capacity to defend the sporting interests of *all* South Africans, will therefore depend upon its ability to attract urban Africans living permanently in white areas. The challenge of *unity* is the critical issue facing the non-racial movement in the coming decade. Let us therefore ask to what extent SACOS has shown proof of its willingness to meet this challenge.

The first thing to be said is that the non-racial principle itself promotes unity. It was among the factors which originally made it possible for black associations to co-operate and merge in the 1950s, and it remains a powerful restraint on sectarianism. Many sportsmen and women join SACOS affiliates precisely *because* they are non-racial, and in purely sporting terms non-racialism has assisted the growth of organized black sport and the establishment of correctly administered national sports bodies.

In this sense, non-racialism, far from being an abstraction, has shown itself to be a valuable and practical rule of organization for black sport. The more radical wing of the movement would go further and argue that the independent black sports movement should be *defined* in terms of its non-racial principle, in other words by its refusal to make concessions, or temporize with the official (racial) sports establishment.

This radical interpretation of non-racialism has not been universally accepted. A number of sports officials have defended a policy of guarded, self-interested co-operation, which would use the system to discredit and destroy it. This point of view was defended by SACOS's first President,

Norman Middleton, in 1975.

> I believe, gentlemen, that at least for the time being and particularly in the absence of any form of democracy in this country, that we must use all types of platforms created for us in this country. The difference being that we use these platforms on our own terms, as platforms of free expression, to confront and embarrass the whole system. I agree that anybody using these created platforms for his own ends and without exposing the situation has no right to claim or belong to any of our non-racial organizations . . . .
>
> I believe that SACOS under the present prevailing circumstances should summon all its lawful position in the struggle for non-racialism and that those involved in this struggle should use vigorously the legal platforms provided by the system.[3]

Middleton's strategy balanced complete rejection of 'multi-nationalism' and wholehearted support for the international boycott, against calculated exploitation of all forms of influence within and outside the system. He argued that unqualified application of 'pure' non-racialism would marginalize and impoverish the independent sports movement, whereas segregation and racism would collapse from within in time and given the right conditions, if sportsmen and women from all backgrounds could unite around their general non-racial ideals. In effect, Middleton was propounding the 'snowball' theory, today defended by officials like Mr Rashid Varachia, President of the official Cricket Union, who claims to be working from within the system to change it. 'If you nibble at the wall,' argued Varachia in 1979, 'it becomes weaker every year.'[4]

This view — which has many partisans, stretching from moderate non-racial sportsmen to the P.F.P., and including prominent sports officials from racial federations and from abroad — has two damning faults. The first is that there is really no evidence that collaboration has ever weakened segregation in South African sport whereas there is a good deal of support for the opposite view that non-cooperation and isolation have produced change. The second is that, in its crudest form, the 'bridge-building' and 'snowball' theory are contradictory, for they describe sport as an activity which is (or should be) at one and the same time *separate* from society ('sport not politics') and a potent influence for change *within* it. This is totally at odds with the SACOS slogan 'No Normal Sport in an Abnormal Society', which affirms that sport is neither independent of society nor a primary influence upon it.

Between 1975 and 1977, a gap opened between 'moderates' and the more radical majority within SACOS. The Soweto Revolt, Koornhof's definition of the 'multi-national' policy in 1976 and the crises in football and cricket successively hardened attitudes. Non-cooperation became explicitly associated with the idea of non-racial sport, comparable to support for the moratorium and opposition to 'multi-nationalism'. As a result the non-racial sports movement undoubtedly changed direction: SACOS affiliates no longer tried to compete with racial sports bodies, either literally or in organizational terms (in numbers, size, etc.). Opposition to apartheid and adherence to non-racial principles alone qualified a sports association to join the non-racial movement. Implicit in this approach was the idea that if players or clubs were lost along the road, this was to be seen as one of the necessary costs of upholding principles.

We have already discussed the major shortcoming of this 'unconditional' interpretation of non-racialism. It can be put quite simply. For those who can afford to do so, it is relatively easy to refuse to collaborate; Indian and Coloured sportsmen have successfully boycotted official sport for several decades. For many Africans, in contrast, non-cooperation means a complete end to their organized sport — and perhaps worse. It is, of course, this racial divide which Government policy is designed to widen.

One, therefore, has to ask whether the principle of non-collaboration, which has been the non-racial movement's most powerful weapon of defence, tends to divide rather than unite black sportsmen, and marginalize the movement by confining its membership to the black minorities. If so, unconditional applications of non-racial principles will merely reinforce the aims and strategy of the 'multi-national' policy, with potentially catastrophic implications for the non-racial movement. One could point to the football crises, which as we have seen, not only caused serious damage to the non-racial Federation but resulted in the wholesale loss of almost all African footballers to the racial African football body, which enclosed them within 'multi-national' structures.

Several remarks must be made here. The first is that there are no grounds for supposing (as interested critics have suggested) that the radicalization of SACOS policy is due to the authoritarian manipulation of the membership by a clique of officials. On the contrary, SACOS's capacity to function efficiently, and certainly its claims to represent the non-racial movement, depend upon the support, firstly, of its national affiliates and, secondly, of the general membership. Its radical swing in policy since 1976 reflects the feelings of non-racial sportsmen and women in South Africa: indeed, any policy of non-collaboration would be quite unworkable if the majority of the membership did not support it.

Secondly, the policy of non-collaboration must be seen in its context, for it is the fruit of long — and bitter — experience. In this respect, the history of sport runs alongside the general history of the struggle of black South Africans to free themselves from racial oppression. In both cases, other forms of recourse — negotiation, protest, critical co-operation — have one by one been frustrated or crushed by the authorities. Blacks have consistently been pressured to concede the principle of racial equality, over which they refuse to make concessions, before negotiations even begin. Many black South Africans, from many motives, have experimented in the past, have associated themselves with the various structures, multi-national or other, which have been marketed by the Government. Almost all of them have either been discredited or deceived. In cricket, a recent example, the vast majority of non-racial cricketers who left the SACOS affiliate to join the official SACU, returned to the S.A. Cricket Board after just one season.

Thirdly, it should not be forgotten that, if African sportsmen have no choice between collaborating or giving up sport altogether, responsibility does not lie with the non-racial movement, but with the white sports authorities, who have consistently blackmailed African associations into submission whenever they have claimed their rights. Indeed, white sports associations have begun to pay attention to African sport in the 1970s largely *because* the successes of the non-racial sports movement have forced them to do so. In the 1950s and 1960s, no interest at all was shown by white federations in African sport, at a time when the non-racial bodies were not only playing, but attempting to merge on equal terms, with their African counterparts. The threat of such mergers caused white associations to intervene to prise African federations away, and place them safely under white control, with associate and dependent status (Chapter 8); and then, under international pressure, to grant limited *material* concessions, in the form of training facilities, etc. (Chapter 11). Sport thus provides a good example of the positive effects which the pressure of international opinion can have *inside* South Africa, and an illustration of the marginal 'benefits' which can accrue to black federations from white reactions.

The successes of the international boycott should not be an excuse for complacency, however. For those who need reminding, the experience of the Black People's Sports Council in 1977 proved that sport is not sacrosanct, and that sports associations are not immune from repression, as some critics of SACOS have proclaimed. The Black People's Sports Council was formed by about one hundred lawyers, doctors and journalists associated with the Black Consciousness Movement who saw SACOS as too 'liberal'. Almost at once, the Council was banned by the Government and dissolved.[5] This confirms the argument that SACOS affiliates are protected from repression primarily by the level of international support which the non-racial movement has won for its policies over the last two decades. It also suggests that Africans are virtually precluded from setting up autonomous sports associations. Despite international support SACOS affiliates remain subject to extremely close surveillance and individual officials have to endure perpetual harassment, which drives some to resignation and hardens the obstinacy of others, like Morgan Naidoo or M.N. Pather, who have suffered real hardship in the course of their sporting duties.[6]

The problem is therefore highly complex. African sportsmen have benefited from the struggle waged by the non-racial movement for all sportsmen, primarily because the white associations have been forced into buying their allegiance. At the same time, some of the policies which SACOS has introduced to defend itself appear to drive African sportsmen and women into the arms of the Administration. Although it is certainly the African population which is first and foremost trapped in this vicious circle, to some degree it affects all sportsmen. The debate about how to apply non-racial principles diverges in two directions which are not easily reconcilable.

The first approach interprets non-racialism in its more limited, legalist sense. Its proponents are prepared to promote sporting activity which *multiplies* inter-racial contact because they believe this will eventually *dilute* the colour bar. In the short term, it is a strategy which undoubtedly encourages unity and can more easily take account of the specific handicaps faced by Africans. It assumes a more 'liberal' approach to change, cumulative in character — and was no doubt shared by some supporters of SACOS, like the P.F.P., who today oppose its policies, as well as by some non-racial sports officials like Norman Middleton.

The second approach represents current opinion within SACOS at the beginning of the 1980s. According to this view, the liberal approach puts at risk the *future* of non-racial sport, and wrongly equates the *issue* of non-racial sport with the *quantity* of multi-racial events. Such critics believe that the non-racial sports movement should identify itself with black unity, and eventually South African unity. In their view, the issue will not, and cannot be resolved on sports fields; unity will be forged, not in multi-racial matches, but by the experience of resisting apartheid in all areas of society, not just in sport. It is an approach which clearly gained ascendancy within SACOS after the Soweto Revolt of 1976 and its increasing influence is at least partly due to the rise of a new generation of young players and officials who are much less willing to compromise with official institutions of all kinds.

These remarks do not imply that the second group is any less interested in the strictly sporting interests of South Africans. On the contrary, those who support a non-cooperative approach would argue that it is irresponsible to support a national sports policy which entirely disregards the interests of all those who have no opportunity of playing sport of any kind, because they have no access to, or have been deprived of, pitches, facilities, training and equipment — not to speak of education, proper nourishment, freedom of movement, etc. They argue that it is the 'moderates' who do a disservice to sport, by perpetuating the belief that black sports officials who co-operate with official sports bodies can remedy the inequalities from which their members suffer even though they are not democratically represented either on sports councils or in Parliament.

These criticisms have a certain weight. Nevertheless, is it not still true that when the poor and disenfranchised refuse to co-operate with the rich and powerful, they simply make themselves poorer and weaker? By their own acts, don't they reinforce the privileges of those who oppress them? And if this is so, does not SACOS's refusal to collaborate, a policy which claims to defend the interests of the mass of sportsmen and women, in fact serve to promote the *class* interests of the minority of black sportsmen and women who can best afford to isolate themselves? Once again, we are confronted by the potential cleavage between the African majority and the small black elite which is disproportionately represented in organized sport and in black sports associations.

Alternatively, should one conclude that the uncompromising line of

SACOS reflects the faith of its members in the capacity of the African majority to throw off apartheid, in spite of the particular burden it imposes on them?

Certainly, we do not pretend in this book to be able to answer these questions — or the central issue of non-racial unity which they embody. They are deeply rooted in the past, and their solutions depend upon many factors outside the control of those who are today having to deal with them. We do believe, however, that one cannot mistake the sense which the majority of SACOS members and officials wish to give to their activity, and to non-racialism. Dominated by Indian and Coloured players and officials, deeply influenced by its urban roots and with a largely urban membership, the non-racial movement nevertheless represents the feelings of black sportsmen and women in South Africa and, to a degree, the aspirations of the black population as a whole. Its principles and its past record both justify SACOS's claim to represent black sportsmen and women and, eventually, South African sport in the future, when the country has been freed from apartheid.

Knowing the conditions under which Africans have to live, it is equally indefensible to argue that, because they take part in 'multi-national' or official sport, Africans condone it or the apartheid system, or have little sympathy for SACOS and the non-racial movement. The evidence runs the other way. In certain sports, notably rugby and tennis, increasing numbers of Africans are joining non-racial clubs at considerable risk and cost. At the beginning of the 1980s, SACOS was effectively advocating policies and ideals which matched, in sporting terms, the themes running through the history of black resistance to injustice and apartheid: non-racialism, non-collaboration, rejection of apartheid laws and racial exploitation. Silent the African majority may often be forced to be, but that does not imply that it has not reached an opinion.

The increased confidence and assertiveness which can be detected in the public statements of SACOS probably bear witness to this tacit support, and contrast sharply with the tone of the early 1970s. When Norman Middleton opened the first biennial conference in 1975, he appealed to members to stand firm. 'We are living in a bedevilled and troubled time,' he said, 'when the forces of suppression, hatred and personality rise like tidal waves about the shores of justice . . . . I have no fear about the struggle of our non-racial organizations, even if our motive is at present misunderstood. Abused and scorned by those that do not agree with us, our destiny is nevertheless tied up with the rest of the world.'[7] In 1977, Hassan Howa was far more abrasive when he spoke of 'the numerous dishonest and insincere strategists of Racist sports bodies and Racist authorities' and of 'the concept of Multi-National sport with its inquisitious use of stooges and renegades in an attempt to hoodwink the reporting world.'[8]

In 1979, the tone was firmer still:

> We are told 'Do not mix politics with Sport'. We wish to remind those people who shout the loudest that . . . we are committed to remove

311

politics from sport. Those that wish to retain politics in sport must certainly be racist. We do not need them in our circle.

I am not opposed to dialogue and I have been always prepared to listen to the other's point of view. But I shall not be dictated to by persons or organizations that offer an ideology other than non-racialism. I will not accept subservient membership or consider associate levels. Any form of membership based on ethnic lines will not be tolerated by this organization. I will welcome a policy in the interest of all South Africans without sacrificing the essence of non-racialism. . . .

In conclusion, I wish to state that our struggle is an uphill battle. Numberwise we are very strong. We have the backing of all disenfranchised people. Naturally we cannot be weak. But we do not have sufficient funds, sponsorships and the various other things that could make our organization, *the organization* . . . . We are not alone in this struggle — equality for all in sport. World support . . . is forever mounting.

We can only win. And we must.[9]

Certainly, SACOS officials assert that it is impossible to practise truly non-racial sport under apartheid; here they are nevertheless adopting the tone and responsibilities of an organization which claims to represent black, indeed South African, sport. It does so not out of bravado or abstract radicalism, as its critics argue, but because its non-racial principles *can*, in fact, unite the oppressed population of South Africa and all sportsmen and women. 'No normal sport in an abnormal society' is neither the 'recipe for conflict, for bitterness, etc,' denounced by the P.F.P., nor a piece of theatre: it condenses into one phrase SACOS's refusal to restrict its action to the narrow interests of its own members, and proclaims the willingness of non-racial sportsmen to speak for the silent majority of black South Africans, whose conditions of life are such that they cannot play sport. Put another way, SACOS may be described as an anti-apartheid organization which, in the name of all South Africans, seeks to free sport from institutionalized racism, and to create the conditions for a non-racial alternative.

The political ambiguities inherent in its policies do not of course disappear if SACOS is described in this manner. The non-racial movement must still prove in the course of events, in action, that it is willing to improve life and sport for the population as a whole. Above all, it must still prove that it is able to promote black unity. Only when the non-racial movement has won the support of all sections of the black population will it be able to claim justly that it is representative, or potentially non-racial. In saying this, we do not imply censure or judgement; the difficulties and risks inherent in any attempt to defend non-racial values in South Africa are all too evident. Without unity, however, SACOS cannot fulfil the role, or programme, which it has set for itself, and the non-racial movement will remain a minority movement.

The political delicacy of its position is evident from another angle, for

SACOS has all the strengths, but also the weaknesses, of 'popular front' organizations. It is supported by all strata of urban society, from the factory worker who is a keen footballer, to the tennis-playing lawyer or businessman. Non-racial sport also has a rare capacity to excite popular sympathy in all social groups, within a single broad-based organization and around a general principle of very wide application. The non-racial sports movement has been remarkably free from political sectarianism: people from all political and non-political backgrounds contribute to its campaigns, from the A.N.C. to the Unity Movement, and Black Consciousness to the Coloured Labour Party or the Indian Congress. In this respect, SACOS's membership is almost unique.

However, when the social background of most sports officials is combined with the 'spolitical' ideology of sport, it is necessary to face the risk that a movement like SACOS may come to serve the interests of a minority. The Double Standards Resolution is an attempt to safeguard the movement against certain forms of compromise, but (as we have seen) it may be used to promote, in other circumstances, the interests of those who can afford not to collude. After all, no resolution can efface differences of class interest between groups or communities. On a more political level, the unifying energy of the non-racial principle itself might also come to be substituted for political reflection; the movement might be tempted, in the name of unity, to avoid divisive issues and settle politically for the area of common ground. In such a case, resounding principles would tend to conceal an absence of political content, and the ideal of non-racialism would again tend to provide an alibi to the black elite, which will continue, no doubt, to run national sports associations.

These are not insuperable obstacles, however. The greatest limitation upon SACOS and upon any non-racial sports organization is imposed by its function. As we have seen, sport is historically associated with urbanization, education and a relatively prosperous section of society. SACOS is a sporting organization, and therefore *necessarily* issues from a minority of the population. Even if, as we believe, SACOS's ideals and policies express the aspirations of the majority of black South Africans, its role and function inevitably reduce its focus and its mandate. In this sense, SACOS represents its membership, relatively privileged (but still oppressed) minority of sportsmen whose claims and interests are not identical with those of all the black population. This gap between the *aspirations* of the black majority and the *interests* of the (non-racial) sporting minority, corresponds precisely with what we have called the 'non-racial space' — that crucial area, both sporting and political, over which SACOS and the 'multi-national' federations dispute possession.

Political organizations opposed to apartheid speak first and above all of the bantustans, of the racial exploitation of African labour, of the denial of fundamental human rights to the African population, of the grossly unjust distribution of land: these are the fundamental issues raised by apartheid. In contrast, SACOS, as an anti-apartheid *sports* organization, is led to give priority to the laws of apartheid, and particularly to the laws affecting *all racial groups* in *urban areas* (the Group Area Act, Reservation of Separate Amenities Act etc.). The character of the sports issue and the ideology of sport cause non-racial sportsmen to campaign around citizens' legal rights — freedom of movement, equal access to public facilities, unencumbered social intercourse, etc. It is extremely difficult for them to speak for those who have lost or are about to lose, their citizenship altogether, who are not just discriminated against but banished from the towns, and forced to live quite outside the *jurisdiction* of 'South African' Law, in the bantustans. However lucid and critical they may be, because of the nature of the organizations for which they are responsible, non-racial sports, officials *cannot* address themselves to the fundamental political issues upon which all others, including sport, eventually depend.

This banal conclusion, that sport is not capable of provoking changes which can transform society, is not without consequences. For one thing, it leads us to reject once and for all the various 'nibbling', 'bridge-building' and 'snowballing' arguments. To believe that small changes on the sports field will gradually transform the entire system, or that the spread of multi-racial sports teams will dissolve or destroy segregation, not only underestimates the resources and character of apartheid, but surrenders abjectly to the illusion that, because the sports issue provokes social agitation, it lies at the heart of South African society. Bridge-building has proved to be a one-way traffic, which has always served in the past to delay change. This is not a book about the international sports campaign. We would like to end, however, by remembering that those who have given up so much to achieve non-racialism in South African sport are able to campaign with relative freedom because South Africa is isolated in most of the major sports. In no other area has South Africa been isolated to anything like the same extent, and those who campaign against apartheid outside sport (in trade unions, education, for political rights) suffer far more violent repression. Since the 1960s, very large numbers of people all over the world, individually and from within organizations, have given remarkable and moving support to South Africans in the non-racial sports movement. Their concern and anger, their protests and boycotts, have not just discomfited the Government and the official sports establishments, but certainly protected many South African sportsmen from harassment and arrest. For this reason alone South African sport should remain isolated. But a further contribution could be made by all those who despise apartheid, by lobbying in favour of international recognition for the non-racial sports associations. If these were granted associate status by their international bodies — as SACOS is an associate member of the Supreme Council for Sport in Africa, and as the S.A. Table Tennis and Darts Boards of Control are respectively members of the I.T.T. and the World Darts Federation — the strength of the non-racial sports movement would be greatly enhanced, and an important, if modest, advance would be made in the general struggle of the people of South Africa to liberate themselves from apartheid.

Certainly it is true that sport will not free South Africa from racialism;

it is also true that sport cannot be played non-racially while apartheid is enforced. But if we wish seriously to support the struggle against apartheid, we cannot pretend to do so by ignoring the appeals of those within South Africa who are today struggling in the most difficult circumstances, for freedom, and for freedom in sport. *They* have called upon the outside world to boycott South African sport; as sportsmen, they have voluntarily isolated themselves. Isolating South Africa is therefore an act of solidarity with the peaceful resistance of non-racial sportsmen and women to an inhuman system. Within a society of stark repression and acute tension, the non-racial sports movement remains one of the few national organizations in South Africa which is able to speak out publicly, not only for South Africa's sportsmen and women, but for all black South Africans. Can we remain deaf?

Robert Archer and Antoine Bouillon.
1982

References

1. 'While the bear (USSR) is at our door, there are still people who quarrel about the Immorality Act and Sport'. Prime Minister Botha, 8 March 1980, in the Cape. (translated from French).
2. *Le Monde*, 11 March 1980 (translated from the French).
3. President's address, SACOS, 1975, pp. 10-11.
4. *Sunday Post,* 14 October 1979.
5. S.A.I.R.R. *Survey* 1977, p. 558, and 1978, p. 487.
6. The homes of several SACOS officials, including Mr Naidoo and Mr Pather have also been attacked, presumably by right-wing white vigilantes.
7. SACOS, 1975, p. 11.
8. SACOS, 1977, p. 25.
9. SACOS, Report of the Third Biennial Conference, 1979, pp. 31-2.

Chronology of South African Sporting History

Dates	Political Events	Sporting Events
1497	Vasco de Gama rounds Cape of Good Hope.	
1648	The Haarlem, belonging to Dutch East India Co., shipwrecked off Cape; crew remain on land for a year. Van Riebeeck lands at Cape with 100 men.	
1652		Importation of the first horses.
1658	Importation of first slaves.	
1667-1744	Importation of Malay slaves.	
1685	Whites forbidden to marry their slaves.	
1688	Huguenots arrive from France.	
1702	First clashes with Xhosa.	
1717	White immigration forbidden. Mixed marriages banned.	
1779	First 'Kaffir War'.	
1789	Second 'Kaffir War'.	
1795-1802	First British Occupation of Cape.	First horse races; foundation of first horseracing club (1802)
1799-1803	Third 'Kaffir War'	Cricket starts. Thoroughbred horses imported
1803	Arrival of LMS missionaries.	
1806	Second and final British Occupation of the Cape.	
1807	Slave trade banned.	
1808		First recorded cricket match, 5 January.

Dates	Political Events	Sporting Events
1811-12	Fourth 'Kaffir War'.	
1814	Britain annexes Cape.	
1818-19	Fifth 'Kaffir War'.	
1834	Abolition of slavery.	
1834-39	Great Trek begins; Natal and then Transvaal are settled; the first African reserve is established. Sixth 'Kaffir War'.	
1838	Battle of Blood River.	
1842	Natal annexed by Britain.	
1853		Pietermaritzburg Cricket Club.
1854	Boer independence beyond Orange River recognized.	Hottentot-Boer cricket match.
1856	Constitution promulgated in Transvaal.	
1860	First Indian labour migrants arrive.	
1862		Rugby-Football appears.
1867	Diamonds discovered.	
1868	Basutoland (Lesotho) declared a British protectorate.	
1872	Self-government accorded to Cape Colony.	
1876		First rugby club established (Cape). First Coloured and African cricket clubs (Kimberley, Port Elizabeth).
1877	British occupation of Transvaal.	
1879	British victory over Zulus.	First football club (Pietermaritzburg).
1880-81	First Anglo-Boer War.	First athletics club (Port Elizabeth).
1881		First cycling club (Port Elizabeth).
1882		First tennis (Natal), golf (Cape), horseracing (Port Elizabeth), bowls (Port Elizabeth), professional boxing and croquet clubs.

317

Dates	Political Events	Sporting Events
1884	Bechuanaland (Botswana) and Swaziland become British protectorates.	
1886	Gold discovered on Witwatersrand.	
1888-89		First British cricket tour — Currie Cup. First gymnastics club (Johannesburg). Formation of white rugby federation (SARB). First Coloured cricket tour.
1890	Rhodes becomes Prime Minister	White cricket federation formed (SACA). Newlands stadium opened in Cape for rugby and cricket.
1892		The M.C.C. plays a Malay cricket XVIII Formation of the white football federation (FASA). Inauguration of Currie Cup (rugby). Formation of the white athletics association.
1896	Introduction of first colour bar laws.	Formation of first black rugby federation (SACRFB).
1899-1902	Second Anglo-Boer War.	White swimming federation formed. Rugby match played between the two armies (29 April 190 Coloured cricket federation formed (SACCB).
1903		White tennis federation forme
1904		White bowling federation formed.
1906	Last 'Kaffir War'.	
1908		White Olympic Committee formed (SAOEGA); South Africa participates for first time in Olympic Games.
1909	National Education Policy passed — free school equipment for white State schools.	White golf federation formed
1910	Union of South Africa created; Botha becomes Prime Minister.	

318

Dates	Political Events	Sporting Events
1911	Mines and Works Act includes colour bar provisions.	
1912	A.N.C. formed.	
1913	Native Land Act passed. White miners strike on Rand. Free compulsory education introduced for Whites. Indian immigration banned.	
1914	Afrikaner National Party formed.	
1918	Broederbond formed.	
1919	Smuts becomes Prime Minister.	
1922	Major strikes on Rand.	
1923	Native Urban Areas Act passed.	White hockey federation formed.
1924	Hertzog becomes Prime Minister.	
1927	Native Administration Act passed.	
1926	Afrikaans becomes second official language.	
1928		White rifle-shooting federation formed.
1931		White motor-racing association formed.
1933		White basketball federation formed.
1934	Malan founds new purified Afrikaner National Party.	
1936	Native Trust & Land Act passed; Native Representative Councils created.	
1938	The Oxwagon Trek. The Institute of National Christian Education defines Afrikaner education policy.	Introduction of a national physical education programme.
1939	Smuts becomes Prime Minister; United Party comes to power.	
1940		White jukskei federation formed.

Dates	Political Events	Sporting Events
1943	The word 'apartheid' appears for first time, in *Die Burger*.	
1946	Strikes of black miners.	The Non-Racial Table Tennis Board recognized by the international body. Multi-racial cricket association formed (SACBOC).
1948	National Party elected; Malan becomes Prime Minister.	
1949	Mixed marriages declared illegal.	
1950	Population Registration Act and Group Areas Act passed. Introduction of anti-Communist legislation.	
1951	African tribal authorities are created	Multi-racial football federation created (SASF).
1952	ANC organizes passive resistance campaigns to pass laws.	
1953	Reservation of Separate Amenities Act passed. Government powers of repression increased.	
1954	Strijdom becomes Prime Minister.	
1955	Congress of the People adopts Freedom Charter.	Blacks excluded from new Bloemfontein stadium.
1956	Extension of the Urban Areas Act.	Non-Racial Table Tennis Board accorded exclusive recognition by the international federation. Several black federations demand international recognition. Official sports policy is defined for the first time.
1957	Native Laws Amendment Act passed.	
1958	Verwoerd becomes Prime Minister.	South African Sports Association (SASA) formed.
1959	Segregation of university education. Bantu Education Department created. Bantustans granted 'self-government'.	Inaugural conference of SASA, which runs its first campaigns. Passports refused to non-racial sportsmen (table-tennis, football).

Dates	Political Events	Sporting Events
1960	Sharpeville massacre; A.N.C. and P.A.C. banned and go underground; they declare armed resistance.	Black federations make transsition towards non-racialism (1959-62). Several black federations affiliate with dependent status to white federations.
1961	South Africa becomes Republic and leaves Commonwealth.	
1962	Transkei becomes 'self-governing'.	Albert Luthuli calls for boycott of racist sport. White judo and trampoline federations formed. SASF (football) and SACBOC (cricket) become non-racial; non-racial tennis union (SALTU) is formed. Formation of the South African Non-Racial Olympic Committee (SAN-ROC).
1963	Liquor Amendment Act passed. Rivonia Trial of leaders of A.N.C.	
1964		South Africa excluded from Olympic Games. SASA and SAN-ROC leaders harassed. Formation of white bodybuilding and white surf-riding federations.
1965	Extension of Group Areas Act; Proclamation R.26.	Verwoerd refuses visas to Maoris.
1966	Verwoerd assassinated; Vorster becomes Prime Minister.	SAN-ROC regroups in exile. Formation of non-racial swimming federation (SAASwiF). Minister of Sport & Recreation appointed. South Africa is excluded from Olympic Games. The Basil d'Oliveira Affair (cricket). Formation of white karate association.
1969	S.A.S.O. formed; growth of the Black Consciousness movement.	

321

Dates	Political Events	Sporting Events
1970	The 'Multi-national' policy declared. Bantustans offered 'independence'.	South Africa expelled from Olympic Movement; and excluded from most major sports. The Second South African Games take place. The South African Non-Racial Sports Organization formed (SASPO).
1971		The 'multi-national' policy introduced in sport; Dr Koornhof becomes Minister of Sport; SACOS formed.
1973	Extension of Group Areas Act; Proclamation R.228.	The Third South African Games take place.
1976	The Soweto riots. Transkei becomed 'independent'.	The 'multi-national' sports policy by Dr Koornhof (September). The first 'multi-national' confederations formed. The African tennis federation leaves white association.
1977	Steve Biko assassinated; Black Consciousness organisations banned.	'Multi-national' confederation formed in football. Multi-racial cricket federation formed.
1978	Muldergate — President Vorster resigns and P.W. Botha becomes Prime Minister. Bophuthatswana becomes 'independent'.	'Multi-national' confederation formed in rugby. De Klerk appointed Minister of Sport.
1979	Venda becomes 'independent'.	New non-racial tennis federation formed (TASA). Non-racial golf federation formed (SANRAGA). Janson appointed Minister of Sport and Ministry becomes responsible for sport in all communities.
1980	Schools boycott by Indian and Coloured schoolchildren	The British Lions tour South Africa (rugby). Publication of the Human Sciences Research Council's report on sport.

Dates	Political Events	Sporting Events
1981		Ireland tours South Africa (rugby). The Springboks tour New Zealand (rugby).

Appendices

Appendix 1: Basic Population Statistics

(1) The South African Population, 1904-80

Year	Africans	Coloureds	Indians	Whites	Total
1904	3,490,000	445,000	122,000	1,117,000	5,175,000
1921	4,697,000	545,000	164,000	1,521,000	6,927,000
1936	6,596,000	769,000	220,000	2,003,000	9,588,000
1946	7,830,000	928,000	285,000	2,372,000	11,416,000
1960	10,928,000	1,509,000	477,000	3,080,000	15,994,000
1970	15,340,000	2,051,000	630,000	3,773,000	21,794,000
1975	18,136,000	2,368,000	727,000	4,240,000	25,471,000
1980 (estimate)	22,500,000	3,000,000	880,000	4,400,000	30,780,000
In % (1977)	71.9%	9.0%	2.8%	16.2%	100%

(2) The Population by Province, 1904, 1970 (%)

	Africans		Coloureds		Indians		Whites	
	1904	1970	1904	1970	1904	1970	1904	1970
Cape Province	40.8%	25.4%	88.7%	87.3%	8.2%	3.5%	51.9%	29.7%
Natal	25.9	21.4	1.6	3.4	82.8	83.5	8.7	11.7
Transvaal	26.8	44.0	5.4	7.5	9.0	13.0	26.6	50.6
Orange Free State	0.0	9.2	4.3	1.8	—	0.0	12.8	8.0
Total	100	100	100	100	100	100	100	100

(3) Urban Population Growth, 1921, 1960, 1970

	Africans	Coloureds	Indians	Whites	Total
Johannesburg*					
1921	622,831	56,951	27,069	153,544	290,196
1960	809,595	82,639	39,348	389,690	1,096,541
1970				501,061	1,432,643
Cape Town					
1921	65,625	365,475	9,134	117,027	220,502
1960	107,877	598,952	11,263	278,555	718,189
1970				378,505	1,096,527
Durban					
1921	204,071	25,638	231,385	61,098	168,743
1960	224,819	43,699	317,029	194,276	655,370
1970				257,780	843,327
Pretoria					
1921	202,359	7,225	7,805	45,590	74,347
1960	234,695	11,343	11,047	202,664	420,053
1970				304,618	561,703
Port Elizabeth					
1921	n.a.	n.a.	4,265	26,236	52,753
1960	111,651	60,914	5,280	94,085	270,815
1970	202,334	112,260		149,574	468,577

Note: The whole Witwatersrand conurbation in the Southern Transvaal has a population nearly twice that of Johannesburg.

(4) Relative Urbanization by Group, 1904-1970 (%)

	Africans	Coloureds	Indians	Whites
1904	10.4%	49.2%	36.5%	53.6%
1921	14.0	52.4	60.4	59.7
1936	19.0	58.0	69.5	68.2
1946	24.3	62.5	72.8	75.6
1960	31.8	68.3	83.2	83.6
1970	33.0	74.1	86.7	86.8

Appendix 2: The South African Government's Official 'Multi-national' Sports Policy

In September 1976, Dr P.G.H. Koornhof, Minister of Sport, announced the basis of 'multi-national' sport which remains Government policy to this day.

The federal council accept that, taking into account the applicable legislation and regulations, the interests of South Africa and all its people in respect of sport can best be served in terms of the following policy:

(1) That white, Coloured, Indian and black sportsmen and women should all belong to their own clubs and that each should control, arrange and manage its own sporting fixtures;

(2) That wherever possible, practical and desirable, the committees or councils of the different race groups should consult together or have such contact as would advance the interests of the sport concerned;

(3) That intergroup competition in respect of individual types of sport be allowed at all levels, should the controlling bodies so decide;

(4) That in respect of team sports, the councils or committees of each racial group should arrange their own leagues or programmes within the racial group;

(5) That where mutually agreed, councils or committees may, in consultation with the Minister of Sport, arrange leagues or matches enabling teams from different racial groups to compete;

(6) That each racial group should arrange its own sporting relationships with other countries or sporting bodies in accordance with its own wishes and that each should award its own badges and colours;

(7) That if and when invited or agreed, teams comprising players from all racial groups can represent South Africa, irrespective of whether the type of sport is an Olympic sport or not, and that such participants can be awarded badges or colours which, if so desired, can incorporate the national flag or its colours;

(8) That attendance at sporting fixtures be arranged by the controlling bodies.

Appendix 3 : SACOS Sports Policies

1) Aims and Objects

The objects of the Council are:

) To foster a spirit of goodwill, equality and fraternity among all people, without any discrimination whatever on the grounds of race, colour or creed, and further carry out the provisions of the Statutes of IOC and other International Bodies controlling sport in the world and also to prevent racial, colour, religious or political discrimination among sportsmen.
•) To assist a member of this Council to affiliate to International Bodies controlling their particular branch of Sport.
) To foster friendly relations among the National Associations, Officials and Players in the Republic of South Africa and overseas.
l) To assist affiliated members of the Council to promote, control and administer their particular branch of sport in keeping with the rules and principles laid down by the International Bodies.

Extract from SACOS Constitution

2) On 'Multi-nationalism'

l) We reaffirm the Resolution passed at the inaugural Conference in 1973, that merit selection is possible only if all participants in sporting events are able to compete with each other freely at all levels, and the call made at that Conference to sporting organisations to reject any system or scheme which does not offer equal opportunity, equal facilities, equal training and equal experience at all levels.
l) Confirms our assessment in 1973 that the system of multi-national sports events which has been offered as a substitute for non-racial sport was a negation of the principles of non-discrimination in sport and congratulates those organisations which refuse to participate in same, thereby exposing to the world at large the farcical nature of these events. This meeting calls on those few sporting bodies which insist on participating in such events to accept that by continuing to do so, they are perpetuating racism in sport and delaying the entry of all sportsmen, irrespective of colour, caste and creed, into international competition and asks them to forthwith desist from continuing to participate in same.

Resolutions 1 and 2, SACOS First Biennial Conference, 1975.

3) On the Moratorium on Sports Contacts with South Africa

SACOS, in a declaration of its solidarity with the Supreme Council for Sport in Africa, hereby rejects all forms of racialism and discrimination in sport, condemns all stooges of apartheid and accepts a complete moratorium on all sports tours to and from South Africa until all the laws and institutions of apartheid have been removed from South African Sport.

Resolution 2, Third Biennial Conference, 1979.

4) On Sponsorship

We condemn those business organisations that sponsor and actively assist the continuation of racially orientated sports bodies and deny assistance to those bodies which stand for and campaign for the participation in sports on a non-racial basis.

Resolution 3, First Biennial Conference, 1975.

(5) On Double Standards

a) Any person, whether he is a player, an administrator or a spectator, committed to the non-racial principle in sport, shall not participate in or be associated with any other codes of sport which practise, perpetuate or condone racialism or multi-nationalism.

Players and/or administrators disregarding the essence of this principle shall be guilty of practising double standards, and cannot therefore be members of any organisation affiliated to SACOS.

Statement on Double Standards issued on 6 April 1977.

b) The South African Council on Sport (SACOS) shall have the power to suspend, expel, fine or otherwise deal with any official, member or affiliate guilty of a breach of the rules, aims and/or objects of SACOS, and/or guilty of any conduct which is adjudged by the Council of SACOS and/or a committee appointed by it, to be prejudicial to the aims and/or the objects of SACOS:

Without prejudice to the generality of the aforegoing, conduct which may be adjudged prejudicial to the aims and/or objects of SACOS may include:

Cooperation with or support of any person or body of persons which, in the opinion of the Council and/or committee appointed by it, pursues a policy inconsistent with the policy of non-racialism enunciated by the SACOS.

Resolution of General Meeting of SACOS, October 1978.

c) No member of SACOS shall in any way condone, encourage, foster or advocate racialism or discrimination in any form and no individual associated with SACOS, or its members, shall in any way condone, encourage, foster, advocate racialism or discrimination in any way whatsoever, and for the purpose of this clause, the participation in association with, or support of all forms of government bodies designed to entrench and/or promote the separateness of people via bodies such as 'the Coloured Persons Representative Council, the South African Indian Council, Local Affairs Committees, Community Councils, Management Committees and the like', or any successors thereto, shall be deemed to condone or encourage or foster or advocate racialism or discrimination.

Resolution 5, SACOS Third Biennial Conference, 1979.

Appendix 4: Sports Bodies Affiliated to the Non-Racial Sports Movement, 1973-81

1973	1975	1977	1979	1981
S.A. Sports Federation	S.A.S.F.	S.A.S.F.	S.A.S.F.	S.A.S.F.
S.A. Amateur Swimming Federation	S.A.A.SwiF.	S.A.A.SwiF.	S.A.A.SwiF.	S.A.A.SwiF.
S.A. Amateur Athletics & Cycling Board of Control	S.A. Amateur Athletics Board	S.A.A.A.B.	S.A.A.A.B.	S.A.A.A.B.
	S.A. Cycling Association	S.A. Cycling Board		S.A.C.B.
S.A. Table Tennis Board	S.A.T.T.B.	S.A.T.T.B.	S.A.T.T.B.	S.A.T.T.B.
S.A. Weight-lifting & Body-Building Federation	S.A. Amateur Bodybuilding Federation	S.A.A.B.B.F.	S.A.A.B.B.F.	S.A.A.B.B.F.
	S.A. Amateur Weightlifting Federation	S.A.A.W.L.F.	S.A.A.W.L.F.	S.A.A.W.L.F.
S.A. Lawn Tennis Union	S.A.L.T.U.	S.A.L.T.U.	S.A.L.T.U.	Tennis Association of S. Africa
S.A. Women's Hockey Board			S.A.W.H.B.	S.A.W.H.B.
S.A. Men's Hockey Board	S.A.M.H.B.		S.A.M.H.B.	S.A.M.H.B.
S.A. Secondary Schools Sports Association		S.A.S.S.S.A.	S.A.S.S.S.A.	S.A.S.S.S.A.
S.A. Darts Board of Control	S.A. Cricket Board of Control	S.A.C.B.O.C.	S.A.C.B.O.C.	S.A.C.B.O.C.
		S.A.D.B.O.C.	S.A.D.B.O.C.	S.A.D.B.O.C.
	S.A. Badminton Association			
	S.A. Rugby Union		S.A.R.U.	S.A.R.U.
		S.A. Primary Schools Association	S.A.P.S.S.A.	S.A.P.S.S.A.
		Durban Golf Club		
			S.A. Non-Racial Golf Association	S.A.N.R.A.G.A.
			S.A. Softball Association	S.A.S.A.
				S.A. Netball Union
				S.A. Professional Boxing Union
			Councils of Sport (E. Province, Natal, Transvaal, W. Province)	Councils of Sport (Border, Boland, E. Province, Natal, Transvaal, W. Province)

Appendix 5: South Africa's Position in International Sport, 1980

Aeronautics	Full member
Angling	Suspended
Archery	Full member
Athletics	Expelled in 1976
Badminton	Full member (barred from world championships)
Baseball	Full member (inactive)
Basketball	Expelled in 1978
Bobsleigh and tobogganing	Not a member
Body-building	Full member
Bowling	Full member
Boxing (amateur)	Expelled in 1968
(professional)	Member of WBA; expelled from WBC
Canoeing	Suspended (participates in international competition)
Chess	Suspended
Cricket (men's)	Membership cancelled
(women's)	Full member
Croquet	Participates in competition
Cruising	Participates in competition
Cycling (amateur)	Expelled in 1970
(professional)	Participates in competition
Darts	White federation is unrecognised; Non-racial SADBOC is recognised
Equestrian sport	Full member
Fencing	Full member (suspended from world championships)
Fishing and angling	Participates in competition
Football	Expelled in 1976
Golf	Full member
Gymnastics	Full member
Handball	Not a member
Hockey	Full member (does not take part in world championships)
Ice hockey	Full member
Judo	Not a member
Karate	Full member
Life-saving	Participates in competition
Luge	Not a member
Masters' athletics	Participates in competition
Model boating	Participates in competition
Motor sports	Full member
Netball	Expelled
Olympic Games	Expelled in 1970
Orienteering	Not a member
Paraplegic sports	Full member
Pentathlon and biathlon	Full member
Pin bowling	Not a member

Polocrosse	Participates in competition
Powerboating	Participates in competition
Roller skating	Full member
Rowing	Full member (does not take part in world championships)
Rugby	Full member of IRB; not a member of FIRA
Shooting	Full member
Silent sports	Full member
Skating	Full member
Skiing	Not a member
Softball	Full member
Squash rackets	Full member
Surf-riding	Participates in competition
Swimming	Expelled in 1973
Table-tennis	White federation is not recognised; the non-racial SATTB is.
Taekwondo	Not a member
Tennis	Full member
Trampolining	Full member
Tug of war	Full member
Underwater sports	Participates in competition
University sports	Not a member
Veteran and vintage cars	Participates in competition
Volleyball	Not a member
Water-skiing	Full member (excluded from world championships)
Weight-lifting	Expelled in 1972
Wrestling	Expelled in 1970
Yacht racing	Full member

Compiled from: Ramsamy, 'Racial Discrimination in South African Sport', April 1980, UN Centre Against Apartheid, Notes and Documents.

Appendix 6: Principal Sports Organizations in Campaign to Isolate South African Sport

South Africa:
South African Council on Sport (SACOS)
Suite 203
Victoria Heights
56/58 Victoria Street
Durban 4001

International:
South African Non-Racial Olympic Committee (SAN-ROC)
30 Seymour Street
London W.1.

Supreme Council for Sport in Africa
B.P. 1363
Yaounde
Cameroon

United Nations Centre Against Apartheid
Department of Political & Security Affairs
United Nations
U.N. Plaza
New York
U.S.A.

Other:

Britain:	Stop all Racial Tours (SART) c/o British Anti-Apartheid Movement 89 Charlotte Street London W.C.1.
Ireland:	Irish Anti-Apartheid Movement 20 Beechpark Road Foxrock Dublin 18
New Zealand:	HART/The New Zealand Anti-Apartheid Movement PO Box 9204 Courtenay Place Wellington
United States:	ACCESS PO Box 518 New York New York 10025
France:	French Anti-Apartheid Movement 46 Rue de Vaugirard 75006 Paris

Bibliography

South Africa: General

Apartheid-Non! bimestriel du Mouvement Anti-Apartheid (CAO) in parti-
  cular, *Un Peuple sous les verrous, le dossier de la répression en République
  Sud-africaine,* (second ed.), No. 32, 1979, 129p; *Du côté noir du tableau,
  le système d'enseignement bantou en Afrique du Sud,* No. 34, 2nd quarter
  1980, *Sport and Apartheid,* No. 30, April-May 1979.
Bunting, Brian, *The Rise of the South African Reich,* London, Penguin, 1964.
Callinicos, Alex and Rogers, John, *Southern Africa after Soweto,* London,
  Pluto Press, 1977.
Catholic Institute of International Relations, *South Africa in the 1980s,*
  London, 1980.
C.F.D.T.-Information, *Afrique du Sud, la vérité,* Paris, 1978.
Cohen, Barry and Schissel, Howard, *L'Afrique australe de Kissinger à Carter,
  le rapport Kissinger sur l'Afrique australe et ses prolongements français,*
  Paris, L'Harmattan, 1977.
Cornevin, Marianne, *L'Afrique du Sud en sursis,* Paris, Hachette, 1977.
————— *L'Apartheid, pouvoir et falsification historique,* UNESCO, Paris,
  1979.
Davidson, B., Slovo, J., Wilkinson, A.R., *Southern Africa, the New Politics
  of Revolution,* London, Penguin, 1976.
De Kiewiet, *A Social and Economic History of South Africa,* 1941.
First, R., Steele, J., Gurney, C., *The South African Connection, Western
  Investment in Apartheid,* London, Penguin, 1972.
Goguel, Anne-Marie and Buis, Pierre, *Chrétiens d'Afrique du Sud face à
  l'apartheid,* Paris, L'Harmattan, 1978.
Hepple, Alex, *Les travailleurs livrés à l'apartheid, le syndicalisme dans la
  République d'Afrique du Sud,* Genève, Fonds International de Dfense et
  d'Aide pour l'Afrique Australe et Mouvement anti-apartheid de Suisse, s.d.
  (1970).
————— *Verwoerd,* London, Penguin, 1967.
Herbstein, Denis, *Whiteman, we want to talk to you,* London, Penguin, 1978.
Hirson, Baruch, *Year of Fire, Year of Ash,* London, Zed Press, 1979.
Horrell, Muriel, *South Africa, basic facts and figures,* Johannesburg, SAIRR,
  1973.
Johnstone, F., Legassick, M., Wolpe, H., Morris, M., paper presented in
  Messiant C. and Meunier, R., *Apartheid et capitalisme, le système économique*

337

de l'Afrique du Sud, Paris, Maspero, 1979.

Kuma, N'Dumbe III, A., Hitler voulait l'Afrique, Paris, Harmattan, 1980.

Lachartre, Brigitte, Luttes ouvrières et libération en Afrique du Sud, Paris, Syros, 1977.

Laurence, John, Race, Propaganda and South Africa, London, 1979.

Lefort, René, L'Afrique du Sud, histoire d'une crise, Paris, Maspero, 1977.

Lesourd, Jean-Alain, La République d'Afrique du Sud, Paris, P.U.F. 'Que sais-je?', 1963.

Meillassoux, Claude, Les derniers blancs, le modèle sud-africain, Paris, Maspero, 1979.

Modisane, B., Blame Me on History, London, New York, Panther, 1965.

Review of African Political Economy, No. 7, Special issue on Southern Africa, London, Sept-Dec. 1976.

Naidoo, R.S., 'The Indian Community', Race Relations News, November 1976.

Rogers, Barbara, Diviser pour régner, les bantoustans en Afrique du Sud, London, IDAF, 1978.

Tabata, I.B., Education for Barbarism in South African Bantu (African) education, London, Pall Mall Press, 1960.

Taillefer, Bernard, Le Dernier Rempart, France-Afrique du Sud, Paris, La Sycomore, 1980.

Thion, Serge, Le Pouvoir pâle ou le racisme sud-africain, Paris, Seuil, 1969.

Van Rensburg, P., Guilty Land, London, Penguin, 1962.

Walsh, P., The Rise of African Nationalism in South Africa, the African National Congress, 1912-1952, London, C. Hurst, 1970.

Welsh, David, The Growth of Towns, in Wilson, M. and Thompson, L. (eds.), Oxford History of South Africa, Volume II, 1870-1966, London, Oxford University Press, 1971.

Wilson, Monica and Thompson, L. (eds.), Oxford History of South Africa, Volume II, 1870-1966, London, Oxford University Press, 1971.

Sport: General

'Aimez-vous les stades?', les origines historiques des politiques sportives en France (1870-1930), edited by Alain Ehrenberg, Recherches No. 43, April 1980.

Alderson, Frederick, Bicycling, a story, Newton Abbot, David and Charles, 1972.

Bourdieu, Pierre, La Distinction, critique sociale du jugement, Paris, Minuit, 1979.

Bowen, Rowland, Cricket, a history of its growth and development throughout the world, introd. by C.L.R. James, London, Eyre and Spottiswood, 1970.

Brohm, J-M, Critiques du sport, Paris, Ch. Bourgeois, 1976.

Brohm, J-M and Field, Jeunesse et révolution, Paris, Maspero, P.C. No. 152, 1975.

Corps et politiques, Paris, PUF, 1975.

Daniel Denis, 'Aux chiottes l'arbitre' à l'heure du Mundial, ces footballeurs qui nous gouvernent . . ., supplement to Politique Aujourd'hui, No. 5, June 1978.

Durry, Jean, *La véridique histoire des géants de la route*, Paris, Denöel, 1973.

Duthen, George, *Le rugby*, with the co-operation of Walter Spanghero, Paris, Denöel, 1976.

L'Encyclopédie mondiale du sport, Paris, in press.

L'Equipe, daily newspaper.

Garcia, Henri, *La fabuleuse histoire du rugby*, (preface by Antoine Blondin), Paris, O.D.I.L., 1973.

——————— *Guide du rugby*, Guides Horay, Paris, Horay, 1976.

——————— *Le rugby: champions, compétitions, palmarès, techniques*, preface by Lucien Mias, Paris, Larousse, 1978.

Gaulton, A.N., *The Encyclopaedia of Rugby League Football*, London, Robert Hale, 1968.

Golesworthy, Maurice, *The Encyclopaedia of Association Football*, London, Robert Hale, 1973 (1956).

——————— *The Encyclopaedia of Cricket*, London, Robert Hale, (fifth edition), 1974 (1962).

——————— *The Encyclopaedia of Boxing*, London, Robert Hale, (fifth edition), 1975 (1960).

——————— *The Encyclopaedia of Rugby Union Football*, London, Robert Hale, (third edition), 1976 (1958, 1966).

Hawkes, Ken and Lindley, Gerard, *The Encyclopaedia of Bowls*, London, Robert Hale, 1974.

Heaton, Peter, *Histoire du Yachting*, Paris, Denöel, 1972.

Lalanne, Denis, *Le grand combat du XV de France*, (preface by Jacques Perret), Paris, La Table Ronde, 1962.

——————— *Le conquérants du XV de France*, Paris, La Table Ronde, 1970.

——————— and Garcia H., *XV coqs en colère*, Paris, La Table Ronde, 1968.

Magnane, G., *Sociologie du Sport*, Paris, Gallimard, col. Idées, 1964.

Mulligan, Andrew, *Ouvert l'après-midi, dix ans de rugby*, (translated from the English by J. Arnaud), Paris, La Table Ronde, 1965.

Partisans, *Sport, Culture et répression*, Paris, Maspero, 1976.

Quel Corps?, (collective), Paris, Maspero, 1978.

Robertson, Max (ed.), *The Encyclopaedia of Tennis*, London, George Allen & Unwin Ltd., 1974.

Stent, R.R., *Rugby Football in South Africa*, in Rosenthal, Eric, *Encyclopaedia of Southern Africa*, London and New York, Frederick Warne & Co. Ltd., (sixth edition), 1973.

Summerhays' Encyclopaedia for Horsemen, compiled by Summerhays, revised by Stella A. Walker, London and New York, Frederick Warne & Co. Ltd., 1975 (1952).

Webster, Evans, *The Encyclopaedia of Golf*, London, Robert Hale, (second edition), 1974 (1971).

South African Sport

Abrahams, Peter, *Tell Freedom*, London, Faber and Faber, 1954.

Annual Report of the Department of Sport and Recreation, Pretoria, South African Department, 1978.

Annual Report of the Department of Sport and Recreation, Pretoria, South

African Government, 1979.

Apartheid and Sport, Sechaba, May 1979.

A.S.S.A., *Southern Africa, First Congress,* Durban, University of Natal, 1973.

Barber, James, *South Africa's Foreign Policy, 1945-1970,* London, New York, Cape Town, Oxford University Press, 1973.

Benabdallah, Abdelkader, *L'Alliance Raciste Israel—Sud-Africaine,* Montreal, Canada-Monde Arabe, 1979.

Biko, Steve, *I Write What I Like,* London, Bowerdean Press, 1978.

Black Review 1972, (ed.) Khoapa, B.A., Durban, Black Community Programmes, 1973.

Black Review 1973, (ed.) Gwala, Mafika Pascal, Durban, Black Community Programmes, 1974.

Black Review 1974-1975, Durban, Black Community Programmes, 1976.

Black Review 1975-1976, (ed.) Rambally, Asha, Lovedale, Black Community Programmes, 1977.

Bokwe, R.T., Foley, B.N., Nkosinkulu, Th., *'The Beer Question', November 1941,* in *South African Outlook,* vol. 106, No. 1224, September 1976.

Botha, Graham, *Social Life in the Cape Colony,* Cape Town, C. Struick (Pty) Ltd., 1970.

Brauer, Joshua, *The Jewish Sportsmen of South Africa,* Johannesburg, Central News Agency, 1939.

Brickhill, Joan, *Race against Race. South Africa's 'Multinational' Sport Fraud,* London, I.D.A.F., July 1976.

Brutus, Dennis, 'Childhood Reminiscences' in Wastberg, Per (ed.), *The Writer in Modern Africa,* Uppsala, Scandinavian Institute of African Studies, 1968.

——————— 'The Sportsman's Choice' in la Guma, Alex (ed.), *Apartheid, a Collection of Writings on South African Racism by South Africans,* London, Lawrence & Wishart, 1972.

Buchan, John, *The African Colony, Studies on Reconstruction,* Edinburgh and London, William Blackwood & Sons, 1903.

Burger, John, *The Black Man's Burden,* London, New York, Port Washington Kenniket Press, 1943.

Caffrey, K., *The British to Southern Africa,* London, Gentry Books, 1973.

Child, Daphne, *Saga of the South African Horse,* London, Howard Timmins, 1967.

Churchill, Lord Randolph, *Men, Mines and Animals in South Africa,* London, Sampson Low, Marston & Co. Ltd., (second edition), 1892.

Committee Against Racial Discrimination in Sport, (C.A.R.D.S.): pamphlets (various).

Couzens, Tim, *Moralizing Leisure Time: the Transatlantic Connection and Black Johannesburg, 1918-1936,* Centre of International and Area Studies, University of London, [Unpublished].

Currey, R.F. and Haarhoff, J.J., *South African Nationality, its Meaning, Possibilities and Limitations,* in *Coming of Age, Studies in South African Citizenship and Politics,* Cape Town, Maskew Miller Ltd., 1930.

Deane, D.S., *Black South Africans, 57 Profiles of South Africa's Leading Blacks, a Who's Who,* London and Johannesburg, Oxford University Press, 1978.

de Broglio, Chris, *South Africa: Racism in Sport,* London, I.D.A.F., 1970.

de Villiers, D., *The Case for South Africa*, London, Tom Stacey, 1970.

Dommisse, John, *The Psychological Pathology of Apartheid Sport*, African Studies Association Convention (ed.), November 1977, (mimeo).

Draper, Mary, *Sport and Race in South Africa*, Johannesburg, S.A.I.R.R., 1963.

Duff Gordon, Lady, *Letters from the Cape*, London and Cape Town, Oxford University Press, 1927.

Edmunds, Jean, 'Horses and Riders in South Africa', in *Summerhays' Encyclopaedia for Horsemen*, London and New York, 1975.

F.A.O., *Coordonnateur CMCF6Action pour de Développement: Apartheid, idées et actions*, bulletin 126/7/8, 1978.

Figg, David, 'The South Atlantic Connection: Growing Links between South Africa and Latin America, in *Britain and Latin America 1979*, London, Latin America Bureau, 1979.

Ganga, J-Cl., *Combats pour un sport africain*, Paris, Harmattan, 1979.

Gordon-Brown, A. (ed.), *Year Book and Guide to Southern Africa 1958*, London, Robert Hale Ltd., (for Union Castle Steamship Co.), 1958.

The Great White Hoax. South Africa's International Propaganda Machine, London, The Africa Bureau, 1977.

Hain, Peter, *Apartheid in Sport Today*, s.d., (mimeo).

————— *Don't Play with Apartheid: the background to the Stop The Seventy Tour Campaign*, London, George Allen & Unwin, 1971.

Hansard Debates, Sports Debate: South African Parliament, May 21 1979.

H.A.R.T., *The Commonwealth and the International Campaign against Apartheid in Sport*, Wellington, New Zealand, 1980, (mimeo).

Hattersley, Alan F., *South Africa, 1652-1933*, London, The Home University Library, Thornton Butterworth Ltd., 1937.

————— *Pietermaritzburg Panorama*, New York, Shuter & Shooter, 1938.

————— *Portrait of a Colony: the Story of Natal*, Cape Town, Cambridge University Press, 1940.

Hellmann, Ellen, *Problems of Urban Bantu Youth*, Johannesburg, SAIRR, 1940.

————— (ed.), *Rooiyard: a sociological survey of an urban native slumyard*, Cape Town, Oxford University Press, 1948.

————— (ed.), *Handbook on Race Relations in South Africa*, Cape Town, London, New York, S.A.I.R.R. and Oxford University Press, 1949.

Hickson, Mike, 'The Aurora Cricket Club and South Africa since isolation', in *Reality*, July 1979.

Hirson, Baruch, *Tuskagee: the Joint Councils and the All African Convention*, Institute of Commonwealth Studies, London University, May 1978, (mimeo).

Horrell, Muriel (ed.), *Survey of Race Relations in South Africa*, annually, in particular 1945-1964, 1974-1979, South African Institute of Race Relations (S.A.I.R.R.), Johannesburg.

————— *Legislation and Race Relations*, S.A.I.R.R., Johannesburg, 1971. Revised edition 1971 plus supplement: legislation of 1972, 1973 and first half of 1974.

Huddleston, Trevor, *Naught for your Comfort*, London, Collins, 1956.

Jokl, E., Preface to the Annual Report of the Bantu Sports Club, 23 July 1943.

————— *Physical Education, Sport and Recreation*, in Hellman, E. (ed.), *Handbook on Race Relations in South Africa*, Cape Town, London, New York, S.A.I.R.R., and Oxford University Press, 1949.

Kerr, A., *Fort Hare 1915-1948: the evolution of an African College*, London,

C. Hurst & Co., 1968.

Kuper, Hilda, *Indian People in Natal,* Natal University Press, 1960.

Kuper, Leo, *The African Bourgeoisie,* Yale University Press, 1965.

Lapchick, Richard E., *The Politics of Race and International Sport: the case of South Africa,* Connecticut and London, Greenwood Press, 1975.

Laurence, John C., *Race, Propaganda and South Africa: the Manipulation of Western Opinion and Politics by the Forces of White Supremacy,* London, Victor Gollancz, 1979.

Lever, Henry, *Ethnic Attitudes of Johannesburg Youth,* Johannesburg, Witwatersrand University Press, 1968.

——————— *South African Society,* Johannesburg, Jonathan Ball Publishers, 1978.

Maasdorp, G., Humphreys, A.J.D. (eds.), *From Shantytown to Township: an Economic Study of African Poverty and Rehousing in a South African City,* Cape Town, Johannesburg, Durban, Juta & Co. Ltd., 1975.

Mafeje, Archie, *Leadership and Change, a Study of two South African Peasant Communities,* University of Cape Town, (thesis), 1963.

Marais, J.S., *The Cape Coloured People (1652-1937),* Johannesburg.

Marie, Bernard, *Report of the French Parliamentary Commission of Inquiry to South Africa,* Paris, 1980, mimeo.

Mayer, P., 'Townsmen and Tribesmen', in Mayer (ed.), *Xhosa in Town: Studies of the Bantu Speaking Population of East London, Cape Province,* Vol. 2, Cape Town, Oxford University Press, 1961.

Melik-Chakhnazarov, Achot, *Le Sport en Afrique,* Paris, Presence Africaine, 1970.

Millin, Sarah Gertrude, *The People of South Africa,* London, Constable & Co., 1951.

——————— *The South Africans,* London, 1926 (1934).

Mouvement Anti-Apartheid C.A.O., SART, in collaboration with ACCESS and IAAM, *Le Sport Sud-Africain, pourquoi l'isolement?* in *Apartheid-Non!,* 1980.

Mweli Skota, T.D., *The African Yearly Register, being an illustrated National Biographical Dictionary (Who's Who) of Black Folks in Africa,* , Johannesburg, Esson & Co. Ltd., 1932.

Naidoo, Morgan, *Sports Sponsorship, Black and White,* Durban, 1972, (mimeo).

Newnham, Tom, *L'Apartheid et les Sports, boycottage international d l'apartheid dans le domaine des sports,* New York, Centre Against Apartheid of the United Nations, *Notes and Documents* No. 15, July 1976, (mimeo).

——————— *By Batons and Barbed Wire: A Response to the 1981 Springbok Tour of New Zealand,* Auckland, Real Pictures Ltd., 1981.

Norman, J., *Sporting and other recreational facilities available in Coloured and Indian townships along the Reef,* Johannesburg, S.A.I.R.R., 1974, (mimeo).

Norton, Conrad, *Opportunity in South Africa,* London, Rockcliff, 1948.

Odendaal, André (ed.), *Cricket in Isolation: the politics of race and cricket in South Africa,* Cape Town, published by the author.

Panorama, (South African weekly): among other numbers, No. 94, *Mixed Sport exists in South Africa,* June 1979, and No. 105, *Rugby for All,* July 1980.

Parker, G.A., *South African sports: cricket, football, athletics, etc. . . ,* South Africa, 1897.

Pather, M.N., *Le racisme dans les sports en Afrique du Sud*, New York, Centre Against Apartheid, United Nations, *Notes et Documents* 12/80, April 1980.

Paton, Alan, *Hofmeyr*, London and Cape Town, Oxford University Press, 1964.

Patterson, Sheila, *Colour and Culture in South Africa: a study of the status of the Cape Coloured People within the social structure of the Union of South Africa*, London, Routledge & Kegan Paul, 1953.

Pauw, B.A., 'The Second Generation', in Mayer (ed.), *Xhosa in Town, Studies of the Bantu-Speaking Population of East London, Cape Province*, Vol. 3, Cape Town, Oxford University Press, 1963.

Phillips, Ray, *The Bantu are Coming*, London, Student Christian Movement Press, 1930.

Phillips, Ray, *The Bantu in the City: a study of cultural adjustment on the Witwatersrand*, Lovedale, Lovedale Press, 1936.

Ramsamy, S., *Non-Racial Sport in South Africa*, New York, Centre Against Apartheid, United Nations, *Notes and Documents*, Lagos Conference, 1977, (mimeo).

———— *Racial Discrimination and Sport in South Africa*, (mimeo).

———— *It is necessary to isolate South Africa from international sport: it is necessary to denounce the fraudulent sporting policy of apartheid*, New York, Centre Against Apartheid, United Nations, *Notes and Documents*, 11/80, April 1980.

Report of the National European-Bantu Conference, Cape Town, February 6-9, 1929, Lovedale Press, 1929.

Report of the South African National Conference on the Post-War Planning of Social Welfare Work, 25-29 September 1944, Johannesburg, University of Witwatersrand, 1944.

Richards, Trevor, *No New Ball Game, Apartheid in Sport Continues*, in *Southern Africa*, Vol. X, No. 5, June-July 1977.

———— *Sports Boycott: Recommendations for International Action*, seminar on South Africa, April-May 1975, New York, Centre Against Apartheid, United Nations, (mimeo).

———— *Apartheid in Sport: Business as usual*, New York, *Objectif-Justice* (UNO), winter 1977-1978, vol. 9, No. 4.

Ritchie, W., *The History of the South African College, 1829-1918*, 2 volumes, Cape Town, T. Maskew Miller, 1918.

Roberts, Brian, *Kimberley, Turbulent City*, Cape Town, David Philip, 1976.

Roman, Roger, 'Don't Play with Apartheid, Isolate It', in *South African Reality*, November 1973.

Rosenthal,.Eric, *Encyclopaedia of Southern Africa*, London and New York, Frederick Warne & Co. Ltd., (sixth edition), 1973.

Ryan, John, 'The Donald Woods I Know', in *South African Outlook*, November 1977.

Saron, Hotz, *The Jews in South Africa*, London, Oxford University Press, 1955.

Savage, Michael, 'Bantu Beer', in *South African Outlook*, vol. 106, No. 1224, September 1976.

Schlemmer, L., 'External Pressure and Local Attitudes and Interests', in Clifford-Vaughan, F.M.A. (ed.), *International Pressures and Political Change in South Africa*, Cape Town, Oxford University Press, 1978.

Shepherd, Robert, *Lovedale, South Africa — the Story of a Century*, Lovedale

Press, 1941.

Shorten, John R., *Cape Town,* City Council of Cape Town, Shorten, 1963.

Sikakane, Joyce, *A Window on Soweto,* London, I.D.A.F., June 1977.

Silburn, Colonel P.A., *South Africa, White and Black — or Brown?* London, George, Allen & Unwin Ltd., 1927.

South Africa 1977, Official Yearbook of the Republic of South Africa, (fourth edition), Johannesburg, Perskor Printers, 1979.

South African Amateur Swimming Federation, *Memorandum to the Fédération Internationale de Natation Amateur (FINA),* February 1978, (mimeo).

South African Council on Sport (S.A.C.O.S.), *Memorandum to the International Tennis Federation Commission of Inquiry,* February 1978 (mimeo)

South African Council on Sport (S.A.C.O.S.), *Minutes of the Third Biennial Conference,* September 1st 1979, (mimeo).

South African Council on Sport (S.A.C.O.S.), *Minutes of a general meeting of S.A.C.O.S.,* October 14 1978, (mimeo).

South African Council on Sport (S.A.C.O.S.), *Third Biennial Conference, Report,* September 1979, (mimeo).

South African Council on Sport (S.A.C.O.S.), *First Biennial Conference, Report,* October 1975, (mimeo).

South African Council on Sport (S.A.C.O.S.), *Second Biennial Conference, Report,* October 1977, (mimeo).

SAN-ROC/MAA-CAO, *Le Rugby Sud-Africain,* Paris, 1980.

SAN-ROC/Irish Anti-Apartheid Movement: *Sport,* contribution to the International Conference on the Common Market and South Africa, Dublin, 27-28 January 1979, (mimeo).

South African Non-Racial Olympic Committee (SAN-ROC) and Irish Anti-Apartheid Movement, *South Africa's Apartheid Rugby: the facts,* London, 1980 (mimeo).

South African Institute of Race Relations, cf. Horrell, Muriel.

South African Olympic and National Games Association (S.A.O.N.G.A.) *Questions and Answers on South African Sport* (prepared by S.A.O.N.G.A. for the British Sports Council delegation's visit to South Africa, January 1980), Director of Information, S.A. Embassy, London, 1981.

————— Jaarverslag Annual Report, Johannesburg, June 1976, (mimeo).

South Africa's Standing in International Sports, New York, United Nations Anti-Apartheid Centre, *Notes and Documents,* July 1978, (mimeo).

Southern Africa Lawn Tennis Union (S.A.L.T.U.), *Secretarial Report and Treasurer's Audited Final Accounts, period ended December 1978,* (mimeo)

Sports Council of Great Britain, *Sport in South Africa, report of the Sports Council's fact-finding delegation,* London, January 1980, (mimeo).

Sproat, Iain, M.P., *Cricketers' Who's Who 1981,* London, Cricketers' Who's Who Ltd., 1981.

State of the Union, *Year Book for South Africa,* 1958.

State of South Africa, *Yearbook, 1974,* Johannesburg, 1974.

Stiebel, Victor, *South African Childhood,* London, André Deutsch, 1968.

Stent, R.K., *Rugby Football in South Africa,* in Rosenthal, E., *Encyclopaedia of Southern Africa,* 1973.

Themba, Can, *The Will to Die,* London, Heinemann Educational, African Writers' Series, No. 104, 1972, pp. 46-57.

Thompson, Richard, *Retreat from Apartheid: New Zealand's Sporting*

Contacts with South Africa, London, Melbourne, New York, Oxford University Press, 1975.

Tracy, Hugh, *African Dances of the Witwatersrand Gold Mines,* photographs Severn, Merlyn, Johannesburg, African Music Society, 1952.

Trainor, Luke, 'The Primacy of Internal Policy: National, Sport and External Relations 1975-78', in *Political Science,* Vol. 30, December 1978, Canterbury, New Zealand, pp. 63-78.

Transkei Annual, 1974.

Transvaal Council on Sport, *Report Presented to the First Annual General Meeting* held at the AEL Centre, Johannesburg, May 21 1978, (mimeo).

Troup, Frieda, *Forbidden Pastures,* London, I.D.A.F., 1976.

UNESCO (ed.), *L'Apartheid, ses effets sur l'éducation, la science, la culture et l'information,* (second edition), Paris, 1972.

United Nations, *The South African Republic and the politics of Apartheid, statistical data,* New York, 1978.

Valderrama (reporter), *Measures taken by governments against South Africa in the field of sports,* United Nations Anti-Apartheid Centre, New York, April 1975, (mimeo).

van der Merwe, Hendrick, W., Buitendab, J.J., 'Political, Ethnic and Structural Differences among White South Africans', in A.S.S.A., *Sociology, Southern Africa,* 1973.

Warner, Sir Plum, *The M.C.C. in South Africa,* London, Chapman & Hall, 1906.

Wastberg, Per (ed.), *The Writer in Modern Africa,* Uppsala, Scandinavian Institute of African Studies, 1967.

Watts, H.L., *South African Town,* Institute of Social and Economic Research, Grahamstown, Rhodes University, 1966.

Wells, A.W., *South Africa: a Planned Tour of the Country Today,* London, J.M. Dent & Sons, 1949, (first edition 1939, revised 1944 and 1947).

Western Province Council of Sport, *Chairman's Address, Secretarial Report and Financial Statement for the period ending 18 November 1979,* (mimeo).

Whisson, M.G., 'The Legitimacy of Treating Coloured People in South Africa as a Minority Group', in A.S.S.A., *Sociology Southern Africa,* 1973.

Wilkins, Ivor, Strydom, Hans, *The Broederbond,* London, New York, Paddington Press, 1979.

Willan, Brian, *An African in Kimberley: Sol T. Plaatje 1894-1898,* s.d., (mimeo).

Wilson, Monica and Mafeje, Archie, *Langa: a study of social groups in an African Township,* London, New York, Cape Town, Oxford University Press, 1963.

Woods, Donald, 'Sport Policy 1976', in *Race Relations News* (S.A.I.R.R., Vol. 38, No. 12, December 1976.

———— *Steve Biko,* London, Penguin, 1978.

Work in Progress, *Rugby in the Eastern Cape,* South Africa, No. 17, April 1981.

Wright, Noël, *Glimpses of South Africa,* London, A. & G. Black Ltd, 1929.

Index